The
101 BEST
OUTDOOR TOWNS

The
101 BEST
OUTDOOR TOWNS

Unspoiled Places to Visit, Live & Play

First Edition

Sarah Tuff & Greg Melville

The Countryman Press
Woodstock, Vermont

Frontispiece: *Winter light glows through the trees in Fort Atkinson, Wisconsin.*
(© Fort Atkinson Chamber of Commerce)

We welcome your comments and suggestions. Please contact
The Countryman Press, P.O. Box 748, Woodstock, VT 05091,
or e-mail countrymanpress@wwnorton.com.

ISBN 978-0-88150-766-9

Book design, composition, and map by Hespenheide Design
Cover photos: Top © Terry Donnelly/Getty Images; bottom left and center © Getty Images; bottom right of Salida, CO © David Brownell

Published by The Countryman Press, P.O. Box 748, Woodstock, Vermont 05091
Distributed by W. W. Norton & Company, 500 Fifth Avenue, New York, NY 10110

Printed in the United States of America

10 9 8 7 6 5 4 3 2 1

This book is dedicated to

Carlton Dunn and Ann Marie Johnson,

who make our own adventures possible.

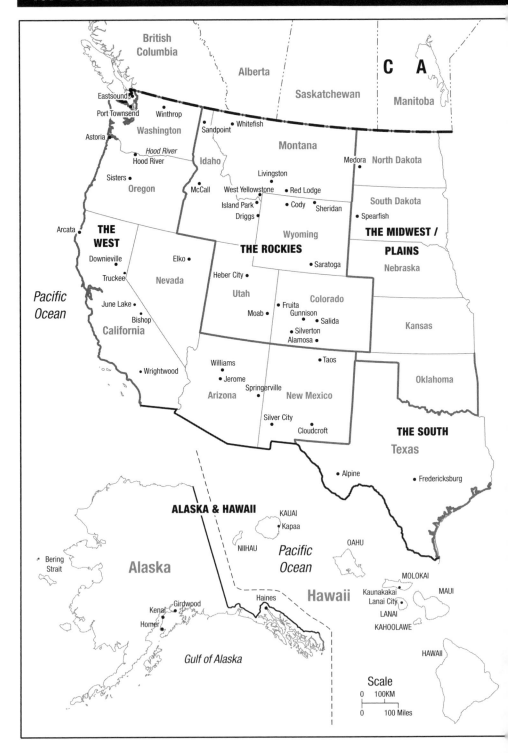

British
Columbia

Alberta

Saskatchewan

C   A

Manitoba

Eastsound
Port Townsend   Winthrop
Astoria   Washington   Sandpoint   Whitefish

Montana

Medora   North Dakota

Hood River
Hood River   Idaho

Livingston

Sisters
Oregon   McCall   West Yellowstone   Red Lodge

South Dakota

Island Park   Cody   Sheridan
Driggs   Spearfish

Arcata   **THE
WEST**

Wyoming

**THE MIDWEST /
PLAINS**

THE ROCKIES   Saratoga

Nebraska

Downieville   Elko

Heber City

Truckee   Nevada

Utah   Colorado

*Pacific
Ocean*   June Lake
Bishop

Fruita
Moab   Gunnison
Salida

Kansas

California   Silverton
Alamosa

Wrightwood

Williams   Taos

Jerome   Oklahoma

Springerville
Arizona   New Mexico

Silver City

THE SOUTH

Cloudcroft   Texas

Alpine   Fredericksburg

ALASKA & HAWAII   KAUAI
Kapaa

NIIHAU   *Pacific
Ocean*   OAHU

* Bering
Strait   Alaska

MOLOKAI
Kaunakakai   MAUI
Lanai City
LANAI
KAHOOLAWE

Kenai   Girdwood   Haines   Hawaii

Homer

Gulf of Alaska

HAWAII

Scale
0   100KM

0   100 Miles

N A D A

Newfoundland

Gulf of
St. Lawrence

Québec

Ontario

New
Brunswick

Maine

Kingfield

Novia
Scotia

Newport

Bethel Southwest
Harbor

East Burke
Montpelier

Bemidji   Ely

Minnesota

Bayfield   Michigan

Jackson

THE

Brainerd   Petoskey

Lake Placid
Middlebury   Vt.   Wolfeboro

NORTHEAST

Sturgeon Bay   N.H.

Haywood   Cadillac

Peterborough

Stillwater

Wisconsin

Williamstown   Mass.

Lanesboro

Michigan

New York New Paltz   Lenox
Cornwall   Tiverton

Fort Atkinson

Conn.   R.I.

THE MIDWEST /

Saugatuck

Wellsboro   Milford

PLAINS

Pennsylvania

Iowa

Harpers Ferry   New Jersey

THE MID-ATLANTIC

Illinois   Indiana   Ohio

Ohiopyle

Milford

Md.

Delaware

West
Virginia

Davis

St. Michaels

Missouri

Staunton   Crisfield

Carbondale

Fayetteville Slatyfork

Rolla

Kentucky

Virginia

Damascus

Edenton

Boone

Gatlinburg   North Carolina

Tennessee   Bryson City   Brevard

Arkansas

Ellijay

South
Carolina

Mena

Oxford

Alabama

Alexander
City

Georgia

Beaufort

Mississippi

North

THE SOUTH

Atlantic
Ocean

Louisiana

Apalachicola

Cedar Key

Florida

Gulf of Mexico

THE BAHAMAS

Scale

0   500 Kilometers

0   500 Miles

Acknowledgments

In addition to recreation and wilderness agencies, gear shops, chambers of commerce, and tourism bureaus and their public relations representatives, Jon Taylor and Justin Turner were helpful in the research and production of this book. Current populations indicated in each town are based on 2005 estimates from the U.S. Census. While each town provided information on their strongest industries, access to nearby airports was obtained from www.city-data.com, which also contains information on current median home prices and other livability factors and is a useful Web site for researching American towns.

Thank you to Kermit Hummel, Amy Rost, and Jennifer Thompson for their invaluable editorial expertise.

Contents

The Middle Atlantic 71

The South 121

The Midwest/Plains 185

The Rockies 255

The West 331

Alaska and Hawaii 413

Introduction

everal years ago, Greg Melville and I became friends while working for *Men's Journal* magazine, whose offices are found in a skyscraper on Manhattan's Avenue of the Americas. We researched and wrote about outdoor gear and outdoor places, but actually getting to use the gear or go to the places? Not as much as we would have liked. Most of the time we were way too cooped up in our cubicle life, helping to put out a magazine.

One fall day, the magazine arranged an editorial staff photo to be taken on the Brooklyn Bridge. Instead of taking the subway or bus, we decided to ride bikes. Greg kept one at his apartment, while my brother had left his at mine. The novelty of riding a mountain bike in New York City was exhilarating; I'll never forget navigating the city streets and pedaling along the East River to meet Greg. It was such a simple thing, but suddenly I knew I had to move to a place where riding a mountain bike—or taking a hike, going for a trail run, or skiing fresh snow—wouldn't involve dodging cabs.

By the next spring, Greg and I had each left New York City and found adventure havens: Lake Placid, New York, from where Greg freelanced, and Park City, Utah, from where I commuted to Salt Lake City to edit publications for the 2002 Olympic Winter Games. And then, serendipitously, we both found ourselves in Burlington, Vermont, a college town whose playground includes Lake Champlain, the Adirondacks, and the Green Mountains, not to mention seven nearby ski resorts. We both now get to use the gear and go to the places we write about, but there are times when even Burlington seems irked by big-city woes: traffic on the arteries from the interstate, crime, and inflated real estate.

So Greg and I began to devise our own dream list of the new outdoor towns. Through a process that is more scientific than you'd guess from a couple of travel writers, we used U.S. Census data and chamber of commerce information to weed out the spots that were too big, too pricey, or simply too far from a major airport for those who might want to stay. Then we threw in some of our own individual adventure experience and parallel backgrounds in writing for outdoor magazines. (And taking into account our dependency on coffee and a microbrew or two, we also mandated that each town must have a decent café and watering hole.)

The end result is what you hold in your hands, a coast-to-coast catalog of mostly undiscovered adventure capitals. Sure, maybe mountain bikers have discovered Moab, Utah, or windsurfers Hood River, Oregon, but these remain places, along with the other ninety-nine selections, that haven't been gobbled up by Gucci boutiques and billion-dollar condominium developments.

101 Best Outdoor Towns gives you the lowdown on what makes these outdoor towns unique and appealing, from where to find the best singletrack ride or hiking trail to where to grab a burger when you're done (sometimes down to the name of the person who flipped it). We hope it will inspire you to escape the cubicle life for a weekend—or maybe much longer—and experience them for yourselves. Don't be so surprised if you run into one of us while you're there.

The Northeast

Cornwall, Connecticut

Don't be fooled by the covered bridges that lend an air of antique-cute placidity to this corner of northwest Connecticut. These wooden structures span one of the most ferociously fun fishing rivers in New England, the Housatonic, which is shared by canoeists, kayakers, and even rafters. And these Litchfield County bridges are also surrounded by the state's other chief sources of outdoor and adrenaline fixes: the Appalachian Trail for hiking, the rolling hills for pedaling, and Mohawk Mountain for skiing and snowboarding. Spend some time around Cornwall and its neighboring communities, Cornwall Bridge and West Cornwall, and you may theorize why there's so much antique furniture in good condition—it's perhaps because a sizeable chunk of the population has never had much time to sit in it.

Population: 1,489
Action: Fishing, paddling, hiking, downhill and cross-country skiing, road biking

Cornwall, Connecticut's Housatonic River is one of the premier fly-fishing rivers in the Northeast. (© Connecticut Commission on Culture and Tourism)

First, the fishing. As the guides at Housatonic River Outfitters will tell you, there are few more premier stretches of water for fly-fishing for trout and smallmouth bass in the Northeast. Flowing more than 130 miles from the Berkshires in Massachusetts to Long Island Sound, the Housatonic is by no means pristine—for years, it was contaminated with PCBs from a Massachusetts General Electric plant and changed colors regularly. But today, the ten miles of river around Cornwall are blue—as in blue ribbon. Local anglers on the Housatonic have, of course, their secret spots, but some of the best areas are right at the West Cornwall covered bridge and at such holes as Split Rock, White Birch, Rainbow Run, and the Ledges. The nearby Farmington River also teems with fish.

Class I and II rapids along the Housatonic also create whitewater kayaking holes, that quiet down to flatwater for canoeing; through Clarke Outdoors, rafters can travel a ten-mile section of the river from Falls Village to Housatonic Meadows. It is so quiet that it can be difficult to believe, at times—especially during fall foliage season in September and October—that one is following a route that parallels State Route 7, one of the busiest thoroughfares in northwest Connecticut.

Some of the least busy thoroughfares are the twenty-four runs—with such area-appropriate names as Pine and the Rapids—at Mohawk Mountain, the ski and snowboard area that sits in Cornwall's backyard. True, it's no Crested Butte, but there's a good variety of trails, many lighted for night skiing.

The surrounding Mohawk State Forest has another thirty miles of trails for snowshoeing, cross-country skiing, and hiking. At more than 3,700 acres, it's another spot where you're not likely to run into traffic of any kind. And with so many visitors to this area ogling those covered bridges and antique shops, it's likely to stay that way.

Start the Day

The Wandering Moose Café (421 Sharon Goshen Turnpike [next to the covered bridge], West Cornwall; 860-672-0178): Full-service breakfast options include omelets, buttermilk pancakes, corned-beef hash and eggs, and bagels with smoked salmon.

Gear Up

Clarke Outdoors (163 Route 7, West Cornwall; 860-672-6365): Canoe, kayak, and raft rentals, and guided trips on the Housatonic River, plus canoe and kayak sales.

Housatonic River Outfitters (24 Kent Road, Cornwall Bridge; 860-672-1010): Fly-fishing supplies and guides, plus hiking and camping gear, snowshoes, and canoe and kayak sales.

Refuel

Bairds General Store (25 Kent Road, Cornwall Bridge; 860-672-6578): The place for big, post-fishing sandwiches and camping supplies.

Cornwall Inn Restaurant (270 Kent Road, Cornwall Bridge; 800-786-6884): Chef Stefan Kappes creates potstickers, oven-fried organic chicken and herb-crusted Australian lamb; the adjacent tavern features local musicians many Fridays.

Bunk

Housatonic Meadows State Park (Route 7, Sharon; 860-672-6772): On the banks of the Housatonic River, ninety-seven campsites with access to fly-fishing and paddling.

Cathedral Pines Farm (10 Valley Road; 860-672-6747; www.cathedralpinesfarm.com): Two-room bed-and-breakfast in a farmhouse surrounded by llamas and lilacs.

Cornwall Inn & Lodge (270 Kent Road, Cornwall Bridge; 800-786-6884; www.cornwallinn.com): Five rooms in the inn and an additional eight pet-friendly rooms in the separate lodge; restaurant and tavern on site.

Can't Leave?

Nearest airport: Bradley International, Windsor Locks, Connecticut (47 miles)

Primary industry: Tourism

The Wild Side

Lime Rock Park

If anything can shatter northwest Connecticut's bucolic image, it's Lime Rock Park, just north of Cornwall and the covered bridges. It's not the kind of park with trees and streams but rather one with speeds and screams, as race-cars whip around the paved track. Among the events that Lime Rock hosts are vintage Ferrari races, stock-car 200s, and the Le Mans series. But you don't have to just sit there and wave rally flags, thanks to the Skip Barber Racing School, which hosts one of the country's most renowned racing programs here every spring, summer and fall.

Bethel, Maine

Population: 2,583
Action: Hiking, paddling, fishing, downhill and cross-country skiing, mountain biking

One of the sweetest summer sights in Maine is, yes, a buttered hot-dog roll loaded with chunks of lobster. But now rivaling that sight for top honors are the views from the 3,000- and 4,000-foot summits studding the Grafton Loop, a new, thirty-nine-mile hiking circuit near Bethel that overlooks the White Mountains, the Mahoosuc Range, and the blue ribbon of the Androscoggin River. It's the first major new Northeast trail in thirty years, and a testament to Bethel's firm belief in the bounty of its surroundings, sometimes overlooked by those headed for the Maine coast.

Bethel was incorporated in 1796, given a book of Genesis name that means "house of God"—and its location was, and is, certainly closer to the heavens than many other spots in New England, thanks to a perch at the northern end of the White Mountain National Forest. But unlike some of its New Hampshire neighbors, Bethel has avoided becoming overrun with year-round Christmas shops and cutesy theme parks. Instead, there are bandstand concerts on the Bethel Common, community road runs, adventure triathlons, and canoe and kayak races on the Androscoggin River. (Bethel is one of Maine's most athletic communities, but the sixty-mile-long Androscoggin is just gentle enough for more placid paddling, or casting a fly into its currents. The "Upper Andro" teems with rainbow and brown trout and also has salmon and smallmouth bass.)

Despite its eighteenth-century beginnings, Bethel didn't really land on the outdoor map until the arrival of Sunday River Ski Resort in 1958. Since then, Sunday River has spilled across eight different peaks and has 131 trails known for consistent conditions. Perhaps tracing back to its higher-power moniker, Bethel has been named the greatest ski town in the universe. The surrounding area also boasts the family-

Snow frosts a covered bridge in Bethel, Maine. (© Bethel Area Chamber of Commerce)

friendly Mount Abraham, the nearby Black Mountain, more than 120 miles of groomed nordic ski trails, and boundless backcountry options. Just southwest of Bethel, the Telemark Inn trains a team of Alaskan huskies to race mid-distance events—and to take guests dogsledding and skijoring around Caribou Mountain and the White Mountains. So quintessentially Maine is the area, that the Telemark's horse-drawn sleigh was once featured on an L.L. Bean winter catalog.

Upping the ante on the local athleticism, Sunday River also hosts a wife-carrying championship, during which teams compete for the wife's weight in Red Hook beer. (Losers can drown their sorrows at the Sunday River Brewing Company.)

But before the beer, to get your bearings, head for the new Grafton Loop. With seven tent sites—two to nine miles apart and all with fresh-water spigots—the trail is ideal for a long-weekend backpacking trip. Starting from the trailhead at Grafton Notch, head east to hear tales from Appalachian Trail thru-hikers who have just tackled their toughest mile before breaking away from the A.T. at the 3,812-foot summit of East Baldpate. The next stretch of the Grafton Loop, on the eastern side, is sprinkled with waterfalls, swimming holes large enough for laps, and warm sunning rocks. You'll stay high for several more miles before dipping down through old-growth forest and over brooks, to connect with the western side. Here, the Grafton Loop Trail climbs up Bald and

The Wild Side

The Trek Across Maine

The Trek Across Maine, a fundraising and cycling event for the American Lung Association of Maine, begins in Bethel every June. The 180-mile, three-day ride takes 2,000 cyclists toward the seaside city of Rockland. The ride includes five meals per day, rest stops every fifteen to twenty-five miles, lodging, luggage transport, and more. Call 800-499-5864 for more information and registration forms.

Stowe mountains and then hits the alpine blueberry bushes on Sunday River Whitecap, a 3,335-foot exposed summit from which you'll peer down at the Rangeley Lakes and diminutive farmhouses sending up curls of woodstove smoke. If time is short, it's a seven-mile round-trip up Puzzle Mountain, whose views inspired locals to build the Grafton Loop.

Still looking for that lobster roll? Bethel's just a ninety-minute drive from the Maine coast. But near the Grafton Loop trailhead, stop by Puzzle Mountain Bakery, whose warm berry and apple pies, sold through an honor-system deposit box on the side of the road, will have you reconsidering the crustacean cuisine.

Start the Day

Café di Cocoa (119 Main Street; 207-824-5282): Tasty vegetarian and vegan treats, plus strong coffee.

Gear Up

Bob & Terry's Ski and Sports Outlet (61 Sunday River Road; 207-824-2323): Ski rentals and outdoor gear.

Refuel

Sunday River Brewing Company (29 Sunday River Road; 207-824-4253): Wash down wings, nachos, and burgers with a Sunsplash Golden Ale or 420 IPA.

Millbrook Tavern and Grille (on the Common; 207-824-2175): Thick steaks, huge salads, and live entertainment in the sports bar at the Bethel Inn.

L'Auberge Bistro (15 L'Auberge Lane; 207-824-2774): French-fusion cuisine.

Bunk

**Bethel Outdoor Adventure &
Campground** (121 Mayville Road; 800-
533-3607): Riverside resort within walking distance of downtown Bethel.

Bethel Inn Resort & Country Club
(on the Common; 800-654-012): Less
fancy than the name sounds, with 160
rooms, fitness center, and golf course.

The Sudbury Inn (151 Main Street;
207-824-2174): Cross-country skiing
and snowshoeing, eighteen rooms, and
the Suds Pub.

Can't Leave?

Nearest airport: Portland
International, Portland, Maine (63
miles)

Primary industries: Skiing, snowboarding, recreation, lumber

Local Legend

Mahoosuc Notch

Appalachian Trail thru-hikers refer to
Mahoosuc Notch, northwest of Bethel,
as the toughest mile on the trail. The
section is, by many accounts, the most
torturous stretch, thanks to the maze of
slabs and boulders that force hikers to
throw off their backpacks and wriggle
through the rock, following painted
white arrows that seem to point to
nowhere. But others relish the challenge and the underworld of caves and
crevices. Decide for yourself by undertaking the 10.2-mile hike through the
area. Bedeviled or delighted, you can
gain further appreciation of the A.T.'s
many personalities.

Kingfield, Maine

Population: 1,117

Action: Downhill and cross-country skiing, mountain biking, fishing, paddling, rafting, hiking

When you live more than twenty miles from the closest chain supermarket, you tend to be pretty innovative (and, many would agree, pretty lucky). The outdoor-minded residents of Kingfield, Maine, a whisper of a town wedged between two of the state's highest mountains, are no exception. Kingfielders seem to be constantly dreaming up new ways to ski and hike their mountains, and fly-fish and raft their rivers. The local newspaper is called *The Irregular;* the local gossip is about who the hottest area ski racer is or what might be the best dry fly for the opening of the angling season. Put on the map by Sugarloaf/USA ski area, but still off the well-trod path of most Maine tourists, this quiet corner of Maine's western mountains somehow stays refreshingly offbeat and updated.

Actually, quirky ingenuity was part of Kingfield's culture long before the adventure boom. Founded in 1816, the town is the birthplace of F. E. and F. O. Stanley, who invented and manufactured the Stanley Steamer, the 1890s car that would later be featured in land-speed records. The Stanley twins also created dry plates for photography and made violins, in a slight nod to Kingfield's reputation as a woodworking center in the 1800s. (Long before the antitobacco movement, they also denounced smoking in their writings. Much of their work is displayed at Kingfield's Stanley Museum.) Though invested heavily in the logging industry, the town also made such whimsical items as knitting-mill bobbins and yo-yos.

Kingfield's most significant invention, however, was one that had been around for thousands of years: the 4,237-foot Sugarloaf Mountain. In 1951, a local shopkeeper named Amos Winter began cutting an access road and trails around the peak, while other Kingfield skiers began organizing themselves into a ski club. Since then, Sugarloaf/USA has turned into a sprawling four-season resort with 1,400 skiable acres and some of the most continual vertical feet (2,820) in New England. Though it's a haul from East Coast metropolises, Sugarloaf draws a large number of loyal road-trippers, who put up with the drive and the sometimes frigid temps to see the mountain suddenly appear around "Oh my gosh corner," and then to ski its steep flanks on Narrow Gauge and Bubblecuffer.

Sugarloaf/USA is one of a few Northeast resorts with a well-established village at its base, so après ski means leaving the ski boots on for a few rounds at the Bag & Kettle and then retiring to a condo or hotel without having to climb back in the car. Culturally, Sugarloaf Mountain also defines Kingfield life; activities and amenities are described as on- or off-mountain. Nearby is one of the country's premier boarding schools for skiers and snowboarders: Carrabassett Valley Academy, where Seth Wescott snowboarded before winning the first-ever Olympic snowboard-cross gold medal. For the less vertically inclined, winter means cross-country skiing the 105 kilometers of trails at the Sugarloaf Outdoor Center (which also has thirty kilometers of snowshoeing trails) and the surrounding hills and lakes, or snow-mobiling at the Bigelow Preserve.

Come summer, Sugarloaf/USA shifts into mountain-biking season with fifty miles of marked trails and a shuttle that runs between Carrabassett Valley Town Park and the mountain. (Dozens of other loops can be found on old logging roads around Kingfield.) Sugarloaf/USA also has an eighteen-hole, Robert Trent Jones, Jr.–designed golf course and

Even in the spring and summer, Mount Abraham lures outdoor-sports enthusiasts to Kingfield, Maine. (© KingfieldUSA.com)

a golf school. A three-mile hike to the summit on the Burnt Mountain Trail, meanwhile, provides views of the Carrabassett Valley.

More hiking trails surround Kingfield. The Appalachian Trail runs nearby, and many thru-hikers start to taste completion of their trek at Katahdin. Mount Abraham, Bigelow Mountain, and Bigelow Preserve all offer hikers panoramic rewards.

Even Maine feels the July and August heat, and area swimming holes abound. West Mountain and Poplar Stream Falls are two of the best, along with Riverside Park on the Carrabassett River.

The Carrabassett is often dotted with canoes and kayaks, thanks to its Class II and III whitewater; more serious stuff lies along the Dead and Kennebec rivers, while the nearby Flagstaff Lake and the Rangeley Lakes offer placid paddling and angling options. Not that fly-fishers will ever need to leave the Carrabassett Valley—the abundance of fish may be one reason why the nearest chain supermarket is more than twenty miles away.

Start the Day

The Orange Cat Café (329 Main Street; 207-265-2860): Breakfast burritos, bagels, and pastries, plus salads and sandwiches; take the jalapeño chicken salad to go.

The Woodsman (Route 27; 207-265-2561): Breakfast only (with some lunch items on the weekends) in this Maine cabin; go for the blueberry pancakes.

Gear Up

Sugarloaf/USA Outdoor Center (207-237-6830): Cross-country skiing in the winter, plus mountain bikes, moose cruises, rafting, hiking maps, and more in the summer.

Sugarloaf Sports Outlet (207-265-2011): Alpine, snowboard, and nordic equipment to buy and rent, plus apparel and accessories for discount purchase.

Kingfisher River Guides (207-265-5823): Driftboat and hike-

and-wade fly-fishing trips on the Kennebec, Dead, and other trout-rich rivers, with longtime guide Todd Towle.

Refuel

Longfellows Restaurant (247 Main Street, 207-265-4394): Overlooking the Carrabassett River, with two-for-one specials on Tuesday nights and Italian night on Wednesdays.

Nostalgia Tavern (Route 27; 207-265-2559): Prime rib, steak tips, and a lively bar.

The Bag & Kettle (Sugarloaf; 207-237-2451): Legendary après-ski bar with equally legendary Bag Burgers, whose ingredients are top secret.

Bunk

Deer Farm Camps (Tuft's Pond Road; 207-265-4599; www.deerfarmcamps .com): Cabins and tent sites, twenty minutes from the Appalachian Trail.

The Herbert Grand Hotel (246 Main Street; 207-265-2000; www.herbertgrandhotel.com): 1917 Beaux-Arts–style hotel with twenty-six rooms. One wintery day in 1982, the owners walked away and never returned; the hotel is now refurbished, with a dining room, free wireless Internet access, and thick bedding and towels to keep winter at bay.

The Inn on Winter's Hill (33 Winter Hill Street; 800-233-9687; www.wintershill.com): Designed by the Stanley twins, this was the first home in Maine to have central heat; modern amenities include a pool, hot tub, and tennis courts.

Can't Leave?

Nearest airport: Portland International, Portland, Maine (92 miles)

Primary industries: Tourism, wood products

The Wild Side

The Backside Snowfields

The bald summit of Sugarloaf Mountain is not only a welcome beacon to weary travelers, but also a destination in itself, thanks to its fabled Backside Snowfields. This is the only place on the East Coast where you can ride a lift to above-treeline powder skiing—provided Mother Nature cooperates, of course. Open only when there is a significant amount of the white stuff, the Snowfields and their double-black terrain have become legendary among eastern skiers, who call each other to proclaim, "The Snowfields are open!"—or keep the secret all to themselves.

Southwest Harbor, Maine

Population: 1,983

Action: Sailing, kayaking, hiking, mountain and road biking, rock climbing

At some 5,500 miles long, the Maine coast is dotted with so many coves, lighthouses, and lobster shacks that sometimes—unless you're a Down Easter yourself—it can be trying, to tell one place apart from another. But Southwest Harbor, the largest town on Mount Desert Island, stands alone. First, it lies on Somes Sound, the only natural fjord on the East Coast. (Think Alaska or Greenland, only warmer and much, much closer to Boston.) Second, it's the only place you'll find Beal's, a working lobster pound. Third, while summer mansions are lined up like sentinels on other parts of the coastline, they taper off around here. And fourth, it's the gateway to the only national park in New England: the 47,000-acre kayaking, hiking, and climbing playground of Acadia.

Mount Desert Island, or MDI, is 108 square miles, much of it alternatively heaved up in twenty-six mountains or sunk into lakes, ponds, creeks, and coves. It was named by French explorer Samuel de Champlain, who landed here in 1604, when Native Americans had already inhabited the island for thousands of years. When Hudson River School painters Frederick Church and Thomas Cole—whose landscape paintings inspired city-dwellers to vacation throughout the northeastern United States—began sharing images of MDI in the mid-1800s, families began to summer here. At first, these families were known as the "rusticators," as they adjusted to the rugged life on the island; later, the summer population brought plenty more creature comforts into their so-called cottages.

But Southwest Harbor was mostly left to the lobstermen and the boatbuilders. Today, it remains one of Maine's top commercial fishing harbors; all those colorful vessels, lobster pots, and piles of nets aren't just for the benefit of tourists. This is also home base for the Hinckley Company, which has been building top-notch yachts since 1928 and

Brisk winds, protected coves, and rocky islands make the sailing around Southwest Harbor, Maine some of the country's best. (© Southwest Harbor/Tremont Chamber of Commerce)

today offers bareboat or fully crewed charters around the Maine coast in the summer.

Whether you're on your own boat or a charter, the sailing around Southwest Harbor is some of the best on the east or west coast of the country, thanks to the brisk winds, hundreds of protected coves, and rocky islands. The sailing is rivaled only, perhaps, by the paddling, which has long been adding the sight of red, yellow, and orange sea kayaks to the natural hues of seals, minke whales, and porpoises in the blue waters of Acadia National Park.

Acadia was first envisioned by George Dorr, a conservationist who summered on MDI and founded the Hancock County Trustees of Public Reservations in 1901, as a way to protect the island against the threat of development from the new gas-powered sawmills. By 1916 the group had donated more than 6,000 acres to the federal government, which declared it a national monument and then, in 1919, Lafayette National Park; the Acadia name change came in 1929. The

The Wild Side

Bass Harbor Marsh

With more than three million visitors per year, Acadia might not seem to have many secrets left. And Bass Harbor Marsh, a few miles from Southwest Harbor, is certainly known to many canoeists and kayakers. (Only tourists paddle here when the tide is low—and then proceed to get their boats stuck in the mud.)

Less known, however, is the appeal of a nighttime paddle. Pack a few beverages and watch the tidal and lunar charts for when the tide is high and the moon is full. Drift through the swollen marsh under the star-laden sky, and you'll see the best nightlife in Southwest Harbor.

park now sprawls across some two-fifths of MDI, rolling along the mountains and spilling down to the sea. Bald eagles and ospreys live and breed in the area near the water, building nests as large as six feet high.

The surrounding peaks and steep cliffs create not only first-rate kayaking drama, but also premier hiking and climbing routes. Of the 120-plus miles of hiking and running trails in Acadia, some of the most challenging—and rewarding—near Southwest Harbor are the winding, wooded paths up Western Mountain and Acadia Mountain. The highest point is the 1,532-foot Cadillac Mountain and is one of the most popular hikes. You'll find fewer people scrambling up the sixty-foot seacliffs of Otter Cliffs, Great Hand, and South Wall; the park offers climbing pitches up to 5.12, plus bouldering problems. Forty-five miles of old carriage roads create smooth mountain-biking trails, while cycling routes in and out of the park career through fishing villages, along seawalls, and around marshes. One of the top picks is the twenty-seven-mile Park Loop Road; go early in the morning to find the gawk-worthy journey all to yourself.

Back in Southwest Harbor, you'll find much of the action (if there is any) centered on Clark Point Road, which is crisscrossed with docks, and on Main Street, where there are only local shops (no chain stores). You'll also find galleries displaying work from artists who have picked up where Cole and Church left off in the 1800s—and who have the remarkable discipline to hold paintbrushes or charcoal sticks in their hands when there are waters, mountains, and lobsters to crack open.

Start the Day

Café 2/Eat-a-Pita (326 Main Street; 207-244-4344): Blueberry-stuffed french toast, starting at 8 AM, plus pita sandwiches and salads for the kayak or backpack.

The Deacon Seat (Clark Point Road; 207-244-0033): A locals' breakfast spot, with free refills on coffee.

Gear Up

Acadia Adventures (19 Clark Point Road; 207-244-0680): Bicycles for rent and guided kayak tours of the western shores of Mount Desert Island.

Maine State Sea Kayak (254 Main Street; 207-244-9500): Guided sea-kayak tours around Somes Sound, Western and Blue Hill Bays, and the Cranberry Islands.

Downeast Friendship Sloop Charters (207-266-5210): Crewed sailing charters for day trips, sunset sails, lobster-bake cruises, and overnight excursions that end with blueberry pancakes at breakfast.

Refuel

Beal's Lobster Pier (182 Clark Point Road; 207-244-7178): A no-frills lobster pound on the pier, with some of Maine's best seafood and moorings for boaters.

Local Legend

Acadia Triathlon and Oktoberfest

Every October, when the tourists have turned south and the trees have turned colors, Mount Desert Island celebrates with one of the best combos since chocolate met peanut butter: a triathlon and Oktoberfest.

The first is a 4.1-mile run, 13-mile bike, and 4-mile canoe race that spares athletes from swimming in frigid fall Atlantic water. Teams and individuals compete. (If you enter alone, you're considered an "iron person"—not bad for an event that's a fraction of the real Ironman Triathlon, whose world title is contested in Hawaii every October.)

The second refuels depleted glycogen stores with two dozen types of Maine microbrews, local wine, and an ideal ratio of protein, carbs, and fat in the pretzel and sausage stands.

Café Drydock & Inn (357 Main Street; 207-244-5842): Burgers, seafood, and vegetarian options; outside deck and, if it gets too late, an upstairs inn with eight rooms; also rents a waterfront cottage on Branch Lake.

Red Sky Restaurant (14 Clark Point Road; 207-244-0476): Bistro with fresh local organic produce and vegetarian options, along with excellent meats and dessert.

Bunk

The Claremont (Claremont Road; 207-244-5036; www.theclare monthotel.com): 1884 hotel with Southwest Harbor's best views;

twenty-four rooms and cottages plus croquet courts, tennis, and the Boathouse restaurant, a local hangout for harbor-watching.

The Moorings Inn (Route 102A; 207-244-5523): Nineteen rooms on the waterfront, plus canoes and kayaks; next door to the Hinckley Yacht Yard.

Smuggler's Den Campground (20 Main Street; 207-244-4072; www.smugglersdencampground.com): Full-service campground with tent and RV sites, cabins, a pool, and even lobsters in the camp store.

Can't Leave?

Nearest airport: Portland International, Portland, Maine (144 miles)

Primary industries: Boatbuilding, fishing, tourism

Lenox, Massachusetts

Lenox, Massachusetts, is synonymous with Boston Symphony Orchestra's summer home at Tanglewood, the Kripalu Center for Yoga and Health, and the spa at Canyon Ranch. But there's another side to Lenox, and it chooses slightly less refined escapes. So while the rest of the world has its nose buried in a musical program or a massage table, a quiet squadron of hikers and bikers is out tackling the trails of Kennedy Park, exploring the 1,300-acre Pleasant Valley Sanctuary, paddling the waters of Goose Pond and cycling long, traffic-free loops around the town of Great Barrington. These are the Berkshires, after all, a rolling section of the Appalachian Mountains interlaced with swift rivers and cobalt blue lakes, and while these hills are one of the country's top cultural seats, there are those who prefer the saddle of a bicycle.

Population: 5,156
Action: Mountain and road biking, hiking, downhill and cross-country skiing, paddling

One of Lenox's top in-town resources is Kennedy Park, 500-plus acres of woods woven with trails for mountain biking, hiking, trail running, and cross-country skiing. The park lies just north of Main Street, and toward the center of the park lie ruins that tell some of Lenox's history. These are the ruins of Aspinwall Hotel, an upscale lodge built in 1902 for wealthy vacationers who had fled Boston and New York for a spell in the Berkshires. Early on, Lenox had been a community of farmers and small-industry workers; the town held its first meeting in 1767 and tapped into its underground vein of iron ore and the Berkshire soil. But by the mid- to late-nineteenth century, thanks in part to promotion by writers such as Herman Melville and Nathaniel Hawthorne, Lenox had become one of the East Coast's top locales for summer cottages, known as the "inland Newport." The Tanglewood concerts first arrived in 1937 and, coupled with the arrival of the Kripalu Center and Canyon Ranch, firmly rooted Lenox as a retreat for

With rooms priced at $500 to more than $1,000 per night, Blantyre, a Tudor mansion with a spa and 117 acres of grounds, is one of the more sumptuous places to bunk in Lenox, Massachusetts. (© Massachusetts Office of Travel and Tourism)

wellness and the well-to-do. Shops and restaurants around the town's compact center cater to such a clientele.

But near the trailhead for Kennedy Park, you'll find Arcadian Shop, which is geared strictly to those who have discovered that Lenox lies among three state forests and near the Housatonic River and Appalachian Trail. Head out from here to fly-fish the Housatonic, a 130-mile waterway that teems with trout as it flows southward toward Long Island Sound. The river is also a prime paddling destination. A four-mile section near the town of Great Barrington is good for flatwater kayaking and canoeing, riffled with Class I and II rapids among the cottonwoods, sycamore trees, and green and gold farms. In Lee, the connected glacial lakes of Goose Pond and Upper Goose Pond create a quiet 5.2-mile paddle, while the 16,500-acre October Mountain State Forest (the largest in Massachusetts), east of Lenox, has more access points.

In the past few years, October Mountain—named as such by Herman Melville—has also become a mountain-biking destination. Try the nine-mile, mostly doubletrack Ashley Lake Loop or climb the singletrack trails around the 1,948-foot October Mountain. Bikes are not allowed on the Appalachian Trail, which runs through the eastern side of the state forest. This part of the trail is an easy hike, just over nine miles with an elevation gain of less than 1,000 feet, and there is a lean-to for picnics on sweltering days. More hikes abound on the thirty miles of trails in the 10,000-acre Beartown State Forest, south of Lenox, and on thirty more trail miles at Pittsfield State Forest, where there are also sixty-five acres of wild azalea fields.

All three state forests become the playground of snowshoeing and nordic-skiing locals. The trails at Kennedy Park are groomed and closed to motor vehicles, while Canterbury Farm Ski Touring Center in Becket, Notchview Reservation in Windsor, and Lenox's own Cranwell Resort are full-service cross-country areas. For alpine skiing and snowboarding, several areas dot the Berkshire hills surrounding Lenox, from Butternut's twenty-two trails to Jiminy Peak's 172 acres.

In the winter, Lenox turns into a much quieter town, without the Tanglewood crowds and the sounds of the symphony in the air, which become a welcome ritual after a summer's day hiking and biking the Berkshires. Until then, there are yoga classes at Kripalu and spa treatments at Canyon Ranch, which seem even sweeter when you've really earned them outdoors.

Start the Day

Berkshire Bagels (18 Franklin Street; 413-637-1500): Coffee, fifteen flavors of bagels, homemade cream cheeses, muffins, and sandwiches.

Carol's (8 Franklin Street; 413-637-8948): Scrambled eggs with lox, feta, tomato, and spinach omelets, thick french toast, and crispy homefries.

Gear Up

Arcadian Shop (91 Pittsfield Road; 413-637-3010): Rent bikes, kayaks, skis, and snowshoes and get the lowdown on local trails, rivers, ponds, and road rides.

Refuel

Church Street Café (65 Church Street; 413-637-2745): Internationally inspired American bistro with such specialties as local organic salads, crispy Thai shrimp and crab cakes, and Moroccan-spiced free-range chicken.

The Wild Side

The Deerfield River

Some of the wildest water in Massachusetts is not on the oft-maligned Charles River, but on the Deerfield, where dam releases from April through October create Class II and III rapids at the Zoar Gap and Class IV at the Dryway. Book a rafting trip with Zoar Outdoor (www.zoaroutdoor.com), an outfitter in the town of Charlemont, which is northeast of Lenox.

Local Legend

Canyon Ranch

Located on 120 wooded acres, Canyon Ranch has evolved from a simple spa, first opened in 1989, to a world-class fitness facility. There's a 100,000-square-foot complex with tennis courts, swimming pools, and gyms, while instructors teach more than fifty fitness classes per day. Outside, Canyon Ranch boasts places to paddle, hike, and cross-country ski.

Olde Heritage Tavern (12 Housatonic Street; 413-637-0884): Burgers, wings, pizza, and beers, plus darts and a pool table, in an old wooden house.

Gateways Inn (51 Walker Street; 413-637-2532): Upscale Italian restaurant with grappa-marinated lamb, grilled paninis, and late-night light meals at La Terraza Bar.

Bunk

October Mountain State Forest (256 Woodland Road, Lee; 413-243-1778; www.mass.gov/drc/parks/western /octm): Forty-six sunny and grassy campsites across from the Housatonic River.

The Village Inn (16 Church Street; 800-253-0917; www.villageinn -lenox.com): Centrally located, 1771 bed-and-breakfast with thirty-two rooms and reasonable rates.

Blantyre (16 Blantyre Road; 413-637-3556; www.blantyre.com): Expansive (and expensive) resort in a Tudor mansion with a spa and 117 acres of grounds.

Can't Leave?

Nearest airport: Albany International, Albany, New York (45 miles)

Primary industries: Tourism, technology

Williamstown, Massachusetts

Population: 8,238

Action: Hiking, mountain biking, downhill and cross-country skiing

I n the late 1820s, the president of Williams College created an annual event called Mountain Day, when students could escape from the rigors of their studies and hike into the surrounding Berkshire Mountains. Nearly two centuries later, the tradition continues. On one of the first three Fridays in October when the weather is clear, the school bells will ring out "The Mountains" in the morning, announcing the start of Mountain Day and excusing the roughly 2,000 students from classes. Shortly after, hundreds of kids begin making their way up the Hopper Trail to the top of Stony Ledge to see views of the Hopper Valley and the peak of 3,500-foot Mount Greylock—the tallest mountain in Massachusetts. This enlightened appreciation for the outdoors is shared by the townsfolk of cultured Williamstown, who are known to take a Mountain Day—or five—themselves when the conditions are right and head onto the scores of biking, hiking, and ski trails in the area.

Often overshadowed by the sprawling Adirondacks to the northwest and the Green Mountains to the north, the Berkshires of western Massachusetts offer their own dose of action—only three hours from Boston and three and a half hours from New York City. The outdoor hub is Mount Greylock State Reservation, where you'll find seventy miles of trails among its 12,500 acres, including a short stretch of the Appalachian Trail. Climb to Mount Greylock's summit on a clear day, and from the tower there you can see into five states.

Williamstown sits next to the north edge of the reservation, in the top corner of Massachusetts near the borders of New York and Vermont. It was first settled as West Hoosac in the mid-1750s, but the name was changed in 1765 at the bequest of Colonel Ephraim Williams, who had just been killed in the French and Indian War. He stipulated in his will that in exchange for donating land and funds to start a school, the

The view from Mount Greylock is stunning in autumn. (© Berkshires Visitors Bureau)

village would need to be incorporated as Williamstown. In the early 1790s, Williams College accepted its first students.

Williamstown has the stately feel of a college town, with artsy boutiques, upscale coffeehouses, and restaurants and distinguished Victorian, Georgian, and Federal homes shaded beneath birches, oaks, and maples that radiate with color in the fall. The town is a haven for culture and art, even apart from the students and professors. Every summer, it attracts some of the world's best actors and actresses for the Williamstown Theatre Festival, a presentation of 200 performances and plays, along with workshops and readings. It's also home to the Sterling and Francine Clark Art Institute, where you'll find works by Homer, Renoir, Gauguin, and Degas. After taking a tour, you can spend time walking on the trails among its 140 acres of woods, fields, and meadows. Or better yet, head into the untamed wilderness outside its borders.

Drive less than a couple of miles from the center of town on Bulkley Street, and you'll reach the Hopkins Memorial Forest, managed by the Center for Environmental Studies at Williams. There are several short but heart-pounding hikes in this 2,500-acre preserve, which stretches across the New York and Vermont borders. Bikes are prohibited, but catch the thirty-five-mile-long Taconic Crest Trail as it exits on the south side, and you'll ride through prime singletrack and rugged old forest roads toward the grueling ascent of Mount Berlin. Or pedal over to Mount Greylock State Reservation and head on the Cheshire Harbor Trail, with its near-vertical 2.5-mile climb that peaks near the mountain summit. Roughly one-quarter of the park's trails are open to mountain biking, and almost all of them can be used by backcountry skiers in the winter. The Mount Greylock Ski Club, founded in 1937, also maintains seventeen downhill-ski trails with a vertical of 350 feet on the mountain. The whole operation is manned by member volunteers, who do everything from operating the three ancient rope tows to cutting logs for the wood-burning stove in the lodge.

Skiers looking for a more modern experience can drive about fifteen minutes to Jiminy Peak. The vertical there may be only 1,400 feet on its forty-three trails, but when a Nor'easter dumps a foot of snow on the area, Jiminy makes for an ideal quick powder escape—or maybe even a Mountain Day.

Local Legend

Williams Outing Club

In 1830, Professor Albert Hopkins and a group of Williams students cleared the Hopper Trail to the summit of Mount Greylock. This event marked the birth of student involvement in the outdoors at the college. A half-century later, the Williams Outing Club was formed, and it continues to flourish today. The club leads weekly hikes and operates a ropes course in Hopkins Forest, and it runs a 2,000-square-foot climbing wall at the campus's Herbert S. Towne Field House. It also publishes the *North Berkshire Outdoor Guide,* the definitive guidebook on the area's hiking trails; the guide is available at the Mountain Goat.

Start the Day

Tunnel City Coffee (100 Spring Street; 413-458-5010): Spend enough time among the students and faculty at this coffeehouse, where the pastries are made from scratch, and you'll feel like you've enrolled in classes at Williams.

Chef's Hat (905 Simonds Road; 413-458-5120): The hearty Sunday brunches at this down-home restaurant will make you glad that you waited in the short line for a table.

Gear Up

The Mountain Goat (130 Water Street; 413-458-8445): The area's main outdoor outfitter; also rents mountain bikes.

The Spoke Bicycles (279 Main Street; 413-458-3456): The source for road bikes and info on the best local road rides.

Refuel

Pappa Charlie's Deli (28 Spring Street; 413-458-5969): Choices like the Paltrow (eggplant and parmesan) at this popular sandwich shop and juice bar are named after the celebrities who have performed at the theater festival or are tied to the town in some other way.

Mezze Bistro and Bar (16 Water Street; 413-458-0123; www.mezze inc.com): Upscale restaurant that would fit as well in Manhattan as in Western Massachusetts; serves entrées like Flying Pig Farm confit of pig, and sea scallops with cauliflower purée, hen-of-the-woods mushrooms, and truffle vinaigrette.

Bunk

Bascom Lodge (Notch Road; 413-743-1591; www.naturesclassroom .org): A stone-and-wood lodge built by the Civilian Conservation Corps in the 1930s at the summit of Mount Greylock. Open May to October.

Williams Inn (Routes 2 and 7; 413-458-9371; www.williamsinn .com): A refined, 100-room inn on the Williams campus.

Can't Leave?

Nearest airport: Albany International, Albany, New York (45 miles)

Primary industries: Education, health care, service

Jackson, New Hampshire

I t's an easy mistake to call Jackson, New Hampshire, the quintessential New England town, given that it comes complete with a red, wooden covered bridge that leads to a village center filled with historic colonial homes and the requisite white, steepled church. But the truth is, there's nowhere else quite like it. For starters, Jackson's hiding spot within the Mount Washington Valley of the White Mountain National Forest gives it views of the stark surrounding peaks that are the undisputed envy of all other resort communities in New England. Second, and most important, it's the only place in New England where it makes more sense to cross-country ski from your bed and breakfast to the pub across town in winter; the town's impressive ninety-five miles of neurotically manicured trails make getting around on two planks so much faster than walking or driving.

Population: 885
Action: Cross-country and downhill skiing, hiking, rock climbing, mountain biking

This gift to the nordic world—and pub crawlers alike—is the work of a local not-for-profit organization called the Jackson Ski Touring Foundation, created about three decades ago. Before that time, the town had suffered through a decades-long decline, as it sat in the shadow of nearby North Conway, an outlet-store-filled haven and jumping-off spot for tourists and adventurers in the White Mountains. Jackson was incorporated in December, 1800, and originally called Adams, after President John Adams. The name was switched to its current one in the 1850s in honor of another commander-in-chief, Andrew Jackson, after his success in the Battle of New Orleans, according to the Jackson Historical Society. A couple of decades later, the railroads deposited well-heeled vacationers from Portland, Maine, and Boston into the area, giving rise to several grand hotels—two of which, the Eagle Mountain House and Wentworth Resort, still operate in the

Holiday lights adorn the gazebo at the Christmas Farm Inn in Jackson, New Hampshire. (© NHDTTD/Candace Cochrane)

village. After World War II, though, tourism largely dried up, and Jackson didn't regain its spit-shine until recent times.

The town's ski trails vary from those for beginners to those for extreme experts, and their main launching pad is the foundation's Touring Center on Main Street. As they wind among maple forests and farm pastures, they dip into three mountain valleys and eventually connect with the backcountry trails in the White Mountains National Forest, a federal preserve the size of Yosemite National Park and accentuated by the tallest peaks in the Northeast, including 6,288-foot Mount Washington. For a long, leisurely ski, try the seven-mile Ellis River Trail, which follows the mostly flat west bank of the Ellis River, and take a break at the trail's warming hut. For a more thrilling route, there's the Wildcat Valley Trail, which starts at the summit of the Wildcat Mountain Ski Area and descends along a ridgeline more than 3,000 feet over its eleven-mile length into Jackson village.

Wildcat is one of two alpine-ski resorts within a fifteen-minute drive from town. It's an old New England throwback; there's no development on the slopes except a base lodge, and more than three-quarters of its forty-seven trails are designated as intermediate or expert. Black Mountain is the second of the pair. A family-owned and family-oriented operation, it has a vertical drop of 1,100 feet, and its forty runs are mostly wide and easy. A handful of other resorts lie within an hour of Jackson, and the backcountry options for down-hillers are almost endless within the Whites.

Although the town stands out for its skiing, the summer has also become a busy time here. Some of the area's cross-country trails open to mountain bikers, and hikers use the town as a base for tackling the Presidential Range in the Whites, where eight summits stand taller than 4,000 feet. Mount Washington is the most imposing. A crossroads for weather systems approaching from three different directions, it's home to the highest wind speed ever recorded on earth, an astounding 231 miles per hour. Just a short drive up U.S. Highway 16 from Jackson is Pinkham Notch, where an Appalachian Mountain Club visitor's center stands at the base of several trails, which lead above the treeline to the rocky, tundralike mountaintop. Pinkham Notch is also the access point to the nearby Appalachian Trail, and it marks the approach for the fabled rock- and ice-climbing area Huntington Ravine, on the east side of Mount Washington.

Head farther up the U.S. Route 16, and you'll reach the Mount Washington Auto Road, a paved route that leads all the way to the summit. Across the highway from the entrance are the Great Glen Trails, an outdoor complex with twenty-five miles of carriage roads and singletrack that double as cross-country ski trails in the winter. Here you can choose the level of exertion, ranging from a flat and easy ride on the valley floor at 1,400 feet in elevation, to a route that climbs nearly up the side of the mountain, past 2,000 feet. In the winter, you'll probably want to stick with the trails in Jackson, though. You're closer to the pubs that way.

Start the Day

As You Like It Bakery and Café (Route 16B; 603-383-6425): Organic espresso and breakfast pastries are always in ready supply here.

Yesterdays Restaurant (Route 16A; 603-383-4457): Breakfast joint open from 6:15 AM to 2 PM every day, and beloved for its banana-nut pancakes.

Local Legend

Honeymoon Bridge

The 121-foot-long wooden covered bridge on U.S. Route 16B has been ushering visitors over the Ellis River and into Jackson since 1876, when it was built by a local dairy farmer, according to the Jackson Historical Society. Not wide enough to fit two vehicles driving in opposite directions, the bridge forces you to slacken your pace as you cross it. Locals call it the Honeymoon Bridge, and they'll tell you that newlyweds do often get their pictures taken beneath its block-letter "Jackson, N.H." sign, although how the bridge got its nickname is still unclear.

The Wild Side

Tuckerman Ravine

The broad glacial bowl on the eastern side of Mount Washington known as Tuckerman Ravine has been the premier backcountry skiing challenge in the East for nearly the past century. Its position and shape make it the collection bin for blowing snow, so depths can reach up to seventy-five feet in spots, resulting in prime spring skiing when the treacherous weather of the White Mountains begins to soften. The ravine was named for botanist Edward Tuckerman, who explored the area in the 1830s and 1840s, but its sheer 800-foot headwall wasn't conquered by skiers until the 1920s. There are now more than twenty established descents, and thousands of people each year make the three-hour slog to the top to ski down it. Many of them are unprepared for the icy climb, quickly changing weather conditions, potential for avalanches, and the ravine's surprising fifty-plus–degree pitch in spots. The access trail to Tuckerman Ravine starts at the Appalachian Mountain Club visitor's center at Pinkham Notch, off U.S. Route 16, north of Jackson.

Gear Up

Nordic Skier (153 Main Street; 603-383-9355): A nordic-ski rental and sales shop operated within the Jackson Ski Touring Foundation's lodge in the village center.

Great Glen Outfitters (Mount Washington Auto Road, Pinkham Notch; 603-466-3328): An outdoor outfitter at the Great Glen Trails Outdoor Center complex, where you'll also find a café with a fieldstone fireplace and twenty-five-foot indoor climbing wall.

Red Jersey Cyclery (Route 16, Intervale, New Hampshire; 603-356-7520): An impressive full-service bike shop, and the sponsor of many local bike races.

Refuel

Thompson House Eatery (Route 16A; 603-383-9341; www.thompsonhouse eatery.com): A nearly 200-year-old farmhouse and barn where the lamb, steak, and fish entrées are simple, but exquisite enough to lure foodies all the way from Boston.

Inn at Thorn Hill (Thorn Hill Road; 603-383-4242; www.innatthornhill .com): The food served in the dining room in this stately inn is as impressive as the selections from its 3,000-bottle wine list.

Red Fox Bar and Grille (Route 16; 603-383-4949): Steak is prepared on a wood-fired grill at this friendly eatery and bar, and live jazz is served with brunch on Sundays.

Bunk

Eagle Mountain House (Carter Notch Road; 603-383-9111; www.eaglemt.com): This sprawling ninety-three-room inn grew from a farmhouse into a grand hotel and retains its historic charm with modern comfort.

Wentworth Resort Hotel (1 Carter Notch Road; 603-383-9700; www.thewentworth.com): The other grand hotel in town, it was built in 1869 in the heart of the village and has undergone an impressive recent restoration.

Can't Leave?

Nearest airport: Portland International, Portland, Maine (71 miles)

Primary industries: Retail, recreation, tourism

Peterborough, New Hampshire

Population: 6,073

Action: Hiking, paddling, cross-country and downhill skiing

What's the most popular peak in the world to climb? For a while, folks had their money on Mount Fuji. But now, according to some sources, odds are that Mount Monadnock, a 3,165-foot peak in southwestern New Hampshire, has more hikers on its flanks every year than any other peak on the planet. Once you reach the top, the reasons are fairly obvious: like those of Fujiyama, the views here are staggering. Imagine peering down at features from all six New England states (including Boston's skyscrapers to the southeast and the Granite State's own Mount Washington to the north) from perfect picnic ledges with only a couple of hours of hiking behind you—the immediate payback's irresistible. But there's a lesser-known and equally good reason why climbing around here should top a mountaineer's list: the tiny town of Peterborough, where the Contoocook River winds by churches and taverns straight out of a Currier & Ives print.

The people of Peterborough, however, are serious mountaineers, paddlers, and skiers whose energy would explode a Currier & Ives woodprint into splinters. They live, after all, on the doorstep of New Hampshire's first state park, Miller (created in 1891), where another mountain, Pack (Native American for "little") Monadnock, provides a 2,290-foot alternative to its big brother. Peterborough also protects the Casalis State Forest, a 228-acre reserve where locals like to hike, horseback ride, and snowshoe, and the smaller Shieling State Forest, which offers in-town trail running, a wildflower preserve, and forestry education on forty-eight acres of tree-covered ridges and valleys.

On Nubanusit Brook, the town's Edward MacDowell Dam creates the eponymous, 165-acre shallow lake. Forgotten by most mapmakers, the lake is one of the best places in southern New Hampshire for an evening canoe trip, as great blue herons, Canada geese, and tree

A bird's eye view of Peterborough, New Hampshire. (© Gerard Gleeson)

swallows are often the only other creatures sharing the lake's shallow marshlands and delicate inlet fingers. In the surrounding Monadnock region, paddlers can find more than 200 other hidden lakes, ponds, and streams, ranging from the placid to the heart palpitating.

You'll also find tucked-away ski areas, the last of a snow-sports era whose 570-plus mom-and-pop operations have mostly been lost. In nearby Keene, the long-closed Pinnacle Ski Area reopened in 2003 as Granite Gorge, and its north face, protected from the wind, holds some good powder stashes. (For larger ski areas, Crotched Mountain is a quick drive away, while many of New England's major resorts are within a two-hour drive.)

On cross-country skis or in hiking boots, it's easy to get lost yourself around Peterborough. The twenty-one-mile Wapack Trail—a yellow-blazed backpacker's dream thanks to its doable distance and ridgeline route—runs right through Peterborough, while other trails of nearly every length lead out of town. There's the streamside Wheeler Trail at less than a mile, the 49-mile Monadnock/Sunapee Gateway, the 2.5-mile Old Railroad Trail, and the 22 miles of hiking and cross-country trails on the grounds of the Sargent Center, an outdoor-education facility owned by Boston University. Even the Monadnock Community Hospital, just north of Shieling Forest, has its own 1.5-mile fitness trail with exercise stations.

For more cerebral workouts, Peterborough retains the type of culture that led to the creation of the country's oldest public-supported library in 1833. The MacDowell colony was one of the first artists' communities in the United States and has helped produce works from Aaron Copeland, Alice Walker, and Leonard Bernstein. In 1938, Thornton Wilder wrote *Our Town* while at the MacDowell retreat.

The Wild Side

Contoocook River

Flowing in an unusual north-northeasterly pattern some seventy-one miles from the New Hampshire town of Rindge, near Peterborough, to the state capital of Concord, the Contoocook (*con-TOOK-cuck*) River is a Granite State gem. Stretches around Peterborough offer flatwater paddling among archaeological sites that give you a glimpse into the salmon-fishing and farming life of the Penacook people. You can also fish for young Atlantic salmon or see some of the 117 species of birds, from bald eagles to eastern bluebirds, that populate the riverbanks. Closer to Concord, a drop of 700 feet creates Class III and IV whitewater runs, including the Class IV "Freight Train Rapids," one of New England's best stretches of whitewater. For guided tours, instruction, or canoe or kayak rentals, contact the Contoocook River Canoe Company at 603-753-9804.

Of course, the real drama lies in the outdoors, and act one might begin on Mount Monadnock itself, where it's possible to find the kind of quiet that inspired so many artists. Avoid the traditional, 4.4-mile White Cross trail and instead opt for the Pumpelly Trail, a nine-mile footpath that leads up from Dublin Lake. You'll hike six or seven hours past the timberline, gaining 1,700 feet of elevation, a new appreciation of New Hampshire, and the very best of the views that draw more people here than Mount Fuji draws to Japan.

Start the Day

Nonie's Restaurant & Bakery (28 Grove Street; 603-924-3451): Baked goods and coffee.

Peterborough Diner (10 Depot Street; 603-924-6202): Since 1949, a favorite spot for omelets, steak and eggs, french toast, and frappes.

Gear Up

Eastern Mountain Sports (1 Vowse Farm Road; 603-924-7231): Tents, backpacks, kayaks, and telemark or cross-country skis for rent or sale, plus books, clothing, and other outdoor essentials.

Refuel

Harlow's (3 School Street; 603-924-6365): Ten beers on tap, burgers, and burritos; live bands every Friday and Saturday night.

Acqua Bistro (Depot Square; 603-924-9925): Ginger-crusted salmon, Gorgonzola bistro burgers, and smoked-salmon, thin-crust pizza; wine dinners in winter.

R. A. Gatto's (6 School Street; 603-924-5000): Italian-influenced seafood and pasta, from calamari to eggplant parmesan, from a Culinary Institute of America chef.

Bunk

Jack Daniels Motor Inn (80 Concord Street; 603-924-7548): Seventeen rooms overlooking the Contoocook River; with basic amenities plus free wireless Internet access.

Peterborough Manor Bed & Breakfast (50 Summer Street; 603-924-9832): Seven rooms within walking distance of downtown; rents kayaks, bikes, boots, and more on site.

Can't Leave?

Nearest airport: Manchester-Boston Regional, Manchester, New Hampshire (37 miles)

Primary industries: Manufacturing, hospital services, education, retail

Wolfeboro, New Hampshire

Population: 6,660
Action: Paddling, sailing, fishing, cross-country skiing, mountain and road biking

Perhaps the oldest outdoorsy getaway in America is Wolfeboro, New Hampshire, on the southern shores of Lake Winnipesaukee. This town of 6,000 year-round residents has been a popular retreat since colonial governor John Wentworth built a summer estate here in 1771. He knew a few things about prime real estate, being the surveyor of the king's woods for North America and a rugged outdoorsman. Wentworth chose Wolfeboro, no doubt, because of its lake-filled location between the Ossipee and Belknap mountain ranges in New Hampshire's Lakes Region. It's also easy to access from Boston (100 miles); Portland, Maine (65 miles); and Concord, New Hampshire (40 miles).

Wolfeboro is the southern commercial hub of Lake Winnipesaukee, the sixth-largest natural body of freshwater completely within the country's borders. The lake stretches nearly twenty-six miles and has more than 250 islands and 288 miles of shoreline (including the islands). Formed by glaciers, it's well known for its clean water—all 625 billion gallons of it. In town, Main Street bustles year round with pedestrians, who hail mostly from Massachusetts and southern New England and are called Flatlanders by the locals. They mill about the sporting goods, clothing, and craft shops housed by the 100-year-old downtown buildings. In warm weather, kayaks and sailboats bob atop protected Wolfeboro Bay, and bass boats buzz off to the many hidden fishing nooks in the nearby coves. In winter, people come to town for its fifteen miles of immaculately maintained cross-country ski trails and to ice fish within the mini village of shanties formed on the frozen water near the municipal beach.

Proof that the town is the area's undisputed sporting center is everywhere—from the water-ski jump and slalom course in tiny Back Bay

Wolfeboro, New Hampshire's position on the southern shores of Lake Winnipesaukee make the town a premier sailing destination. (© NHDTTD/William Johnson)

(accessed by passing beneath a bridge in Main Street), to the steady stream of joggers constantly flowing through town, to the bikes on racks atop cars parked outside of the coffee shops and grocery stores.

The paddling opportunities on Winnipesaukee seem endless. All of the lake's hidden nooks would take nearly a lifetime to discover in a canoe or kayak. Then there are three other, quieter bodies of water to explore within town: Lake Wentworth, Rust Pond, and Crescent Lake. On Winnipesaukee, the other popular sport is sailing, and on a breezy day you'll spot everything from tiny Sunfish to thirty-foot-yachts taking advantage of the weather. Nearly everyone who lives on the lake seems to own a power boat, and the diving is some of the most interesting in the Northeast, because the wrecks of a handful of old passenger vessels still lie on the relatively shallow lake bottom.

On land, the road biking is spectacular, as quiet, wide-shouldered country roads wind into the White Mountain National Forest to the north of town and toward the Maine and New Hampshire coasts in the east. Every August, the town welcomes an invasion of riders for the Granite Man Triathlon, the athletic event of the year that includes a .75-mile swim in Winnipesaukee, a 15-mile ride, and 4.2-mile run. Then in the fall, as the trees turn to bright red and orange during peak foliage, the riding becomes hands down the most picturesque in North America.

Although there are no prime footpaths within Wolfeboro itself, the town is a short drive from rugged half-day hikes up and down peaks like Mount Major and Gunstock Mountain (the latter a ski mountain in the winter), which provide wide views of the lake below. For an even broader panorama, the major trailheads leading up the bald alpine summits of the towering Presidential Range—including 6,288-foot Mount Washington—of the White Mountains, are less than an hour away.

Once the lakes freeze in Wolfeboro and the snow begins to fall—in abundance, usually—the Flagg family, owners of the Nordic Skier Sports shop, haul out their grooming equipment and get to work on the roughly twenty miles of curvy, hilly local cross-country ski trails. They maintain two networks, Abenaki and Sewall Woods, joined by a black-diamond connector. The nordic skiing in town has been a popular winter draw for a long time, although not quite as far back as when Governor Wentworth called the woods here his home.

Local Legend

Bailey's Bubble

Why are the lines always so much longer outside the nondescript Bailey's Bubble ice cream stand downtown than at the Ben & Jerry's just a few doors away? Two words: hot fudge. The thick, gooey, and diet-busting chocolate topping poured over the Bailey's Bubble ice cream has drawn crowds for three generations. It was the creation of the owner's grandfather, who opened Bailey's Restaurant, a fixture on South Main Street for roughly sixty years until it closed and the Bubble took its place. You can buy jars of the hot fudge at the local IGA, but the recipe is a closely guarded family secret.

Start the Day

Wolfeboro Diner (3 North Main Street; 603-569-2997): Traditional stick-to-your-ribs diner food in the center of downtown.

Lydia's Café (33 North Main Street; 603-569-3991): The place to find fresh cappuccino, bagels, and local gossip in the morning.

Gear Up

Nordic Skier Sports (47 North Main Street; 603-569-3151): Sells bikes, cross-country skis, snowshoes, skates, and apparel.

Wolfeboro Bay Outfitters (15 South Main Street; 603-569-1114): Sells fishing tackle and outdoor gear.

Refuel

Huck's Hoagies (4 Valley Lane; 603-569-6122): Hard to find down a back street, but serves the best subs in town.

Wolfe's Tavern (90 North Main Street; 603-569-3016; www.wolfeboroinn.com): Located in the Wolfeboro Inn, an old-fashioned pub serving burgers and beer in fireplace-heated rooms.

Wolfe Den (14 Union Street; 603-569-0444; www.wolfetrap.com): Known for its raw bar and martini bar; accessible by water through Back Bay.

Bunk

The Wolfeboro Inn (90 North Main Street; 603-569-3016; www.wolfeboro inn.com): Clean, comfortable, and the largest hotel in town—and the only one with access to Winnipesaukee.

Tuc' Me Inn (118 North Main Street; 603-569-5702; www.tucmeinn.com): A 150-year-old Federal-style Inn on a hill above downtown; the town's best cross-country ski trails are practically in its back yard.

The Lake Motel (280 South Main Street; 603-569-1258; www.the lakemotel.com): On Mirror Lake and within walking distance of downtown.

Can't Leave?

Nearest airport: Manchester-Boston Regional, Manchester, New Hampshire (48 miles)

Primary industries: Tourism, health care, education

The Wild Side

Castle in the Clouds

In 1914, shoe-making mogul Tom Plant built an opulent Arts and Crafts–style country estate high in the Ossippee Mountains, overlooking Lake Winnipesaukee. His creation, known as Castle in the Clouds, and the 5,500 acres of wilderness surrounding it—which encompasses seven mountain peaks—are now owned by a conservation trust. The house, about twenty minutes north of Wolfeboro in Moultonborough, is open for tours, and hikers can explore the property's forty-five miles of well-maintained trails, converted from old, wide carriage roads that ascend several peaks, including the tallest on the property, 2,975-foot Mount Shaw. The wilderness here is so pristine that its spring water is bottled at the source and sold under the Crystal Geyser label.

Lake Placid, New York

Population: 2,638

Action: Downhill and cross-country skiing, hiking, mountain biking, boating

Crowned by jagged peaks and packed year-round with fleece-wearing adrenaline seekers, Lake Placid looks and feels like a mountain-resort destination out West, minus the altitude—and, argue some locals, the attitude. This welcoming hideout at 1,100 feet of elevation is wedged between the large body of water that bears the same name and tiny Mirror Lake, about two and a half hours north of Albany. It's the jumping-off point for adventure in the surrounding six-million-acre Adirondack Park, a state-run preserve of public and private lands big enough to fit the entire state of Vermont within its borders, along with the borough of Brooklyn thrown in for good measure. The park is crisscrossed by more than 2,000 miles of trails, which wind to the tops of the state's tallest summits and among the wilderness's 3,000 lakes and ponds.

Lake Placid is probably best known as the only place in North America to host two Olympic Winter Games, in 1932 and 1980. On a drive through town, you'll see the impeccably maintained speed-skating oval in front of the high school and, next door, the indoor rink complex where the U.S. hockey team's "Miracle on Ice" occurred. You'll pass the old Olympic Cauldron, towering above the bleachers beside the local running track, and spot the tops of two ski jumps looming over the trees on the edge of town like concrete lookout towers from some science-fiction fantasy. These venues aren't merely relics of Lake Placid's sporting past, though. Nearly all of them, from the cross-country ski trails to the luge run, are still used as training facilities for Olympic hopefuls, as sites for World Cup events, or as public recreation areas.

Surprisingly, even more visitors flock here in the summer than in winter. The two biggest events of the year are the Lake Placid Horse

Lake Placid, New York nestles between its namesake waters and tiny Mirror Lake.
(© Lake Placid/Essex County Visitors Bureau)

Show—one of the country's largest for hunter and jumper competitions—held in early July, and the Ironman Triathlon later in the month.

Established as a farming community in the late eighteenth century, Lake Placid transformed into a vacation resort about a hundred years later when the railroad connected it to New York City. The connection lured wealthy families, who built massive rustic homes, called Great Camps, on the nearby lakes. Train service has long since vanished, as have the droves of well-heeled Manhattanites and their teams of servants. They've largely been replaced by outdoorsy types from across the country and Quebec, who spend their days among the water and trees and their evenings milling about the restaurants, hotels, brew pubs, outfitter shops, gift stores, and book shops that occupy the eclectic mix of alpine-style buildings on Main Street, along the edge of Mirror Lake.

Lake Placid is the focal point for adventure largely because nearly every path in the Adirondacks seems to converge upon it. By far the most popular starting point for backpacking trips in the park is the Adirondack Loj, a rustic lodge operated the Adirondack Mountain Club on the outskirts of town. It sits on the edge of a quiet lake and in the shadow of New York's tallest peaks, at the terminus of trails leading to most of them. The favorite stretch of singletrack trail for mountain biking and cross-country skiing in the area—and a connection to several other major trail networks—is the Jackrabbit Trail, which forms the geographical spine of town. An exploration of the park's most beautiful and remote lakes and streams can begin on the shore of Lake Placid and a put-in at the town marina, about two minutes off Main Street.

In winter, Lake Placid becomes a popular destination for alpine skiers thanks to Whiteface Mountain, which boasts the longest vertical drop in the East: 3,430 feet. The mountain hosted the skiing events for both Olympics and has 75 trails on 221 acres, including 35 acres on the Slides, the ungroomed, tree-lined chutes that open when the snow is deep enough and conditions are right. Because Whiteface, which is actually fifteen minutes away in Wilmington, is part of the protected lands of the park, there's no slopeside development on it—no shops, no condos, no nothing—only pines and maples.

Of course, there are other reasons to come to Lake Placid in cold weather, starting with the East's best mountaineering, ice climbing, and backcountry skiing. There's also the cross-country skiing on the thirty-one miles of former Olympic trails at the Olympic Sports Complex. Finally, there's the romantic luxury of staying at one of the town's rustic inns and enjoying the scenery by taking a horse-drawn sleigh ride around Mirror Lake—all altitude- and attitude-free.

Local Legend

Local Legend: UBU Ale

Folks in Lake Placid will disagree about many things, like which nearby summit is the toughest to hike, where the best swimming hole is hidden, or who among the three generations of Winter Olympians in the local Shea family was truly the greatest athlete. But the undisputed favorite beverage in town is the UBU Ale, which is poured in great quantities in the former church that now houses the Lake Placid Pub and Brewery. This überstrong amber beer has an alcohol content of 7 percent and is served straight from the keg either upstairs in the dining room or downstairs in the English-style pub. Word has it that President Bill Clinton had three cases of bottled UBU sent to the White House after tasting it while in town during Hillary's first campaign for New York's U.S. Senate seat.

Start the Day

Howard Johnson (98 Saranac Avenue; 518-523-9555): A real HoJo's bacon-and-egg breakfast with coffee, the way you remember it.

Coff E Bean Internet Café and Coffee Bar (Alpine Mall; 518-523-3228): For a quick cappuccino or latte.

The Black Bear Restaurant (2573 Main Street; 518-523-9886): Breakfast all day; famous for its rib-sticking pancakes.

Gear Up

High Peaks Mountain Adventures (2733 Main Street; 518-523-3764): Brian Delaney, the owner of this one-stop outfitter, is an expert on the biking trails and rock-climbing routes in the Adirondacks.

Maui North (134 Main Street; 518-523-7245): The best combination ski and snowboard shop in the area.

Placid Planet (2242 Saranac Avenue; 518-523-4128): A bike shop with a cult following among local Ironman triathletes.

Refuel

The Cottage (5 Mirror Lake Drive; 518-523-9845): A low-key dining spot on the edge of Mirror Lake, offering postcard-perfect views of Whiteface.

Nicola's on Main (2617 Main Street; 518-523-5853): The creations from its wood-fired oven and open kitchen give Lake Placid some Mediterranean zest.

Brown Dog Deli & Wine Bar (3 Main Street; 518-523-3036): Check out the Stephen Huneck lithographs as you wait for your roasted chicken breast with pancetta on sourdough and glass of Sonoma Cabernet Sauvignon.

Bunk

The Mirror Lake Inn (5 Mirror Lake Drive; 518-523-2871; www.mirror lakeinn.com): A fixture on the shores of

The Wild Side

Mount Marcy

At 5,344 feet in elevation, Mount Marcy is the tallest mountain in New York and the centerpiece of the High Peaks region of the Adirondacks, located about ten miles outside of Lake Placid. The shortest trek to the top is via the steep, 7.4-mile Van Hoevenberg Trail, which starts at the Adirondack Loj and emerges above the treeline onto the rocky, alpine scrub–garnished summit. The trip makes for a long day hike or a leisurely two-day backpacking expedition. The payoff is the view from the top, which stretches across the Adirondacks to the Green Mountains of Vermont. The Van Hoevenberg Trail is also a popular route for backcountry skiers and snowboarders in winter. Powderhounds usually take a few runs on the snow-covered summit before facing the perils of the entire 3,100-foot, tree-filled descent.

Mirror Lake since the late nineteenth century and one of the finest spas in the country.

Art Devlin's Olympic Motor Inn (2764 Main Street; 518-523-3700; www.artdevlins.com): A top bargain opened by a ski-jumping legend.

The Adirondack Loj (867 Adirondack Loj Road; 518-523-3441; www.adk.org): A lakeside lodge and bunkhouse built in 1927 and operated by the Adirondack Mountain Club.

Can't Leave?

Nearest airport: Burlington International, Burlington, Vermont (80 miles)

Primary industries: Service, biotech, parks, Olympic Region Development Authority

New Paltz, New York

When the upper crust of Manhattan escapes to the Hamptons of Long Island for the weekend, earthier New Yorkers head for the hills ninety miles north of the city, to the quiet village of New Paltz. Surrounded by the farmlands along the northern ridge of the Shawangunk Mountains, it's a place where the people are so back-to-nature that Green Party candidates receive more votes in local elections than Democrats or Republicans. The gossip at the latte houses centers on rock climbing rather than social climbing, and there's plenty to dish on this subject. The roughly thousand routes on the cliffs of the Mohonk Preserve, about ten minutes from downtown, make for the most popular and history-laden rock-climbing destination in the country.

Population: 14,008
Action: Rock climbing, hiking, mountain biking, paddling

Known collectively as the Gunks—short for Shawangunks —the cliffs were spotted in 1935 by German climber Fritz Weissner, who noticed vertical walls rising as high as 300 feet and covered with deep overhangs and challenging angles. He made his first ascent up what is now called Old Route wearing thick hiking boots and carrying hemp ropes. In the decades that followed, the Gunks became the premier climbing destination in the East, attracting the world's greatest climbers, from Patagonia founder Yvon Chouinard to Royal Robbins to John Stannard. In 1988, the placement of new pitons and bolts was forbidden in order to protect the rock and to encourage traditional techniques. Today, over fifty thousand climbers a year converge upon the Gunks. Most of the cliffs lie completely within the 6,500-acre Mohonk Preserve, the largest private protected natural area in the state. It was created in 1963 by the Smiley family, who owned the land and the adjacent Mohonk Mountain House lodge, which is still in operation.

An approach trail to the famed cliffs known as the Gunks, in the Mohawk Preserve, outside New Paltz, New York. (© Mohawk Preserve)

Beneath the rock walls, its 100 miles of trails and carriage roads are popular among runners, mountain bikers, hikers, and horseback riders—and, to a lesser extent, cross-country skiers in the winter. The preserve is also home to 1,400 known plant and animal species, such as bobcats, bears, and timber rattlesnakes; that total includes forty rare animals and plants, such as the long-tailed shrew and the dwarf pitch pine.

Just north of the preserve is the even larger Minnewaska State Park. Also former Smiley property, it encompasses 14,500 acres of the Shawagunk Mountains, punctuated by two pristine lakes. While the climbing isn't quite as sensational there, the park's fifty miles of trails and carriage roads are probably more attractive because the crowds are significantly smaller.

Camping is limited to twenty sites in the Mohonk Preserve, and Minnewaska is day use only. Most visitors stay in the farmhouse bed-and-breakfasts in the outlying area and spend their evenings at the funky restaurants and browsing through the antique shops, boutiques, and independent book shops in the heart of New Paltz. The town itself was established in 1692 by twelve Huguenot families fleeing Protestant persecution in France, and some of their original stone homes still stand on Huguenot Street, a national historic district. Those early residents certainly chose a magnificent spot. New Paltz sits in a valley bisected by the quiet, north-flowing Wallkill River, which eventually joins with Rondout Creek and drains into the Hudson River. The valley has spectacular views of the Catskill Mountains to the northwest, as well as the Shawangunks, a chain in the Appalachians that stretches all the way into northern New Jersey.

Much of the youthful vibe in town comes from the 7,000 students of the nearby New Paltz Campus of the State University of New York. They provide a ready audience for the many cultural events and performances that come to the area and enliven the night scene by packing the bars and music clubs. As outdoorsy as the year-round folk, they can also be found paddling on the quiet Wallkill and biking or jogging on the 12.2-mile Wallkill Valley Rail Trail. And rock climbing, of course.

Start the Day

The Bakery (13a North Front Street; 845-255-8840; www.ilovethebakery .com): A bake shop with coffee bar, gardens, outdoor café, and delectable danishes.

Mudd Puddle Coffee Roasters & Café (10 Main Street, #312; 845-255-3436; www.muddpuddlecoffee.com): Where to get egg-bagel sandwiches to go along with your latte.

Gear Up

Rock and Snow (44 Main Street; 845-255-1311): This climbing store is a local institution.

The Bicycle Rack (15 Main Street; 845-255-1770): Sells bike gear and has information on all of the best local rides.

New Paltz Outfitters (188 Main Street; 845-255-2829): An impressive selection

Local Legend

Dick Williams

Telling the history of the Gunks without mentioning Dick Williams would be like telling the history of the United States without mentioning Thomas Jefferson. No one knows their 1,000-plus routes better or was more influential in their culture over the last four decades. In the 1960s, Williams was known as one of the ringleaders of the Vulgarians, an anti-establishment group of partygoing, world-class climbers credited with hundreds of first ascents in the Gunks. He has written five definitive climbing guidebooks and was the owner of Rock and Snow, the popular outfitter shop in New Paltz, from 1970 until he retired and sold it to his longtime business partner in 2000.

The Wild Side

Catskill State Park

Overshadowed by the Adirondacks to the north, and too often associated with summer resorts from bygone days—and *Dirty Dancing* movie fame—the Catskills remain a relative secret among outdoor adventurers in the Northeast. Yet Catskill State Park, just west of New Paltz, is only 100 square miles smaller than the entire state of Rhode Island, and within its boundaries are thirty-five mountain peaks over 3,500 feet, three major ski areas, two massive reservoirs, and 300 miles of trails. Much like Adirondack Park, the preserve is a patchwork of private and public lands, and more than one-third of it, or roughly 290,000 acres, is protected as forever wild. The park has some of the best, and quietest, fly-fishing, camping, hiking, biking, and backcountry nordic skiing in the East, even if no one knows about it.

of hiking boots, plus assorted hiking and backpacking gear.

Refuel

Harvest Café (10 Main Street; 845-255-4205; www.harvestcafenp.com) "New American" cuisine including a selection of vegan soups; owned by a graduate of the nearby Culinary Institute of America.

Main Street Bistro (59 Main Street; 845-255-7766; www.mainstreet bistro.com): Funky and traditional variations on pasta, burritos, burgers, stir-fry, wraps, and vegetarian entrées—all in hearty, delicious, and relatively inexpensive portions.

Gilded Otter Brewing Company (3 Main Street; 845-256-1700; www.gildedotter.com): The Stone House Imperial Stout is reason enough to visit this brew pub by Huguenot Street, but the burgers and chicken schnitzel are equally tasty.

Bunk

Mohonk Mountain House (1000 Mountain Rest Road; 800-772-6646; www.mohonk.com): An 1869 Victorian hotel on a lake, established and still owned by the Smiley family, who created the adjacent Mohonk Preserve. Recently opened an impressive new spa.

Mountain Meadows Bed and Breakfast (542 Albany Post Road; 845/255-6144; www.mountainmeadowsbnb.com): This quaint bed-and-breakfast offers stunning views of the Gunks from its pool.

Lefèvre House Bed & Breakfast (14 Southside Avenue; 845-255-4747; www.lefevrehouse.com): A pink, converted nineteenth-century Victorian farmhouse offering Versace linens in the color-themed rooms, plus amazing breakfasts.

Can't Leave?

Nearest airport: Stewert International, Newburgh/New Windsor, New York (18 miles)

Primary industries: Higher education, agriculture, health care

Tiverton, Rhode Island

Population:

15,336

Action: Kayaking, sailing, fishing, road biking

Along wide Bellevue Avenue in Newport, Rhode Island, there are 130,000-square foot mansions made of Indiana limestone and modeled after Italian palazzos of the sixteenth century. Drive north from here, past the strip malls and movie theaters of Middletown and the fancy, black-lacquered signs and vineyards of Portsmouth toward Fall River and Boston, and you'll hit—but almost miss—the tiny town of Tiverton. Sitting among a cluster of sailboats, fishing and lobster boats, and kayaks, below the bridge between Aquidneck Island and the mainland, on the Sakonnet River, Tiverton is as understated as Newport is ostentatious. Its rough, sea-worn edges have yet to be coated in any kind of lacquer. Lined by beaches, farms, and seafood drive-ins, it's one of the last places in the Ocean State where you can not only play on Narragansett Bay, but also actually afford a place with a view of the ocean.

In fact, Tiverton once belonged to the Bay State, as it was incorporated in 1694 as part of the Massachusetts Bay Colony, but after a longstanding tug of war, the town—along with its now tonier neighbors of Little Compton, Barrington, Bristol, and Cumberland—eventually joined Rhode Island in 1746. Farming, fish-oil production, fishing, and boat construction long served as the town's financial lifeline; today, there is also a boost from tourists attracted to the rural, restored colonial village of quaint shops at Tiverton Four Corners. It's among these artisanal cheese markets and art galleries that some of the area's best cycling routes begin—or at least pass through—and where cyclers can stop for a picnic of pâtés, baguettes, and manchego from the Milk & Honey Bazaar. Rhode Island Route 77 leads to scenic Little Compton and pristine Sakonnet Point, while a web of wide country roads connects Tiverton to the seaside community of Buzzards Bay in Massachusetts.

At Tiverton, Rhode Island, sailboats and commercial fishing and lobster boats share the waters of Narragansett Bay. (© Rick Barrette)

The roads are almost entirely empty of fellow cyclists, chiefly because most everyone else with some recreational time to kill is out on Narragansett Bay, where there are 147 square miles and 700 billion gallons of sailing and fishing waters, and more than 250 miles of shoreline to explore by sea kayak. Tiverton's sailing community revolves around the appropriately subtle Tiverton Yacht Club, housed in a white colonial home along the Sakonnet River. Membership dues are a mere $400 per family, and the social calendar is filled with potluck dinners rather than prom-style balls. Anglers, meanwhile, load up on lures and baits for the bay's bluefish, flounder, tuna, and stripers, and beachgoers swim off Fogland Beach, near Four Corners, and Grinnell's Beach, off Rhode Island 77.

The Sakonnet River, a wide, somewhat protected passage of open water between Mount Hope Bay and the main Narragansett Bay, is one of Rhode Island paddlers' top picks for kayaking a mix of flatwater, marshes, and surf. It's a fifteen-mile trip from Tiverton to Sakonnet Point, or kayakers can cross over to Sachuest Point National Wildlife Refuge on Aquidneck Island. From here, it's a short paddle—but light years from Tiverton—to the mansions of Newport.

Weetamoo Woods

Hidden among the rural roads, colonial houses, and sea-sprayed beaches of Tiverton is a nearly 500-acre preserve of endangered plants, stone bridges, crumbling sawmills, Native American history, and trail running. Yep, trail running in Rhode Island. It's at Weetamoo Woods, named for the wife of a Wampanoag Pocasset chief; *Weetamoo* means sweetheart. A six-plus-mile loop at the preserve winds through the pink lady's slipper, mountain laurel, and ginseng that bloom here.

Start the Day

Coastal Roasters (1791 Main Road; 401-624-2343): Fresh-roasted, fair-trade organic coffee, plus bagels, breads, pastries, and cookies, in a bright yellow outpost on the Sakonnet River.

Gear Up

Sakonnet Boathouse (169 Riverside Drive; 401-624-1440): Kayak rentals and lessons, including lessons on kayak fishing, surf kayaking, and Eskimo rolls, under the Sakonnet River Bridge.

Refuel

Evelyn's Drive-in (2335 Main Road; 401-624-3100): Lobster rolls, fried clam strips, chowders, and grilled cheese; plus beer, wine, dinner plates, and dessert; dine at the picnic tables overlooking Nannaquaket Pond.

Four Corners Grille (3841 Main Road; 401-624-1510): Pub grub such as jalapeño poppers and wings, along with shrimp Mozambique, fried scallops, and towering desserts.

Bunk

Ferolbink Farms Bed & Breakfast (993 Punkateest Neck Road; 401-624-4107): Six-room bed-and-breakfast on a 550-acre farm.

The Stone House Club (122 Sakonnet Point Road, Little Compton; 401-635-2222; www.stonehouseclub.com): Thirteen rooms, some with ocean views, in a country inn.

Can't Leave?

Nearest airport: T. F. Green International, Providence, Rhode Island (16 miles)

Primary industries: Fishing, boatbuilding, retail

East Burke, Vermont

urke Mountain may be the only ski resort in the country that's more famous for its mountain biking than its skiing and snowboarding. The reason: the resort is incorporated into the Kingdom Trails, a 100-mile network of magnificently kept, well-marked, singletrack and old dirt roads interlaced around the village of East Burke. Filled with more thrills than a Seven Flags amusement park, the trails lie entirely on private property—a remarkable feat achieved through the hard work of committed local riders—and are enticement enough to come to northeastern Vermont, even without the maple syrup, deep blue lakes, majestic red barns, and mountain views. The action doesn't die off in winter, as nordic skiers take over many of the paths and downhillers converge upon the ski resort from as far away as Boston (three hours south) and Montreal (two and a half hours northwest).

Population: 1,676

Action: Mountain biking, cross-country and downhill skiing

When you drive among the dairy farms up State Route 114, you might truly miss the town if you blink. Its grassy center consists of little more than an old general store, a post office, a sport shop, an inn, and the white clapboard Burke Mountain Club House and gazebo, built in 1920. Officially, East Burke is one of three villages—along with Burke Hollow and West Burke—contained within the 1,676-person municipality of Burke, but each is considered its own separate community. The area was settled in the 1780s and became a center for lumber, manufacturing, and then agriculture. The most influential family in East Burke's history was the Darlings, wealthy longtime landowners who brought electricity to the town, built the Club House, and donated the property—complete with two miles of ski trails—on Burke Mountain that would later make up part of the resort, according to the Center for Rural Studies at the University of Vermont.

In the snowless seasons, Burke Mountain beckons to mountain bikers in East Burke, Vermont. (© Hannah Collins)

The Kingdom Trails are a part of much more recent history. In the mid-1990s, locals Doug Kitchel, who was a former owner of the ski area, and John Worth, a co-owner of the East Burke Sports shop, pushed the idea of creating an organized mountain-biking area out of the trails already carved. Attracted by the prospect of bringing more tourists to the village in summer, landowners jumped on board, and the nonprofit Kingdom Trail Association was born. The network is the most extensive in the Northeast and is a fern-fringed mix of beginner, intermediate, and expert trails all marked with green circles, blue squares, and black diamonds. Its spine is the tall, slim ridge known as Darling Hill, where the dirt surface is almost as smooth as slickrock—at least on dry days. The rides lead you through pine and maple forests, through flowery fields, and over creeks. You'll find grassy vistas with open views of the countryside as you navigate the chutes and twists of trails like Coronary, Pines, the ultrapopular Poundcake, and Dead Moose Alley.

The official welcome center for the association is behind the general store, but don't even think about hitting the trails without first stopping at Worth's shop for some route planning first.

When the snow falls—250 inches of it annually—the Kingdom Trails maintains about thirty miles for cross-country skiing, including about fifteen miles on Burke Mountain resort property. On the downhill side, Burke Mountain's forty-five trails, four chair lifts, and vertical drop of 2,000 feet won't compare with what you'll find on the larger ski areas in Vermont, but then again, East Burke is the kind of friendly, old-timey place where the lifties will be greeting you by name by the end of the week. It's also home to the oldest ski academy in the country, the Burke Mountain Academy, which produces slews of Olympic hopefuls every year—proof that the skiing can be world-class within its cozy confines, even if it is overshadowed by the mountain biking.

Start the Day

Inn at Mountain View Farm (Darling Hill Road; 802-626-9924; www.innmtn view.com): Located on the road to the trails; serves hearty breakfasts with food that comes largely from local farms.

Bailey's & Burke (466 Route 114; 802-626-9250; www.baileysandburke.com): The general store in town; serves hot breakfast sandwiches, fresh-baked pastries and muffins, and coffee.

Gear Up

East Burke Sports (Route 114; 802-626-3215): Not only the authority in local mountain biking, but also sells paddling and backpacking gear.

Village Sport Shop (511 Broad Street, Lyndonville; 802-626-8448): Located in the next-door town, it sells and rents snowboards and skis, and in the summer is a mountain-bike, kayak, and fishing shop.

Local Legend

Bailey's & Burke

Old general stores in rural Vermont are nearly as ubiquitous as maple sugar shacks. But most have evolved from being the social and commercial hubs of their towns into tourist attractions hawking penny candy and gewgaws with the words "Green Mountains" printed on them.

Not so with Bailey's & Burke, in East Burke, where you can browse for a good bottle of wine, a fresh-baked pie, or a painting by a local artist as the ancient hardwood floors groan beneath your feet. Built in 1897, it underwent a huge restoration eighty years later. It was revitalized again in 1999 by new owners Billy Turner and Jody Fried, who broadened the selection of staple goods, began selling pizza and wine in it, and turned the pub in back of the building into the area's favorite watering hole.

The Wild Side

Lake Willoughby

When the glaciers that enveloped the landscape of northeast Vermont retreated, they left behind Lake Willoughby, a clear blue body of water about twice the size of Central Park and reaching depths of more than 300 feet. Its southern half, flanked by the 300-foot vertical cliffs of Mount Pisgah to the east and Mount Hor to the west, lies within the 7,300-acre Willoughby State Forest, just up State Route 5A from East Burke. In the summer, anglers stalk the salmon, perch, and trout in the lake's waters or on the thirty-two miles of streams in the park, and hikers take to the twelve miles of trails that lead to three mountain peaks. In the winter, the frozen waterfalls coating the multipitch cliffs—especially on Mount Pisgah—become the premier ice-climbing challenge east of the Canadian Rockies.

Refuel

The Pub Outback (482 Route 114; 802-626-1188; www.thepuboutback.com): Out back of the general store, hence its name, this pub in a red barnlike building has very good burgers and onion rings and even better atmosphere.

Tamarack Grill (223 Sherburne Lodge Road; 802-626-7333): The Burke Mountain resort restaurant; fancy feasting on the likes of tempura tuna rolls and Muscovy duck.

Trout River Brewing Company (Route 5, Lyndonville; 802-626-9396): Home for many popular regional brews, such as Hoppin' Mad Trout; brew samplings on Friday and Saturday evenings include pizza.

Bunk

Inn at Mountain View Farm (Darling Hill Road; 802-626-9924; www.innmtnview.com): One of the finest inns in the country; located on a 440-acre farm adjacent to Kingdom Trails.

Village Inn of East Burke (606 Route 114; 802-626-3161; www.villageinnofeastburke.com): A quiet, refined place to stay; in an old house in the center of town.

Wildflower Inn (2059 Darling Hill Road; 802-626-8310; www.wildflowerinn.com): An inn on 570 acres, offering ice skating, sleigh rides, and sledding in the winter; also on the Kingdom Trails.

Can't Leave?

Nearest airport: Burlington International, Burlington, Vermont (80 miles)

Primary industries: Manufacturing, retail, health care

Middlebury, Vermont

Population: 8,152
Action: Hiking, mountain and road biking, downhill and cross-country skiing, kayaking

Upon graduation from Middlebury College, students are presented with a cane—not exactly the most appropriate symbol for a school and a town obsessed with running, hiking, kayaking, and skiing. A more well-suited, though perhaps less portable, parting gift might be a piece of the Green Mountain National Forest. In the early 1900s, Middlebury owned much of central Vermont's mountainous, western-lying land, but eventually sold it to the federal government. The land became the 821,000-acre Green Mountain National Forest, over which early birds in Middlebury watch the sun rise. (Night owls watch it set over the Adirondacks and Lake Champlain by hiking up Snake Mountain, a peak so tame that you could walk it with a cane—or a keg of beer, as some Middlebury students have done successfully.)

The town, one of the state's earliest, was first chartered in 1761; the college, which today has 2,350 students, was founded in 1800. The school's campus is one of the two striking features of the town, thanks to its marble buildings that stand stalwart on the top of a hill. The marble was not imported, but mostly quarried right in Vermont. That local marble has produced impressive libraries, science centers, and sports buildings, all open to the public. Quarries once pocked the rolling hills, and in the 1930s, the Vermont Marble company produced more of the stone than anywhere else in the world. Though the Omya mining company still quarries marble in Middlebury today, the main factory area has been converted into Marble Works, a commercial complex with everything from yoga studios and independent pharmacies to delis and wood-fired pizza bakeries.

Middlebury's second first impression is the Otter Creek, which is not so much a creek as a 100-mile river that tumbles from marshlands on Mount Tabor to Lake Champlain at the town of Ferrisburgh. Just

Kayakers can run Otter Creek Falls, located just off Main Street in Middlebury, Vermont.
(© Addison County Chamber of Commerce)

off the center of Middlebury's Main Street, the river drops nearly twenty feet to create Otter Creek Falls, whose rushing sound soothes downtown strollers or picnickers—and captivates kayakers, who run the falls. For calmer waters, paddlers head to Lake Dunmore in the nearby town of Salisbury or to Lake Champlain itself, where a recently developed Paddlers' Trail links put-ins, campsites, and wilderness areas.

There are more challenging hiking options than the low-lying Snake: along the ridgeline of the Green Mountains, you'll find strenuous climbs up 4,006-foot Mount Abraham or 3,623-foot Mount Grant; more moderate choices include the 6.8-mile hike up Mount Roosevelt. The Long Trail, a 270-mile backcountry route that stretches the length of Vermont, passes near Middlebury at Breadloaf Mountain. (Near the mountain, the college maintains its Bread Loaf campus of yellow buildings, housing an English graduate program and a writers' conference in the woodsy wilderness where Robert Frost once walked.) Though some parts of the Green Mountain National Forest are off-limits to mountain bikers—and it will cost you if you're caught—you can find old fire roads and singletrack near the Bread Loaf campus. The twenty-three-mile Natural Turnpike loop and eleven-mile Steammill Road loop are two top picks in the area, which also abounds with a network of quiet, rolling roads for cycling and swimming holes for cooling off on steamy summer days. (If you're pedaling near the town of Bristol, just northwest of Middlebury, plan to dip into Bristol Falls and then into a creemee, or soft-serve ice cream, at the Village Creemee Stand, which has some of the best views, and cones, in the state.)

Just past the Bread Loaf campus lies one of the reasons many students choose Middlebury over other New England liberal-arts schools: the college's own ski hill. Though visitors don't get quite the cut rates that Midd kids enjoy, the 110-acre Snow Bowl is still one of the best ski bargains in the Northeast. It could even serve as a morning warmup for larger mountains at Sugarbush or Mad River Glen. The college's Rikert Ski Touring Center is also open to the public. After taking part in all of Middlebury's action, you might just pine for one of the college's walking sticks yourself.

Start the Day

Otter Creek Bakery (14 College Street; 802-388-3371): Fluffy croissants, sugary pastries, and coffee drinks.

Steve's Park Diner (66 Merchants Row; 802-388-3297): The place for pancakes and eggs.

Noonies (137 Maple Street, Suite B; 802-388-0014): Thick sandwiches on hearty breads for the trail.

Gear Up

The Alpine Shop (6 Merchants Row; 802-388-7547): The Green Mountain gurus of just about anything with spokes or edges; get your bikes and skis spruced up here and find a wide selection of clothing, shoes, boots, and accessories.

The Wild Side

The Catamount Trail

At 300 miles, the Catamount Trail is the longest ski trail in North America. If you've never heard of it, you're hardly alone, as its warm-weather equivalent, the Long Trail, gets much more attention than this skinny-ski sister. Starting from Readsboro, on the Massachusetts border, and ending at the Canadian border, the Catamount traces the backbone of Vermont, connecting nordic-ski centers with snow-blanketed farms, frozen rivers, and lung-busting, hairraising peaks. At about its halfway point, the backcountry trail travels by Middlebury College's Rikert Ski Touring Center, and a one-day, fifteen-mile tour in the area is one of the most scenic of the Catamount. For directions, maps—many of them courtesy of Middlebury's geography students—and group tours, visit www.catamounttrail.org.

Local Legend

Wolaver's

Going organic is big even in Japan, where you can find six-packs of Wolaver's, a certified organic ale produced by Otter Creek Brewing—Middlebury's hugely popular house of hops, malts, water, and yeast. (Those are the only four ingredients you'll find in the nearly twenty types of beer.) The brewing company is open Monday through Saturday from 10 a.m. to 6 p.m.; there are tours at 1, 3, and 5 p.m., and free samples of beers and beer mustards all day long. Try the flagship, German-style Copper Ale, the citrusy 'Otter Summer, or the Wolaver's Wit Bier. Then pick up a "growler" (a half-gallon jug) or a discounted case of "seconds" (with label misprints or other small imperfections) for an evening picnic along—where else?—the Otter Creek.

Refuel

Tully & Marie's (7 Bakery Lane; 802-388-4182): A contemporary eatery and art gallery along the Otter Creek; much on the menu is local and organic.

The Storm Café (3 Mill Street; 802-388-1063): Also on the banks of the Otter Creek; Stormy Thai stew, chipotle- and cheese-stuffed pasta, and other eclectic, ethnic fare.

Eat Good Food (51 Main Street; 802-388-9100): Panini, homemade sausage and lentils, and inventive ravioli in a friendly, funky atmosphere.

Bunk

Blue Spruce Motel (2428 Route 7 South; 802-388-4091): Convenient location between downtown and the Green Mountains; some kitchenettes and cottages.

Inn on the Green (71 South Main Street; 802-388-7512): Victorian home with eleven rooms in downtown Middlebury; continental breakfasts served to each room.

Middlebury Inn (14 Court Square; 802-388-4961): A Middlebury landmark with seventy-five rooms; opened in 1827 and within walking distance of Otter Creek.

Can't Leave?

Nearest airport: Burlington International, Burlington, Vermont (32 miles)

Primary industry: Education, tourism, manufacturing, service providers

Montpelier, Vermont

The most exclusive ski resort in Vermont—maybe even the world—is found in Montpelier. And it doesn't cost a penny to ride the single rope tow. The membership fee is a friendship with a Montpelier high-school science teacher, who installed a 400-foot-long rope tow in his backyard and bought a Model-A engine to power the lift so that his kids could learn how to ski on the supercheap. Now fellow teachers on telemark skis, teenagers filming stunts off little jumps, and toddlers trying out their first turn all spend their Saturdays and Sundays at this "resort."

Population: 8,000

Action: Road and mountain biking, paddling, downhill and cross-country skiing

It's this kind of innovative, independent spirit that defines Montpelier, the nation's smallest capital city at 8,000 people and the only one without a McDonald's. Vermont's famously progressive politics find a gathering point here, beneath the golden dome of the statehouse, which is topped with a statue of Ceres, the Roman goddess of agriculture. (Farming—at small, independent farms—still reigns around here.) At the New England Culinary Institute, or NECI (*NECK-y*), future chefs create inventive dishes using local, often organic ingredients, to feed the masses at three different Montpelier eateries. And at Bear Pond Books, the state's literary minds gather to find inspiration in the art of procrastination.

Outdoor adventurers around Montpelier share the same free thinking; unlike other of the state's resort towns, such as Stowe, which package sports neatly, Montpelier lets you do the planning, so it helps to have a primer in the lay of the land. Montpelier's front door is Interstate 89; the back door opens to some of the most spectacular cycling in the state. Start with the 16.5-mile East Montpelier loop, which climbs out of the compact city into back roads lined by sugar-maple groves, behemoth barns, and bright green fields dotted with stone walls. Or cycle along Route 2 to Plainfield, where the River Run restaurant's buttermilk

The dome of the Vermont state capitol peeks through the pines of Montpelier. (© Central Vermont Chamber of Commerce)

biscuits, fried catfish, and blueberry pancakes will let you leave the PowerBars to stiffen in your hydration pack. Don't like catfish? Visit the provenance of the band Phish at nearby Goddard College. You can also find cheese, naturally, in Cabot, and maple treats at dozens of roadside sugarhouses.

A new, unpaved twenty-mile biking route explores the historic hamlet of Calais, while another five-mile newcomer spins around Berlin Pond; you'll find more tours in the Mad River Valley area or around the town of Northfield, many with covered bridges and swift rivers to cross.

Just south of Montpelier, the granite town of Barre contains the area's most exciting mountain biking, thanks to a new network of trails weaving among abandoned quarries at Millstone Hill. The trail system—forty miles and growing each summer—leads bikers on shady, birch-lined singletrack past boom derricks, railroad cars, and more than forty quarries. Overlooks atop jumbles of rock reward riders with views of the turquoise surface of water-filled quarries below and a panoramic look at the 4,083-foot peak of Camel's Hump, the Knox Mountains, and rolling farmlands. Because some of the quarries are so deep, there's a cooling sensation when you ride by them—and an even cooler one when you jump in for a swim on a hot summer day.

Kayakers and canoeists, meanwhile, dip into the ninety-mile Winooski River, which runs through downtown Montpelier toward Lake Champlain. (*Winooski* means "wild onion," so it is sometimes called the Onion River.) There's a popular seven-mile stretch accessible right off Lower State Street, and city officials are working on creating new put-in points for paddlers along the Winooski. Whitewater runs on the Winooski south of Montpelier, or over on the Mad River

The Wild Side

Mount Mansfield

Montpelier is just a thirty-minute drive from the trailhead to Vermont's highest point: 4,393-foot Mount Mansfield, whose ridgeline is characterized by the humanlike features of a nose, chin, forehead, lips, and Adam's apple. The lazy way up is by gondola at Stowe Mountain Resort, but the 6- to 7.9-mile hike is worth every step to the arctic-alpine summit. And if you decide to skin up on backcountry skis in the winter, you can stay in the Stone Hut near the top of Mount Mansfield. After a night of swapping tall tales over taller mugs of brandy-laced cocoa by the wood burning stove, you and eleven friends will get first tracks, guaranteed. (Well, unless you go overboard with the brandy.) The only hitch? The limited available slots at the hut are awarded by an annual lottery, so you'll have to wish upon a star to see the stunning night skies here. Call 802-253-4010 or 802-253-4014 for information.

near the towns of Waitsfield and Warren, which are also home to the Sugarbush and Mad River Glen ski areas.

These winter-sport options are just a thirty-minute drive from the city. Morse Farm, a legendary maple mecca just three miles north of Montpelier, run by seventh-generation Vermonters, has cross-country skiing trails designed by an Olympian. You can reach the alpine and backcountry areas of Stowe, Smuggler's Notch, Cochran's, and Bolton Valley before you finish your morning cup of coffee. But stick around Montpelier long enough, and you just may become friends with a certain high school science teacher who'll invite you to his backyard powder party.

Local Legend

Quarries

The landlocked state of Vermont once had its own Ellis Island, thanks to the flood of immigrants who arrived during the 1800s to work in the quarries of Barre, just south of Montpelier. By the early 1900s, Barre had become an unlikely but popular vacation for New York and Boston dwellers, who took train rides to peer into the deep gouges in the earth and the tiny figures of toilers taking out the rock for gravestones, garden adornments, and kitchen counters. Today, the area still pulls in millions from the granite industry, and visitors can tour the Rock of Ages quarry. But one of the best places to get a glimpse of where Barre granite has gone is at the city's eighty-five-acre Hope Cemetery, where a race car, an armchair, and an airplane are among the 10,500 gravestones.

Start the Day

Capitol Grounds Café & Roastery (27 State Street; 802-223-7800): Twenty-five types of coffee, plus bagels, baked goods, and soups in a building once coveted—but never attained—by McDonald's.

Gear Up

Onion River Sports (20 Langdon Street; 802-229-9409): The center of the city's cycling scene, with road and mountain bike, snowshoe and cross-country ski rentals; also offers weekly rides, plus packs, tents, and a next-door boot store.

Refuel

Finkerman's Riverside Bar-B-Q (188 River Street; 802-229-2295): Yep, real ribs, grits, pulled pork, and other cool 'cue in Vermont; local farmers are providers.

Black Door Bar & Bistro (44 Main Street; 802-223-7070): Burgers and steaks with a stylish, citified twist and a jazzy, 1930s New Orleans atmosphere.

Positive Pie 2 (22 State Street; 802-229-0453): Pizza (traditional or gourmet, white or wheat crust), pasta, and a live music lounge.

Bunk

Capitol Plaza (100 State Street; 802-223-5252): Stately downtown hotel with fifty-six rooms; first opened in 1826.

Betsy's Bed & Breakfast (74 East State Street; 802-229-0466): Twelve rooms; breakfast includes migas—eggs with green chiles, cheese, and tortilla chips—and other filling fare.

Can't Leave?

Nearest airport: Burlington International, Burlington, Vermont (43 miles)

Primary industries: Government, insurance

Newport, Vermont

Population: 5,207

Action: Paddling, downhill and cross-country skiing, mountain biking, rock climbing

The most fluid border crossing in the country might be near Newport, Vermont, where the thirty-three-mile-long Lake Memphremagog slips into Quebec as quietly as a paddle dips into the sapphire-blue surface. The two countries and cultures are so intermixed here, in fact, that you might feel as if you're in a French Canadian village rather a tiny American city. Meanwhile, the surrounding mountains of Vermont's Northeast Kingdom actually belong to New Hampshire's White Mountains, geologically speaking.

Any identity crisis, however, quickly dissolves when it comes to Newport's ties with the outdoors. The connection begins with the dairy farms that perch on hilltops, continues through the fact that cycling company Louis Garneau has chosen to locate its American headquarters here, and culminates in the grueling Jay Challenge adventure race that takes place here every July. First held in 2002, the event puts competitors through the rigors of three of Newport's favorite sports: paddling, trail running, and mountain biking. (The only sport missing, due to obvious logistical reasons, is skiing.) And in the spirit of the hardy Northeast Kingdom, there's a tough twist to each part. The paddle, known as the crossover, is twenty-six miles across Lake Memphremagog, whose name means "beautiful waters" in Abenaki—but try telling that to racers on a windy, choppy day. The mountain bike portion includes sixty-five miles of knotty, tight trails with 10,000 feet of climbing. Finally, the marathon actually measures 30.5 miles, not 26.2, and sends runners bushwhacking on a steep course up and down 3,968-foot Jay Peak. Finishing times for the marathon alone are typically six hours and more, while more than a third of participants in the Jay Challenge end up dropping out. Taking on all three parts of the race yourself, rather than dividing them

The ski area at Jay Peak, in Newport, Vermont, receives an average of 358 inches of snow each year. (© Christopher Smith)

among team members, can feel equivalent to taking on an Ironman— or worse.

Whether or not they're training for the Jay Challenge, Newport locals regularly slice across Lake Memphremagog—into which the Black and Barton rivers flow—in multicolored kayaks. Or they find calmer waters, along with rock-climbing routes, at nearby Lake Willoughby. The 100-mile network of singletrack known as the Kingdom Trails provides ample mountain-biking opportunities, while the 270-mile Long Trail finishes up just beyond Jay Peak to the north.

Even if the mountain didn't host part of the now famous Challenge, Jay Peak would still have plenty of bragging rights, thanks to its position in North American weather patterns. Swirling storms dump an average of 358 inches of snow on the ski area, where nearly 350 acres of skiing and riding terrain drop through thick glades, bump over moguls, and bottom out at a funky lodge with more French-Canadian feel. (You can pay in U.S. or Canadian dollars here.) Jay Peak has been called the Jackson Hole of the East; its backcountry is wide open to powderhounds, too, and rewards them with thirty-five-degree slopes and the muffled silence of plowing through waist-deep snow. From Jay Pass, it's just thirteen or so miles to the Canadian border by cross-country skis on the Catamount Trail. But there's a fence and a guard station, so you'll feel slightly less freedom than when paddling Lake Memphremagog.

The Wild Side

The Northern Forest Canoe Trail

One of the nation's newest—and oldest—trails is the 740-mile Northern Forest Canoe Trail, which traces Native American travel routes from Old Forge, New York, to Fort Kent, Maine. One of the NFCT's most difficult sections, known as the Grand Portage for its many overland carries, ends at Lake Memphremagog. Tempted to canoe the whole thing? Organizers caution that only the most skilled of paddlers should attempt a thru-paddle, and that only four people have ever achieved the feat.

Start the Day

Brown Cow (350 East Main Street; 802-334-7887): Blueberry pancakes and omelets in a 1950s atmosphere.

Gear Up

The Great Outdoors of Vermont (177 Main Street; 802-334-2831): Everything you need for biking, camping, paddling, skiing, and snowboarding.

Refuel

Eastside Restaurant & Pub (25 Lake Street; 802-334-2340): Steaks and chicken overlooking the lake.

Newport Natural Foods (194 Main Street; 802-334-2626): Organic produce, natural groceries, and health products.

Lago Trattoria (95 Main Street; 802-334-8222): Pizzas and other Italian fare.

Bunk

Prouty Beach Campground (802-334-7951): A thirty-six-acre downtown public park with four tent sites, tennis courts, and canoe rentals on Lake Memphremagog.

Newport City Motel (444 East Main Street; 802-334-6558): A sixty-four-room motel with indoor pool.

Cliff Haven Farm Bed & Breakfast (5463 Lake Road; 802-334-2401; www.cliffhavenfarmbedand breakfast.com): Three rooms on a 300-acre dairy farm.

Can't Leave?

Nearest airport: Burlington International, Burlington, Vermont (74 miles)

Primary industries: Agriculture, recreation

Local Legend

Memphre

Scotland has the Loch Ness Monster, while Burlington boasts of Champ. And in Newport, Vermont, it's Memphre, the sea serpent that is said to swim Lake Memphremagog. A Quebec newspaper first mentioned the monster in 1847, and today two international dracontology societies on either side of the border collect sightings. Around Newport, Memphre has stirred up not only a mystery but also a controversy, as one local woman claims a copyright to the name.

The Middle Atlantic

Milford, Delaware

Population: 7,201

Action: Road biking, paddling, fishing, diving

Hardly more than a decade ago, practically the only reason to stop in Milford was to get gas on the way to Rehoboth Beach, about twenty miles southeast. Now this rejuvenated historic town on the Mispillion River is a worthy destination in itself—even if almost no one knows it yet. The whirlwind of change began with the creation of a mile-long greenway along the river; the greenway's wide red-brick path has encouraged people to jog, walk, and just plain loiter downtown at the end of the day. In return, the storefronts have been spruced up and the gingerbread Victorian homes have been revitalized. There are also tentative plans to extend the greenway, known as the Mispillion Riverwalk, and create a paddling trail alongside it. Yet even without future improvements, there's enough biking in the outlying countryside—and paddling, hiking, fishing, and diving—to lure you to the new, improved Milford and entice you to stay for a while.

Milford was incorporated in the late 1700s and for more than 150 years was known as a port and boatbuilding community. Several shipyards once lined the river, and more than 600 vessels were built there. When the industry vanished after World War II, the vitality of the downtown gradually withered. But now the bustle is back on Walnut Street, and sailors have been replaced by attorneys, accountants, and workers from the giant dental-supply manufacturer nearby. The local waterways are still a focal point of people's lives there, but in a more recreational sense. Within Milford there are a handful of small lakes and ponds open for fishing and boating, and about ten minutes from town the Mispillion drains into Delaware Bay, the broad, 782-square-mile estuary at the mouth of the Delaware River. It's not hard to find a local charter boat captain to take you out there to stalk the bluefish, flounder, stripers, weakfish, and blackfish that lurk in its depths and

Paddlers take to the Mispillion River in Milford, Delaware. (© Daniel Bond)

in the nearby Atlantic. The bay and the marshlands that fringe its shores are also prime territory for paddling and viewing the millions of migratory birds that stop there during their annual travels up and down the Eastern Flyway.

Some of Milford's most exciting action can only be seen through a dive mask. At the mouth of Delaware Bay, you'll find the China Wreck, a 160-foot ship sunk at a depth of about fifty feet and laden with old English china. Close to it are the remains of a 120-year-old tugboat. Further south, unbeknownst to the millions of people who line the magnificent beaches there, the Delaware coast is littered with the wrecks of ships sunk in its shallow waters over the past three centuries. If you're looking for a quiet way to appreciate the sand, get up early in the morning and bike on the wide-shouldered roads through Bethany, Dewey, and Rehoboth, grab breakfast, and then head back to town. Stopping in Rehoboth to gas up before heading to Milford—now there's a novel concept.

Start the Day

Baked Fresh Bakery (215 NE Front Street; 302-424-3587): By the waterfront; try their sticky buns.

Nancy's Riverfront Café (1 North Walnut Street; 302-424-2393): Combination coffeehouse and breakfast joint.

Gear Up

Bikes Etc. (3 North Walnut Street; 302-422-8030): Friendly, full-service bike shop.

Quest Fitness & Kayak (1239 NE Front Street; 302-422-8808): A fitness center that doubles as a kayak shop and touring outfit.

Refuel

Milford Diner (1042 North Walnut Street; 302-422-6111): The jam-packed crowds aren't wrong about this half-century-old diner.

Dolce (36 North Walnut Street; 302-422-5760): For dessert, try their cheesecake on a stick.

Bunk

The Towers Bed and Breakfast (101 NW Front Street; 302-422-3814; www.mispillion.com): A restored, antique-filled Victorian built in 1783. Check out the music room, complete with grand piano and a Victrola that still works.

Pink Haus Bed & Breakfast (109 Church Street; 302-422-2754): A century-old Arts and Crafts–style house, surrounded by gardens; four rooms.

Can't Leave?

Nearest airport: Salisbury–Ocean City Wicomico Regional, Salisbury, Maryland (41 miles)

Primary industries: Health care, manufacturing, retail

The Wild Side

Prime Hook National Wildlife Refuge

Every year in late spring, millions of horseshoe crabs spawn on the shores of Delaware Bay, which makes this spot one of the most popular rendezvous points in the Western Hemisphere for migrating shorebirds. These birds include the nearly extinct red knot, which makes the trip all the way from the frigid southern tip of South America. To witness this annual avian event, head to the 10,000-acre Prime Hook National Wildlife Refuge. Bring your binoculars as you hike its four footpaths among the marshlands, coast, and hardwood forests, or, if you're really ambitious, paddle on its impressive seven-mile canoe trail.

Crisfield, Maryland

Population: 2,808
Action: Fishing, sailing, kayaking

Examine a map of Maryland, and you'll see that the town of Crisfield clings to a point of land so far south on the Eastern Shore, it looks like it could drop into the Chesapeake Bay with one or two shakes of that chart. Indeed, Crisfield is so immersed in the watery culture of the Chesapeake that around the town's marshes and marinas it's sometimes hard to distinguish where the land ends and the bay begins. As one of the last real watermen's towns on the Chesapeake, Crisfield also makes it difficult to determine when the night ends and the day begins, as workers shuck oysters, empty crab pots, and pack softshell crabs in shipping crates long before sunrise. For a town celebrated for its seafood, its access to nearby Tangier and Smith islands, and, now, its wealth of paddling waters, Crisfield's crest—which includes two crossed oars, a crab, an anchor, and undulating waves of water—nearly says it all.

If you headed directly west across the Chesapeake Bay from Crisfield, you'd hit the Potomac River and end up in Washington, D.C., but the town might as well be oceans away from the nation's capital. Instead of a swamp, Crisfield's foundations settle into the shells of oysters, which helped it prosper in the mid-1800s. Originally, it was called Annemessex, or "bountiful waters," and then Somers Cove, but when John Crisfield lobbied to bring the Eastern Shore Railroad here—to help carry seafood to outlying markets—the town was renamed in his honor. While other small businesses cropped up, including a squadron of sewing experts who helped clothe Wall Street, it was still oysters, and then crabs, that helped Crisfield hang on to the edge of the bay. Today, the Chesapeake's bounty of crustaceans has become seriously depleted: according to a 2005 *National Geographic* article, the annual oyster harvest has dropped from a million bushels two decades ago to 26,500 in 2004, while only a quarter of the watermen of the 1970s are still crabbing. But Crisfield still ekes a living from the water.

Crab shacks and fish-cleaning stations sit alongside some 500 berths for boats at Somers Cove Marina in Crisfield, Maryland. (© Maryland Office of Tourism)

Part of the town's current welfare depends on tourism and recreation, along with fishing, and you'll find the center of the social and business scene at Somers Cove Marina, where crab shacks and fish-cleaning stations sit alongside some 500 berths for boats. the Chesapeake is one of the world's best places to sail—whether you're racing or cruising—and Crisfield is well located for excursions along the East Coast and back home again. Ensuring that visitors never stray too far from the water, the marina even has a swimming pool, laundry rooms, picnic tables, and grills. The marina is the departure point for the town's fishing-charter operations, which head out to reel in striped bass, bluefish, trout, flounder, and more in Tangier and Poconoke sounds. The best all-around fishing times are in June, when the Scorchy Tawes Pro-Am Fishing Tournament offers daily 500-dollar awards for the heaviest trout, rockfish, croaker, and flounder, or the fall, when cooling temperatures mean hot fishing.

Somers Cove is also the departure point for ferry rides to Tangier Island, a carless speck of land with 850 residents and a single schoolhouse, and the marshy and more touristy Smith Island, just eight miles long and four miles wide. Both are worthy day trips, but better visited by kayak if you can handle the twelve-mile crossing. You'll be able to slip through the stilt town of crabbers on Tangier, feast on softshells, and sleep on the beach, before taking on the seven-mile stretch of water to Smith Island, stopping to pick up treasures on tiny strips of sand along the way. If you want to stay closer to Crisfield, kayak through Janes Island State Park, where fifteen miles of wind- and current-protected water trails snake through more than 3,000 acres of marshes and beaches.

The Crisfield Heritage Foundation leads kayak tours of the 330-acre Cedar Island Marsh Sanctuary, across from Somers Cove. The sanctuary is a good place for an immersion in the town's seafood-rich history. All along the Delmarva peninsula, shared by Delaware, Maryland, and Virginia, are hundreds of miles of flat cycling routes punctuated by grassy dunes, crab houses, breweries, and beaches.

But you'll want to get back to Crisfield in time for sunset over the Chesapeake Bay, as views like these might not last forever. A few condos are popping up, and there may soon be a day when Crisfield does not cling to the water in quite the same way.

Start the Day

Circle Inn Restaurant (4012 Crisfield Highway; 410-968-1969): Diner with all-day breakfast including omelets, pancakes, egg sandwiches, and coffee.

Gordon's Confectionary (831 West Main Street; 410-968-0566): Opens at 4 AM to serve fishing-boat workers; go here for coffee and the photo-filled cigar boxes.

The Wild Side

Assateague Island

With 11,600 miles of coastline to explore, there are plenty of kayaking waters on Chesapeake Bay, but none like the final approach to Assateague Island, where the wild ponies are even friendlier to paddlers than to other visitors. You'll need to drive to Ocean City first, and then paddle across Chincoteague Bay. Once you reach the thirty-seven-mile-long barrier island, you can camp on the beach.

Gear Up

Chesapeake Angling (26952 Holly Avenue; 410-968-3286): Fly-fishing and saltwater light tackle with Captain Matt Tawes from Janes Island State Park.

Prime Time Fishing (Somers Cove; 410-968-0074): Captain Keith Ward leads trolling, bottom fishing, and chumming expeditions for stripers, blues, trout, and flounder.

Refuel

Side Street Seafood Restaurant (204 South Tenth Street; 410-968-2442): The place to go for a platter of steamed crabs; overlooks Somers Cove Marina.

The Watermen's Inn (901 West Main Street; 410-968-2119): Backfin lump crab cakes, fried shrimp dinners, steaks, and Chesapeake-crab soups, plus salads and homemade deserts.

The Cove Restaurant (718 Broadway Street; 410-968-9532): More crabs, crab cakes, and seafood, along with big salads, steaks, and fried chicken at Somers Cove.

Bunk

Janes Island State Park (26280 Alfred Lawson Drive; 410-968-1565; www.dnr .state.md.us/publiclands/eastern/janes island.html): Five rustic cabins and 104 campsites, along with four bedrooms in the conference center; located on canoeing and kayaking waters.

Local Legend

The Blue Crab

From the Soft Shell Spring Fair in May to the Hard Crab Derby and Fair on Labor Day weekend, Crisfield has an unparalleled celebration of the crustacean. For the most meat for your money, don't miss the Crab and Clam Bake in July, when a thirty-five dollar donation gets you all the steamed crabs (plus a mallet), fried fish, clams (any way you like 'em), french fries, corn on the cob, onion rings, and watermelon you can eat—and frosty beer in a commemorative mug.

Bea's Bed & Breakfast (10 South Somerset Avenue; 410-968-0423): Two rooms at reasonable rates, in a 1909 Victorian built by John Handy, founder of a softshell crab company.

Somers Cove Motel (700 Robert Norris Drive; 410-968-1900): Basic accommodations with air conditioning at Somers Cove.

Can't Leave?

Nearest airport: Salisbury–Ocean City Wicomico Regional, Salisbury, Maryland (35 miles)

Primary industries: Seafood, poultry, education

St. Michaels, Maryland

Population: 1,193

Action: Sailing, boating, kayaking, road biking

If you took Annapolis, shrank it a bit, dropped it onto the opposite shore of the Chesapeake Bay on a hidden, slim neck of land, and subtracted the crowds, the result would be something like quiet St. Michaels, Maryland. This historic village is one of the East Coast's prime sailing and paddling enclaves, although it lies largely off the tourist radar. Its protected location—sandwiched between the Miles River to the north and Broad Creek to the south—and quick access to the open, brackish waters of the Chesapeake has made St. Michaels a busy port for much of three centuries. It's so well concealed that even British ships couldn't find it when they tried to attack one night during the War of 1812. Their cannon fire overshot their intended mark when locals blacked out their windows and hung lanterns from the trees as a diversion. Legend says that only one home was hit in what became known as the Battle of St. Michaels. (The trees didn't fare so well, though.)

Today the only vessels patrolling its shores are captained by fishermen, recreational sailors, and pleasure boaters lured by the picturesque scenery, steady breezes, and consistently blue summer skies. Visiting adventurers can commandeer their own boats from the many local marinas or take a ride on an ancient skipjack or charter sailing yacht. The 189-mile-long Chesapeake Bay is the largest estuary in the United States, covering 4,400 square miles and having nearly 11,700 miles of shoreline. And the opportunities for exploring it are limitless.

Originally, St. Michaels was an important boatbuilding center, and although it's no longer filled with ship's carpenters, St. Mary's Square downtown still has the ancient bell that rang three times a day to sound out the start and end of work. More striking reminders of the past are the eighteenth- and nineteenth-century Colonial, Federal, and Victorian homes on Talbot Street and the outlying avenues.

A 129-year-old lighthouse adorns the Chesapeake Bay Maritime Museum in St. Michaels, Maryland. (© Maryland Office of Tourism)

Immaculately preserved, the homes are now filled with upscale galleries bookstores, antique stores, inns, and restaurants serving the area's specialty, Chesapeake blue crabs. No visit to town is complete without at least a half day spent among the ten exhibit buildings and eighty-five boats at the Chesapeake Bay Maritime Museum on the edge of the Miles River. You can climb the steps of the three-story, 129-year-old lighthouse, wander through the working boatyard where wooden vessels are restored, or get a look at an authentic crabber's shanty.

Another magnificent way to enjoy the bay—and the streams and rivers that pour into it—is by kayak. Only a few outfitters operate in the area, so you're better off bringing your own boat, if you've got one. You can tour the likes of the Blackwater National Wildlife Refuge, created in 1993 and a major stopover for birds in the Eastern Flyway. More than 50,000 waterfowl use its 27,000 acres of tidal marsh, forests, meadows, and rivers as a rest area during migration periods, and it's home to 165 species of threatened or endangered plants. Three color-coded kayaking trails snake through the refuge, providing access to its hidden nooks and giving up-close glimpses of bald eagles, peregrine falcons, Delmarva fox squirrels, and Southern leopard frogs. The land is the site of a former fur farm for muskrats and nutria, a nonnative rodent species that was single-handedly destroying acres of marshland in the area until it was recently eradicated. On terra firma, the refuge can be explored by biking the 6.5-mile loop called Wildlife Drive, which winds through forest and marshes, or on two routes—one 25 miles, the other 20—that encircle it. St. Michaels is also a popular stop for riders, drawn by the Eastern Shore's flat, empty and scenic roads that wind among the fertile farmlands. Yes, landlubbers are welcome there, too.

Start the Day

Blue Crab Coffee (102 South Fremont Street; 410-745-4155; www.bluecrabcoffee.com): Unique blends like Jamaican Me Crazy and Grandma's Chocolate Snicker Cookie are house specialties.

Sherwood's Landing at the Inn at Perry Cabin (308 Watkins Lane; 410-745-2200; www.perrycabin.com): The Caramel Pecan Twist is worth the price in this dining room of the area's finest hotel.

The Wild Side

Jean Ellen duPont Shehan Audubon Sanctuary

It doesn't get wilder on the Chesapeake than in the 952-acre Jean Ellen duPont Shehan Audubon Sanctuary, about fifteen minutes from downtown St. Michaels. Named after the woman who donated it to the Audubon Society in 1997, the sanctuary is a former farm bordered by three creeks. Almost 200 bird species and nearly the same number of different animals make their homes among its vast pastures, shoreline, and woodlands of pine, willow, and oak. On most Sundays and Mondays, when it's open to the public, the sanctuary is a favorite quick escape for locals, who come for a walk or jog on its ten miles of paths. It also conducts nature courses for kids and adults, and puts on an annual monarch butterfly watch (410/745-9283; www.audubonmddc.org).

Gear Up

Tilghman Island Marina (6140 Mariners Court, Tilghman; 410-886-2979): "Captain" Ron and Nancy Cicero operate fishing charters; rent powerboats, sailboats, canoes, and kayaks; and help chart routes.

Eastern Shore Adventure Company (28290 St. Michaels Road, Easton; 410-820-8881): Drops off and picks up its rental kayaks at several different locations in the area.

Refuel

Crab Claw Restaurant (304 Mill Street at Navy Point; 410-745-2900; www.thecrabclaw.com): A legendary local seafood shanty that is a tourist destination in itself.

Foxy's Marina Bar (125 Mulberry Street; 410-745-4340; www.foxysstmichaels.com): For crab cakes and beer served outside by the water.

Bistro St. Michaels (403 South Talbot Street; 410-745-9111; www.bistro stmichaels.com): A cozy French bistro with creative seafood offerings.

Bunk

St. Michaels Harbour Inn, Marina and Spa (101 North Harbor Road; 800-955-9001; www.harbourinn.com): Stay in one of the well-appointed rooms, or in your boat, docked at one of the marina's fifty slips.

Parsonage Inn (210 North Talbot Street; 800-394-5519; www.parsonage -inn.com): A nineteenth-century red-brick Victorian and former church that is now the top bed-and-breakfast in town.

Inn at Perry Cabin (308 Watkins Lane; 410-745-2200; www.perrycabin.com): A luxurious and romantic former estate right on the Miles River.

Can't Leave?

Nearest airport: Baltimore/Washington International, Baltimore, Maryland (41 miles)

Primary industries: Fishing, tourism, health care

Local Legend

Cannonball House

This impressive Colonial-style brick home at 200 Mulberry Street, on the edge of St. Mary's Square, was built by the shipwright William Merchant two centuries ago. Legend has it that the lone British cannonball to hit the village in the Battle of St. Michaels in August, 1813, surprised Merchant's wife and daughter by crashing through the roof and rolling downstairs from the attic. (Other accounts say that all women and children were evacuated from town before the attack.) Because it's a private residence, it can't be toured, but you can find out more about it at the nearby St. Mary's Square Museum (409 St. Mary's Square; 410-745-9561), which is open from May through October.

Milford, Pennsylvania

Population: 1,214
Action: Hiking, paddling, rock climbing

Philadelphians might find something familiar about Milford—besides the fact that, like their home, the Delaware River runs through it. When Milford's founders created this town, etched into a valley in the Poconos, in 1796, they modeled it after the grid of the City of Brotherly Love, right down to naming one of the main thoroughfares Broad Street. There are some slight differences, though. Fewer people live in Milford than in a Philly high rise; its section of the Delaware is littered with hidden fishing nooks and stretches of whitewater, as opposed to being just plain littered; and the eagles you see in the area don't sign autographs or wear football helmets—they're too busy looking for prey.

Milford lies at the northern tip of the Delaware Water Gap National Recreation Area, a once-popular natural attraction for wealthy urbanites from New York to Baltimore, but now largely overlooked. The dramatic craggy chasm that gives the park its name drops as far as 1,200 feet below the peaks of the Appalachian Mountains and stretches a mile wide at its widest point. The park flanks forty miles of the river, covering 169,269 acres straddling Pennsylvania and New Jersey. Within its borders you'll find ninety-five miles of hiking trails (twenty-five of which belong to the Appalachian Trail), several stocked lakes and side creeks, and more than 200 rock-climbing routes. On the river, the mostly flat-water paddling is more relaxing than challenging.

Milford was transformed from a stagecoach stop into a village in the late eighteenth century by Judge John Biddis, who named six of its streets after his daughters. It was later home to one of the nation's first conservationists, Gifford Pinchot, the first head of the United States Forest Service and co-founder of the Yale University School of Forestry. He died in 1946, but his chateau-style mansion, built on a hill above town in 1886, still stands and is open to the public. This house

The Delaware Water Gap National Recreation Area flanks 40 miles of the Delaware River south of Milford, Pennsylvania (© Michelle Jacques)

and the many Victorians and stone storefronts also erected in the nineteenth century are reminders of when grand hotels used to fill the Delaware Water Gap area.

For outdoor action outside of the park, a twenty-minute drive west is Lake Wallenpaupack, a sliver of water fifteen miles long and fifty-two miles around, created in 1926 for hydroelectric energy. Replacing the farmers who once lived in this now-flooded valley are a healthy population of smallmouth bass, stripers, walleye, brown trout, and perch. Try getting that in Philadelphia.

Start the Day

Milford Diner and Restaurant (301 Broad Street; 570-296-8611; www.milforddiner.com): A good old-fashioned American diner located downtown.

Waterwheel Café (150 Water Street; 570-296-2383; www.waterwheel cafe.com): Scones, croissants, danish, and pancakes in a restored nineteenth-century mill.

Gear Up

Pike County Outfitters (106 Route 6; 570-296-9492): Specializes in fishing gear, but sells some camping equipment. Inside, say hello to the eleven-foot mounted Alaskan brown bear.

Action Outfitters (546 Routes 6 and 209; 570-296-6657): Well-stocked and energetic snowboard, bike, and paintball shop.

Refuel

Apple Valley Restaurant (104 Route 6; 570-296-6831): Burgers, sandwiches, and, on the last Friday of every month, karaoke.

Dimmick Inn Steakhouse (Broad and Harford streets; 570-296-4021): An 1828 inn with a pub from the same era,

The Wild Side

The Delaware Water Gap

There may be taller mountains than the Poconos—which are actually just the remains of an eroded high plateau—in the East, and ones that have superior rock climbing, skiing, and hiking. But when it comes to waterfalls, especially around the Delaware Water Gap, the Poconos are unmatched in number and quality. Within the preserve itself, don't miss Raymondskill Falls, which has three separate cascades that drop a total of 105 feet, and Dingmans Falls, a 130-foot hemlock-flanked cascade. You can get a view from the top of Dingmans Falls by climbing a set of roughly 250 steps. The most spectacular waterfall is in the privately owned Bushkill Falls park, where you can watch the fern-garnished Bushkill Creek plummet 100 feet straight down the main falls.

where you can eat on the wraparound porch.

Bunk

Milford Motel (1591 Route 6; 570-296-6411): A clean, friendly, nineteen-room motor lodge.

Myer Country Motel (600 Routes 6 and 209; 800-764-6937; www.myer motel.com): Quaint collection of white cottages, each with its own front porch.

Cliff Park Inn (155 Cliff Park Road; 800-225-6535; www.cliffparkinn.com): An upscale, fourteen-room country lodge on 500 acres.

Can't Leave?

Nearest airport: Stewart International, Newburgh/New Windsor, New York (50 miles)

Primary industries: Tourism, electronics, retail

Local Legend

The Ferry

In 1735, Andrew Dingman began operating a toll ferry across the Delaware River seven miles south of Milford, connecting New Jersey to Pennsylvania. Today you have to pay a whopping seventy-five cents to get across at the same spot that the pioneers did nearly two centuries ago, on the Dingmans Bridge. The first bridge built by the Dingman family to span the river was completed around 1850, but was washed away after several years. So they restarted the ferry service, which ran on and off—but mostly on—until the turn of the twentieth century, when a wrought-iron overpass built atop stone supports replaced it. The 530-foot-long structure still stands and is the only remaining toll bridge on the Delaware—and one of the last privately owned ones in the country.

Ohiopyle, Pennsylvania

Population: 76

Action: Paddling, rafting, hiking, mountain biking

For some people, getting out of Ohiopyle is more fun than being there. Not that they aren't charmed by this four-square-block oasis of civilization within the vast, rugged forest tract of the Laurel Mountains known as Ohiopyle State Park. Instead, there's a good chance that they've just hopped onto on the powerful Youghiogheny (pronounced *yock-a-GAIN-ey*) River, at the start of a stretch of whitewater that makes most eastern rapids seem like a lazy tube ride. Or they're heading onto the spectacular rail trail that traces the water's banks, or among the seventy-five miles of backpacking trails that navigate the park. Another reason they're happy to leave is that they probably know they're coming back that evening to swap stories about their adventures over drinks at one of the town's cozy watering holes.

Given its size and obscurity, Ohiopyle seems an unlikely candidate to be the hub of outdoor recreation in southern Pennsylvania. The area was settled in the early nineteenth century, mostly by farmers, but when the Baltimore and Ohio railroad arrived in town in the early 1870s, a boom in lumber and tourism followed. Resort hotels soon arose, and Ohiopyle became a popular destination for people willing to pay the one-dollar train ticket to get there from Pittsburgh, seventy miles away, according to the Pennsylvania Department of Conservation and Natural Resources. As the trains dwindled in the twentieth century, so did visitors. The hotels were abandoned and torn down, and in the 1960s the state purchased the land that now makes up the park. Now rafting outfitter shops, bike stores, general stores, and restaurants occupy the historic downtown commercial buildings, and replacing the resorts is a smattering of guest rooms in the vintage clapboard houses along the short streets.

Of the old structures in Ohiopyle, maybe the most impressive is the restored wooden train depot, now a visitor's center and trailhead

Ohiopyle, Pennsylvania is an oasis of civilization within the Laurel Mountains and vast Ohiopyle State Park. (© Stacie Faust)

for the Youghiogheny River Trail. A seventy-mile bike path of crushed limestone atop the former Baltimore and Ohio railroad bed, nearly one-third of the river trail stretches through the park, running alongside the river and crossing it occasionally while offering impressive vantages of the many rapids. The trail also connects to the Great Allegheny Passage, a network of paths that reach as far as Washington, D.C., on the Chesapeake and Ohio (C&O) Canal towpath. For hikers, the town is the western terminus of the seventy-mile-long Laurel Highlands Hiking Trail, which climbs Laurel Ridge and exits the park after six miles as it meanders toward Johnstown. Most of the other footpaths in the park extend between two and three miles, often leading through thick pine stands to hidden waterfalls or scenic water vistas. On the Ferncliff Peninsula, created by a hairpin turn on the river next to town, you can take short hikes past the remains of the old hotels that once sat there.

Yet the main reason people come to Ohiopyle, is for the paddling on the Youghiogheny or "Yough." Rafting outfits usually divide the river into three sections—upper, middle, and lower. The ten-mile upper section starts in Maryland and barrels down the mountains in one long stretch, leading paddlers through more than twenty Class IV and V hazards and an average drop of 115 feet per mile. On the scenic, ten-mile, family-friendly middle section, the Yough flattens to Class I and II rapids until the take-out just above Ohiopyle Falls. More than 100,000 padders arrive at the launch in town each year for the seven-mile lower section, making it the most popular whitewater run east of the Rockies. Starting almost immediately with the Entrance Rapid, they're challenged with a steady barrage of Class III and IV rapids until the take-out after Bruner Run—when they get ready to head back to town to swap stories, of course.

Start the Day

Falls Market and Inn (69 Main Street; 724-329-4973): Is it a market? Is it a down-home restaurant? Is it a three-room inn? It's all three.

Local Legend

Frank Lloyd Wright

Ever wonder where, exactly, in southern Pennsylvania you can find Fallingwater, the famous home created by architect Frank Lloyd Wright? The people of Ohiopyle don't, because it's less than ten minutes from town. They're lucky enough to live in the natural setting that inspired Wright to conceive what the American Institute of Architects once voted the "best all-time work of American architecture." The house, completed in 1939 for a wealthy Pittsburgh family, has a natural waterfall cascading beneath it. Fallingwater's cantilevered design makes its limestone walls seem almost like a natural extension of the rugged surroundings.

Firefly Grill (25 Sherman Street; 724-329-7155): A vegetarian-friendly, chalet-style restaurant next to the train depot visitor's center.

Gear Up

Ohiopyle Trading Post (Whitewater Street; 724-329-1450): A bike shop, paddling outfitter, guide service, and tourist knickknack store.

Wilderness Voyageurs (Commercial Street; 800-272-4141): A rafting outfitter that runs an outdoor-gear shop, provides paddling and rock-climbing instruction, and rents and sells bikes.

Refuel

Falls City Pub (112 Garrett Street; 724-329-3000; www.fallscitypub.com): Wash down your nachos and pub burger with a Youghiogheny Red microbrew, served on tap.

Ohiopyle House Café (144 Grant Street; 724-329-1122): A restaurant inside a house beside the bike path; the specialties are steak, seafood, and pasta.

Bunk

Ohiopyle Lodge (138 Grant Street; 800-419-7599; www.ohiopyle lodge.com): Four units in three adjacent ranch houses.

Ohiopyle Guest Houses (Grant Street; 800-472-3846): Guest rooms in three quaint downtown homes.

Can't Leave?

Nearest airport: Pittsburgh International, Pittsburgh, Pennsylvania (86 miles)

Primary industries: Forestry, agriculture, retail

Wellsboro, Pennsylvania

Population: 3,342

Action: Rafting, paddling, hiking, rock climbing, mountain and road biking, cross-country skiing, fishing

There's a reason why Wellsboro, Pennsylvania—with its colonial homes, its downtown of boulevards and gas lights, and its streets lined shaded by maples and elms—smacks of New England: the town was originally part of the Connecticut Grant issued by the king of England. But this town easily beats its northern neighbors when it comes to jaw-dropping gorges, for it sits ten miles east of a forty-seven-mile-long gash, up to 1,450 feet deep, in the Endless Mountains of north-central Pennsylvania. Here you can take your pick of paddling Class II and III rapids, hiking nearly 1,500 miles of trails, rock climbing quartzite conglomerate, and mountain biking from sunup to sundown along the Pine Creek Gorge. After a day that begins with a ninety-nine-cent cup of coffee at an authentic diner and ends with rolling out the Primaloft in a lakeside yurt, you may feel you're closer to the wild West than New England.

Like its Rocky Mountain brethren, Wellsboro is near ghost towns, abandoned when the coal mines and timber operations went bust in the late 1800s and early 1900s. Wellsboro, incorporated in 1830, managed to hang on, and today has begun to bank on its bevy of outdoor resources, as well as its factories, small businesses, and the North Campus of the Pennsylvania College of Technology.

Much of the signage and tourist literature around town touts the Grand Canyon of Pennsylvania, which is the Pine Creek Gorge, formed by retreating glaciers during the Ice Age and declared a national landmark in 1968. The gorge ticks off the seasons with a reassuring regularity: burning with orange, red, and yellow foliage in the fall; freezing up ice-climbing routes in the winter; spilling waterfalls down its exposed rock formations in spring; and blooming with mountain laurel, the Pennsylvania state flower, to herald the arrival of summer.

With its boulevards, gas lights, and tree shaded Main Street, Wellsboro, Pennsylvania could be mistaken for a New England village. (© Tioga County Visitors Bureau)

(Wellsboro's Laurel Festival and the twenty-four-mile Laurel Flyer Road Race happen in June, while September means the Laurel Classic Mountain Bike Race in loops of eleven or twenty-two miles.) Spring is the best time to raft or whitewater kayak the free-flowing Pine Creek, a tributary of the west branch of the Susquehanna River. Take a day-long, seventeen-mile trip to a multiday, seventy-mile trip. The lower water levels of autumn, meanwhile, lure paddlers in Old Town canoes, who drift along riffles while spotting eagles and scouting out campsites among the changing colors of the forested riverbanks.

Even with the rafters, kayakers, and canoeists, anglers find plenty of elbow room on the Pine Creek for fly-fishing for wild brown and brook trout; in the surrounding lakes and creeks of the north-central region there is also fishing for rainbows, bass, muskies, walleyes, and catfish. For ice fishing, head to the 407-acre Hills Creek Lake at Hills Creek State Park, one of three state parks surrounding Wellsboro. You'll find the 368-acre Colton Point State Park on the west rim of the Pine Creek Gorge, while Leonard Harrison State Park, at 585 acres, sits on the eastern rim and offers expansive views of the gorge below it.

But you'll need to venture farther than the terraced overlooks to really experience the panaroma of Pine Creek. Hiking and cross-country trails easily outnumber roads in this wilderness area. For back-packing, enter the 159,466-acre Tioga State Forest, which is littered with rock-climbing and bouldering routes, and follow the thirty-mile West Rim Trail. This trail parallels the gorge and connects to the Mid-State Trail, a 168-mile-long system of footpaths winding from the Mason-Dixon Line to the New York border. Other nearby backpacking trails include the forty-two-mile Black Forest Trail and the eighty-five-mile Susquehannock Trail.

Hikers also hit the sixty-two-mile Pine Creek Trail, which runs the length of the canyon at river level, but the mostly flat, crushed-limestone rail trail is better suited to a long, easy mountain-bike ride. Find tougher stuff on the state park and state forest trails, or switch to a road bike to join the group rides leaving from the Wellsboro green on summer Thursday evenings. After pedaling the country roads that spiderweb in every direction, head back to Main Street and dismount at the Arcadia Theatre, an old-fashioned cinema that sometimes serves supper along with its screenings. See if you can stay awake long enough to catch the movie's ending.

Local Legend

First National Bank

Stay in Wellsboro long enough, and you just might start doing business in one of its handful of banks. Just be thankful that they're more secure than the First National Bank, the site of a notorious bank robbery. In 1874, seven men captured First National's president, John Robinson, and his family, at their house and ordered his son, a cashier, to accompany a few of them to the bank and open the vault. News of the robbery along the local telegraph line was delayed, and the robbers fled with more than $50,000 in cash, securities, and bonds. Eventually, two of the robbers were captured, but the rest escaped.

Start the Day

Wellsboro Diner (19 Main Street, 570-724-3992): An authentic diner car, established in 1939, that serves all-day breakfast items including omelets, french toast, and hot cakes.

Gear Up

Pine Creek Outfitters (Route 6; 570-724-3003): Guided rafting trips on Pine Creek, plus canoe, kayak, raft, and wet-suit rentals; hiking guides; shuttles; and bike rentals.

Wild Asaph Outfitters (12389 Route 6; 570-724-5155): Hiking, backpacking, camping, and rock-climbing equipment, rentals, and information.

Country Ski & Sports (81 Main Street; 570-724-3858): Skiing, snowboarding, biking, and paddling gear for sale; cross-country skis for rent.

Refuel

The Native Bagel (One Central Avenue; 570-724-0900): A Wellsboro lunch spot, selling soups, salads, homemade bagels, and bread with dozens of toppings.

The Steak House (29 Main Street; 570-724-9092): Find zucchini parmesan, roast turkey with trimmings, salad platters, steak, and seafood, all reasonably priced.

Timeless Destination (77 Main Street; 570-724-8499): Pizza, pasta, and such other Italian specialties as chicken Sorrentino and veal Marsala; burgers at lunch.

Bunk

Hills Creek State Park (111 Spillway Road; 570-724-4246; www.dcnr.state.pa.us): Includes a 102-site camping area, plus camping cottages, cabins, and yurts.

Bear Mountain Bed & Breakfast (8010 Route 6; 570-724-2428; www.bearmountainbb.com): A three-room lodge near the Pine Creek Gorge; breakfast is a ticket to the Wellsboro Diner and a trail picnic.

Coach Stop Inn (4755 Route 6; 800-829-4130; www.thecoach stopinn.com): A thirty-room tavern turned motel, restaurant, and lounge with one cabin; continental breakfast included.

Can't Leave?

Nearest airport: Elmira-Corning Regional, Elmira, New York (41 miles)

Primary industries: Manufacturing, education, lumber services

Damascus, Virginia

Population: 1,083

Action: Hiking, mountain and road biking

In Virginia, all paths lead to Damascus—or at least it seems that way. At the center of this hamlet in the Blue Ridge Mountains, the Appalachian Trail converges with the rugged Iron Mountain Trail, Virginia Creeper Trail bike path, TransAmerica Bike Trail, and Daniel Boone Trail driving route. Yet the townsfolk have embraced the intrusion of people passing through town by foot, bike, and car.

Given the location of Damascus it's hard to figure out exactly why so many trails meet at this coordinate on the map—as spectacular as it is. It's not like the town lies along some old trade route, or in the geographical center of the state, or at the confluence of two mighty rivers. Instead, it's sandwiched between the Cherokee National Forest and Mount Rogers National Recreation Area by the Tennessee border, near the northwestern corner of North Carolina. At the turn of the twentieth century, it was a whistle stop on the Virginia Carolina Railroad line that carried lumber and iron ore extracted from the area. Since the trains closed in 1977, it has transformed into a beacon for travelers, most notably Appalachian Trail hikers. The 2,175-mile footpath descends from the south through the outlying ridgetops before crossing Beaverdam Creek and running alongside First Street through the three-block heart of the village.

A.T. backpackers who start their journey at Springer Mountain, Georgia, reach Damascus around their 450th mile—and up to that point, it's one of the few places where the footpath intersects with some semblance of civilization. For that reason, almost all of them recharge their batteries for at least a night at the hostel called "The Place," located in the old house behind the Baptist church; resupply at Mount Rogers Outfitters; and devour at least one meal at Baja Café. In 1987, the town hosted the first of what would become an annual Trail Days reunion event for thru-hikers. Held the weekend after Mother's Day,

Beautiful Beaverdam Creek flows through Damascus, Virginia. (© Suzanne Bullard)

it's now attended by more than 20,000 people each year and includes live bands, displays from gear manufacturers, a beauty pageant, a townwide yard sale, an Appalachian Trail Jeopardy game, and free medical check-ups for backpackers and their dogs.

As the A.T. exits town across Laurel Creek and heads north, it piggybacks for a short distance with the mostly cinder Virginia Creeper Trail, a thirty-four-mile bike path that has arisen from the remains of the old railroad bed. From its western starting point in the nearby town of Abington, the bike path crosses forty-seven trestles and climbs almost 1,600 feet before reaching its eastern terminus near Whitetop. More than 200,000 people travel to the area to take their bikes onto Virginia Creeper Trail each year. Meanwhile, the A.T. ascends into the high peaks of Virginia and skirts the bald 5,279-foot summit of Mount Rogers, the highest point on the trail until New England.

The forty-seven-mile Iron Mountain Trail actually used to be part of the Appalachian Trail, before the route was altered a few decades ago. The twenty-three miles of the path south of Damascus are still open to only hikers, while mountain biking and horseback riding are permitted on the northern twenty-four miles north that lead to Iron Mountain Gap. Riders usually don't need to go much farther than eight miles up the path from town, though, to the junction of Forest Road 90, where a treasure trove of singletrack trails lay hidden in the woods. These routes are mostly short, between two and three miles long, but vary from flat and bumpy to hair-raisingly steep and fast. Adventure Damascus Bicycles can give you the lowdown on them, and even arrange a shuttle for you and your bike there. If you prefer something smoother, you can always follow the section of the TransAmerica road-biking trail that passes through the area, on its 4,200-mile route from Yorktown, Virginia, to Astoria, Oregon. Or you can linger in Damascus and, like the locals, welcome all of the riders, hikers, and drivers as they come into town.

Local Legend

The Virginia Creeper

The Virginia Creeper Trail occupies a route first forged at the turn of the twentieth century by the Virginia-Carolina Railroad Company to carry people, timber, iron ore, and coal back and forth between Damascus and Abingdon. The train was nicknamed the Virginia Creeper, because of the vines that grew alongside the tracks and because of how it crept up the mountainsides when filled with cargo. It was the source of vitality to the communities along its route, which stretched to Todd, North Carolina, past Whitetop, Virginia; during the railroads gradual decline from the late 1920s until 1977, these towns suffered with it. The Virginia Creeper train is still legendary among the people in the region, and the trail, drawing tens of thousands of tourists a year, has become a worthy replacement.

Start the Day

Lazy Fox Inn (133 Imboden Street; 276-475-5838; www.lazyfoxinn.com): Serves bottomless plates of eggs, cheese grits, waffles, whatever.

Gear Up

Mount Rogers Outfitters (110 Laurel Avenue; 276-475-5416): One of the favorite outfitter shops on the A.T; carries a wide inventory of backpacking gear. Also provides shuttle service to trailheads within 100 miles.

SunDog Outfitter (331 Douglas Drive; 866-515-3441): Steve Webb, a.k.a. SunDog, is a two-time thru-hiker of the A.T., and his shop sells backpacking gear.

Adventure Damascus Bicycles (128 West Lauel Street; 276-475-6262): Bike sales and rentals; offers trail shuttles.

Refuel

Baja Café (103 South Shady Avenue; 276-475-6005): Mexican food served by an A.T. thru-hiker, Jared Yelton.

Dairy King (511 East Third Street; 276-475-3942): Cheeseburgers, cheeseburgers, cheeseburgers.

Sicily's Italian Restaurant and Pizzeria (142 West Laurel Avenue; 276-475-5753): Watch an emaciated A.T. hiker eat a whole large pie singlehandedly. It might ruin your appetite, but it's a fascinating sight.

Bunk

The Victorian Inn Bed & Breakfast (203 North Legion Street; 276-475-5059): An antique-filled 1903 country Victorian with two rooms, a guest cottage, and a front-porch swing.

Dancing Bear Vacation Rentals (203 Laurel Avenue; 276-475-5900): Four rental units behind the house come equipped at least with a microwave, if not a whole kitchenette.

Can't Leave?

Nearest airport: Tri-Cities Regional, Bristol, Tennessee (44 miles)

Primary industries: Manufacturing, retail, health care

The Wild Side

Mount Rogers

While the Blue Ridge Mountains above the Shenandoah Valley in Virginia get all of the accolades, the beauty of the 150,000-acre Mount Rogers National Recreation Area is largely overshadowed. In the 2,000-acre crest zone, which covers several ridges and the peaks of Stone and Pine mountains, the open grasslands and rocky outcrops leave a spectacular, uninhibited backdrop for your entire hike. The landscape also makes it easy to spot the wild ponies that live there. Not much can overshadow the 5,729-foot summit of Mount Rogers, the tallest peak in the state, which can be accessed off a half-mile side trail from the A.T. In all, there are 400 miles of trails within the park.

Staunton, Virginia

Population:
23,337
Action: Hiking,
mountain and
road biking

It's easy to understand why so many pioneers in the 1700s ended their westward travels upon reaching Staunton (pronounced *STAN-ton*). After taking a look at the wide, fertile Shenandoah Valley, carved between two long mountain ranges and marbled by gentle rivers teeming with fish, they probably decided that it would be tough to find anywhere nicer. Nowadays, city slickers an hour away in Washington, D.C., know they don't need to go any farther than this old-timey gateway near Shenandoah National Park to find epic biking and hiking—not to mention an inviting place to grab a bite to eat, watch a play, and admire an impressive cluster of nineteenth-century architectural gems.

There are plenty of other friendly towns fringing the 300-square-mile national park, which envelops the Blue Ridge Mountain ridgeline in northwestern Virginia, but none have as much culture, history, and character. After spending the morning hiking or biking in the backcountry, you can use the afternoon to browse for art in the galleries housed in the old Victorian buildings crammed together downtown. Then you can maybe catch an American Shakespeare Center performance of Macbeth at the 300-seat Blackfriar's Playhouse, the world's only recreation of the Bard of Avon's indoor theater. (Planning is also underway on a replica of the legendary Globe Theatre.) Or you can simply recover from the day's workout the way the students of local Mary Baldwin College do: with an espresso and a book at Blue Mountain Coffees.

With so many trails in the outlying backcountry, you're best served by browsing a guidebook with that cup of java. There are more than 500 miles of hiking paths in the Shenandoah park, including a 100-mile stretch of the Appalachian Trail that parallels spectacular Skyline Drive through the spine of the Blue Ridge. If you want to avoid the

An outdoor adventure in Staunton, Virginia comes with a side order of local history: the birth-place of native son Woodrow Wilson. (© Virginia Tourism Corporation)

Local Legend

Thomas Jasper Collins

Perhaps an even bigger hometown hero than Woodrow Wilson–whose birthplace and presidential library are in Staunton–is Thomas Jasper Collins. A Washington, D.C. architect who moved to the Shenandoah Valley in 1890 for a company that soon went belly-up, he designed and remodeled more than 200 buildings in town between 1891 and 1911, according to the Historic Staunton Foundation. Name a historic home or commercial building that suits your fancy in Staunton, and odds are that Collins, an expert in the many design styles that fell under the Victorian label, had something to do with its look or design. Or if he didn't, his son Sam, who retired in the 1950s, did.

A.T. crowds and stick close to town, try the Rocky Mount hike, a nine-mile circuit that dips 1,500 feet before ascending sharply to the top of Rocky Mount, where you'll find broad views of the park. Mountain bikes aren't allowed in Shenandoah, but they're free to roam the endless miles of old doubletrack and established single-track routes in the high-rising, million-acre George Washington National Forest, south and west of Staunton. Within a quick drive you'll find everything from easy trails like the flat, nine-mile out-and-back North River Gorge that makes dozens of creek crossings, to more technical ones like the rocky, thirteen-mile Lookout Mountain Trail, which has a climb to the ridgeline that will leave your thighs begging for mercy.

Even more accessible than the hiking and mountain biking is the road riding around Staunton. Just head out the back door of your bed-and-breakfast, and you're into the heart of the Shenandoah Valley, a verdant quilt of hills, farms, pastures, and rivers accentuated by a mountain backdrop that was called the breadbasket of the Confederacy during the Civil War. The town was established around 1745 by a Scottish family, and it later became a major train stop and important supply post for roads leading west. The old depot still stands, as do many of the Victorian warehouses—now filled with shops and restaurants—in what's called the Wharf District. The railroad was also largely responsible for generating the wealth that built the hodgepodge of Greek Revival, Italiante, Federal, Queen Anne, and Colonial Revival homes before the 1920s and that have been so magnificently restored over the past couple of decades. Amtrak cars still make regular stops in town, before heading into the countryside that's now empty of pioneers, but still full of people who couldn't imagine living anywhere else.

Start the Day

Blue Mountain Coffees (12 Buyers Street; 540-886-4506; www.damnfinecoffee.net): A coffeehouse and sandwich shop.

Gear Up

Wilderness Adventure Outfitters (25 Middlebrook Avenue; 540-885-3200): A backpacking, hiking, and paddling shop by the train depot. Leads twice-monthly guided hikes in the national park and surroundings from April through December.

Black Dog Bikes (121 South Lewis Street; 540-887-8700): An impressively stocked bike shop near the old Wharf District buildings.

Refuel

The Depot Grille (42 Middlebrook Avenue; 540-885-7332): In the former freight depot, it has booths that are pews from an old church and a forty-foot wooden bar from an ancient luxury hotel in Albany, New York. Try the prime rib with the house seasoning.

Wright's Dairy-Rite (346 Greenville Avenue; 540-886-0435; www.dairy-rite.com): A half-century-old drive-in restaurant that serves up seven different hamburgers and makes a mean pineapple shake.

Mrs. Rowe's Restaurant and Bakery (74 Rowe Road; 540-886-1833; www.mrsrowes.com): A down-home Southern comfort-food institution in Staunton since Mildred Rowe opened for business in 1947. Mrs. Rowe has turned the reins over to her son, but she still makes the apple dumplings.

Can't Leave?

Nearest airport: Charlottesville-Albemarle, Charlottesville, Virginia (44 miles)

Primary industries: Manufacturing, government, retail

Davis, West Virginia

Population: 624

Action: Mountain biking, downhill and cross-country skiing, hiking, rock climbing

Whoever thinks that the southern Appalachians don't see much snow has never been to Davis in the winter. This cozy hideout at the base of two ski mountains gets buried beneath 150 inches of the white stuff a year—about twice as much as what Burlington, Vermont gets. At 3,200 feet, Davis is the highest town in West Virginia and shares the shallow, fourteen-by-three-mile Canaan Valley on the northeastern fringe of the Monongahela National Forest with its sister village, Thomas, about a five-minute drive away. The two also share the duty of hosting the small but dedicated crowds of skiers, bikers, hikers, and rock climbers smart enough to make the three-hour trip from Pittsburgh or the three-and-a-half-hour one from Washington, D.C.

If the scenery around Davis reminds you of New England or southern Canada, it should. The hemlocks, spruce, and balsam fir that line the hundreds of miles of hiking and biking trails snaking through the outlying mountainsides are usually only found hundreds of miles to the north. Loggers established Davis as one of the state's first lumber towns in the 1880s partly because of its rare, abundant hardwoods. Twenty years later, it boasted three hotels, two banks, and five restaurants among the eighty businesses that catered to its 3,000 citizens. Now, the seven-block tic-tac-toe board of streets downtown isn't nearly as packed with buildings or people, but the quirks of the town's wild surrounding landscape still provide its allure.

Canaan Valley, the highest-elevation valley in the East, is crowned by flat mountains rising 1,000 feet above it and bisected by the Blackwater River, a popular rafting and fishing stream whose waters are tinted black by the tannic acid from spruce and hemlock needles. A few minutes to the south on State Route 32 are the Canaan Valley and Timberline Four Seasons ski resorts, which bear the brunt of the

Blackwater Falls State Park is at the end of the Davis Trail in Davis, West Virginia. (© David Fattaleh)

winter storms. Their vertical can't quite compare to what you would find in the West or even the Northeast, but your quads will still get a satisfying burn from the double-diamond steeps and bumps of Off the Wall at Timberline and the slingshot turns of Dark Side of the Moon at Canaan. Nordic skiers who come to Davis will find the area's deepest, most consistent snow base on the town's ten miles of groomed trails and endless supply of backcountry.

When the snow melts, the Blackwater Bikes shop awakens from its winter hibernation. It's the unofficial welcome center for Davis, as mud-hungry fat-tire riders come in throngs for the valley's long, technical rides through rooty forests and wet alpine clearings. Routes are mostly singletrack, including the Davis Trail, which ends in Blackwater Falls State Park, and the legendary twenty-eight-mile Plantation Trail. Hikers can practically fall off the porch steps of their bed-and-breakfast and onto a footpath that will connect them to the hundreds of miles of trails in the 919,000-acre Monongahela Forest. Rock climbers, though, will have to drive about forty minutes to get to Seneca Rocks, a formation of two jagged sandstone camel's humps that

The Wild Side

The Dolly Sods Wilderness

The beauty of the 10,200-acre Dolly Sods Wilderness is in its starkness. This alpine plateau south of Davis reaches as high as 4,000 feet in elevation and is hammered by such strong weather that the few trees interrupting its plains and bogs face the opposite direction of the prevailing winds. Many of its plants and animals—like the snowshoe hare—are more common to Canada and Alaska, and the terrain is so rugged that the U.S. Forest Service, when describing its twenty-five miles of footpaths, warns, "Trails do not have blazes, and may or may not have signs . . . Deadfall trees will be made so they are reasonably passable, but will not be completely cleared." In other words, Dolly Sods offers true, open, backcountry wilderness hiking at its Southern—no, make that Northern—best.

rise as high as 900 feet. Its nearly 400 established routes make for the East's premier climbing outside of the Gunks, though the climbing season here is much shorter than it is in New York—because of the quantity of snow that falls in these parts, of course.

Start the Day

Cabin Mountain Deli (Canaan Valley Stores, Canaan Valley; 304-866-2350): Hot breakfast sandwiches and coffee at the Canaan Valley resort.

Flying Pigs Cafe (Route 32; 304-259-5119; www.brightmorninginn.com): Biscuits and gravy, pancakes, waffles, and breakfast burritos in this eatery in the aptly named Bright Morning Inn.

Gear Up

Blackwater Bikes (Main Street; 304-259-5286): Owned by West Virginia fat-tire luminary Roger Lilly, this is the home shop for some of the nation's top competitive riders. Rents and sells bikes and bike gear.

Timberline Resort (800-766-9464): In the summer, you can buy and rent bikes and bike gear from the Mountain Bike Center and ride for free on the resort's trails. In the winter, the Outdoors Edge shop will outfit you.

Refuel

Blackwater Brewing Company (Route 32; 304-259-4221; www.blackwater-brewing.com): Known for its Blackwater Marzen on tap, Wednesday wing specials, and Friday steak specials.

Muttley's Downtown (Route 32; 304-259-4858): Get steaks, prime rib, burgers, and beer, and play darts at this friendly local hangout.

Bunk

Bright Morning Inn (Route 32; 304-259-5119; www.bright morninginn.com): A former nineteenth-century boardinghouse and saloon turned bed-and-breakfast; next to Blackwater Bikes. Eat breakfast at its restaurant, Flying Pigs Cafe.

Meyer House Bed & Breakfast (Third Street and Thomas Avenue; 304-259-5451; www.meyerhousebandb.com): An antique-filled 1885 Victorian home with—of all things—wireless Internet access for guests in its three rooms.

Can't Leave?

Nearest airport: Morgantown Municipal, Morgantown, West Virginia (46 miles)

Primary industries: Health care, manufacturing, service

Fayetteville, West Virginia

Population: 2,657

Action: Rafting, rock climbing, mountain biking, fishing

What's the difference between a river runner and a mutual fund? A mutual fund matures when it gets older. You'll find that there's a grain of truth to that old joke in Fayetteville. On a summer evening, go to a hangout like the Cathedral Café, and there will be guides from as many as thirteen different rafting outfits, fresh from leading clients down the rip-roaring rapids of the New and Gauley rivers—all good naturedly acting like anything but full-grown adults. They've come to this town in southern West Virginia because it's a nexus for paddlers, mountain bikers, rock climbers, and fly-fishers who embrace their inner, nature-loving delinquent by escaping—at least for a while—the mature world of traffic jams, office cubicles, and, yup, mutual funds.

Fayetteville and its century-old brick-faced buildings and homes punctuate the northern tip of the New River Gorge National River, a 70,000-acre preserve containing fifty-three miles of the New River, downstream from Hinton, West Virginia. Thought to be the second-oldest river in the world, the New flows north from North Carolina, slicing through the Allegheny Mountains until it converges with the Gauley River, about fifteen minutes northwest of Fayetteville. In the spring and summer, its consistent flow within the 800-foot-deep gorge churns up a lively gauntlet of Class I through III rapids for recreational kayakers, and then gets hairier about fourteen miles upstream from town. This final section before Fayetteville makes for one of the most popular runs in the East—passable by river guides skilled enough to handle the massive walls of water and boat-sucking whirlpools of its Class V hazards. The Gauley is even more adrenaline-packed during the dam releases of September and October. It drops more than 650 feet over a twenty-eight-mile stretch before converging with the New, and

The bridge for State Route 19 towers over the New River gorge east of Fayetteville, West Virginia. (© David Fattaleh)

the high volume churns up more than 100 Class III through V+ roller-coaster rapids.

Fayetteville's reputation as a world-class paddling destination has overshadowed the biking, climbing, and fishing in the area. Small-mouth bass flourish in the New, as do largemouth and stripers, and you'll also find your share of walleye, crappie, bluegill, and carp in the area's waters. The river has carved spectacular climbing cliffs in the sandstone of the gorge, and there are 1,400 established routes, varying from 30 to 120 feet high. The most renowned spot for rock hounds is in the shadow of the towering State Route 19 bridge, just east of town.

For mountain bikers, there are more than twenty miles of trails near Fayetteville in the national river area. Most notable is the Cunard-Kaymoor route, a rolling seven-mile (one-way) ride above the gorge. Past the old Kaymoor mine site, only hikers are allowed on the trail. There are several prime hiking paths snaking above the gorge, offering

Local Legend

Bridge Day

Built in 1977, the bridge on State Route 19 in Fayetteville is one of the longest steel-arch spans in the world, at 3,030 feet. It's also the second highest, standing 875 feet above the New River. On the third Saturday in October every year, it's the site of a massive celebration called Bridge Day, which attracts adrenaline junkies from throughout the Mid-Atlantic. The bridge is packed from end to end with spectators who come for the demonstrations on rappelling, and competitors in the BASE-jumping accuracy event, where parachutists try to (softly) hit the bull's-eye in the landing zone below.

views of the rapids below and the river runners passing by and showing no signs of maturing anytime soon.

Start the Day

Cathedral Café (134 South Court Street; 304-574-0202; www.cathedral cafe.com): In the morning, grab an espresso in this café and river-guide hangout in a century-old former church. In the evening, come for an after-dinner ice cream.

Smokey's on the Gorge (Ames Heights Road, Lansing; 800-252-7784; www .class-vi.com): A homey restaurant in a timber-frame cabin at the edge of the gorge. Opens very early and serves breakfast buffets by reservation only. Operated by a local rafting guide service.

Gear Up

Water Stone Outdoors (101 East Wiseman Avenue; 304-574-2425): A hard-core outdoor-gear shop and the authority on all of the rock-climbing routes in the area.

ACE Adventure Center (Minden Road, Oak Hill; 304-469-2651): A rafting outfitter on 1,500 acres that rents mountain bikes and operates an outdoor-outfitter shop.

Refuel

Gumbo's (103 South Court Street; 304-574-4704; www.wvgumbo .com): Pick your entrée from the chalkboard menu at this small, spicy Cajun eatery downtown.

Pies and Pints Pizzeria (103 1/2 Keller Avenue; 304-574-2200): All of its melt-in-your-mouth pizzas are made with a mozzarella-provolone cheese blend and dough brushed with garlic oil.

Bunk

Country River Inn (Gatewood Road; 304-574-0055; www.country riverinn.com): A clean, welcoming inn in a renovated 1929 school-house, near the gorge.

Historic White Horse Bed & Breakfast (120 Fayette Avenue; 304-574-1400; www.historicwhitehorse.net): A rustic, 100-year-old country mansion turned twenty-room bed-and-breakfast that serves hearty comfort-food breakfasts.

Can't Leave?

Nearest airport: Greenbrier Valley, Lewisburg, West Virginia (50 miles)

Primary industries: Education, government, service

Harpers Ferry, West Virginia

Population: 313
Action: Hiking,
road biking, rock
climbing,
paddling

In 1783, Thomas Jefferson stood on a rock ledge above Harpers Ferry and, upon looking down at the confluence of the Potomac and Shenandoah rivers below, wrote that the landscape that unfolded before him was "perhaps one of the most stupendous scenes in nature." Clearly, he had yet to take the wife and kids on a family trip to the Grand Canyon or Yosemite, but you get his point: this is one special place. Best of all, it's only an hour from Washington, D.C., and you, like Jefferson, don't even need a car to get there. It's a gentle sixty-mile ride from Georgetown on the dirt and gravel towpath of the C&O Canal, or a 995-mile hike from Springer Mountain, Georgia, on the Appalachian Trail. Take your pick.

Harpers Ferry sits on the eastern tip of the West Virginia panhandle, at a junction with Maryland and Virginia. The ravine that contains it was dug so deep by the two rivers there that it's officially the lowest point in West Virginia, at 247 feet in elevation. In 1963, Congress turned almost the entire town into a national historical park because of its significance before and during the Civil War.

One of the first settlers to the area was Robert Harper, who operated a ferry in the 1760s across the Potomac. Early the next decade, the town of Shenandoah Falls at Mr. Harper's Ferry was incorporated. Its strategic location as a gateway through the Appalachian Mountains to the west and on the wide river that leads east to Chesapeake Bay wasn't lost on George Washington, who successfully pushed for a national armory to be built there. It was this facility that abolitionist John Brown and eighteen others seized on October 16, 1859, before their defeat two days later by Colonel Robert E. Lee of the U.S. Army. During the Civil War, the town was traded back and forth between the Union and Confederacy several times, and it was the site of a battle in

St. Peter's Catholic Church fills the skyline above Harpers Ferry, West Virginia.
(© Courtesy of Harpers Ferry NHP)

which more than 10,000 Union troops were taken prisoner by Stonewall Jackson's men.

Many historic structures of Harpers Ferry remain, thanks to the preservation efforts of the National Park Service. In Lower Town, where the main streets converge at the peninsula called the Point—formed by the junction of the Potomac and Shenandoah—there's an old dry goods store, clothes shop, boarding house, and blacksmith's shop, to name a few of the sights, along with Robert Harper's home, built sometime in the 1770s or 1780s. The most important building to outdoor adventurers, though, is a white house in a section above the park boundary, on Washington Street, that houses the headquarters for the Appalachian Trail Conservancy, the organization that oversees the A.T.

This house is considered the psychological halfway point for thru-hikers, who have just completed the 550-mile slog through Virginia. Nearly all of them get their pictures taken in front of the office, sign the register there (author Greg Melville's name can be found in the 1996 book), and weigh themselves on the scale in the bathroom.

On the way out of town, the A.T. crosses the Potomac into Maryland on a footbridge and follows the towpath of the C&O Canal for about three miles before parting ways. The canal makes for perhaps the most serene bike ride in the Mid-Atlantic. Stretching 185 miles from Cumberland, Maryland, to Georgetown in Washington, D.C., it parallels the Potomac and was completed in 1850. The barges that sailed up and down it—hauling coal, mostly—were pulled by mules. The canal closed in 1924, and the towpath is now open to bikers, runners, and horseback riders. It is protected as part of the Chesapeake and Ohio Canal National Historical Park. Its terrain isn't challenging, but you'll never be bored as you pass the remains of old locks and lock houses and get spectacular glimpses of the river and rolling countryside.

Local Legend

Jefferson Rock

Take a short detour off the A.T. in the Low Town section of Harpers Ferry, near the ruins of St. John's Church, and you'll find a cluster of shale boulders that are now collectively known as Jefferson Rock. This is the place where the Declaration of Independence author stood on October 25, 1783, and surveyed the area, making his famous observations that are boastfully repeated in town. According to the Potomac Appalachian Trail Club, the original boulder on which he stood—and carved his name—was pried loose and pushed down the steep hill below it in 1800, by a group of men who opposed his campaign for president that year.

The A.T. footbridge crossing the Potomac out of Harpers Ferry also gives access to the multipitch rock climbs on the cliffs of Maryland Heights. The twenty or so routes vary in level of difficulty from 5.1 to 5.11 and in height from 20 to over 100 feet. The remains of Civil War fortifications and the views of the town and its surroundings from the top are worth hauling a camera with you—just don't be disappointed if it's crowded with tourists who took the side trail to get there.

A slightly more restful way to appreciate the scenery is by inner tube on the Shenandoah. Several outfitters offer half-day float trips down the mostly flat and occasionally Class I whitewater before town. During high water, you can also paddle down the nearby Class II and III rapids on the Potomac or sign on for a rafting trip. It isn't quite the same as the Grand Canyon, but as Jefferson might attest, it's still pretty nice.

Start the Day

Coffee Mill (High Street; 304-535-1257): Folks will come just for the home fries, but the small restaurant also serves eggs and bacon, pancakes and waffles. Located in a stone-and-mortar building on the corner of High and Potomac streets, this is pretty much the only place in town to grab a bite to eat in the morning.

Gear Up

The Outfitter at Harpers Ferry (180 High Street; 304-535-2087): As you would expect with a shop in any town where the A.T. runs right through it, this one has every piece of gear a backpacker might need. Located in a pre–Civil War building, it also sells climbing equipment and rents bikes for the C&O Canal towpath.

River & Trail Outfitters (604 Valley Road, Knoxville, Maryland; 301-695-5177): Sells canoes, kayaks, and paddling gear, and guides rafting and tubing trips down the Shenandoah, Potomac, and North Branch of the Potomac; three miles east of Harpers Ferry in Maryland.

River Riders (408 Alstadts Hill Road; 800-326-7238): Rents bikes and guides fishing trips and paddling expeditions on the local waterways.

Refuel

Armory Pub (109 Potomac Street; 304-535-2469): Soups and sandwiches across from the train station.

The Anvil Restaurant (1290 West Washington Street; 304-535-2582): Crab balls, crab dip, crab salad, crab cakes, crab with country ham—you can figure out what the specialty of this homey downtown restaurant is.

Yellow Brick Bank (201 East German Street, Shepherdstown; 304-876-2208): Housed in a former bank building

The Wild Side

The Potomac

Once almost barren of fish due to runoff from coal mines, the North Branch of the Potomac River, which forms the border of Maryland west of West Virginia's panhandle, is becoming a fly-fisherman's paradise. Brown, brook, rainbow, and cutthroat trout are all starting to thrive in the river for the first time in over a century. The revitalization is largely the result of clean-up and stocking efforts by the Maryland Department of Natural Resources. Twice in the spring and twice in the fall, the Jennings Randolph Dam, near Elk Garden, West Virginia, releases water, creating nearly seven miles of nonstop Class I through III rapids.

constructed in 1904, this high-end—but worth it—restaurant makes its own pastas and breads.

Bunk

The Angler's Inn (867 West Washington Street; 304-535-1239; www.theanglersinn.com): A bed-and-breakfast in an 1880s Victorian home, offering a fishing guide service on the area's waters.

Jackson Rose Bed & Breakfast (1167 West Washington Street; 304-535-1528): A red-brick home where Stonewall Jackson based his headquarters briefly during the Civil War.

Can't Leave?

Nearest airport: Washington Dulles International, Dulles, Virginia (35 miles)

Primary industries: Tourism, recreation, government

Slatyfork, West Virginia

T hey say that if you learn to ski in the East, you can
handle any terrain. The same goes for mountain biking in Slatyfork. If you can master the eastern pot-
pourri of rocks, roots, steeps, chutes, stream crossings, and
tight switchbacks among the knobby mountains of these
parts, then tackling the likes of Moab's roller-coaster
slickrock will seem like a leisurely day in the park. Then
again, after mountain biking here, you may not feel like going out West
at all. Outside Slatyfork's back door in east-central West Virginia, more
than 500 miles of trails—roughly 200 of them pure singletrack—
interconnect through the maples, oaks, and spruce of the rugged southern Monongahela National Forest. Exploring it all could take you years,
especially when there are so many rich trout streams nearby to distract
you. And then there's the long winters, which aren't so good for biking, but do make for prime conditions on the slopes of Snowshoe
Mountain ski resort.

Slatyfork is an unincorporated smattering of homes and a post
office in Pocohontas County near the junction of State Route 66 and
U.S. Highway 219, about twenty miles from the Virginia border. If there
is an unofficial city hall, it's the Elk River Touring Center, which makes
owners Gil and Mary Willis the co-mayors. On their 150-acre property
fringing the Elk River, they operate a bed-and-breakfast; a restaurant;
a bike, snowboard, and tackle outfitter; and mountain-biking and fly-
fishing guide services. The unofficial downtown lies five miles away at
the village at Snowshoe. The resort, with its 4,848 summit elevation
and 1,500-foot vertical, is the premier ski destination in the state and
the summer home to 125 miles of well-maintained mountain bike trails
and an impressive freeride center.

The real riding action, though, lies in the untamed Monongahela
itself. The section of national forest around Slatyfork is one of the

Population: 163
Action: Mountain
biking, fishing,
downhill skiing

quietest stretches of backcountry in the Virginias, and its endless network of trails and forest roads stays remarkably empty—even the most famous routes, like the Greenbrier River Trail. Rated as one of the top converted rail trails in the country, the Greenbrier starts just outside of town and rambles north seventy-five miles, crossing thirty-five bridges and passing through two tunnels as it traces the banks of its namesake river. Much less forgiving than the one-percent-graded Greenbrier, but almost equally well known, is Props Run, a roughly fifteen-mile loop with a six-mile plummet down an old railroad bed.

For a sampler of all of the different hazards and terrains of the area, take the Gauley Mountain Trail, an undulating ten-mile out-and-back with short, steep ups and downs, through hardwood forests and over varying surfaces of rocks, soft earth, roots, and creek beds. Be sure to get a map from Elk River Touring Center, and while you're there ask

Snowshoe Resort and its 4,848-foot summit outside of Slatyfork, West Virginia, make for the state's premier ski and snowboard distinction. (© *Snowshoe Mountain Resort*)

about hiring a fishing guide for a day. Even if the closest you've come to fly-fishing is watching *A River Runs Through It,* you can't miss the opportunity to cast a line while you're in Slatyfork. The cold Elk, Greenbrier, Cranberry, New, and James rivers, among others, are all packed with hungry brook, rainbow, and brown trout. After all, if you learn to fly-fish in these parts, you can fly-fish anywhere—or something like that.

Start the Day

The Boathouse (Snowshoe Drive; 877-441-4386; www.snowshoemtn.com): On Shavers Lake at Snowshoe; an alpine-style eatery open in the summer and winter.

Gear Up

The Ski Barn (Routes 219 and 66; 304-572-1234): An impressively well-stocked ski and board sales and rental shop.

Local Legend

The Wild 100

If you want to explore the route of the annual Wild 100 backcountry bike race in Slatyfork before you compete in the event, you're out of luck. Officially, there is no course. There are simply six checkpoints that you must reach in sequence. You choose the best route for getting to them. But no matter how you go, you're guaranteed to be pedaling at least 100 kilometers (62 miles) before you're done and hitting most of the best trails surrounding town. On the morning of the race, you're given a laminated trail map of the area with the checkpoints marked. So bring your navigation skills, along with a lot of endurance.

Mountain Adventure Center (Snowshoe Drive; 877-441-4386): The gear shop, bike rental center, and mountain-biking nerve center at Snowshoe resort.

Elk River Touring Company (Route 219; 304-572-3771): The one-stop outfitter for mountain biking, fly-fishing, and snowboarding in Pocahontas County.

Refuel

The Restaurant at Elk River (Route 219; 304-572-3771; www.ertc .com): Known for its light menu, the restaurant at the Elk River Touring Center is open Thursday through Sunday evenings.

Foxfire Grille (Snowshoe Drive; 877-441-4386; www.snowshoe mtn.com): A lively barbecue joint—with homemade sauces—in the resort village; open summer and winter.

Bunk

Morning Glory Inn (Route 219; 304-572-5000; www.morning gloryinn.com): A cozy, six-room bed-and-breakfast, with an emphasis on the breakfast. It serves belly-filling meals every morning.

Mount Airy Bed and Breakfast (Route 219; 604-572-5208; www.mtairybnb.com): A friendly bed-and-breakfast on a hilly perch with mountain views; waterbeds in most bedrooms.

Can't Leave?

Nearest airport: Roanoke Regional, Roanoke, Virginia (60 miles)

Primary industries: Outdoor recreation, retail, government

The South

Alexander City, Alabama

I f you're kitesurfing or wakeboarding on Lake Martin, you'll be comforted to know that the mouthful of water you got is so clear and clean. You won't be so happy if you're fishing, because the water's twenty-foot visibility means that the swarms of cagey largemouth and spotted bass will see you more easily. That's why so many anglers in Alexander City, on the northern shore of Lake Martin, hit the water at night during the summer, coming out in broad daylight only for occasions like the tournaments held at Wind Creek State Park. Of course, there are worse problems than having an impeccably clean body of water—one that covers an area almost half the size of nearby Montgomery—in your backyard.

Population:
14,957
Action: Fishing, paddling, sailing

When the Alabama Power company dammed the Tallapoosa River in 1926 to control floods and generate hydroelectric power, it created Lake Martin—the largest reservoir in the world at the time. In the process, Alexander City transformed into an outdoor destination. Named for the president of the rail line who brought trains to its doorstep, the town was previously known as the home of an underwear-manufacturing outfit founded by Ben Russell at the turn of the twentieth century. That company is now Russell Corporation Athletic Apparel and Equipment, and it has powered the local economy for decades. To stem the tide from recent downsizing there, though, the town has increasingly turned toward tourism. It promotes the allure of its historic downtown and attracts visitors with events such as the Alexander City Jazz Festival in early June—held at the 2,500-capacity Lake Martin Amphitheatre and other venues in town—and Oktoberfest in early fall.

The lake is still the prime reason to come to Alexander City, though, and fishing is by far the most popular sport. Spotted, largemouth, and striped bass, along with sunfish, bluegill, and record-

The waters of Lake Martin make for superb paddling, boating, and fishing in Alexander City, Alabama. (© Alexander City Chamber of Commerce)

setting white crappie, thrive within its 750 miles of steep shoreline. Locals will tell you that the most fertile area lies around the U.S. Highway 280 bridge by Wind Creek State Park; the park itself, a 1,400-acre preserve, has a 210-foot fishing pier and marina. Farther south, the fish may not bite as well, but the wider waters lure schools of sailboats on breezy days. The popular Dixie Sailing Club in town organizes races and other events almost weekly throughout most of the year.

During the peak summer season, the kayaking on the smooth waters is superb early in the morning, but the higher the sun rises, the more you'll be buzzed by powerboats. The waterways draining into Lake Martin are the midday alternative, offering plenty of solitude. For flatwater paddling, head for the Tallapoosa River above the Horseshoe Bend National Military Park, and to get your foam fix, try the Class I through III rapids on a two-mile stretch of Elkahatchee Creek just outside of town. Be sure to get back to town early, though, so you'll have plenty of time to rest up for some night fishing.

Start the Day

Collegiate Deli (1675 Cherokee Road; 256-215-4007): A friendly deli on the Central Alabama Community College campus; opens at 6 AM for early risers.

Gear Up

Lake Martin Bait & Tackle (6752 Highway 280; 256-329-9107): For fishing tackle and the ins and outs of all of the local waters.

Lakeside Marina (9160 Highway 280; 256-825-0940): Marina and boat dealer located by the river bridge.

Coosa Outdoor Center (172 River Drive, Wetumpka; 334-201-5510): Sells kayaks and leads trips on local waterways; located between Alexander City and Montgomery.

Refuel

Chuck's Pizza (237 Marina Road, Dadeville; 256-825-7733): A pizza joint at a marina on the edge of the water.

Cecil's Public House (243 Green Street; 256-329-0732): Popular pub in a century-old house downtown.

Bunk

Mistletoe Bough Bed & Breakfast (497 Hillabee Street; 256-329-3717; www.mistletoebough.com): This century-old, five-room Queen Anne mansion has porches on both floors and is surrounded by gardens.

The Wild Side

Talladega National Forest

If you want to stick to terra firma for a day or two, the Talladega National Forest is about twenty minutes northwest of Alexander City. Within this long, densely forested, 375,000-acre preserve, the Appalachian Mountains start. Explore it on the 102-mile Pinhoti National Recreation Trail, which extends from Piedmont to near Talladega.

Wind Creek State Park Campground (4325 Alabama Highway 128; 256-329-0845): Largest state-operated campground in the country; has more than 600 well-kept campsites, many of them on the water.

Can't Leave?

Nearest airport: Montgomery Regional, Montgomery, Alabama (50 miles)

Primary industries: Textiles, education, health care

Mena, Arkansas

L ike the kid in the family who hogs all of the attention, the Ozark National Forest in Arkansas has long
overshadowed its sibling to the south, the Ouachita
National Forest. But don't think the better-known destination is the better adventure destination. The trails
crisscrossing the jagged ridges of the Ouachita Mountains
make for some of the best hiking and mountain biking
between the Mississippi and Rockies; and the paddling on the rip-
roaring Class IV and V rapids of the Cossatot River have been scaring
the lunch out of people since before the Caddo Indians named the
waters "head crusher." Just as important, the Ouachitas have Mena, a
town as inviting as the park surrounding it.

Population: 5,608
Action: Hiking,
mountain biking,
paddling

Mena, about eighty miles west of Hot Springs at the foot of 2,681-
foot Rich Mountain, was established in the mid-1890s as a railroad stop
for tourists headed to nearby country resorts. But as the relevance of
passenger trains shrank in the twentieth century, so did the town's reputation as a destination. But recently Mena has rebounded as an outdoor haven. Walk downtown and you'll still see many of the same
rectangular brick buildings that lined the streets more than fifty years
ago, as well as the same magnificent train depot—restored in 1987.
There's also the old 1851 log cabin inside ten-acre Janssen Park that
served as a post office, city hall, and hospital at different times. Odds
are that you won't be spending much time window shopping among
the antique and craft stores, though, given all there is to do in the
town's backyard.

Within the 1.8-million-acre Ouachita National Forest, there are
more than 700 miles of hiking and biking trails among the lakes, rivers,
and mountains. The granddaddy of them all is the 192-mile Ouachita
National Recreation Trail, a footpath that spans the east-west length
of the forest. It's interrupted by enough old roads that you can access

The restored historic train depot in Mena, Arkansas reminds visitors that the town was established as a railroad stop in the late 1800s. (© Arkansas Department of Parks and Tourism)

pretty much any peak, overlook, or hidden water cascade within the course of a day's trek. About 130 miles of the trail are open to mountain bikes, but most them are too rugged to be fun. Besides, there's enough prime riding around it to keep you busy.

If you only have a day or two to bike in the area, head first for the Womble Trail, a thirty-seven-mile (one-way) singletrack route that occasionally climbs the high bluffs of the Ouachita River. If you have more time, head for the ten-mile roller-coaster Athens Big Fork Trail and switchback-filled Earthquake Ridge, one of the more difficult of six interconnected loops about two miles outside of town. On it, don't be surprised to run into members of the Ouachita Cycling Club, a surprisingly active group of local road and mountain bikers who maintain area trails, organize races, and hold informal group rides—mostly on dirt—on Tuesdays, Saturdays, and Sundays.

Paddlers can choose from a float on the flat Ouachita River or take a trip on the Cossatot, a twenty-six-mile, rapid-packed river that deposits into Gilham Lake. The adrenaline builds as you go, starting with a handful of Class III rapids and then climaxing near the end with Cassatot Falls, a 500-yard gauntlet of waves, rocks, and drops. Kind of makes you wonder why the Ozarks get all of the press, doesn't it?

Start the Day

Friendship House (517 Sherwood Avenue; 479-394-2385): Coffeehouse and sandwich shop by the depot.

Grumpy's Café (1311 Highway 71; 479-394-4324): Opens at 6 AM and serves hearty traditional breakfasts.

Gear Up

Arkatents Outdoor Gear (3856 Highway 88; 479-394-7893): Not many local retail stores can compete with Wal-Mart in this part of the country, but Arkatents does, with camping, backpacking, and paddling gear.

Parkside Cycle (719 Whittington Avenue, Hot Springs; 501-623-6188): Rents and sells mountain and road bikes. Even though they're in Hot Springs, they can clue you in on the routes and trails through the Ouachita.

Refuel

Chopping Block Steakhouse (Highway 71; 479-394-6410; www.menachopping block.com): A log-cabin restaurant where they grind the beef for burgers and cut their own steaks.

Papa Poblano's Mexican Restaurant (1100 Highway 71 North; 479-394-6461): The Sanchez family serves true Mexican creations.

Bunk

Queen Wihelmina Lodge (3877 Highway 88; 800-264-2477; www.queen wilhelmina.com): A thirty-eight-room stone lodge in Queen Wilhelmina State

Local Legend

Talimena Scenic Byway

For a condensed experience in the Ouachita Mountains, take the Talimena Scenic Byway. At fifty-four miles long, it doesn't quite match the Blue Ridge Parkway in scale, but the views from this two-lane drive—stretching from eastern Oklahoma into Mena—can be nearly as postcard worthy. The route, constructed in the mid-1960s, twists and turns its way over peaks such as 2,681-foot Rich Mountain and Winding Stair Mountain, and through wooded valleys as low as 1,100 feet in elevation. There are enough overlooks along the way that you'll be recharging your camera's batteries at the end of the day.

Park, at the top of Rich Mountain, the state's second-highest peak.

Sun Country Inn (1309 Highway 71 North; 479-394-7477; www.suncountryinn.com): A clean, well-lit—and, most importantly, affordable—motor lodge downtown.

Raspberry Manor (300 Raspberry Lane; 479-394-7555; www.raspberrymanor.com): A quaint four-story bed-and-breakfast down a three-mile driveway on seventy-eight mostly wooded acres.

Can't Leave?

Nearest airport: Fort Smith Regional, Fort Smith, Arkansas (55 miles)

Primary industries: Poultry processing, retail, health care

Apalachicola, Florida

W hen you're talking about bars in Apalachicola on the Florida panhandle, it's usually not the kind with swivel stools and pickled eggs. Nope, the best watering holes around here are the oyster bars, where "tongers," who use two scissor-style rakes that resemble tongs, harvest some 2.5 million pounds of the mollusk each year from their twenty-foot boats. Apalachicola celebrates the shellfish every November with an oyster roast and seafood festival and just about nightly with gatherings of oyster-mad locals. So it's no surprise that oyster shell litter can be found in the streets, in the alleyways, and, yes, in your kayak as you share Apalachicola Bay and the Gulf of Mexico with the oystermen and explore the 246,000 acres of the Apalachicola National Estuarine Research Reserve. (As warm as these waters are, you'll want to wear some type of shoes while paddling to protect your feet from the ferociously sharp shells.)

Population: 2,340
Action: Fishing, paddling

Thanks to the 200-plus historic homes from the nineteenth century in Apalachicola (established in 1831), the town tends to draw landlubbing history buffs, who seem content with the antique shops and galleries. Indeed, the earth around here was a rich resource, providing lumber from the large cypress forests. But Apalachicola's real past lies in those oyster-filled waters, from which Native Americans pulled oysters and created ceremonial shell mounds; they also gave the area its name, which is loosely translated to "land of the friendly people." More recently, the cotton and logging industries have faded, but fishing remains as vibrant as the multicolored Victorians of downtown.

For anglers, the 106-mile-long Apalachicola River (Florida's largest, in terms of water discharged) is abundant with largemouth and striped bass in its upper reaches and stripers (stocked annually by the U.S. Fish and Wildlife Service) in the lower river. Where the river meets the bay near downtown, there are redfish. And in the sprawling bay framed by

Apalachicola, Florida is a paradise for paddlers. (© Apalachicola Bay Chamber of Commerce)

the towns of Apalachicola and Eastpoint, and St. George and St. Vincent islands, it's tarpon time. Thanks to the abundance and variety of fish, there's no off-season around here: spring means redfish, largemouth bass, and mackerel, while summer sends anglers out for tarpon and shark. And while much of the rest of the country is winding down for fall and winter, Apalachicola stays lively with flounder and stripers.

The same islands that create Apalachicola Bay make excellent paddling destinations. From Indian Pass, just west of Apalachicola, it's only about a quarter mile to the 12,500-acre St. Vincent Island National Wildlife Refuge, an undeveloped home for eagles, wild pigs, alligators, nesting loggerhead sea turtles, deer, and deserted beaches speckled with bits of Native American pottery. South of St. Vincent (via the half-mile-wide West Pass) lies the equally wild Little St. George Island, a nine-mile-long boomerang of shell-studded beaches, primitive campsites, and lighthouses separated from St. George Island by the man-made Bob

Sikes Cut. (There was once a single, thirty-seven-mile long island, but it was severed by the Army Corps of Engineers in 1954 so that shrimp boats could more easily access the Gulf of Mexico.)

On twenty-eight-mile-long St. George Island, paddlers will find more civilization, seen in the seaside cottages, condos, and cafés strewn along the central shores. A four-mile-long bridge connects the barrier island to the fishing town of Eastpoint; to the northeast is St. George Island State Park, where another nine miles of dunes and untouched beaches create rest stops for migratory birds—and paddlers. Off the tip of the park lies 6.8-mile-long Dog Island, much of it owned by the Nature Conservancy.

Back around Apalachicola, you'll discover marshes, bayous, and estuaries teeming with wildlife, as the river's drainage basin supports more than 1,300 species of plants, 180 species of fish, 315 species of birds, and more than 360 species of marine mollusks. That includes the ever-present oyster, which is best appreciated at the more typical types of bars easily found throughout Apalachicola: the kind with ice-cold beer and cocktail sauce.

Start the Day

Café con Leche (39 Avenue D; 850-653-2233): Coffeehouse and Internet café, serving light breakfast fare, pastries, and lunches.

Gear Up

Forgotten Coast Outfitters (94 Market Street; 850-653-9669): An Orvis dealer with fly-fishing gear, books, and clothing.

Robinson Brothers Guide Service (152 Seventeenth Street; 850-653-8896): Private fishing charters, with six guides for the flats and bay.

Journeys of St. George Island (240 East Third Street, St. George Island; 850-927-3259): Naturalist Jeanni McMillan guides kayak, canoe, and

Local Legend

The Original Garden of Eden?

You won't find an apple tree, but you will find a snake—the eastern diamondback rattlesnake or the rare eastern indigo snake—in the area that some folks around Apalachicola claim is the original Garden of Eden. It's the Apalachicola Bluffs and Ravines Preserve, a 6,300-acre chunk of land in Bristol. Protected by the Nature Conservancy, the preserve is open only to hikers, who are drawn to the 3.5-mile Garden of Eden Trail. The footpath climbs along the river, through a forest of Florida torreya and Florida yew, to a bluff overlooking the Apalachicola. Adam and Eve would have been well protected here, as there are ferns, magnolias, trillium, and wild ginger; their company would have been salamanders, warblers, cottontail rabbits, and wild turkeys.

The Wild Side

Apalachicola National Forest

Though much of the action around Apalachicola is water based, there are campgrounds and more than eighty-five miles of hiking, mountain-biking, and horseback-riding trails in the Apalachicola National Forest. At more than a half-million acres, it's the largest national forest in Florida and home to part of the statewide Florida National Scenic Trail. If you don't mind a few alligators and a few inches (or, sometimes, a few feet) of standing water, take on the challenging eighteen-mile section of the Bradwell Bay Wilderness Area, which is wide open to backpackers and thick with titi trees.

powerboat trips and rents all three vessels to the public.

Refuel

Boss Oyster (123 Water Street; 850-653-9364): A can't-miss spot for oysters, cooked seventeen ways (from jalapeño to Greektown) by "King Ken," along with grouper, steamed blue crabs, and sandwiches.

Apalachicola Seafood Grill (100 Market Street; 850-653-9510): This eatery, established in 1903, serves the world's largest fried-fish sandwich—or at least one of them.

Tamara's Café Floridita (17 Avenue E; 850-653-6111): Tropical and Spanish-influenced seafood specialties, from paella and margarita scallops to a Caribbean banana split.

Bunk

Bay City Lodge (1000 Bay City Road; 850-653-9294): Cabins and motel units for anglers; includes a marina, fishing guides, a bait-and-tackle store, and fish-cleaning service on the premises.

Apalachicola River Inn (123 Water Street; 850-653-8139; www.apalachicolariverinn.com): Rooms on the Apalachicola River; adjacent to Boss Oyster and within walking distance of downtown.

The Gibson Inn (51 Avenue C; 850-653-2191; www.gibsoninn.com): They say that room 309 is haunted by a sea captain, but this 100-year-old, thirty-room lodge is more likely to mystify you with its wraparound veranda and rockers.

Can't Leave?

Nearest airport: Panama City–Bay County International, Panama City, Florida (57 miles)

Primary industries: Fishing, tourism

Cedar Key, Florida

f you want to experience a little old-time Florida island living, skip the T-shirt stands and tourist traps of Key West and go about nine hours northwest to Cedar Key. Never heard of it? That's exactly the point. The town, ninety minutes from Gainesville, is spread over a few tiny islands connected to the Gulf Coast mainland by three miles of causeway. You can't find a doctor or pharmacy there, but finding somewhere to paddle, fish, hike, camp, or share drinks with friendly strangers until the wee hours of the morning is as easy as walking out your hotel door.

Population: 1,958
Action: Paddling, fishing, hiking

Surrounding Cedar Key are tens of thousands of acres of protected islets, marshes, rivers, and swamps beside the gulf waters, cultivating an unspoiled habitat for herons, egrets, ibis, roseate spoonbills, white pelicans, crabs, and raccoons. Within paddling distance of the downtown Big Dock is the Cedar Keys National Wildlife Refuge, a preserve of thirteen islands accessible only by boat, where the white sandy beaches are open to the public but hardly ever used. Among its gems are a seabird rookery, a nineteenth-century lighthouse, and Atsena Otie Key, where the town was first settled before storms and fire forced residents to vacate. Atsena Otie Key still contains old ruins and is the only island in the refuge with inland hiking trails to explore.

Cedar Key was established in the 1840s as a resort town and home for sawmills and pencil factories harvesting the juniper trees that grew so abundantly there. With its deepwater access, it also became a major port for sending shipped goods from the Gulf of Mexico to the Atlantic Ocean, via a direct rail line between Cedar Key and Amelia Island on the state's east coast. The railroad is long gone, and now the town is spread among Way Key and two other keys, across a small channel from Atsena Otie. Today, the primary occupation, and passion, among the natives is fishing. Its farm-raised clams are the local delicacy and a

The Big Dock in downtown Cedar Key, Florida is a favorite fishing spot for locals, regardless of their species. (© Stacey Brown)

multimillion-dollar industry. Each fall, the town holds its annual two-day October Seafood Festival, which attracts thousands of hungry visitors. The other big local event is the Sidewalk Art Festival in April, which shows off the works of the town's surprisingly large artist population.

Sportfishing is perhaps the most popular draw among the trickle of tourists who come to town the rest of the year. There are eight different guide services operating in the waters offshore, and they can take you to some of the richest mackerel waters anywhere, about ten miles south by Seahorse Reef. Trout and redfish are just as abundant close to shore. The social way to cast a line, though, is from the municipal fishing pier on Dock Street (damaged by a hurricane in 2004, but recently repaired); see if you can find a good spot among the crowd of locals who show up on warm, sunny days, angling for mullet and flounder.

If you decide to spend a lot of time doing nothing while you're there—that's another favorite pastime in Cedar Key—you'll likely be doing it on Dock Street. Most of the restaurants and shops are situated within its white buildings, constructed with oak frames, and on the parallel Second Street, where the Island Hotel lies.

One of the few reasons to escape Cedar Key for the mainland is to head to one of the two state conservation areas nearby. The 32,000-acre Waccasassa Bay Preserve to the east is one of the largest state parks in Florida, yet it doesn't have a single marked trail. Instead, the way to explore its woods, marsh, and islands—home to bears, panthers, eagles, alligators, manatees, and bald eagles—is by canoe or kayak. Cedar Key Scrub State Reserve is 5,000 acres of mostly hardwood forest and pine scrub with twelve miles of trails for biking and hiking among them. There is also fishing and paddling within its salt marshes. There aren't any campsites at the park, which is no big deal, because odds are there are vacant rooms back in Cedar Key—another refreshing difference from Key West.

Start the Day

Dock Street Depot (490 Dock Street; 352-543-0202; www.dock streetdepot.com): This relatively new breakfast hangout for locals has a view of the dock.

Annie's Café (Highway 24; 352-543-6141): Serves hearty, down-home food like biscuits and gravy.

Gear Up

Kayak Cedar Keys (First and A streets; 352-543-9447): Owners Tom and Sherry Liebert rent kayaks and guide tours among the preserves near town.

Nature Coast Expeditions (12717 State Road 24; 352-543-6463): Operates kayak tours and overnight island camping trips.

Cedar Key Island Hopper (302 Dock Street; 352-543-5904): Rents sixteen- to twenty-one-foot-long skiffs for the day.

Refuel

Frogs Landing (420 Dock Street; 352-543-9243; www.frogslanding.net): The

The Wild Side

Lower Suwannee National Wildlife Refuge

One of the largest undeveloped wildlife estuary systems in the country lies just outside of Cedar Key, a short drive north on the mainland of Florida's west coast. The Lower Suwannee National Wildlife Refuge is home to alligators, bald eagles, white ibis, and ospreys, who live among the scrub pine forests, tidal creeks, and cypress swamps on its 52,935 acres. There are about ten miles of hiking trails and nearly nine miles of canoe trails within the reserve.

Local Legend

The Island Hotel

The Victorian building on Second Street, with its wraparound porches on both floors and made of oyster-shell-tabby walls supported by oak beams, has survived storms, war, Prohibition, and the slings and arrows of age to remain perhaps the most colorful piece of Cedar Key's history. Its name is the Island Hotel. Built in 1859 as a general store, it later housed boarders. After falling into disrepair in the early twentieth century, it was restored and turned into a hotel. Locals say that the hotel sold whiskey during Prohibition and was a bordello after the Great Depression. The hotel has cleaned up its act dramatically, and its King Neptune Lounge has become a wholesome—and legal—place to buy a drink at the end of the day.

shrimp pie and crab bisque are as exquisite as the sunset views from this popular hangout.

The Island Room Restaurant at Cedar Cove (192 Second Street; 352-543-6520; www.islandroom.com): Chef Peter Stefani prepares locally caught shellfish with exquisite flair, but at inexpensive prices.

Blue Desert Café (12518 Highway 24; 352-543-9111): Seafood pasta, seafood pizza, and seafood burritos in a cozy shack.

Bunk

Island Hotel (373 Second Street; 352-543-5111): This nearly 150-year-old local institution is on the National Register of Historic Places.

Cedar Key Harbour Master Suites (390 Dock Street; 352-543-9146; www.cedarkeyharbourmaster.com): Its suites hang over the Gulf of Mexico.

Island Place (550 First Street; 352-543-5307; www.islandplace-ck.com) Comfortable one- and two-bedroom rental condos on the water.

Can't Leave?

Nearest airport: Gainesville Regional, Gainesville, Florida (65 miles)

Primary industries: Commercial fishing, clam farming, tourism

Ellijay, Georgia

Population: 1,519

Action: Mountain and road biking, kayaking, rafting, hiking

Georgia peaches? The folks in Ellijay prefer to brag about their apples; some 600,000 bushels are picked each year in this town that seems to fall backward rather than fast-forward in time. (The former Hyatt Hotel is now the Gilmer County Courthouse, while Ford Mustangs are still raffled off at old-fashioned Fourth of July jubilees.) But while popular fall festivals celebrate the apple, Ellijay's bikers, hikers, kayakers, and rafters have mostly kept mum about the other outdoor fruits around this tidy square of a town in the North Georgia Mountains, where the rolling hills rumple into Appalachia and rivers twist seemingly in every direction. Ellijay's adventurers don't mind that most of the visitors are here for the apples, the boiled peanuts, and perhaps a bite of Colonel Poole's Bar-B-Q. They're too busy harvesting their own goods in the 60 percent of surrounding Gilmer County that is protected wilderness.

There's really no off-season for mountain biking around here, thanks to Georgia's mild climate. Just west of Ellijay, near a sparkling blue lake, the Carter's Lake Trails are the town's closest thing to a Six Flags. They make for a 5.6-mile roller-coaster ride that winds through the Ridgeway Recreation Area, nearly producing whiplash as they hurl around hairpin turns after scary downhills. Listen to the guys at Cartecay Bike Shop when they tell you to bring your lungs. You'll also find gut-busting climbs at Stanley Gap, where more than twelve miles of trails trace steep ridgelines overlooking the surrounding peaks, and at Bear Creek, where a seven-mile ascent rewards riders with a long, fun downhill. As a bonus, Bear Creek's slightly technical singletrack also passes a 400-year-old poplar tree that's 100 feet high and 20 feet around.

Ellijay is also blessed with bountiful road riding; the Tour de Georgia cycling competition races near or through here every spring.

Ellijay, Georgia is located in the North Georgia Mountains, and sixty percent of the county surrounding the town is protected wilderness. (© Georgia Department of Economic Development)

Ask the staff at Cartecay about the forty-mile Roundtop/Whitestone trip, which mixes an ideal ratio of hills and flats, or the fifty-mile Burnt Mountain Ride, whose name rightly indicates that you'll be climbing up, and whizzing down, a mountain. Cyclists can head in pretty much any direction, as cars are sparse around Ellijay.

There's more traffic along the rivers around the Blue Ridge Mountains. The Upper Ocoee River, just across the border in Tennessee, hosted the whitewater kayaking competitions for Atlanta's 1996 Olympic Games. The river's Class III and IV rapids, such as Hell Hole and Broken Nose, are now open to rafters on summer weekends when water is released. The Chattooga—which many reckon to be the river in James Dickey's *Deliverance*—is one of the Southeast's last free-flowing streams. Lined with rhododendrons and rippled with both rookie and expert rapids for rafters and kayakers, it's east of Ellijay, near South Carolina. Closer to town is the Chattahoochee, whose rapids leave kayakers just enough time to gawk at the blooming dogwoods and azaleas. The Chattahoochee is also a designated trout stream. Ellijay's own Cartecay River delivers a ten-mile stretch of Class II and III whitewater.

The Appalachian Trail begins—or ends, depending on which way you're hiking it—near Ellijay at the 3,782-foot Springer Mountain, whose summit is accessible by the 8.3-mile Approach Trail. The hike is busiest from March to May; for a lesser-known walk in the woods, hit the newer Benton MacKaye Trail. The nearly 300-mile-long foot-path is named after the A.T.'s visionary and runs a rugged, remote way through eight federally designated wilderness areas to the northern edge of Great Smoky Mountains National Park. Less ambitious, but equally aesthetically pleasing, hiking trails around Ellijay include the Bear Creek Trail, the Oak Creek Nature Trail, and the Mountaintown Creek Trail.

Start the day

The Cornerstone Café (76 Main Street; 706-636-2330): Eggs, hash browns, grits, and french toast, listed under such creatively named specials as Floating Down the River and Ooh-La-La.

Gear up

Cartecay Bike Shop (120 Old Orchard Square; 706-635-2453): Mountain bik-ing and cycling shop opened by Atlanta fireman Mike Palmeri; head here for Wednesday rides, rentals, maps, and more.

North Georgia Mountain Outfitters (49 Oak Street; 706-698-4453): Hiking and backpacking gear.

Refuel

Colonel Poole's Bar-B-Q (706-635-4100): A roadside landmark, where twenty dollars gets you a platter of pork and a plywood pig on the Hill of Fame.

Local Legend

Fort Mountain

As weird as the film *Deliverance* are some of the mysteries around North Georgia, such as the inexplicably bald summits on low-elevation mountains. Or take the 855-foot-long rock wall at Fort Mountain in the Chattahoochee National Forest. Nobody has a clue who built it, or when or why. Devise your own theories while mountain bik-ing one of the four loops that wind through Fort Mountain State Park; they include the easy, two-mile Lake Loop to the advanced, fourteen-mile East-West Loop. The park is also filled with streams, blueberry thickets, and even a little beach on the lake. For more infor-mation, call 706-695-2621.

The Wild Side

The Len Foote Hike Inn

If you prefer to earn your sleep at a local lodge, at least through a little burn of the leg muscles, head for the Len Foote Hike Inn (www.hike-inn .com) at Amicalola Falls. Lying one mile from the approach trail to the A.T., the wooden lodge has twenty bunk rooms and was named after a Georgia conservationist. It is reachable only by hiking a five-mile trail that starts at the top of the falls. If you time it right, you can arrive at the end just in time to settle into an Adirondack chair and watch the sun set over the Blue Ridge Mountains. There are bed linens, meals, books, and games at the inn—just bring water, bug spray, clothes, and a flashlight.

Mucho Kaliente (941 Maddox Drive, Suite 232-234; 706-636-4192): Vegetarian fajitas and dozens of Mexican combos, plus karaoke on Wednesday nights.

The Davis House (96 North Main Street; 706-276-7340): Country cooking off Ellijay's main square; try the turkey and dressing or buttermilk-dipped chicken.

Bunk

Whitepath Mountain Retreat (987 Shenandoah Drive; 706-276-7199; www.whitepathlodge.com): Two-bedroom villas with views, plus tennis courts and an Olympic-sized pool.

Forest Cabins of Ellijay (151 Azalea Drive; 706-273-0262): Two pet-friendly log cabins with hot tubs; good for couples.

Can't Leave?

Nearest airport: Hartsfield-Jackson Atlanta International, Atlanta, Georgia (90 miles)

Primary industries: Agriculture, tourism

Oxford, Mississippi

Renowned as the home of Southern literary heavy-weights, Oxford has somehow dodged getting the same attention as the home of many epic bike rides. While locals proudly brag that the likes of Faulkner, Welty, and Grisham have lived among them, they still seem to want to keep the empty, oak-lined roads of green, hilly northern Mississippi to themselves. Some Oxonians are as passionate about riding as they are about literature, barbecue, Ole Miss football, and the blues. The local bike club stokes the fire with group rides nearly every day and time trials and races that are as much social events as competitions.

Population: 13,618

Action: Road and mountain biking, fishing, paddling

Oxford, about seventy miles southeast of Memphis, is so perfectly Southern it seems almost re-created from the fictional works of the great writers who have called this place home. The central Courthouse Square; the Greek Revival, Georgian, and Victorian architecture downtown; and the hospitality of the townsfolk are all just as you expect them to be. The square's tidy storefronts are packed with clothes shops, restaurants, an independent bookstore, and even a department store that dates back to the nineteenth century.

When incorporated in 1835, Oxford consisted of little more than a few homes and a smattering of shops. It took its name from the famous university town in England, hoping that the soon-to-be-established University of Mississippi would be built there. In 1841, the state legislature granted Oxford's wish—by a one-vote majority—and seven years later, Ole Miss welcomed its first students. During the Civil War, General A. J. "Whisky" Smith and his troops torched almost the entire town, and nearly all of its historic buildings were constructed during the ensuing rebuilding effort. Encircling the center square is a ring of strip malls and megastores catering largely to the 11,000

One of Oxford, Mississippi's prized possessions is author William Faulkner's Rowan Oak estate, now owned by the University of Mississippi. (Photo courtesy of the Mississippi Development Authority/Division of Tourism)

college students who live there during the school year, although these chains hardly dampen the overall character of the place.

Most of Oxford's famous residents weren't born here. Instead, they were no doubt attracted by the magnificent scenery, small-town feel, and intellectual and cultural pull of the university. (The university houses a center for Southern culture, the world's largest collection of blues recordings, and impressive literary archives within the walls of its museums and academic buildings.) Faulkner moved here in 1930, living in a home he called Rowan Oak—now owned by Ole Miss—until his death in 1962. He even modeled his fictional Yoknapatawpha County on the people and places of the area.

If you want to immerse yourself in the beauty of the surrounding north Mississippi countryside, which hasn't changed much since Faulkner's time, then there's no better way than by bike. After navigating out of town, you're greeted by open farmlands, thick forests, and long lakes formed by old dams on the interconnected jumble of rivers that flow either south to the gulf or west to the mighty body of water that gives the state its name. The symbiotic Oxford Bike Club and the Oxford Bicycle Company bike shop have mapped out loops that vary from 20 to 100 miles in length and begin and end in town. Finding a riding partner is never a problem—even for strangers who have come for only a day or two.

The off-road riding in town is limited but challenging. Two popular mountain biking spots will give even an expert a workout. The first is the Clear Creek Recreation Area, where the singletrack is narrow, rooty, and hardly ever straight as it hugs the shoreline of a local lake and climbs into the hills above it. The second is off Old Taylor Road, south of the town center, where the trails intertwine with an old railroad bed. It ascends to the fire tower on Thacker Mountain, which, at more than 600 feet in elevation, is one of the highest points in Mississippi. (Woodall Mountain is the highest at 806 feet.) Be careful here. Although the main Fruit Loop trail and most of its spurs lie on land owned by the university, some unmarked ones veer onto the property of a local hunting club. So pay attention to the signs.

The prime hiking, paddling, and fishing around Oxford falls largely within the 155,000-acre Holly Spring National Forest. Abutting the edge of town, the forest stretches north almost to the Tennessee line. Within it you could kayak on a different lake each day for a month and still not explore all of them. The water, rich with bass and crappie, is shaded by dogwoods, oaks, and pine and lies on what was largely open farmland before the federal government began protecting it in the 1930s. To the west of the park and town is Sardis Lake, created by the Sardis Dam and covering a 900-acre swath along the Little Tallahatchie River. With its twenty-seven boat ramps, six beaches, and 514 campsites, it doesn't exactly provide

The Wild Side

Puskus Lake

With no electric hookups at its simple campground and no wake allowed on the water, ninety-six-acre Puskus Lake in Holly Springs National Forest weeds out the luxury-seeking types, who wouldn't be caught dead on a pit toilet, to make room for people who want to enjoy a true natural setting within a short bike ride from downtown Oxford. Anyone fortunate enough to reserve one of the nineteen rustic campsites can take full advantage of paddling on the quiet lake, taking a swim, hiking the 1.5-mile nature trail loop (bikes are prohibited), and casting a line for bluegill, largemouth bass, or black crappie. While the experience might not quite be as rugged and solitary as in some places, for parks in Mississippi in general and Holly Springs in particular, hanging out here is downright roughing it. For day users, entry costs three dollars by car and one dollar by foot or bike.

Local Legend

Rowan Oak

Oxford's most prized possession is the mid-nineteenth-century Greek Revival home, surrounded by equally old gardens, on Old Taylor Road. William Faulkner lived here from 1930 until his death in 1962 and named it Rowan Oak after the white-flowered rowan tree, which symbolizes peace, according to the University of Mississippi. While there, Faulkner penned *Absalom, Absalom!, Go Down Moses,* and *The Reivers,* among other works. When working on *A Fable,* he handwrote a plot outline on his office wall, and the scribblings can still be seen today. The university bought the property from his daughter Jill in 1972, and a recent renovation has returned the home to the glory it enjoyed during Faulkner's day. Tours are available Tuesday through Saturday.

a solitary experience, but there's enough room—and fish—for everyone, even on the busiest summer day. Besides, the lake doesn't need to inspire you. If Faulkner, Welty, and Grisham are any evidence, Oxford has proven that it can do the job all by itself.

Start the Day

Bottletree Bakery (923 Van Buren Avenue; 662-236-5000): Cinnamon rolls and chocolate-stuffed fresh croissants. Enough said.

The Ajax Diner (118 Courthouse Square; 662-232-8880): Right in the heart of town, it's known for its hearty, artery-clogging breakfasts and meatloaf dinners.

Uptown Coffee (265 North Lamar Boulevard; 662-513-0905): The couch-filled latte connection for students.

Gear Up

Oxford Bicycle Company (407 Jackson Avenue; 662-236-6507): This bike shop is the epicenter of the cycling community in Oxford.

Active Oxford (720 North Lamar Boulevard; 662-236-9011): Sells running gear and high-end bike gear and accessories.

Buffalo Peak Outfitters (1501 West Jackson Avenue; 662-236-4013): The area's primary camping, backpacking, and paddling outfitter.

Refuel

Proud Larry's (211 South Lamar Boulevard; 662-236-0050; www.proudlarrys.com): Even more inviting than the hand-tossed pizza is the live music. The favorite venue in town, it is where world-famous musicians like Elvis Costello sometimes play.

City Grocery (152 Courthouse Square; 662-232-8080): A former nineteenth-century livery stable, now upscale restaurant, that fuses haute cuisine and traditional Southern cooking. The menu constantly changes, but the brilliance of chef John Currence stays the same.

Handy Andy (800 North Lamar Boulevard; 662-234-4621): Order a pulled-pork sandwich from the counter, pour the barbecue sauce from the container labeled "hot," and enjoy.

Bunk

Puddin Place (1008 University Avenue; 662-234-1250): A white, antique-filled downtown Victorian home with two comfortable suites.

Downtown Oxford Inn and Suites (400 North Lamar Boulevard; 662-234-3031; www.downtownoxfordinnandsuites.com): Nothing fancy, but a clean hotel in the heart of the action.

Can't Leave?

Nearest airport: Memphis International, Memphis, Tennessee (60 miles)

Primary industries: Education, health care, manufacturing

Boone, North Carolina

Population:
13,472

Action: Hiking, paddling, mountain biking, fishing, downhill skiing

Many aspects of the mountain town of Boone, North Carolina, are pretty cool, but its summer weather is the coolest. There's hardly anywhere south of the Mason-Dixon Line, or north of it, for that matter, that can match its imminently pleasant average high temperatures of seventy-three degrees Fahrenheit in June, seventy-six in July, and seventy-five in August. Couple that with its proximity to first-rate mountain biking, paddling, hiking, fishing, and skiing—yes, skiing— among the Blue Ridge Mountains, and you've got an ideal outdoor destination.

Hidden in the quiet northwestern corner of the state, about 100 miles north of Asheville, Boone was first settled in the early nineteenth century as a frontier outpost. It was later named after the legendary Daniel Boone, who spent time in the area. Now it's most widely known as an educational outpost for the 12,000 fleece-wearing, outdoorsy students of Appalachian State University, who inject the town with a youthful vibe and fill the surprising number of coffeehouses, hip restaurants, and bars—when they're not out in the woods and on the nearby streams and rivers. With so much backcountry in the vicinity of Boone, figuring out where to go and what to do can be an even more dizzying task for them than choosing the next semester's courses.

Directly to the south is the half-million-acre Pisgah National Forest, which straddles the spine of the Blue Ridge Mountains and boasts peaks as high as 6,000 feet. (The tallest mountain in the East, 6,684-foot Mount Mitchell, lies just outside its borders.) The spectacular Blue Ridge Parkway traces its spine, and the park is crisscrossed by hundreds of miles of hiking trails, which pass among rare virgin forest, grassy summits, and lush hidden meadows. One of the most-trodden routes is the roughly forty-mile stretch of Appalachian Trail that traces the border

Grandfather Mountain, the highest summit in the Blue Ridge range, is just one of Boone, North Carolina's many hiking options. (© N.C. Division of Tourism, Film & Sports Division)

of the Pisgah between State Routes 23 and 19E, before taking a sharp left into the Cherokee National Forest of Tennessee, almost due west of Boone.

For shorter treks, the local favorite is 3,900-acre Julian Price Memorial Park, just off the Blue Ridge Parkway. There the five-mile Boone Fork Trail hops back and forth over Boone Fork Creek, skirting a twenty-five-foot waterfall and a handful of prime swimming holes. Others prefer the hiking on Grandfather Mountain, the tallest summit in the Blue Ridge range. The Daniel Boone Scout Trail ascends 2,000 feet in 2.6 miles to reach the 5,964-foot apex of the mountain's Calloway Peak. There are ladders in place near the top for easier climbing.

Almost as extensive as the footpaths surrounding Boone is the network of singletrack. The area is packed with thrill rides barely known to anyone but local mountain bikers. Close to town is Wilson Creek Recreational Area, located within the Pisgah near Grandfather

Mountain, where routes like the thirty-mile out-and-back Wilson Ridge Trail interlace with the trout-bloated creeks that carve their way through birch-laden forest. The rugged Dark Mountain Recreational Area, about twenty minutes outside of Boone, offers some of the best roller-coaster twists and turns. For something slightly better groomed, the downhills at Sugar Mountain ski resort, site of a recent National Off-Road Bicycle Association (NORBA) competition, will quickly deposit your heart in your throat.

The Nolichucky and French Broad Rivers draw paddlers from across the country to test their mettle on the frothing Class III and IV rapids that punctuate these two powerful bodies of water. On the flat stretches, the boats inevitably pass the occasional angler, who is privy to the secret that musky, smallmouth bass, and rainbows thrive there. In the winter, the four small ski resorts nearby provide the most action; an average of forty inches of snow falls on Boone each year, and even more dumps on the outlying mountains. Fortunately, the weather at this time of year isn't quite as extraordinarily cool as it is in the summer—although the fun definitely is.

Local Legend

Daniel Boone

How much time Daniel Boone actually spent around the Boone area is up for debate, but what isn't questioned is how beloved he still is there. Each summer since 1952, the locals have put on an outdoor drama based upon his experiences during the Revolutionary War. Called *Horn in the West*, it's performed in the Daniel Boone Amphitheater, which is next to the Daniel Boone Native Gardens. The gardens are a ten-acre collage of wild plants, rhododendrons, stone paths, and meadows designed in 1965. They were donated by Daniel Boone VI, and their iron gates were forged by Daniel Boone IV—both descendants of the frontiersman.

Start the Day

Espresso News (267 Howard Street; 828-264-8850): Well-presented coffees and eclectic crowds in this downtown coffee house and hangout.

Boone Bagelry (516 West King Street; 828-262-5585): The place to get a quick bagel sandwich and cup of go juice before tackling the backcountry.

Troy's 105 Diner (1286 Highway 105 South; 828-265-1344): Where to get a full bacon-and-egg breakfast, even at 11 PM on a Saturday.

Gear Up

Footsloggers (139 South Depot Street; 828-262-5111): A well-equipped outfitter with a thirty-five-foot climbing wall, a massive boot selection and a knowledgeable, fiercely dedicated staff.

Magic Cycles (140 South Depot Street; 828-265-2211): A one-stop shop for mountain- and road-biking gear.

Mountain Adventure Guides (2 Jones Branch Road, Erwin, Tennessee; 866-813-5210): Runs daylong trips on both the Nolichucky and French Broad rivers.

Refuel

Dan'l Boone Inn (130 Hardin Street; 828-264-8657; www.danl booneinn.com): A down-home gem of a country restaurant, where meals are served family style and specialties include ham biscuits, country-style steak, and fried chicken.

The Wildflower (783 West King Street; 828-264-3463): A quiet, well-lit place for sushi and vegetarian fare.

Joe's Italian Kitchen (190 Boone Heights Drive; 828-263-9200): When you load up on pasta and handmade meatballs, you'll feel like you've been transported to New York City, owner Joe's hometown.

Bunk

Lovill House Inn (404 Old Bristol Road; 828-264-4204; www.lovill houseinn.com): This well-preserved farmhouse, built by a former Confederate captain just after the Civil War, gives you a taste of refined country living.

Mountain Villa Motor Lodge (Highway 321 South; 828-264-6166; www.mtvillamotorlodge.com): A friendly, clean, chalet-style motel with a Jacuzzi and pool.

Can't Leave?

Nearest airport: Hickory Regional, Hickory, North Carolina (40 miles)

Primary industries: Education, tourism, Christmas-tree farms

Brevard, North Carolina

Population: 6,643

Action: Hiking, rock climbing, mountain biking, paddling, rafting

Half the U.S. population lives within a day's drive of Brevard, North Carolina, but you'd never guess it from the small-town scene along Main and Broad streets, where Rocky's Soda Shop sits near a spinning barber pole, a downtown movie theater, a folk-music center, independent toy and bookstores, the Transylvania County Courthouse, and an old-fashioned gazebo. If that sounds too good to be true, you'll have an even harder time believing what surrounds Brevard: the gorges, rivers, and waterfalls of the Blue Ridge Mountains.

Brevard is just twenty-five miles from Asheville, but it has more people commuting in than out and maintains an independent livelihood thanks to the Brevard Music Center, Brevard College, and the Porter Center for Performing Arts, the intellectual and cultural chambers of the town. As for the adventure artery, that begins at the north-flowing French Broad River, a 210-mile waterway (the third oldest in the world, younger only than the Nile and North Carolina's New River) that begins a few miles from Brevard and helped attract settlers to the area in the early 1800s. Though French Broad might have been an interesting name for the new settlement, it was eventually named Brevard after a Revolutionary army colonel and surgeon who had written a patriotic predecessor to the Declaration of Independence and then died after being captured in Charleston.

Today, the French Broad has two personalities. It is a quiet, canoeing, kayaking, and tubing destination lined with sycamores, poplars, and dogwood, and is just about the best place to be on a hot, North Carolina summer day. As the river flows north, however, it froths with Class II to IV rapids, drawing whitewater rafters and kayakers to its falls and forks. More whitewater, meanwhile, crashes along the nearby Green, Tuckasegee, and Nolichucky rivers.

The rivers, gorges, and waterfalls of the Blue Ridge Mountains surround Brevard, North Carolina. (Photo Courtesy of NC Division of Tourism, Film and Sports Development)

The same place that turned Asheville into an adventure capital—Pisgah National Forest—also sits at Brevard's back door. The forest has more than a half-million acres and is topped with some of western North Carolina's best hiking summits, including the 6,410-foot peak of Richland Balsam Mountain. The Appalachian Trail, as well as such lesser-known long-distance routes as the Mountains to Sea Trail, the Shut-in Trail, and the Art Loeb Trail, all run through here. And any East Coast congestion can easily be shaken off in the rugged Linville Gorge Wilderness Area, where an 11.5-mile trail runs along the river to picnic-perfect overlooks.

The Linville Gorge is also littered with rock-climbing routes, including the 5.4 to 5.6 routes up Mummy Buttress and a range of ascents up Table Rock. But Pisgah's prime climbing spot is Looking Glass Rock, a giant ship of granite in the sea of surrounding trees. Though Looking Glass, and especially its South Face and Nose areas, is no longer the secret it once was, the rock's Yosemite-like climbs remain some of the South's top year-round proving grounds. Its eponymous water feature, Looking Glass Falls, is equally popular, and the sixty-foot cascade is just a short bike ride from Brevard. (For hidden spots, take your pick—Transylvania County boasts of more than 250 waterfalls.)

If you are on a bike, there's really no wrong way to turn around Brevard. In the Pisgah National Forest, head for the fourteen-mile Laurel Mountain Trail, which rolls past rock caves and through rock gardens and includes some thigh-burning uphills, tight switchbacks, and breathtaking Blue Ridge views. In the Bent Creek area, twenty miles of trails, many recently rebuilt, offer a mix of mostly intermediate rides. If you need more convincing about the Pisgah's prominence in eastern adventures, consider that the North Carolina Outward Bound School leads its mountain-biking courses in the Pisgah.

The Pisgah is hardly the only piece of protected land around these parts. Twenty-five minutes southeast of Brevard lies the 10,268-acre DuPont State Forest, home to Bridal Veil Falls and 3,600-foot Stone Mountain. Nearby Gorges State Park, dedicated in 1999, is one of North Carolina's newest state parks. While other wild places along the Eastern Seaboard are disappearing into development projects, the Brevard area sees land increasingly protected—even as it lies within a day's drive of half the U.S. population.

Start the Day

Bracken Mountain Bakery (42 South Broad Street; 828-883-4034): Fresh bread and pastries.

Brighter Day Coffee (102 College Station Drive, Suite 3; 828-884-2739): Coffee, tea, and espresso drinks, plus bagels, scones, muffins, and cinnamon rolls.

Gear Up

Backcountry Outdoors (49 Pisgah Highway, Suite 6; 828-884-4262): Find bikes, bike rentals, camping equipment, and clothing for the Pisgah National Forest.

Headwaters Outfitters (29 Parkway Drive, Rosnan; 828-877-3106): Canoe, kayak, and inner-tube rentals, plus new and used canoes and kayaks for sale. Also provides shuttle service for the French Broad River. Located eight miles west of Brevard.

Pisgah Whitewater (156 Vorus Circle; 828-883-4026): Whitewater kayaking

Local Legend

The White Squirrels

If a giant white squirrel happens to wave to you upon your entrance to Brevard, don't rub your eyes: that just means it's Memorial Day weekend, when the town celebrates its (ahem) nuttiest residents. Found in only a few other towns in North America, the white squirrels of Brevard reportedly trace their roots to an overturned carnival truck in Florida. At the annual festival, you can see some of the area's top musicians, along with a tennis tournament. You can see the real white squirrels darting through town almost any day of the year.

clinics on the French Broad, Green River, Nolichucky and Tuckasegee.

Refuel

Dugan's Pub (143 East Main Street; 828-862-6527): Irish pub with twenty-ounce "Irish pints" of Guinness, wings, burgers, fish and chips, salads, and shepherd's pie.

Jason's Main Street Grill (48 East Main Street; 828-883-4447): Something for everyone, from Southwest chicken eggrolls and blueberry-spinach salad to lobster ravioli, ribs, and T-bones—even corn dogs for the kids.

The Hob Nob Restaurant (226 West Main Street; 828-966-4662): Brunch on Sundays and daily lunch and dinner; entrées include dill-crusted mountain trout with lemon caper sauce and roasted duck and mushroom risotto stew.

Bunk

Ash Grove Resort Cabins & Camping (749 East Fork Road; 828-885-7216; www.ash-grove.com): Four cabins, twenty tent sites, and five RV sites on fourteen wooded acres.

The Womble Inn (301 West Main Street; 828-884-4770; www.the wombleinn.com): Six-room bed-and-breakfast in downtown Brevard.

Earthshine Mountain Lodge (1600 Golden Road, Lake Toxaway; 828-862-4207): Activity-stocked resort on seventy acres; includes a climbing wall, ten rooms, and a cottage.

Can't Leave?

Nearest airport: Asheville Regional, Asheville, North Carolina (19 miles)

Primary industries: Tourism, relocation, building and construction, real estate

The Wild Side

The Mountains to Sea Trail

The best way from Clingman's Dome to the Atlantic Ocean will one day be along the Mountains to Sea Trail (MST), a 900-mile hiking trail now in development. The MST is actually a network of existing footpaths, roads, and bike routes; there are just some dots to be connected. Right now, it's about half trails and half backcountry roads and bike routes. It's possible to thru-hike the MST, or you can pick one of the dozens of day hikes and weekend backpacking trips, all listed on www.ncmst.org.

Bryson City, North Carolina

Population: 1,361

Action: Hiking, paddling, mountain biking, fishing

If you can't find something exciting to do outdoors in Bryson City—a three-hour drive from both Charlotte and Atlanta—you're not breathing. This speck on the North Carolina map, sandwiched between the Great Smoky Mountains National Park and the Nantahala National Forest, packs a heavier dose of mountain-biking, hiking, and paddling adrenaline per capita than nearly any other town in the East. Want proof? Start by hitting the trails of the Tsali Recreation Area, which can make even mountain bikers from the Rockies froth at the mouth. Then head for the Nanatahala River to paddle alongside members of the U.S. Olympic Kayak Team, who sometimes train on its rapids. Once you dry off, lace up the hiking boots and set out on some of the 800 miles of paths through the Smokies, hitting any of the range's sixteen peaks taller than 6,000 feet. Still not convinced? Then go to Fontana Lake, where the mythic size and quantity of its smallmouth bass will make you want to cast a line forever.

Established in the late 1880s as a lumber and farming community, Bryson City was built on the edge of the flat Tuckasegee River, at 1,700 feet in elevation, among the Blue Ridge Mountains of western North Carolina. Its tiny Appalachian downtown suits the community's stature as the seat of Swain County, with old, well-kept brick storefronts and a proud-looking former courthouse building, complete with clock tower and four front pillars. Now the town is known primarily as the entryway to the national park. More than 40 percent of the Smokies lie within Swain County, including the range's tallest peak, 6,642-foot Clingman's Dome, and some of its most spectacular waterfalls, like eighty-foot Juneywhank Falls, eighty-foot Tom Branch Falls, and hidden Forney Creek Cascade, the latter accessible only to backpackers.

The 2,175-mile Appalachian Trail also enters the park in Swain County, after crossing Fontana Dam. From there, it largely follows the

The former Swain County courthouse stands proud in Bryson City, North Carolina. (© Swain County Chamber of Commerce–David Redman)

high ridgeline for the next seventy miles. To walk the A.T. through this area, start at Newfound Gap—where the park was dedicated by President Franklin Delano Roosevelt in 1940—and follow it through the alpine forest, which is mostly above 6,000 feet in elevation. Take in the views at the occasional overlooks before turning around at the rocky vista known as Charlie's Bunion. Round-trip, the hike is eight miles.

If you'd prefer simply to sympathize with A.T. hikers, stand at Fontana Dam in spring, where you'll find them arriving in droves after completing the rigorous, twenty-one-mile trek from the Nantahala Outdoor Center (N.O.C.). The center is also a whitewater instruction, training, and outfitting facility that attracts paddlers from around the world, including top Americans competing for the Olympics. Embedded within the narrow, deep Nantahala Gorge, the N.O.C. occupies both banks of the Nantahala River, along a short stretch of Class III rapids inside the half-million-acre Nantahala National Forest. The rustic center has an outfitter's shop, three restaurants, and several cabins and bunkrooms. It offers paddling trips not only on the Nanathala, but also on the world-class rapids of the French Broad, Nolichucky, Pigeon, Chatooga, and Cheoah rivers.

The N.O.C. bike shop is one of the prime sources for dirt on the nearby Tsali, which is also in the national forest and known as the East's fat-tire answer to Moab. The roughly forty miles of trails there are hard-packed and relatively hazard free—except for the many creek crossings. These conditions make for fast-paced roller-coaster rides, as you zigzag through pine forests and mountain-laurel thickets that trace the shore of twenty-nine-mile-long Fontana Lake. The twelve-mile Left Loop path and eleven-mile Right Loop are mostly singletrack and have views of the water. Mouse Branch is a slightly more technical six-mile mix of logging roads and singletrack, as is the twisty, up-and-down, 7.9-mile Thompson Loop. If you want to take a fishing break on the lake, its cold depths are a fertile home for walleye, muskie, crappie, largemouth and smallmouth bass, and striper. For those of you who *are* breathing, all of this action is bound to take your breath away.

Start the Day

Everett Street Diner (126 Everett Street; 828-488-0123): Traditional bacon, egg, and grits diner.

Mountain Perks (9 Depot Street; 828-488-9561): Bagels, espresso, and smoothies in the heart of downtown, overlooking the train depot.

Aunt B's Donut and Ice Cream Shop (15 Everett Street; 828-488-0881): The sign on the window says "7 a.m. 'till the donuts are gone!" so don't get there too late.

Gear Up

Nantahala Outdoor Center (13077 Highway 19 West; 800-232-7238): Their extremely well-stocked outfitter shop has everything you need for biking, backpacking, and paddling. Check out the register signed by passing A.T. hikers.

Bryson City Rock-N-Rivers (149 Main Street; 828-488-7555): Sells boats, and guides paddling, biking, and hiking trips.

Refuel

Relia's Garden (13077 Highway 19 West; 800-232-7238; www.noc.com): The fanciest of the three restaurants at the N.O.C., specializing in fresh vegetarian fare.

Pasqualino's Italian Restaurant (25 Everett Street; 828-488-9555): The place to get a good old-fashioned plate of spaghetti and meatballs in Bryson City center.

Bunk

Charleston Inn (208 Arlington Avenue; 828-488-4644; www.charlestoninn.com): A lodge-style bed-and-breakfast with nineteen rooms and a cottage, surrounded by trees and rhododendron.

Lloyd's on the River (5370 Ela Road; 828-488-3767; www.lloydson theriver.com): A quiet motor hotel just outside of downtown, on the Oconaluftee River.

Ridge Top Motel (390 Arlington Avenue; 828-488-6363): A friendly hotel and campground.

Can't Leave?

Nearest airport: McGhee Tyson, Knoxville, Tennessee (50 miles)

Primary industries: Health care, service, recreation

Local Legend

Tsali Recreation Area

The Tsali Recreation Area gets its name from a Cherokee man who was executed in a village that now lies beneath the waters of Fontana Lake. He and his family sought refuge in the mountains of southwestern North Carolina after the federal government ordered the Cherokee nation to be relocated to Oklahoma in 1838. Legend has it that Tsali agreed to turn himself in with his son and brother-in-law, under the condition that others in his group be allowed to stay in the area. The three were executed, and though their burial spot was flooded in the 1930s with the construction of the dam, their memory is ever present.

Edenton, North Carolina

Population: 5,394

Action: Sailing, paddling, fishing

When a town puts the word "Eden" in its name, it can be an easy target for jokes—like, "Um, I don't think Adam and Eve really had oil refineries and smokestacks where they lived." Except in the case of Edenton. This colorful waterfront village in northern North Carolina may not quite be paradise, but to paddlers, sailors, and anyone looking for a folksy, small-town Southern experience, it's pretty darn close.

Edenton lies at the confluence of the two-mile-wide Chowan River and a small bay on the northern bank of Albemarle Sound, one of the largest freshwater sounds in North America. About a ninety-minute drive south of Norfolk, Virginia, and thirty miles removed from the nearest highway, the town feels thousands of miles away from the bustle and commercialism that has overtaken so much of the East. To set the record straight, the town was actually named after former governor Charles Eden when it was incorporated in 1722. At that time, it was one of the region's most important ports, and for a while it was the colonial capital of North Carolina.

Reminders of Edenton's proud and important history are everywhere, from the cannons sent by Benjamin Franklin—in the waterfront park at the foot of Broad Street—to the twenty-five or so eighteenth- and nineteenth-century buildings in the historic downtown area. Among the spotless old homes, the architecture is a mix of Georgian, Federal, Victorian, and Greek Revival. The one characteristic that nearly all of them share is a bilevel wraparound porch, a necessity for surviving the steamy summers. These homes, with their white picket fences and verdant gardens, can be found on King and Water streets by the shore.

The town has evolved into a boatbuilding and tourist community, and nearly everyone who lives or visits there does so because of the

Life and recreation in Edenton, North Carolina revolve around the waters of Albemarle Sound and the Chowan River. (© Chowan County Tourism Development Authority)

water. The popular local social organization is the Edenton Yacht Club. Throughout the summer, it organizes dinghy regattas and other sailboat races, which are usually followed by a barbecue or drinks at a downtown pub. The group is about as pretentious as a bottle of light beer—initiation fees are a mere forty dollars, and annual membership fee is also forty dollars. With steady Atlantic breezes blowing consistently over the wide, protected Albemarle Sound and its deep inlets in the summer, the sailing conditions in these parts are some of the best anywhere south of the Chesapeake.

The kayaking is at least on par with the sailing, as long as the chop isn't too high, and can take you through swamplands, hidden creeks, and wide-open waters. Edenton lies at the heart of the new Albemarle Region Canoe and Small Boat Trails, a 200-mile network of twenty-nine paddling routes, two of which originate at the town boat ramp. The four-mile Pembroke Creek trail follows quiet waterways lined with spanish-moss-canopied oaks. The four-mile Queen Anne Creek trail runs alongside the revitalized century-old Edenton Cotton Mill.

The Cupola House

Relics of Edenton's past as an important port and the first colonial capital of North Carolina are scattered throughout town, but the spacious, wooden Cupola House stands above all others—in both significance and height. It's easy to recognize, thanks to the octagonal tower that extends above the center of the roof like a turret. The house, set among elaborate Colonial Revival gardens, was built in 1758. A rare example of Jacobean architecture in the South, it features an overhanging second story and wide chimneys. It's operated as a museum and decorated with period furniture to offer a perspective on the life of Edenton gentry 250 years ago. The elaborate paneling downstairs is actually a re-creation, because the original was sold to the Brooklyn Museum in New York in 1918 and is still there today.

Albemarle Sound and the Chowan River are historically rich bass waters. Largemouth bass are plentiful, and stripers have recently made a comeback. The largest striped bass ever recorded—more than 123 pounds—was caught outside Edenton in 1891. Pembroke Fishing Center, on Pembroke Creek, organizes nine regional fishing competitions between March and October; the largest, called the Edenton Annual Bass Fishing Tournament, is held the first Saturday in June.

The town hosts two other crowd-pleasing events each year. The first is the mid-June Music and Water Festival, which presents live jazz and blues performances to go with kayak and sailboat races and free boat demos and tours. The second is the Edenton Bay Challenge Sailboat Races in July—a weekend regatta for small sailboats like Lasers and Sunfish. Both events are held at the open, grassy waterfront park, which has postcard-perfect views of the bay. It's a spot that could easily be nicknamed the Garden of Edenton. (Sorry, couldn't resist.)

Start the Day

Acoustic Coffee (302 South Broad Street; 252-482-7465; www.acoustic-coffee.com): Bagels, muffins, and espresso; a hip music venue on Friday nights.

Chicken Kitchen (809 North Broad Street; 252-482-4721): Loved for its fried chicken, but its hearty breakfasts are just as tasty.

Gear Up

Pembroke Fishing Center (802 West Queen Street; 252-482-5343): Has two boat ramps, sells tackle, organizes tournaments, and even serves lunch.

Colonial Edenton Downtown Harbor
(252-482-7352;): The Town of Edenton
rents kayaks by the waterfront park.

Refuel

Waterman's Grill (427 South Broad
Street; 252-482-7733): Seafood served
Southern style, including fried oyster
sandwiches.

Nixon Family Restaurant (327 River
Road; 252-221-2244): Two words:
seafood buffet.

Lords Proprietor's Inn (300 North
Broad Street; 888-394-6622; www
.edentoninn.com): Real sit-down
dinners in a refined setting.

Bunk

Lords Proprietor's Inn (300 North
Broad Street; 888-394-6622; www
.edentoninn.com): The inn's three historic houses have sixteen rooms total.

Trestle House Inn (632 Soundside
Road; 252-482-2282; www.trestlehouse
inn.com): This country house with
wooden cedar beams sits on a lake
beside a wildlife refuge.

The Wild Side

The Charles Kuralt Trail

The Charles Kuralt Trail, named after
the late television journalist and
Tarheel, isn't a true trail—it's a collection of eleven national wildlife refuges
and one fish hatchery in eastern
Virginia and North Carolina. At each
location, there are red-roofed kiosks
informing you what to see and do on
the surrounding scenic paths and
roads. The site closest to downtown
Edenton is the Edenton National Fish
Hatchery, created in 1899 to maintain
the health of native fish populations.
Also within a short drive are stops at
the bottomland forests of the Roanoke
River National Wildlife Refuge, where
migratory waterfowl stop on the
Eastern Flyway, and the Pocosin Lakes
National Wildlife Refuge, a 112,000-
acre habitat for red cockaded wood-
peckers, black bears, and rare red
wolves.

Colonial Edenton Downtown Harbor (252-482-7352; www.town
ofedenton.com): You can get a free overnight slip for your boat for
two nights. Power, restrooms, and showers are
available.

Can't Leave?

Nearest airport: Pitt-Greenville, Greenville, North Carolina
(60 miles)

Primary industries: Agriculture, commercial fishing, health care

Beaufort, South Carolina

Population:
12,058

Action: Paddling, sailing, road biking, hiking

With all of the water surrounding Beaufort, there's much more to do on a beautiful day than sip lemonade and whistle Dixie on one of the wrap-around porches of its antebellum homes. Hidden among the Sea Islands of South Carolina's coastal Low Country, it's a boater's dream destination. Here, kayaking is nearly as reflexive as breathing among the local townsfolk, and sailing isn't too far behind. On land, the pastime is eating—the town is home to a surprising array of exquisite seafood restaurants, each with its own specialty shrimp dish, of course. After all, spending so much time outdoors can make a person work up an appetite.

Even if you've never heard of Beaufort (pronounced *BYOO-fert*), you've probably seen it. The oak-lined avenues of this quintessential Southern town have served as the backdrop for such movies as *The Great Santini, Forrest Gump, The Big Chill,* and *The Legend of Bagger Vance.* About a ninety-minute drive southwest of Charleston, it occupies the eastern thumb of Port Royal Island, bordered by the brackish Beaufort River. It's a popular stop on the Intracoastal Waterway for boaters headed to or coming from nearby Port Royal Sound, the second-deepest natural port on the East Coast. Paddle just a few minutes outside of Beaufort among the rivers and tidal creeks, and your only company will be bottle-nosed dolphins playing in the water and ospreys swooping overhead. Within all of Beaufort County, there are more than 2,000 islands, which occupy almost 600 square miles total.

The haven for local paddlers is the ACE Basin National Wildlife Refuge, about fifteen minutes north of town. The 11,800-acre preserve is where the Ashepo, Combahee, and Edisto rivers (their acronym provides the refuge's name) converge upon St. Helena Sound to form pristine marshes, cypress swamps, hardwood forests, and grasslands. The

The coastal waters surrounding Beaufort, South Carolina make the town a dream destination for boaters and seafood lovers. (© Beaufort Regional Chamber of Commerce)

preserve also contains the remains of old rice plantations. ACE Basin is one of the largest undeveloped estuaries in the eastern United States and provides habitat for wood storks and shortnose sturgeon, as well as migrating ducks, herons, and egrets. Several local outfitters offer guided tours, and you're almost guaranteed a solitary experience, since only 25,000 people visit the refuge each year. The crystal-clear waters make for hundreds of miles of routes that snake far into surrounding untouched, private lands. Just keep your eyes open for the alligators sunning themselves on the water's banks, or you'll start to feel as at-risk as the sixteen endangered species that make this area their home. The refuge is also a prime hiking destination, crisscrossed by trails that are open from sunrise to dusk and offer quiet vantage points for spotting an occasional white-tailed deer or even a bald eagle.

In town, the biggest party of the year is the Annual Water Festival, held in July on the well-manicured grass of the seven-acre Henry C. Chambers Waterfront Park. The event began more than a half century ago as a sailboat regatta, but it has grown to include a craft fair, food, music, and an air show—along with the boat races, of course. Several smaller sailboat races are held by local clubs throughout the summer, and there's no shortage of launching ramps around Beaufort for day cruisers visiting the area.

Spend any time exploring downtown, and it's easy to understand why General Sherman's Union forces spared it from the torch and used it as an encampment. It's also easy to see why it has been named a National Historic Landmark. Some of the gas-lit residential streets in such neighborhoods as the Point—a peninsula on the eastern end of town, where Georgian-style homes are shaded by trees covered in spanish moss—haven't changed much in appearance in the past 150 years.

The Wild Side

Hunting Island State Park

The state park that encompasses undeveloped, 5,000-acre Huntington Island is hardly a secret, as nearly a million people visit its pristine white beach each year. Yet when the sunbathing masses leave this four-mile-long barrier island for the evening, the pine-shaded Atlantic-side waterfront campsites become a quiet, spectacular natural setting. Inland, its eight miles of hiking paths, which wind through marshlands and pine and oak forests, are relatively free from crowds throughout the day, making a pure outdoor experience surprisingly easy to find. Hunting Island State Park is located a short drive from Beaufort (843-838-2111; www.southcarolinaparks.com).

Perhaps the best way to tour the area's present and former glory is on two wheels. Although the countryside is relatively flat, what it lacks in hills it makes up for with the scenic beauty of its quiet, tree-lined country roads, which pass through marshland, beside aged plantations, over bridges, and through thick forests. There are several favorite twenty- to thirty-mile routes frequented by the local cycling clubs, including one called the Forrest Gump ride, which winds through sites used for filming the movie.

Despite Beaufort's cinematic beauty and deep Southern roots, it doesn't feel caught in the past. An influx of young professionals fleeing the bustle of East Coast urban life have ushered in a handful of new bistros, shops, and galleries to mix new vitality into the immaculate old buildings on Bay Street, North Street, and other downtown avenues. You'll notice it on the few spare minutes you have when you're not on the water or striking out on some other adventure.

Start the Day

Firehouse Books and Espresso (706 Craven Street; 843-522-2665): Best coffee in town, served in the old red-brick firehouse, two blocks from the Beaufort River.

Blackstone's Cafe (205 Scott Street; 843-524-4330; www.black stonescafe.com): Authentic Low-Country breakfasts, like shrimp and grits.

Gear Up

Higher Ground of the Low Country (1307 Boundary Street; 843-379-4327): Sells camping, kayak, and climbing gear, and rents cruiser bikes.

Low Country Paddlesports (1109 Boundary Street; 843-379-5292): Rents kayaks, canoes, and surfboards, and leads kayaking tours.

Beaufort Kayak Tours (2707 Oaklawn Street; 843-525-0810): Paddling guide service that offers the most expansive trip list.

Refuel

Kathleen's Grille (822 Bay Street; 843-524-2500): Owner Kathy Bussing's Southern specialties include pan-fried lump crab cakes.

Saltus River Grill (802 Bay Street; 843-379-3474; www.saltusrivergrill.com): Upscale Manhattan-meets-Low-Country cuisine.

The Shrimp Shack (1925 Sea Island Parkway, St. Helena Island; 843-838-2962): A can't-miss seafood shanty renowned for its shrimp burgers.

Local Legend

Beaufort Stew

Also known as Frogmore Stew and Beaufort Boil, Beaufort Stew is a staple food among South Carolinians. Although there are more variations of this concoction in town than anecdotes about local legend Pat Conroy—and that's saying something—it's basically made with shrimp, sausage, corn on the cob, crabs, and Old Bay seafood seasoning, all steamed together. Folks will tell you that the best restaurant version is served at Steamer Oyster & Steakhouse (168 Sea Island Parkway; 843-522-0210).

Bunk

Beaufort Inn (809 Port Republic Street; 888-522-0250; www
.beaufortinn.com): An idiosyncratic, century-old Victorian house
with four-poster beds and fireplaces in the twenty-one guest
rooms.

The Rhett House Inn (1009 Craven Street; 843-524-9030;
www.rhretthouseinn.com): When movie stars come to town, they
stay in one of the well-appointed rooms of this romantic 1820
plantation home.

Old Point Inn (212 New Street; 843-524-3177; www.oldpointinn
.com): A five-room 1898 home in the historic Point neighborhood.

Can't Leave?

Nearest airport: Savannah/Hilton Head International, Savannah,
Georgia (42 miles)

Primary industries: Tourism, fishing, military

Gatlinburg, Tennessee

f or northbound thru-hikers traveling the Appalachian Trail along the ridgeline of Great Smoky Mountains National Park, the lights of Gatlinburg, thousands of feet below the footpath, seem golden. After some 200 miles into their 2,175-mile journey from Georgia to Maine, many A.T. trekkers are already dreaming of fluffy pancakes, fluffier pillows, and a place where they can find not only hot showers, but also a cold microbrew and a cozy bookstore. Meanwhile, ticket sellers at Gatlinburg's Guinness Book of World Records Museum gaze up at the Great Smokies, aching to get back on a trail as soon as the last visitor has gaped at the video of local Dan Netherland breaking fifty-five concrete blocks in one minute with his bare hands. Gatlinburg lies at the juncture of wacky civilization and wonderful wilderness, and it's a lively gateway to the more than a half million acres of misty, mountainous national park.

Population: 4,426
Action: Hiking, fishing

For Revolutionary War veterans who claimed their fifty acres of land in East Tennessee, Gatlinburg was considered the Land of Paradise. Eventually, timbering and creekside homesteads evolved into tourism and hotels. Gatlinburg was named after Radford Gatlin, a shopkeeper who in 1860 was chased out of town for his pro-slavery views. You'll learn this and more should you choose to explore the Ripley's Believe or Not! Museum, a rainy day diversion and one of the many manmade attractions along the thoroughfare known as the Parkway. Lined with candy factories and souvenir stands, the strip is often a sea of tourists, but it's worth checking out the Space Needle for the views and the retro elevator ride.

But Gatlinburg's best attractions are the Mother Nature–made ones especially the 800-plus hiking trails that snake through Great Smoky Mountain National Park. One of the premier day hikes is Ramsey Cascades, a ninety-foot series of falls reachable by an eight-mile

Gatlinburg, Tennessee lies at the juncture of wacky civilization and the wonderful wilderness of Great Smoky Mountains National Park. (© Gatlinburg Dept. of Tourism)

round-trip walk. The area, just east of Gatlinburg, contains tuliptrees, hemlock, and cherry trees in the largest section of old-growth forest in the Smokies, along with a 2,140-foot elevation gain, footbridges and ferns. Other local favorite hikes include the four-mile Chimney Tops, which goes past large buckeye trees toward eye-popping views, and the 11.2-mile round-trip to the tower atop 4,928-foot Mount Cammerer, whose approach traces the Appalachian Trail. In addition to a pair of hiking boots, the best way to beat the slow crawl of cars in the Great Smokies is a road bike or a kayak.

Tennessee isn't exactly known for its skiing, but the town is so consumed with alpinism, it even has a ski area: Ober Gatlinburg. From the Parkway, you take a 120-passenger aerial tram (à la Jackson Hole's old signature lift) to an eight-trail, 600-foot vertical-drop resort with a 3,300-foot summit elevation. The thin, average annual snowfall of thirty-five inches is augmented by an adjacent amusement park, which has rides in both winter and summer.

Spring finds Gatlinburg at its most golden, thanks to the Ribfest and Wings street festival (which seems to cover the Parkway in barbecue sauce), the bluegrass-infused Smoky Mountain Springfest, and the Spring Wildflower Pilgrimmage. (The adjacent towns of Pigeon Forge and Sevierville also feature events, but traveling to them on a weekend could land you in a snarl of Dollywood-bound traffic; it's best to save the car for excursions into the Smokies and take the trolley around Gatlinburg.) The Great Smoky Arts and Crafts Easter Show reveals Gatlinburg's strong cultural side; the town is also home to the Arrowmont School of Arts and Crafts, a refreshing studio and gallery space that seems to have been preserved, in spirit and design, from the 1970s.

Besides the Parkway, Gatlinburg's other main thoroughfare is the Little Pigeon River, where you can fish for trout in the early morning hours. If the trout aren't biting, head for one of the more that 2,100 miles of rivers and streams in Great Smoky Mountains National Park. Or just sneak off into a local pancake parlor, where you're likely to rub elbows with

The Wild Side

The Big Pigeon

Just outside of Gatlinburg, the upper section of the Big Pigeon River has a 6.5-mile stretch riddled with some seventy rapids, including the Class IV Lost Guide, where new rafters are most likely to be launched into the froth. There are quieter parts, such as After Shave and Bombs Lake, but much of the ride is a rollicking one that will squeeze every penny out of the fee you pay Smoky Mountain Outdoors (the original and best rafting company for the area; 800-771-7238)—and leave you squeezing Great Smoky whitewater from your shirt.

Local Legend

Cades Cove

One of the most enchanting areas of Great Smoky Mountains National Park is the Cades Cove area, where a preserved settlement from the 1800s would instantly transport twenty-first-century dwellers back in time—were it not for the parade of minivans and pick-up trucks on the eleven-mile, one-way loop around the place. So keep this local secret in mind: from May through September, from sunup to 10 a.m., only hikers and bikers are allowed into Cades Cove. With the early morning dew still sparkling on the pastures, you can poke through one of the best preserved pieces of Appalachian history, with only the flash of a deer or the flapping of a wild turkey to distract you.

an Appalachian Trail thru-hiker, detoured from the journey by the delights of Gatlinburg.

Start the Day

Village Coffee & Company (613 Parkway #13; 865-430-4280): From almond-amaretto to swiss-chocolate coffees, plus a few pastries and java-junky gifts.

The Pancake Pantry (628 Parkway; 865-436-4724): Flapjacks twenty-four ways, including sausage stuffed, plus eggs to order and speedy service.

Gear Up

The Happy Hiker (905 River Road, Suite 5; 865-436-6000): Located at the doorstep to the Great Smokies; sells tents, packs, snacks, climbing gear, and guided trips.

Refuel

Smoky Mountain Brewery (1004 Parkway; 865-436-4200): A pizza parlor downstairs and brewpub upstairs, with 33.8-ounce mugs of Black Bear Ale.

No Way Jose's Cantina (555 Parkway; 865-430-5673): Margaritas and Mexican along the Little Pigeon River.

Park Grill (1110 Parkway; 865-436-2300): Steaks, ribs, rainbow trout, and a salad bar boasting more than forty items; save room for the Jack Daniel's crème brulée.

Bunk

Bearskin Lodge (840 River Road; 865-430-4330): Private balconies overlooking the Little Pigeon River, and an off-the-Parkway sense of peace and quiet.

Buckhorn Inn (2140 Tudor Mountain Road; 865-436-4668): Nine rooms in the main lodge, plus seven cottages and three guesthouses, which each sleep up to four.

Can't Leave?

Nearest airport: McGhee Tyson, Knoxville, Tennessee (34 miles)

Primary industries: Tourism, arts

Alpine, Texas

Population: 6,065
Action: Hiking, paddling, rafting

In Texas, where everything is, well, Texas-sized, it should come as no surprise that Big Bend National Park and its neighbor, Big Bend Ranch State Park, sprawl across more than a million acres. The hulking landscape, tucked against the border with Mexico, ranges from 1,800 to 7,800 feet in elevation. Big Bend's southern boundary is the equally impressive Rio Grande, which winds more than 1,000 miles and has spectacular canyons plunging up to 1,500 feet in the Chihuahuan Desert. The park's far-reaching geologic and paleontologic history draws intense study by scientists; according to archaeologists who have collected Big Bend artifacts, its human history reaches back 10,500 years. But now, Big Bend is dominated by plants, animals, and birds rather than humans; the area receives only one tenth of the number of visitors that Yellowstone National Park does.

Part of Big Bend's allure is that it's so far from everything else—except the West Texas town of Alpine, found in a valley of the Davis Mountains. Some eighty miles north of the park, Alpine is just distant enough to avoid becoming a fudge-filled tourist trap, but close enough to appreciate all the action. Alpine got its start from a few railroad workers, who in the 1880s pitched a few tents at the foot of a mountain; eventually, the tents became houses surrounded by saloons and a combination drugstore and post office. When Sul Ross State University—named for a Texas ranger, senator, and governor—was founded in 1917, Alpine grew more rapidly, and in the second half of the twentieth century, the town hooked into its proximity to Big Bend to attract visitors and more permanent settlers.

Today, the town's a hotbed for pure West Texas culture, art, and outdoor adrenaline. There are cowboy poetry gatherings, rodeos, theater performances of *Annie Get Your Gun*, the Museum of the Big Bend,

Alpine, Texas is the stepping off point to remote Big Bend National Park, where there are more desert plants, animals, and birds than tourists. (© *Texas Tourism*)

and nearly twenty galleries. Organized triathlons and regular hikes and float trips gobble up locals' calendars.

For an overview of the area, you can rent a bike from the Bikeman; have Marfa Gliders take you on a glider ride from the town of Marfa, just west of Alpine; or hop on a horse at the Madera Hills Ranch in nearby Balmorhea. But chances are you'll want to fill up a large thermal mug of coffee and drive the hour and a half (which feels like much less, especially if you have a sack of pastries on your lap) south to Big Bend National Park to embark on a day hike or backpacking trip. On the park's east side, the four-mile (round-trip) Pine Canyon trail leads to a 200-foot cliff that turns into a waterfall after rain; the fourteen-mile (round-trip) Marufo Vega is a remote and rugged trail that parallels the Rio Grande and is best hiked in the cooler fall and spring months. Big Bend's central Chisos Mountains provide premier backcountry experiences, such as the twelve-mile (round-trip) trail to South Rim, where you can gaze out over Mexico before spending the night under the stars on a high lava plateau. The north end of the park features Devil's Den, a six-mile hike within a limestone slot canyon that is cooled by water runoff. And the prize among serious Big Bend hikers is Outer Mountain Loop, a thirty-mile, three-day circuit through one of the lower forty-eight's wildest and loneliest corners: the Sierra Quemada, or "burnt land." The dangers of the trail, especially in May through October, lead park officials to warn off tenderfeet by posting online the number of folks who fail to complete the loop.

For a more refreshing exploration of Big Bend, you can float the Rio Grande on a kayak, canoe, or raft trip. On the nine- to twenty-one-mile stretch through the Colorado Canyon in Big Bend Ranch State Park, Class II and III rapids roll through igneous rock and limestone, while the twenty-mile, Class IV Rock Slide rapid cuts through the 1,500-foot limestone walls of Santa Elena Canyon.

Alpine is also surrounded by natural hot springs; after your day of activity, you

The Wild Side

Marfa's Mystery Lights

One of the wildest sights in West Texas is the mystery lights of Marfa, reddish orange globes that are visible after dark. First reported by Robert Ellison, a settler who headed west from Alpine to Marfa in 1883 and believed the strange nighttime lights to be Apache signal fires, the lights have since drawn the curious, who chase them using airplanes, jeeps, and radios. Some claim to hear a tinny noise in one ear while viewing the phenomenon; others dismiss the so-called ghost lights as reflections from passing traffic or nearby ranches. Either way, the Marfa mystery lights have earned their own viewing center in between Marfa and Alpine and their own festival, held the first weekend of every September.

can relax in the largest spring-fed pool in Texas—the 77,053 square-foot San Salomon Spring, constructed by the Civilian Conservation Corps and found at Balmorhea State Park. Or you can wind down the way those first Alpine settlers did, with a cold brew at Railroad Blues. Along with live music almost every night, the venue boasts a Texas-sized selection of beer.

Start the Day

Bread & Breakfast Bakery & Café (113 West Holland Avenue; 432-837-9424): Pastries, doughnuts, and coffee, plus lunch and dinner specials; a hangout for local artists.

Alicia's Burrito Place (708 East Avenue G; 432-837-2802): Cheap breakfast burritos and other filling fare for the trails of Big Bend.

Gear Up

Cactus Country Outfitters & Taxidermy (607 East Holland Avenue; 432-294-0053): Where else but Texas could you find a place that will sell you a sleeping bag and skin that animal you bagged?

Bikeman (602 West Holland Avenue; 432-837-5050): Rents bikes and sells accessories.

Far Flung Adventures (800-839-7238): Rafting outfitter in the town of Terlingua, for floats along the Rio Grande.

Refuel

Edelweiss Brewery & Restaurant (209 West Holland Avenue; 432-837-9454): A quirky, German-themed spot (think wiener schnitzel, bratwurst, and knackwurst, along with burgers and big breakfasts) in the Holland Hotel, with the smallest and highest brewery in Texas.

Local Legend

Terlingua Chili

The town of Terlingua is eighty-two miles from Alpine, but on the first Saturday of November, it's worth the drive. That's when Terlingua hosts not one, but two international chili competitions, and peppers, tomatoes, and cubes of beef become the talk of the ghost town. The competition started in 1967, when two newspaper journalists argued over whether beans belonged in chili and decided to settle the matter in the first-ever chili cookoff. The topic of chili is so fiery that the original contest split in two when organizers had a dispute. Now, the Chili Appreciation Society International, Inc. holds one event and the International Chili Society holds the other; the latter has its own newspaper. Both have earned Terlingua the title of chili capital of the world by an esteemed source: the McIlhenny Company, makers of Tabasco.

Reata (203 North Fifth Street; 432-837-9232): Reata is Spanish for rope; in Alpine, it also means cowboy cuisine, which translates to locally raised beef, chicken-fried and served with such sides as jalapeño-and-cheddar grits and Texas margaritas.

La Casita (1104 East Avenue H; 432-837-2842): A popular Tex-Mex joint with vegetarian options.

Bunk

Holland Hotel (209 West Holland Avenue; 800-535-8040; www.hollandhotel.net): Stay in the stylish lofts and basic rooms in downtown Alpine, or at the Holland's funky, one-room adobe Dome or Casita cottage on the outskirts of town.

White House Inn (2003 Fort Davis Highway; 432-837-1401; www.whitehouseinntexas.com): Quiet cottages and suites with kitchenettes.

Antelope Lodge (2310 West Highway 90; 432-837-3417; www.antelopelodge.com): A 1950s-era cluster of cottages with its own museum of rocks and gems.

Can't Leave?

Nearest airport: Cavern City Air Terminal, Carlsbad, New Mexico (142 miles)

Primary industries: Ranching, tourism, law enforcement, education

Fredericksburg, Texas

pend some time in Fredericksburg, and it's easy to understand why there are more than 300 bed-and-breakfasts packed inside its cozy borders. It lies in the midst of the relatively cool, verdant Hill Country, on the lazy, picturesque Town Creek; its German heritage is so apparent in its pedestrian-friendly downtown shops, architecture, and people that you practically think you've set foot in a theme park; and its location, about ninety minutes west of Austin and only an hour north of San Antonio, make it an easy weekend getaway. Yet the best reason to come to town are the rides on quiet, well-paved roads through the rolling countryside, which will make you scream "God Bless Texas!" like you mean it.

Population: 10,432

Action: Road and mountain biking, rock climbing

When you're standing in the heart of town, there are probably more options for biking routes than there are places to spend the night, including a handful of bona fide classics. Fortunately, the local biking community is so strong, and the local Hill Country Bicycle Works shop on East Main Street so helpful, that you can easily find assistance in choosing one ride or finding a riding partner to join you. There are also two unsupported group rides that Fredericksburg cyclists organize each week—a fifty-plus-miler on Saturdays and a thirty-miler on Tuesdays that's usually followed by a meet-up at a pub afterward. The folks in these parts take their beer seriously, too—a trait that can probably be traced back to the original settlers.

Fredericksburg was created in 1846 by a small group of German immigrants, who forged the long, wide Main Street to parallel Town Creek to the way villages paralleled the Rhine in their homeland, according to the Texas State Historical Association. Each family was given a small plot of land in town on which to build their homes and a ten-acre tract on the outskirts for growing crops. As the population grew, farmers started living by their fields and building one- or

Fredericksburg, Texas's German heritage is evident in its pedestrian-friendly downtown.
(© Fredericksburg Convention & Visitor Bureau)

two-bedroom Sunday houses in town, for churchgoing and weekend business. Some of these structures still stand and today are occupied by restaurants or shops. In the twentieth century, the community's economic base evolved from agriculture, to manufacturing, to tourism. Without proper knowledge of Fredericksburg's history, you might find the German pastry shops, brat stands, and various places with the word *haus* in their name to be a bit contrived instead of what they really are— a surprisingly authentic reflection of the past.

Even if the town had no culture or history, it would still be worth visiting for its cycling alone. The mother of all Fredericksburg rides is the fifty-five-mile Willow City Loop (there are variations on every course here), which starts with a few brisk climbs out of town, climaxes with a sharp drop, and ends with a thigh-screaming climb into the town that gives the route its name. When the spring bluebonnets bloom in the meadows that surround this trail, you practically feel like you're on the Yellow Brick Road just outside of Emerald City. A shorter but equally heart-pumping—and enjoyable—ride is the thirty-seven-mile Luckenbach Loop. The highlight of this ride is the town of Luckenbach itself, made famous in a Willie Nelson and Waylon Jennings song and consisting of little more than a general store with a saloon in back that has been open since 1849.

If you're looking for mountain biking, the best rides are a short drive south, in the town of Kerrville. The Kelly Creek Ranch, home to occasional bike races, has more than twenty miles of rocky single-track and doubletrack with creek crossings and white-knuckle chutes. For something less extreme, head to the Kerrville-Schreiner State Park where the six miles of trails by the Guadalupe River are flatter and much more forgiving.

Not all the action around Fredericksburg takes place on two wheels, though. At the Enchanted Rock State Natural area seventeen miles north of town, you'll find a 425-foot-tall dome of pink granite unearthed by erosion. Nicknamed E Rock, the dome occupies 600 acres of the 1,600-acre park and is the prime climbing spot

Local Legend

LBJ

The legacy of thirty-sixth president of the United States, Lyndon Baines Johnson, still casts a long shadow over the Texas Hill Country and Fredericksburg. He was born in the neighboring community of Stonewall and graduated from high school in Johnson City (named after his grandfather), about thirty miles east of Fredericksburg. The local 719-acre Lyndon B. Johnson State Park and Historic Site is divided into two sections. The first, in Johnson City, contains Johnson's boyhood home. The second contains his birthplace and the LBJ Ranch, once nicknamed the Texas White House and still a working cattle ranch.

The Wild Side

Devil's Sinkhole State Natural Area

You can't go inside the 300-foot-deep cavern that gives Devil's Sinkhole Natural Area its name, or even look down the forty-by-sixty-foot shaft. But that doesn't mean there's nothing to see. Every summer evening at this park in Rocksprings, southwest of Fredericksburg, you can watch its population of more than a million Mexican free-tailed bats rise through the hole in a twisting cyclone of black, flapping wings. From April through October, when the colony is at its peak, the Devil's Sinkhole Society offers evening bat-flight tours to view the spectacle.

in Central Texas. There are hundreds of established routes, usually between 5.7 and 5.10—and many of them multi-pitch—on its rough, crack-scarred surface. Get there early on weekends, though, because once the parking lot is full—often well before noon—no more visitors are allowed, and you'll find yourself basking in the German flavor of the Fredericksburg pubs a little earlier than planned.

Start the Day

Fredericksburg Gourmet Coffee and Tea (338 West Main Street; 830-997-8327): Their own coffee blends, like "Remember the Alamo" and "Texas Velvet Hammer," go with the eggs and Opa's German sausage that are served all day.

Old German Bakery and Restaurant (225 West Main Street; 830-997-9084): The best apple strudels in town and piping hot old-time German pastries.

Rather Sweet Bakery and Café (249 East Main Street; 830-990-0498): Owner and renowned pastry chef Rebecca Rather's out-of-this-universe brownies and famous Big Hair Tarts are okay to eat with coffee in the morning. Or you can try more traditional breakfast fare.

Gear Up

Hill Country Bicycle Works (702 East Main Street; 830-990-2609): The ultimate resource for information on local places to ride and group rides, and for all the bike gear you might need.

Hill Country Outfitters (115 East Main Street; 830-997-3761): Sells fly-fishing and kayaking gear, and guides fishing and paddling trips on area waters.

Refuel

The Auslander Biergarten and Restaurant (323 East Main Street; 830-997-7714; www.theauslander.com): The town's biggest beer selection and the best biergarten, where live music is played every Thursday and Saturday. The food is good, too.

Cotton Gin Restaurant & Lodging (12805 South Highway 16; 830-990-5734; www.cottonginlodging.com): The Black Diamond Buffalo Enchiladas and Gulf Shrimp Ranchero are as delectable as the 1800s log-cabin-style restaurant and cottages, which are surrounded by hokey windmills, herb gardens, and a waterfall.

Cottage Cafe (232 West Main Street; 830-990-1037): This upscale Mediterranean café with outdoor seating provides an escape from the German food and décor of the other restaurants in town—and serves up some of the town's best food.

Bunk

Austin Street Retreat (408 West Austin Street; 866-427-8374; www.austinstreetretreat.com): A restored 1867 home and a barn that sometimes served as the local jail are the centerpieces of this courtyard-adorned property; offers five suites in stone bungalows, each with its own terrace.

Das Keidel Inn (403 East Main Street; 830-997-2297; www.das keidelinn.com): The plot that houses the inn has been in the Keidel family since the founding of Fredericksburg, or so the story goes. Its rooms are furnished like an elegant German country house, with pine furniture and chandeliers.

Full Moon Inn (3234 Luckenbach Road; 800-997-1124; www.full mooninn.com): Rustic luxury in an antique-filled 1860s log cabin (with two rooms and a shared bath) and a former smokehouse turned guest cottage.

Can't Leave?

Nearest airport: San Antonio International, San Antonio, Texas (60 miles)

Primary industries: Hospitality, agriculture, retail, health care

The Midwest/Plains

Carbondale, Illinois

E ven though Illinois has fewer acres of protected public lands than all but two other states, its biggest park
is a doozie. The Shawnee National Forest is a diverse,
420-square-mile spread of lakes, forests, steep hills, rocky
bluffs, and grassy floodplains cobbled together within
seven wilderness areas. Shaped like the silhouette of a
dog, with its nose nudging the Ohio River into Kentucky
on the east and its backside bordering the Mississippi
River and Missouri on the west, it stands on the southern tip of Illinois
at a sort of geographical crossroads—where plant and animal species
from all four corners of the country have converged. On the western
side—less than fifteen miles as the heron flies to the Mississippi—you'll
find Carbondale. Part college town and part major gateway to the park
for bikers, hikers, paddlers, and anglers, it lies ninety miles north of
St. Louis.

Population:
24,806
Action: Mountain
biking, hiking,
paddling, fishing

Carbondale arose out of the rolling, rugged countryside as a whistle stop on the Illinois Central Railroad in the late 1850s and, after the
founding of Carbondale College—now Southern Illinois University—
in 1866, gained a reputation as an educational and cultural center. Just
as the Italiante and Queen Anne homes on West Walnut Street have
remained much the same for the past century, so has the town's
dependence on the school and its 22,000 students as a social and economic engine. The park entered the scene in 1939, when the tract it
covers—mostly former farmland rehabilitated by the Civilian
Conservation Corps in the prior two decades—was designated a
national forest by President Franklin D. Roosevelt. Over the years, it
has evolved into a sprawling recreation area, and many of its highlights
lie close to town.

Just below Carbondale is Little Grand Canyon, a 200-foot-deep box
canyon accessed by a steep 3.6-mile loop trail that descends among

Carbondale is home to Southern Illinois University. (© Southern Illinois University Carbondale)

hardwoods and then climbs up to views of the Mississippi and Big Muddy rivers. Nearly adjacent to the southern border of town is 1,750-acre Cedar Lake and its population of largemouth and spotted bass, carp, walleye, crappie, and sunfish. Its forty miles of shoreline are open for exploration by kayak or canoe. The fourteen-mile out-and-back mountain-biking trail that skirts its western shore and loops around Little Cedar Lake is one of the two prime riding spots in southern Illinois—thanks to its rock chutes and packed-dirt singletrack, running beneath towering boulder formations and interrupted by an occasional creek crossing.

The region's other fat-tire destination, Kinkaid Lake, is just northwest of town in the Shawnee National Forest. Its rocky, rooty singletrack twists sharply with the curves of the lake's spectacular western shore for about fifteen miles before dead-ending. About ten miles to the southwest of Carbondale is Devil's Backbone Park, home to a spiny ridge of rocks overlooking the Mississippi; river pirates once used the rocks as a hideout for raids on unsuspecting boats. The park is also home to the western terminus of the River-to-River Trail, a challenging 160-mile footpath slicing straight across the national forest until it meets the Ohio River. Not a bad hike for a state with so little protected land.

Start the Day

Harbaugh's Café (901 South Illinois Avenue; 618-351-9897): Kids from the college pack this eclectic coffee shop for breakfast.

Longbranch Coffee House (100 East Jackson; 618-529-4488): Artsy organic coffeehouse that serves biscuits and gravy and omelets at breakfast, and handmade pizza for lunch and dinner.

Gear Up

Shawnee Trails Wilderness Outfitter (222 West Freeman; 618-529-2313): The local outdoor outfitter sells everything from backpacks to kayaks.

Carbondale Cycle Shop (303 South Illinois Avenue; 618-549-6863): The largest bike store and repair shop in town, staffed by young local gearheads who clearly spend more time on the trails than in class.

Refuel

Tres Hombres (119 North Washington Street; 618-457-3308): A Tex-Mex joint and one of the top music venues in Carbondale.

Quatro's (218 West Freeman; 618-549-5326; www.quatros.com): This three-decade-old college pizza joint is known for its Chicago-style deep-dish pies.

Bunk

Barton House Bed and Breakfast (1655 North Reed Station Road; 618-457-7717;

Local Legend

Mayberry Arboretum

Walking in the footsteps of Abraham Lincoln isn't as hard as you might think when you're in Carbondale. The twenty-four-acre Mayberry Arboretum at the intersection of South Wall and West Pleasant Hill Road claims to have paving stones once stepped on by Honest Abe. They were collected by the former owner of the property, William Mayberry, who said they came from the town square in Jonesboro, where Lincoln and Stephen A. Douglas debated. You'll also find 20,000 plants—6,000 species—around the paths, picnic tables, and pond at this pastoral site, now owned and preserved by the city.

www.bartonhousebedandbreakfast.com): A well-appointed three-suite bed and breakfast in a farmhouse-style home.

Kite Hill Vineyard Bed and Breakfast (819 Kite Hill Road; 618-684-5072; www.kitehillvineyards.com): A three-room bed and breakfast in a Cape Cod house on a working winery.

Can't Leave?

Nearest airport: Southern Illinois, Carbondale (5 miles)

Primary industries: Education, service, government

Cadillac, Michigan

or a place that shares its name with a famous car brand, Cadillac sure is foot-power friendly. There are so many official pathways, walkways, trails, and trail parks within its confines that you'll be burning more calories than gas. Being such a biking and hiking area makes it a standout adventure destination over many of the resort towns on Lake Michigan, forty-five miles to the west. Not that it doesn't have its share of water. Cadillac envelops all of 1,100-acre Lake Cadillac and the eastern half of 2,500-acre Lake Mitchell. It's also the entry point for the ponds, creeks, and rivers that make up the hundreds of miles of waterways in the Manistee section of the Huron-Manistee National Forest, a preserve that covers an area ten times the size of Detroit.

Population:
10,167
Action: Mountain biking, cross-country and downhill skiing, fishing

Like so many other northern Michigan communities, Cadillac was established in the late nineteenth century as a lumber outpost. To transport logs from Lake Mitchell to the trains stationed by the shores of Lake Cadillac, the local mills dug a quarter-mile-long connecting canal that is still used by recreational boaters. (It has been widened and dredged several times over the years.) After the trees inevitably vanished, the town became a center for industry, and manufacturing is still the largest money-maker for the local economy. As a result, the city center has a refreshingly less touristy feel than other towns. When you browse among the shops that fill the two- and three-story brick buildings downtown, you're more likely to find kitchen supplies and furniture than fudge or T-shirts.

More out-of-towners seem to come to Cadillac in the winter. Throngs of snowmobile riders are drawn to the deep snow that covers the 137 miles of local trails and to the North American Snowmobile Festival, held each year on Lake Cadillac. You'll also find alpine skiers heading for the thirty-one trails on the nearby Caberfae Peaks ski area,

Caberfae Peaks in Cadillac, Michigan offers alpine skiers thirty-one trails and the tallest ski hill in the state. (© Caberfae Peaks Ski and Golf Resort)

which has a 1,545-foot ski hill—the tallest in the state. Next to the resort is the 5.5-mile Mackenzie Pathway, one of the handful of classic, groomed nordic-skiing routes the town boasts. Mackenzie meanders through quiet hardwood forests and by Johnson Creek, and, like most cross-country ski trails in the area, it's open for mountain biking in the summer. An alternate popular dual-use path is the Cadillac Pathway in the Pere Marquette State Forest, an eleven-mile track of two loops—one hilly, one relatively flat—attached by a steep two-mile connector. Other biking choices in Cadillac worth pedaling are the rolling, twenty-six-mile stretch of the North Country Trail that approaches town; the mostly cinder and gravel, 100-mile White Pine Rail Trail; and the 7.5-mile bike path around Lake Cadillac.

In summer, people who don't bring a bike with them almost invariably come with a fishing rod in hand. You can cast for walleye, perch, and trout in Lakes Cadillac and Mitchell, and the outlying rivers are also fertile angling waters. The 334-acre Mitchell State Park in town is home to the Carl T. Johnson Hunting and Fishing Center—a regional sporting-history museum with an exhibit hall on local wildlife, an aquarium stocked with native fish, and a 2.5-mile woodchip nature trail. Yes, yet another trail to walk.

Start the Day

World Perk Internet Café (5936 East M-55; 231-775-4677): Espresso house at the Pine Chata Resort on the shore of Lake Mitchell.

Terrace Room Restaurant (7880 Mackinaw Trail; 231-775-9947; www.mcguiresresort.com): Dining room at McGuire's Resort; serves buffet breakfast on Sundays.

Gear Up

McClain Cycle & Fitness (311 North Mitchell; 231-775-6161): The only bike shop in town; rents and sells bikes.

McGuire's Resort (7880 Mackinaw Trail; 800-634-7302): Grooms ten kilometers of its own nordic trails; its ski shop rents cross-country skis to be used on any of the local trails and also sells cross-country gear.

Refuel

Maggie's Tavern (523 North Mitchell Street; 231-775-1810): Old-time family restaurant.

Lakeside Charlies (301 South Mitchell Drive; 231-775-5332): A pub by the shore of Lake Mitchell. For live music, order your food from the bar, Crabby Charlies.

Hermann's European Café (214 North Mitchell Street; 231-775-9563): Select a creation by Austrian chef Hermann Suhs from his chalkboard menu—and be sure to save room for one of his pastries.

Local Legend

The Canal

The 0.3-mile canal connecting Lake Mitchell and Lake Cadillac was designated a state historic landmark by the Michigan Historical Commission because of its unique role in the vitality of the community. But it's unique in another way, as well: it freezes before the two lakes every year—usually in late November—but once they freeze, it thaws out and stays largely open for the rest of the season. No one in town can tell you why exactly. Does the current become swifter? Does the weight of the ice on the lakes force warmer water beneath the surface to bubble into the canal? Is it some cruel practical joke by aliens? You decide.

The Wild Side

The Manistee River

If you can't get out West for a fly-fishing trip, your next-best bet may be the long, lazy Manistee River, where the abundance of hungry trout will put you in a Rockies state of mind. Long a traveling route for Native Americans, it's more than 170 miles long, flowing south from near the town of Mancelona in the north-center of the Lower Peninsula, taking a westward turn before reaching Cadillac, and heading west through two dams before draining into Lake Michigan. The sandy-bottomed upper half is the more fertile stretch, but the lower river, near the lake, is also steelhead and salmon territory.

Bunk

Cadillac Sands Resort (Routes 115 and 55; 800-647-2637; www.cadillacsands .com): Relatively inexpensive lodgings on the shore of Lake Cadillac; rents snowmobiles.

Sunset Shores Resort (1231 Sunnyside Drive; 231-876-3700; www.sunsetshores resort.net): An upscale condo complex on the south shore of Lake Cadillac.

McGuire's Resort (7880 Mackinaw Trail; 800-634-7302; www.mcguires resort.com): Resort on its own 300 acres. Take a ride on its horse-drawn sleigh in winter.

Can't Leave?

Nearest airport: Cherry Capital, Traverse City, Michigan (35 miles)

Primary industries: Manufacturing, health care, tourism

Petoskey, Michigan

ichigan probably isn't the first place that comes to mind when you think of romantic beachside sunsets, but after a clear evening in Petoskey, it might be. The Caribbean has nothing over the view from town as the sun extinguishes into Lake Michigan behind the Creamsicle horizon. Couple that with the back-in-time feel of the artsy downtown Gaslight District, the long beach walks, and the views of Little Traverse Bay from the top of sandy Old Baldy, and you've got one of the most romantic spots in the Midwest. The recreational options aren't too shabby either. You can fish on the fertile waterworld of lakes and rivers in and around town, hike in the local state park, bike on hundreds of miles of nearby trails, and even alpine ski on some of the most famed and best groomed resorts in the region.

Population: 6,198
Action: Hiking, paddling, fishing, road biking, cross-country and downhill skiing

When Petoskey, named after an Ottowa Indian chief, was established in 1879, it thrived on the lumber trade. Legend has it that when Mrs. O'Leary's cow left much of Chicago in ruins earlier that decade, the city was largely reconstructed with wood from this part of Michigan, on the northwestern tip of the Lower Peninsula. Not long afterward, tourists began flocking to Petoskey and never stopped coming. Given its natural beauty and cool summers on the shore of Little Traverse Bay, about an hour north of Traverse City, it's easy to see why. The most famous summer resident was a young Ernest Hemingway, who came every year to stay at his family's home on Walloon Lake until he was in his early twenties.

Exploring Petoskey and its surroundings is easiest on bike, given the expansive network of cycling paths there. The local shoreline trail along Lake Michigan—where you'll find plenty of company from runners, walkers, and inline skaters—winds through the two local waterfront parks and heart of downtown. It then expands into the

Petoskey, Michigan sits at the mouth of the Bear River, a mostly flat, slow-moving stretch of water laden with brown trout and ripe for a quiet paddle. (© Petoskey-Harbor Springs-Boyne Country Visitors Bureau)

nearly completed, mostly paved, twenty-nine-mile Little Traverse Wheelway. From the Wheelway, you can jump onto road routes that lead all the way to the eastern shore of Lake Huron and as far north as Mackinaw City.

The hiking options are just as diverse. The town is a stop on the North Country Trail, a 4,600-mile footpath that stretches from the Adirondacks of New York to North Dakota. A slightly more modest trek is the 2.5-mile Portage Trail in the 300-acre Petoskey State Park; the Portage Trail passes by the park's mile-long beach and two campgrounds, and it connects with a half-mile trail up the Old Baldy dune. While you're there, stop to collect a few Petoskey stones, pieces of shiny, fossilized coral roughly 350 million years old—and now the state rock of Michigan—that can be found only in this area.

Even if you never hit the trails around town, there's plenty of fishing, swimming, and paddling on the local waterways to keep you blissfully busy. Petoskey is surrounded by several small lakes that feed into Lake Michigan, and it sits at the mouth of the Bear River, a mostly flat slow-moving stretch of water laden with brown trout and ripe for a quiet paddle. As if the clear waters don't produce enough fish, the nearby Oden State Fish Hatchery releases a million browns and brookies each year. Traverse Bay, as well as the small lakes like Walloon, Charlevoix, and Crooked, are fished for smallmouth bass, walleye, pike, perch, and rainbows.

In the winter, thoughts turn to ice fishing and cross-country skiing on the trails that were used for biking and hiking during the warm months. Out-of-towners also come to the area for the three local ski mountains. Legendary Boyne Mountain, all fifty-two trails and 500 vertical feet of it, is the site of the first quad and high-speed six-person chairlifts in the United States, and it was the first resort in the country to hire Stein Eriksen, an Olympic gold medalist and the godfather of instruction in North America. The resort was established by skiing pioneer Everett Kircher. Nearly similar in size—though not quite in reputation—are Boyne Highlands and Nub's Nob. Even with the

The Wild Side

Thorne Swift Nature Preserve

The thirty-acre Thorne Swift Nature Preserve won't impress you with its size, but it will with its diversity of plants and wildlife among its dunes, beachfront, and cedar swamps. Created in 1981 when the land was donated to the Little Traverse Conservancy, it harbors critters like frogs, great blue herons, and foxes among its forest and marshy areas, along with delicate showy ladyslippers. You can enjoy all the preserve's plants, animals, and habitats when you follow its tiny network of nature trails, which total about a mile in length. It makes for a quick, pleasant afternoon's escape.

Local Legend

Ernest Hemingway

Petoskey doesn't have much in common with Key West, except for bragging rights as former stomping grounds for Ernest Hemingway. Papa Hemingway summered on 4,000-acre Walloon Lake for most of his youth and set *The Nick Adams Stories* in the area. The Little Traverse History Museum Center celebrates the author with an exhibit on his favorite haunts and the local places described in his works. The people in Petoskey claim that he learned to fish and hunt when he stayed at Windemere, the Hemingway cottage, which still stands. It's still owned by the Hemingway family and isn't open to the public.

powder-seeking crowds at this time of year, Petoskey takes on an even more intimate feel than it usually has. The restaurants in the snow-coated nineteenth-century buildings on Lake Street are quieter, the shop decorations are more festive, and the woods are more inviting. Overall the local scenery looks borrowed from a classic holiday card.

Start the Day

Horizon Books (319 East Mitchell Street; 231-347-2590): An independent bookstore and coffee bar that can compete with the big-name megashops. Opens at 8 AM.

Big Apple Bagels of Petoskey (1125 North U.S. Highway 31; 231-348-1110): Not quite a slice of Manhattan, but by far the best bagel joint in the area.

Gear Up

Bearcub Outfitters (321 East Lake Street; 231-439-9500): An exceptional selection of outdoorsy gear for dogs—and two-footed creatures who hike and camp.

Bahnhof Ski Shops (1300 Bay View Drive; 231-347-2112): There are three Bahnhof shops, one each in Breckenridge, Park City, and Petoskey. They sell a full array of ski gear in the winter and kayak accessories in the summer.

Bear River Canoe Livery (2517 McDougall Road; 231-347-9038): They'll transport you upriver for a leisurely paddle. You can't miss the stopping point—just look for the sign that says, "You are back, pull canoe out of water."

Refuel

City Park Grill (432 East Lake Street; 231-347-0101): A fixture for almost a century in the heart of the Gaslight District, this is the place to grab a steak and listen to live acoustic music.

Mitchell Street Pub and Café (426 East Mitchell Street; 231-347-1801): Pick a song from the jukebox and order a Pub Burger—the tastiest in town.

Bunk

Inn at Bay Harbor (3600 Village Harbor Drive, Bay Harbor; 231-439-4000): Opened in 1998, but designed in the nineteenth-century grand hotel style, this eighty-seven-room resort is decorated with cottage-style furniture and locally commissioned art.

Stafford's Perry Hotel (100 Lewis Street; 231-347-4000; www .staffords.com): The first hotel in Petoskey to be built by brick—and lo and behold, it still stands after more than a century, a romantic icon of a bygone era. Ask for one of the Imperial or Arlington guest rooms, for views of the water.

Can't Leave?

Nearest airport: Cherry Capital, Traverse City, Michigan (60 miles)

Primary industries: Service, health care, education

Saugatuck, Michigan

Population: 1,040

Action: Fishing, road biking, hiking, cross-country skiing

For nearly a century, Midwestern artists have flocked to Saugatuck to be inspired by its dunes, magnificent white beach, and pastoral surrounding countryside. Its central location—within three hours of Chicago, Detroit, Indianapolis, and Milwaukee—doesn't hurt either. But for bikers, hikers, and anglers who come in almost equal numbers, the portrait-perfect background is merely an added bonus.

The first stop in town should be to Oval Beach. To fully savor the experience, get there the way people have been doing it for more than 150 years: by boat. Separated from the rest of Saugatuck by the Kalamazoo River, the beach can be accessed by car if you drive south across the bridge to neighboring Douglas and then head north, but the more adventuresome option is to take the hand-cranked public ferry directly across the water and climb over the dunes to the shore. What will unfold before you is a long, undeveloped stretch of white sand rising out of blue Lake Michigan and buffered from civilization by the grassy bluffs directly above it.

Even though Saugatuck made its name in the mid-1800 as a lumber town—and when the trees were gone, as a fruit-growing town—it doubled as a tourist escape almost from the start. The well-heeled from Michigan, Illinois, and even Missouri came to enjoy the cool summer breezes off the lake by inhabiting many of the Italianate and Greek Revival downtown homes. In the early twentieth century, a handful of artists created a summer school that has since evolved into the flourishing Ox-Bow School of Art and Artists' Residency, affiliated with the Art Institute of Chicago. Creative types get their juices flowing by spending time at the beach, on the river, in the thick forests of pine and hardwoods, and in the rolling farmlands garnished by wildflowers. Outdoorsy types do, too.

A hand-cranked public ferry takes visitors from Saugatuck across the Kalamazoo River to Lake Michigan's Oval Beach. (© David F. Wisse)

The road biking in the area makes for some of the most spectacular in the state. Relatively traffic-free, local loops include the twenty-five-mile round-trip ride to the larger, tulip-filled town of Holland, established on the Black River to the north by Dutch settlers. For the best perspective on Saugatuck, though, take the 282 steps that lead to the pinnacle of the towering, tree-speckled dune called Mount Baldhead, beside Oval Beach. From there, you can look down upon the boats in the town's protected harbor and the sunbathers on the magnificent ribbon of sand below. For a more secluded experience, there's the 1,000-acre Saugatuck Dunes State Park. Several miles of trails within it weave among the tall sandy slopes and hills and along its two and a half miles of Lake Michigan shoreline, including a hardly used public beach, accessed by a half-mile hike.

In the winter, cross-country skiers come to the park for its ungroomed paths and also to make tracks on the roughly twelve miles of trails in the Allegan State Game Area, about ten miles east along the

The Wild Side

Lake Michigan

Lake Michigan is the second-largest Great Lake by volume and the only one completely within the United States; it is also the fifth-largest lake in the world. It has 1,600 miles of shoreline, but no parts are more spectacular than the stretch in sandy Saugatuck. And there are few, if any, better jumping-off points for adventure on its waters (or stopping points *after* an adventure). You can easily make a day of sailing, windsurfing, boating, paddling, or fishing. There are nearly 100 species of fish within the Lake Michigan depths–which reaches up to a whopping 925 feet–from alewife to carp to northern pike to walleye.

Kalamazoo River. This 50,000-acre preserve is spiderwebbed with creeks and streams, and in the summer, paddlers will make the lazy float from it to Saugatuck, passing anglers stalking trout, pike, salmon, and steelhead. The bounty of underwater critters, like walleye, muskie, and largemouth bass, lurking within Lake Michigan near Saugatuck is legendary, and you'll have about as little trouble finding a guide service as you will finding a painting of the area landscape.

Start the Day

Kalico Kitchen Restaurant (312 Ferry Street, Douglas; 269-857-2678; www .kalikokitchenrestaurant.com): Hearty breakfasts served all day at this down-home restaurant.

Uncommon Grounds (127 Hoffman Street; 269-857-3333; www.uncommon groundscafe.com): All of the coffee is roasted on site at this colorful café with a garden patio.

Gear Up

Big Lake Outfitters (640 Water Street; 269-857-4762): A fishing shop on the Kalamazoo that rents canoes and bikes and charters fishing boats.

Running Rivers, Inc. (Wade's Bayou Memorial Park, Douglas; 269-673-3698): Rents kayaks for paddling trips down the Kalamazoo and will provide guide service if you want it.

Refuel

Saugatuck Drug Store (201 Butler Street; 269-857-2300): After more than eight decades, this store still operates a soda fountain in back during the summer, where they serve a mean chocolate malt.

Wally's Bar and Grill (128 Hoffman Street; 616-857-5641): The social, friendly place in town to get a margarita, fresh perch, and some live music.

Boathouse of Saugatuck (449 Water Street; 269-857-2888): On the river, this restaurant serves Mexican and American food and has a happy hour every day.

Bunk

Lake Shore Resort (2885 Lakeshore Drive; 269-857-7121; www.lakeshore resortsaugatuck.com): A thirty-room resort and the only place in town with its own beach on Lake Michigan. Open May to mid-October.

Rosemont Inn (83 Lakeshore Drive; 888-767-3666; www.rosemontinn.com): A romantic fourteen-room bed-and-breakfast with fireplaces in the rooms and views of the lake, just off the beach.

Sherwood Forest Bed and Breakfast (938 Center Street; 800-838-1246; www.sherwoodforestbandb.com): A Victorian home less than a block from the beach. Check out the mural at the bottom of the pool—it depicts a sunken, coral-encrusted Greek ship surrounded by tropical fish. This is an art town, after all.

Can't Leave?

Nearest airport: Gerald R. Ford International, Grand Rapids, Michigan (50 miles)

Primary industries: Tourism, manufacturing, marine services

Local Legend

Saugatuck Dune Rides

In 1954, twenty-one-year-old Ron Jousma bought a tract of dunes in Saugatuck near Goshorn Lake and pimped his 1942 Ford convertible into a dune buggy for paying passengers. About seven years later, he added a couple of trucks, and the area's famed Dune Schooners were born. You can take a thirty-five- to forty-minute ride among the Saugatuck's immense grass-covered dunes in one of the company's Schooners. It's part of the experience of coming to town. Dune Schooners is open from April to October.

Bemidji, Minnesota

Population:

13,296

Action: Paddling, hiking, mountain biking, fishing, cross-country skiing

Hundreds of woodsy hamlets from Washington to Maine say that they're the true birthplace of Paul Bunyan. So even though Bemidji has an eighteen-foot flannel-shirted statue of the big guy, standing next to his blue ox, Babe, the town's claim to fame is hardly unique. What isn't disputed, though, is the fact that the water-pocked wilderness around town is the birthplace of an even bigger American legend: the Mississippi River. The Father of Waters starts its 2,552-mile journey to the Gulf of Mexico at tiny Lake Itasca, trickling north—yes, north—about thirty miles to Bemidji, the first real settlement on its banks. Getting the chance to rock-hop across the shallow headwaters of the Mississippi is just one of many outdoor adventures at the town's doorstep—along with hiking, paddling, fishing, cross-country skiing, and even dogsledding within the hundreds of thousands of acres of nearby preserves.

Bemidji is wedged between Lake Irving and Lake Bemidji in the heart of northern Minnesota, about a five-hour drive from Minneapolis. It was settled in the late nineteenth century as a trading and lumber outpost, but even then the early townsfolk saw its potential as a magnet for summer vacationers. By the early twentieth century they had begun actively promoting tourism. Now it's as much of a college town as an outdoor getaway, home to Bemidji State University and three other schools. The students have brought with them a liberal, creative vibe, embodied by the sculpture displays on the concrete sidewalks, the crowds that pack popular summer-stock theater, and the impressive local exhibits shown at the campus's community arts center.

Stroll among the shops, restaurants, and coffeehouses downtown and take in the impressive historic old homes on Lake Boulevard, and

The headwaters of the Mississippi River can be found at Itasca State Park, near Bemidji, Minnesota. (© Minnesota Department of Natural Resources)

you'll practically forget that you're surrounded by untamed wilderness. Practically. Fringing the eastern edge of town past Lake Bemidji is the 666,000-acre Chippewa National Forest, where you could explore a different lake each day for almost four years without repeating one. That's a lot of water for walleye and northern pike. Also spread among the forest's thick stands of birch, oak, and aspen are 900 miles of rivers, with nine designated canoe routes, and 300 miles of trails—half of which are open to cross-country skiing in the winter. The average snowfall is forty-one inches, giving enough cover to keep people on nordic skis from January through March and to support the annual Paul Bunyan Sled Dog Challenge each February. The Challenge comprises a series of races and provides a townwide excuse to celebrate outdoors. People take their cold-weather sports here very seriously. Bemidji is even considered a talent factory for world-class curlers.

Not that the locals take it easy in the summer. They can swim in Lake Bemidji or cast a line from one of its two fishing piers—that is, if

Local Legend

The Continental Divide

Italian explorer Giacomo Constantino Beltrami came to the region around Bemidji in the 1820s and mistakenly declared Lake Julia, just north of town to be the headwaters of the Mississippi. Little did he know—so the story goes—that the spot where he stood, twelve miles north of town at an elevation of 1,400 feet, actually marked the northern Continental Divide. All waters north of it flow into the Hudson River. All waters south of it flow into the Gulf of Mexico. A historical marker now sits at the site.

they don't feel like fishing on one of the other 400 lakes within twenty-five miles of downtown. They can bike the Paul Bunyan Trail, a 100-mile, mostly paved path, to Brainerd. Or they can simply hike the 1.5-mile loop inside Itasca State Park that leads to the headwaters of the Mississippi—which is more of a quiet, tea-colored creek at this point than a full-blown river—and contemplate whether big Paul ever made his way over there after he was born.

Start the Day

Raphaels Bakery Café (319 Minnesota Avenue; 218-759-2015; www.gr8buns .com): Breakfast starts at 6 AM and includes eggs, hash browns, and french toast made from the bakery's fresh bread.

Cabin Coffeehouse (214 Third Street; 218-444-2899): The stage in back of this espresso shop is a popular music venue with local college kids.

Gear Up

Home Place Bike & Ski Shop (524 Paul Bunyan Drive SE; 218-751-3456): A bike shack that also sells snowshoes and cross-country skis.

Itasca Sports Rental (20758 County Road 2, Shevlin; 218-266-2150): A bike- and boat-rental shop and camp store inside the Itasca State Park.

Refuel

Brigid's Cross (317 Beltrami Avenue; 218-444-0567; www.brigids irishpub.com): An Irish pub with Guinness on tap and traditional pub grub on the menu.

Peppercorn Restaurant (1813 Paul Bunyan Drive; 218-759-2794; www.peppercornrestaurant.com): An upscale steakhouse. Order the walleye.

Bunk

A Place in the Woods Resort (11380 Turtle River Lake Road NE; 218-586-2345; www.aplaceinthewoodsresort.com): Twelve modern log cabins with fireplaces, hidden by spruce, pine, and oak on Turtle River Lake.

Ruttger's Birchmont Lodge (7598 Bemidji Road NE; 218-444-3463; www.ruttger.com): A lodge, built in 1921, and cottages on a property with a 1,700-foot natural beach on the northern end of Lake Bemidji. The dining room is closed fall and winter.

Can't Leave?

Nearest airport: Bemidji Regional (5 miles)

Primary industries: Education, paper manufacturing, health care

Brainerd, Minnesota

Population:
13,684

Action: Fishing, hiking, mountain and road biking, cross-country skiing

In a constellation of sparkling waters around Brainerd, Minnesota, you'll find a lake for every single day of the year—and 100 more. The Brainerd Lakes region, just over two hours from Minneapolis-St. Paul, boasts 465 sapphire lakes within a fifty-mile radius, nearly all of them linked by a thick forest of pine trees.

The equally impressive number of golf holes (520) and lodgings (130) illuminates the facts that Brainerd, which lies at the geographic center of Minnesota and is bisected by the Mississippi River, is no longer a wilderness town and that development is beginning to run rampant. But the town remains one of the Midwest's best gateways for soft outdoor adventure, from fishing easily accessed lakes, pedaling along paved pathways, and piloting a Chris-Craft to a dockside dinner to cross-country skiing through an arboretum and ice skating natural rinks that are frozen solid from November through April. For really soft adventure, there's even a "Mini-Himalaya" ride at This Old Farm, an amusement park graced with a twenty-six-foot tall, animated statue of Babe the Blue Ox's boss. (If that statue seems familiar, it might be because parts of the 1996 movie Fargo were based on a fictional version of Brainerd, one of several Minnesota towns to promote the legend of the oversized lumberjack.)

Paul Bunyan is also the namesake of a 100-mile trail that leads from Brainerd to Bemidji, Minnesota; more than half is now coated with asphalt, though there are soft flanks for knee-concerned runners. The trail is not only a nod to Brainerd's logging industry, but also the town's railroad-oriented growth, as it's built upon the original line of the Burlington Northern Railroad. As one of the country's longest rail-trails, the Paul Bunyan connects more than a dozen towns in central Minnesota. It offers a mix of trailside creature comforts and quiet spots,

The Brainerd Lakes region of Minnesota boasts 465 lakes, nearly all of them linked by a thick forest of pine trees. (© explorebrainerdlakes.com)

and it's a good spot for flat cycling and cross-country skiing. But be prepared for snowmobiles, the only motorized travel allowed on the trail.

For slightly more challenging terrain, mountain bikers head to the 14,800-acre Pillsbury State Forest, located ten miles northeast of Brainerd and crisscrossed with more than twenty miles of rolling gravel roads and grassy trails. The forest is also one of many options for cross-country skiing and snowshoeing in the area; adjacent are the forty kilometers of the Pine Beach Trails, while at French Rapids Cross-Country Ski Area, sixteen kilometers wind along the Mississippi River. (On the subject of rapids, there are some Class I riffles along the Mississippi, creating a swift flatwater paddling site. The stretch from Brainerd to a takeout at Little Falls is just over thirty-six miles.) At the winter-buried gardens of the Northland Arboretum, or the Arb, there are twenty kilometers of nordic trails, five of them lighted for night skiing. The Arb is the site of the Lumberjack Jaunt, an annual series of sixteen-kilometer, six-kilometer, and one-kilometer skinny-ski races, and the Sour Grapes Half-Marathon, started by a group of local runners who had lost the lottery for spots in Minnesota's more famous Grandma's Marathon.

Gull Lake, twelve miles north of Brainerd, rounds out nearby winter fun with a small, twelve-run downhill ski and snowboard area and the yearly Brainerd Jaycees $150,000 Ice Fishing Extravaganza that attracts more than 12,000 anglers with its hefty pot. If that sounds too crowded, keep in mind that, summer and winter, there are 464 other lakes from which to choose.

Start the Day

Coco Moon (601 Laurel Street; 218-825-7955): Coffeehouse with free wireless Internet access.

371 Diner (14901 Edgewood Drive North, Baxter; 218-829-3356): You'll come for the full breakfast and stay for the malts.

Gear Up

Easy Rider (415 Washington Street; 218-829-5516): Road-bike and mountain-bike rentals, plus skis, snowboards, canoes, kayaks, and clothing.

Reeds Family Outdoor Outfitters (Highway 371 North, Baxter; 218-824-7333): A sprawling, 40,000-square-foot superstore with fishing and camping gear and clothing.

Refuel

Eclectic Café (717 Laurel Street; 218-825-4880): Minnesota's Schell microbrews, plus organic, fair-trade, shade-grown coffee, panini, and sushi on Saturdays; live music most Friday and Saturday nights.

Morey's Market & Grille (1650 Highway 371 North; 218-829-8248): Seafood specialties from chowder and Scandinavian caviar to walleye, lobster, and crab, plus a gourmet market.

The Wild Side

Scuba Diving

Scuba diving in Minnesota? You betcha. It happens at Cuyuna State Recreational Area, where more than fifty open-pit mines have filled up with clear, blue-green water since their abandonment in the mid-twentieth century. Through the Minnesota School of Diving (218-829-5953), you can dive among sunfish, underwater mining equipment, and submerged road beds and trees. The visibility is up to fifty feet. Plus, the name, Cuyuna, has a faintly tropical ring, doesn't it?

Last Turn Saloon (214 South Eighth Street; 218-829-4856): Local watering hole with inexpensive soups, sandwiches, and seafood.

Bunk

Gull Lake Recreation Area (10867 Gull Lake Drive; 218-829-3334, www.mvp.usace.army.mil): Thirty-nine campsites, fourteen of them walk-in, near Gull River, the Gull Dam, and Gull Lake.

Lost Lake Lodge (7965 Lost Lake Road, Lakeshore; 218-963-2681; www.lostlake.com): Thirteen private cabins on the Gull Lake Narrows, with canoes, kayaks, fishing boats and tackle, and a fish-cleaning station; reasonable rates include breakfast and dinner.

Cragun's (11,000 Craguns Drive; 800-272-4867; www.craguns .com): Megaresort on Gull Lake; 200-plus rooms and cabins, along with three golf courses, a fishing marina, spa, sports center, and four restaurants.

Can't Leave?

Nearest airport: Brainerd Lakes Regional (5 miles)

Primary industries: Tourism, manufacturing, forest and wood products, health care, building, architecture, finance, technology

Ely, Minnesota

Population: 3,633

Action: Canoeing, fishing, cross-country skiing, hiking, mountain biking

If it simply had been called the Boundary Waters Wilderness, things might be different. We might imagine a thick swath of trees and waters somewhere along the Canadian border, impressive but often impenetrable. But add the words "Canoe Area" to the official title of this 1.1-million-acre chunk of the Superior National Forest, studded with more than 1,000 lakes, and it's like cracking open a can of adventure. We can now picture the dip of a paddle into a dark, glassy surface, our canoe laden with tents, fishing poles, and tin coffee cups for a week, a month, or longer.

At the end of the road (pretty much all the roads in northeast Minnesota) and poking its nose into the Boundary Waters Canoe Area Wilderness is the town of Ely, where canoe outfitters outnumber service stations and where the chamber of commerce is found in an old Finnish lumberjack log cabin. The town, on Miner's and Shagawa lakes, is home to the International Wolf Center, while the tagline of its weekly newspaper, the Ely Echo, is "The Voice of the Wilderness." Ely has called itself the natural-resource Mall of America, but such a nickname automatically carries indoor connotations. Everything here revolves around the outdoors: canoeing, hiking, and fishing in the summer, and cross-country skiing and dogsledding in the winter, when the Boundary Waters is blanketed by snow and ice. You duck inside to grab some last-minute gear, to down your last fix of espresso or microbrew before leaving civilization, to forget the sound of mosquitoes and the smell of bug spray, or to remember what it's like to sleep on a feather-filled pillow surrounded by walls instead of wilderness.

Wilderness wasn't always so chic in Ely, and in some ways, the word still causes a bit of discomfort for a few townspeople, who remember that the town long depended on logging and mining to making a liv-

The outfitters of Ely, Minnesota specialize in helping visitors gear up for trips to the Boundary Waters Canoe Area Wilderness. (© Ely Chamber of Commerce)

ing. In 1888, the same year Ely was incorporated as a village, the Chandler Mine began shipping iron ore out of town on the Duluth and Iron Range trains. The mines employed as many as 1,200 people at one time, and there were twenty-six saloons and six brothels in Ely, according to miners' reports. The last mine shut down in 1967, around the same time that conservation groups were discovering the wealth of wilderness in the Boundary Waters Canoe Area. When Congress officially attached the word "wilderness" to the Boundary Waters in 1978, thereby shutting down heavy-industry access to the area, Ely residents strongly protested. And though tourism has since replaced many of the lost dollars, there are still op-ed pieces in the *Ely Echo* that sound less like the voice of the wilderness than a cry for mining's return.

The Boundary Waters adjoins an additional million acres of canoe trails in Ontario's Quetico Provinical Park, which can make deciding upon a trip a dizzying enterprise. You can avoid ice, blackflies, mosquitoes and most crowds—even on the classic routes—by going for a week in May or September. The thirty- to fifty-mile Knife Lake Loop features a chain of twenty-nine lakes linked by almost as many portages. Nearly every lake in the Boundary Waters has dinner waiting for you—walleye, northern pike, large- and smallmouth bass, and lake trout whose size may exceed that of your frying pan. For the really remote stuff in paddling and fishing, you can arrange for a fly-in canoe trip with one of Ely's many outfitters.

Angling continues into the winter with ice-fishing shacks. Cross-country skiing trails spiderweb in nearly every direction throughout the Superior National Forest and frozen-over Boundary Waters, where you'll find the nearly eighteen-mile long Banadad Trail. As many of the canoe-oriented accommodations remain open year-round, its possible to embark on a lodge-to-lodge trip. Legs still too cramped from the summer's canoeing? Book a dogsledding excursion, during which man's best friend will pull you to some of the area's best meals and accommodations.

But if you've done Ely right, you've already stretched out those legs by hiking and mountain biking before the snow fell. In the Kawishiwi Ranger District lie the fourteen-mile Angleworm Trail and the twenty-two-mile Kekekabic/Snowbank Trail, both ideal for a backpacking trip, while twelve miles of hilly loops in the Hidden Valley Recreation Area, a nordic center, create scenic mountain-biking trails.

Local Legend

The Root Beer Lady

On a backcountry canoe trip in the middle of summer, few things taste better than a frosty bottle of root beer—but the Boundary Waters forbids bottles, and carrying ice is impractical. Enter Dorothy Molter, who lived for fifty-six years in a cabin on Knife Lake and made 12,000 bottles of root beer a year for passing canoeists. Though the Root Beer Lady died more than twenty years ago, you can still buy a bottle of the ice-cold elixir, along with root beer soap, root beer recipes, and "root beerings" at Ely's Dorothy Molter Museum, open May to September.

Start the Day

Northern Grounds Café (117 North Central Avenue; 218-365-2460): Coffee, bagels, and eggs.

Front Porch Coffee & Tea (343 East Sheridan Street; 218-365-2326): Muffins, coffee drinks, and live music on the front porch in the evenings.

Gear Up

Boundary Waters Outfitters (629 Kawishiwi Trail; 218-365-4879): Guided and fly-in canoe and fishing trips, plus outfitting services for self-guided excursions.

Wintergreen Dog Sledding (218-365-6022): Lodge-to-lodge or camping dogsledding trips, from three to four days.

Refuel

Chainsaw Sisters Saloon (1414 North Grassy Road; 218-343-6840): Ice-cold beers, candy bars, chips, and "generator burgers" in an electricity-free outpost eighteen miles north of Ely.

Ely Steak House (216 East Sheridan Street; 218-365-7412): Kansas City steaks, prime rib, and fish, plus darts and foosball in the cocktail lounge.

Burntside Lodge (2755 Burntside Lodge Road; 218-365-3894): Overlook Burntside Lake while dining on walleye with mushroom, walnut, and wine sauce or caramelized-onion steak.

Bunk

Adventure Inn (1145 East Sheridan Street; 218-365-3140; www.ely -motel.com): Affordable, green-minded and pet-friendly motel with newly remodeled rooms.

Grand Ely Lodge (400 North Pioneer Road; 218-365-6565; www .grandelylodge.com): A full-service hotel with sixty-one rooms on Shagawa Lake, one mile from downtown.

Burntside Lodge (2755 Burntside Lodge Road; 218-365-3894; www.burntside.com): On the National Register of Historic Places, this lodge has twenty-one lakeside cabins and a marina on twelve-mile long Burntside Lake.

Can't Leave?

Nearest airport: Duluth International, Duluth, Minnesota (77 miles)

Primary industries: Tourism, logging, mining

The Wild Side

The Border Route Trail

When it's completed, the North Country National Scenic Trail, 4,600 miles of interlinked footpaths in seven states, will be the longest hiking trail in the country. Part of it will be the Border Route Trail, a sixty-five-mile-long route paralleling the Canadian border, northeast of Ely. And with sixteen campsites along the trail (most built for canoeists and therefore near bodies of water) the Border Route makes an excellent multiday hike. Plan for seven to eight days and a rugged, narrow trip, as trees felled in the "Big Blow" storm of 1999 continue to impact conditions.

Lanesboro, Minnesota

Population: 767
Action: Road biking, fishing, cross-country skiing, canoeing

A century ago, the railroad brought prosperity to Lanesboro, and today, its remains do—in the form of the spectacular Root River State Trail, a forty-two-mile paved rail-trail through Minnesota's verdant Bluff Country. It's used by throngs of road bikers in the summer and smaller crowds of cross-country skiers in the winter, and Lanesboro has become its undisputed focal point in recent years. As a result, the town has undergone an impressive rebirth. The old Victorian homes in this very laid-back and friendly Midwestern village are as clean-cut and cared for as the lawns and hedges in front of them, and the bustle among the shops downtown stays vibrant and steady on weekends almost throughout the year. The town caters to visitors from Minneapolis-St. Paul ninety miles to the northwest, and other outdoorsy types from outlying areas looking for a relaxing escape.

The bike path itself largely follows the mostly flat Root River, crossing more than forty-six bridges as it passes through farmlands and stunning, chalky limestone bluffs. Its western trailhead lies in Fountain, and from there its course winds roughly eleven miles southeast before leading into Lanesboro. Over the next thirty-one miles, the river begins to straighten, the Root River Valley flattens, and the trail intersects with five other towns among pastures and woodlands before terminating in Houston, in the bottom right-hand corner of the state. None of the other stops are quite as inviting as Lanesboro, though. Settled in the 1850s, the town became a center for agriculture, lumber, and locally quarried limestone before industry petered out in the 1930s. Now the main revenue source is tourism. Fortunately, Lanesboro has resisted the siren's song of chain stores and cheesy knickknack shops and maintained its stately dignity while catering to visitors.

Bicycling the Root River Trail. (© Explore Minnesota Tourism)

If you decide to rest your weary legs after a day or two of riding, the South Branch of the Root River begs to be canoed—or better yet, tubed. A handful of outfitting companies will drive you to the put-ins west of town, so you can spend the better part of a day floating beneath the area's breathtaking bluffs on the surprisingly chilly, but refreshing, water. The fishing on the area's nutrient-rich rivers and side streams is also the envy of the state. Trout, smallmouth bass, crappies, carp, and pike all flourish here, and you won't find any wader-clad crowds to compete with, even on picture-perfect summer days. People who prefer a more social scene can opt to cast a line from the sixty-four-foot fishing pier at the municipal bass pond just off the bike path, or at the trout ponds in Sylvan Park, which also has basketball courts, volleyball, and sixty tent sites for camping.

When the snow begins to fall, the Root River Trail is maintained by the Minnesota Department of Natural Resources, and a pass—good for all state-groomed trails and sold for a nominal cost—is required. This is the primary nordic route for the area, and some skiers will take a few days to make their way down the length of the trail, staying at different bed-and-breakfasts as they go. For more rolling and challenging terrain, the nearby Forestville/Mystery Cave State Park, about ten miles out of town, grooms nearly nine of its eleven miles of intermediate trails, which wind among deciduous forest and prairie—yet another reason why Lanesboro has become more than just a whistle stop.

Start the Day

Chat 'N Chew (701 Parkway Avenue South; 507-467-3444): A down-home diner with a friendly local clientele and even friendlier service.

Lanesboro Pastry Shoppe (202 Parkway Avenue North; 507-467-2867): Where to grab fresh-baked sticky buns on your way to the trail.

Local Legend

Buffalo Bill

Frontiersman Buffalo Bill Cody rode with the Pony Express, fought for the Union in the Civil War, became a U.S. army scout, and gained his nickname in a buffalo-shooting contest. And for a spell, he spent a bit of time in Lanesboro. The town was the home of a close friend, and after he founded Buffalo Bill's Wild West traveling show in the early 1880s, he brought his troupe to perform there on occasion. In his honor, Lanesboro organizes the annual Buffalo Bill Days festival the first weekend of August. For the event there's a parade, a canoe race, a series of historical reenactments, and live music—all to go with plenty of beer and brats.

Gear Up

Little River General Store (105 Coffee Street; 507-467-2943): Rents and sells bikes, canoes, and kayaks and is the town's foremost seller of souvenirs.

Root River Outfitters (109 Parkway Avenue South; 507-467-3400): Rents canoes, bikes, and tubes; operates canoeing and tubing shuttles; sells fishing tackle.

Refuel

Das Wurst Haus (117 Parkway Avenue North; 507-467-2902): A local institution and authentic German deli, down to the polka music in the background and the tastiest brats in southern Minnesota.

Riverside on the Root (109 South Parkway: 507-467-3663): Sitting on the edge of the bike path and overlooking the Root River, it has a perfect location and a warm atmosphere for enjoying a beer, sandwich, and some live music from April through October.

Bunk

Historic Scanlan House Bed & Breakfast (708 Parkway Avenue South; 507-467-2158; www.scanlanhouse.com): An 1889 Queen Anne house with original stained-glass windows and woodwork, and two-person whirlpool baths in most of the rooms.

Cedar Valley Resort (905 Bench Street, Whalan: 507-467-9000): Located on thirty acres adjacent to the Root River Trail just outside of Lanesboro, it offers eight log-style cabins with three to eight bedrooms for family or group expeditions.

Anna V's Bed and Breakfast (507 Fillmore Avenue South; 507-467-2686; www.anna-v.com): A quaint, three-room 1908 Victorian that serves exquisite breakfasts like strawberry-stuffed french toast.

Can't Leave?

Nearest airport: Rochester International, Rochester, Minnesota (40 miles)

Primary industries: Tourism, government, agriculture

The Wild Side

Mystery Cave

Even if you walked the entire surface area of the rugged, 3,100-acre Forestville/Mystery Cave State Park, you would still be missing its most spectacular sight: the Mystery Cave. Consisting of twelve miles of stalactite-filled passages through ancient limestone, it dips deeper than 100 feet beneath the park and stays at a consistent forty-eight degrees year-round. The rock there is so porous and filled with sinkholes that in dry seasons the South Branch Root River disappears underground entirely as it passes through the cave. Above ground, there are seventeen miles of hiking trails and fifteen miles of horse trails among the hilly prairie, trout-laden streams, and forests of oak, maple, and pine. There's also the restored mid-nineteenth century village of Forestville, which you can tour courtesy of the Minnesota Historical Society.

Stillwater, Minnesota

Population:
17,378
Action: Paddling,
rock climbing, hik-
ing, road and
mountain biking,
cross-country
skiing

from Antiques St. Croix to Woodland Cabinets, there are more than 100 stores in Stillwater, Minnesota, which is fine for the flocks of shoppers who make the thirty-minute drive east from St. Paul—and a big plus for the more outdoor-oriented. The booming business has helped turn this sloping town on the St. Croix River into a mini San Francisco, complete with the microbrew-stocked bars, organic co-ops, and feathery beds one might seek after a day, or several, of adventure. Meanwhile, everyone else is so busy browsing old bookstores or picking out vintage Pucci prints that the St. Croix River, its climbing cliffs, and the surrounding hiking, biking, and cross-country ski trails are left wide open.

Okay, so there's at least one shop to drop by—P. J. Asch Otterfitters, to pick up gear for the St. Croix River valley. At Taylors Falls, forty-five minutes north of Stillwater, are some of the best and most easily accessed climbing routes in the state. They're found at the Dalles of the St. Croix, a place where the river has cut a 200-foot-tall gorge through Precambrian basalt. Pleasure-boaters on scenic paddleboat cruises like to think that gaping up at the bluffs is the best way to see them, but you can top that by peering back down from one of the fifty-plus crack routes rated 5.4 to 5.11 and bearing such names as Piece of Cake, Piece of Pie, and the Real Thing. The surrounding Interstate State Park, so named because it's shared by both Minnesota and Wisconsin, also has hiking trails that wind among large, cylindrical potholes, some of which are up to twelve feet deep, that have been formed in the rock by sand and swirling currents. Also near Taylors Falls is Wild River State Park, which lines the St. Croix River for eighteen miles and is a popular paddling spot; canoe-camping sites are protected by the park. For

The scenic St. Croix River is at the center of most outdoor activities around Stillwater, Minnesota. (© Explore Minnesota Tourism Photo)

hiking and cross-country skiing, there are also backpacking campsites and more than thirty miles of trails.

Less than an hour south of Stillwater, the St. Croix joins the Mississippi River, north of where more climbing opportunities abound; ask about Barn Bluff and other limestone bluffs around the city of Red Wing. Back in Stillwater, one of the numerous put-ins for canoeing and kayaking trips is at Boomsite Landing, part of the St. Croix National Scenic Riverway. From here, paddlers can head south to the riverway's terminus at Prescott (about twenty-five miles) or north all the way to Wisconsin, where the riverway follows the Namekagon River to the Hayward-Cable area. Primitive campsites line the St. Croix, and while the paddling falls shy of a wilderness experience, there are fish to be caught and fall colors to see—and canoes and kayaks beat out cars.

Two wheels trump four, too, of course, and the 2,165-acre Lake Elmo Park Reserve has eight miles of mountain-biking trails. The web

Local Legend

The Joseph Wolf Caves

Of all the losses due to Prohibition, one of the greatest for Minnesota was that of the Joseph Wolf Caves, underneath the Stillwater streets. In the late 1800s, the Joseph Wolf Brewing Company carved the caves out of limestone for a place to brew beer. There it produced 25,000 barrels a year in the consistent temperatures of fifty-two degrees. Despite the ideal, underground location, the brewery shut down in 1919, and though you can still tour the caves today, there are, alas, no free samples.

of country roads in Washington County around Stillwater provides seemingly limitless road-cycling options, and if you really wanted to, you could pedal all the way back to St. Paul on the Gateway State Trail. But why?

Start the Day

Grumpy Steve's Coffee (410 South Main Street; 651-430-3494): Coffee, tea, espresso drinks, and Belgian waffles.

Gear Up

P. J. Asch Otterfitters (413 East Nelson Street; 651-430-2286): Climbing gear and 6,000 feet of indoor climbing, plus kayak and cross-country ski rentals, lessons, and outdoor clothing.

Refuel

BT Doyle's Rib Joint (423 South Main Street; 651-439-2852): Ribs and homemade pies at this bar and restaurant; full breakfasts, including eggs Benedict on the weekends.

Gasthaus Bavarian Hunter (8390 Lofton Avenue; 651-439-7128): German restaurant with Munich beers, schnitzels, vegetarian options, and polka music.

The Dock Cafe (425 Nelson Street; 651-430-3770): Overlooks the St. Croix River and bluffs; bistro menu includes such items as shrimp diablo and prosciutto-wrapped fish.

Bunk

Lake Elmo Park Reserve (1515 Keats Avenue North; 651-430-8370): More than 100 campsites along hiking and horseback-riding trails, southwest of Stillwater.

Elephant Walk Bed and Breakfast (801 West Pine Street; 888-430-0359; www.elephantwalkbb.com): This 1883 Victorian has four rooms decorated with Southeast Asian finds; your own find is a stocked refrigerator, plus complimentary wine and cheese.

Water Street Inn (101 Water Street South; 651-439-6000; www.waterstreetinn.us): Rooms and suites overlooking the St. Croix River; also has an in-house Irish pub.

Can't Leave?

Nearest airport: Minneapolis-St. Paul International, Bloomington, Minnesota (31 miles)

Primary industries: Tourism, manufacturing

Rolla, Missouri

Population:

17,717

Action: Hiking,
mountain biking,
paddling, fishing

If you're using the fishing technique called noodling, a pair of waders won't help you. A rod won't, either. All you need is a bathing suit, a strong pair of lungs, and a little courage. Also known as handfishing, noodling involves reaching deep into underwater holes in muddy river banks and using your arm as bait for catfish that stretch as long as five feet—all the while you're hoping you don't find a beaver, snapping turtle, or water moccasin instead. It's legal in certain stretches of water in Missouri during a short summer season and is an underground pastime in Rolla, about ninety minutes southwest of St. Louis in the foothills of the Ozarks. If you prefer more conventional sports, the town is also a hotspot for hiking, biking, and paddling in the 1.5-million-acre Mark Twain National Forest.

Rolla is the type of place where pickup-driving noodlers can share beers with sandal-wearing granola eaters, who can swap friendly greetings with number-crunching engineering students from the campus of the University of Missouri-Rolla (UMR). Most people in town seem to share a love for the outdoors, and with more than 360 miles of streams to fish and paddle and 750 miles of trails among the deciduous woodlands of the national forest, there's plenty of it to go around. The preserve is a patchwork of six separate districts scattered throughout southern Missouri, established in 1939 to reclaim the vast tracts stripped by timber and mining operations. The Civilian Conservation Corps planted hundreds of thousands of trees, and today the land makes up more than 10 percent of the state's forested areas.

Rolla initially served as an important railroad terminus and then as home to the Missouri School of Mines and Metallurgy—now UMR— founded in 1870. It also became a popular stop for drivers on U.S. Route 66, until the interstate system replaced the legendary road in the

A mini replica of Stonehenge, built by students in the early 1980s, graces the campus of the University of Missouri-Rolla. (© Missouri Division of Tourism)

1950s. As a college community, Rolla kept on an even keel despite the disappearance of the lumber industry and highway. Now the storefronts in the tiny grid of a downtown are occupied mostly with restaurants and pubs catering to the 4,200 students; there are also a smattering of antique stores, thrift shops, and most importantly, Route 66 Bicycles—the meeting house for bikers and outdoor adrenaline junkies.

Owner and UMR graduate Dan Furhmann leads rides, gives the dirt on the best biking spots, and even maintains the zigzagging, 3.5-mile singletrack course he cut through the meadows and cedar groves of a park owned by the Rolla Lions Club. It's the best ride in town, but just one of many fat-tire options. Roughly half of the national forest's trails are open to mountain biking, and epic routes nearby include the Kaintuck Hollow Trail, a twenty-four-mile path divided into nine sections that ramble between groves of oak and cedar, with surprisingly steep climbs and drops among the high, grassy ridges. Just off the trail is a 175-foot-long natural limestone tunnel that you can investigate on foot.

Not far east of Rolla, in the national forest, is the unincorporated town of Berryman, known by local riders as the Moab of Missouri because of the rocky, twenty-four-mile Berryman Trail. This ride has long, switchbacking climbs and drops and a separate switchback that navigates among narrow ridges, small ponds, and even a cave by Brazil Creek Camp that Jesse James supposedly used as a hideout. A portion of the trail is to be incorporated into the Ozark Trail, a 700-mile footpath—with certain sections open to bikes—that is currently under construction; when finished, it will run from the St. Louis area south to Arkansas. Several stretches have been completed around Rolla and make for excellent hiking, even if they can get lost in the forest's quality mix of trails.

If you want to give your feet a rest, you can always explore the forest by canoe or kayak. Although there aren't any raging streams, the lazy rivers often offer the best vantage points for enjoying the natural setting. Just keep an eye out so you don't knock into any noodlers.

Start the Day

Zeno's Steakhouse (1621 Martin Springs Drive; 573-364-1301): This nostalgic restaurant, attached to a motel on old U.S. Route 66, has a full breakfast menu.

Local Legend

Stonehenge

More science project than pagan monument, the mini replica of Stonehenge on the University of Missouri-Rolla campus was built by students in the early 1980s. It's made from more than 160 tons of granite, placed in a fifty-foot-diameter ring. The tallest structures rise fourteen feet high. While the purpose of the English Stonehenge is still a mystery, this Stonehenge serves as a sundial, telling surprisingly accurate time.

Gear Up

Route 66 Bicycles (509 West Fifth Street; 573-368-3001): The daily blog of owner (and local mountain-bike guru) Dan Furhmann is mandatory morning reading for local riders.

Missouri Outfitters (595 Doolittle Outer Road; 573-762-3400): A sprawling, 8,400-square-foot hunting, fishing, camping, and paddling shop just outside of town.

Refuel

Gordoz (1212 Highway 72 East; 573-364-2780): Steak, seafood, and pasta is served in this Mediterranean-style restaurant.

Johnny's Smoke Stak (201 Highway 72 West; 573-364-4838): Missouri is known for its barbecue and Johnny's thick Missouri Classic sauce is known as among the best in the state.

Bunk

The Painted Lady Bed and Breakfast (1127 South Jefferson Street, St. James; 573-265-5008; www.paintedladybandb.com): A luxurious gingerbread Victorian house with four rooms—named Scarlet, Little Tara, Melanie, and Prissy—on a vast spread of land.

Rustic Motel of Rolla (812 South Bishop Avenue; 573-364-6943; www.rusticmotelofrolla.com): Owners Vina and Bob will make you feel at home in this clean, low-cost motel.

Can't Leave?

Nearest airport: Jefferson City Memorial, Jefferson City, Missouri (52 miles)

Primary industries: Health care, education, retail

Medora, North Dakota

Population: 94

Action: Mountain biking, hiking, paddling

When Theodore Roosevelt wanted to escape from the world for a spell in 1884, after his wife and mother died on the same day, he came to his Maltese Cross Ranch in the badlands around Medora. Living in a three-room cabin, he spent his nights putting musings on paper and his days hunting and wrangling. The town had just been established as a cattle and meatpacking outpost about 130 miles west of Bismarck, near the Montana border. If Roosevelt were to walk the four square blocks of Medora today, he might be pleased to see that it still looks and feels like a quiet Western getaway. He could also find his old cabin preserved by the visitor's center of the national park that bears his name and protects 70,400 acres of the domes, spires, ravines, and cliffs that so inspired him. Whether or not he would appreciate all of the references about him during the nightly variety shows performed in the summer at the local Burning Hills Amphitheatre is another matter.

Medora was established in 1883 by the twenty-four-year-old Marquis de Mores, a French aristocrat who started an ambitious beef-production company there, aiming to send fresh meat to the cities in the East. His venture failed after only a few years, and for the next century, the town went on and off of life support until the Theodore Roosevelt National Park was established in 1978 and cemented its reputation as a bona fide tourist destination. The park is divided into three separate sections, the South, North, and Elkhorn Ranch units. The entrance to the South Unit is in Medora, and at the visitor's center there, you'll find Roosevelt's restored Maltese Cross cabin. The North Unit lies about eighty miles north of town. Between the North and South units you'll find the Little Missouri National Grassland and the Elkhorn Ranch Unit. (Elkhorn was the other area ranch that Roosevelt owned.) The South Unit protects a magnificent landscape

Theodore Roosevelt National Park protects 70,400 acres of domes, spires, ravines, and cliffs that once inspired Teddy Roosevelt himself. (© Theodore Roosevelt Medora Foundation)

where bison, elk, and prairie dogs roam among the radiant rock formations and beside the banks of the meandering Little Missouri. A thirty-six-mile scenic road loops through the section, hitting all of the major sights. But a more solitary—and profound—way to experience the area is by foot on its roughly eighty or so miles of trails, especially the sixteen miles that wind through its Petrified Forest Wilderness Area west of the river.

Connecting the South and North units is the ninety-six-mile Maah Daah Hey Trail, open to hikers and horseback riders and known as one of the great extended stretches of singletrack in the country. It rolls through barren canyons and grasslands, making tight turns and steep mesa-top climbs—and plummets—along the way. The only stretches you're not allowed to ride are the ones that go through the park itself, and you can get information about detours in Medora at Dakota Cyclery—a bike shop, tour outfitter, and the leading authority on the Maah Daah Hey. Just be aware that the shop, like much of the village, closes down from early October to late spring.

An equally spectacular and secluded way to tour the area is by floating on the northeast-flowing Little Missouri when the water is high in late spring. It takes about five days to paddle the 110 miles of river between town and the take-out by the North Unit. It only takes about a minute, though, to understand why a rugged outdoorsman like Teddy Roosevelt fell in love with the outlying landscape.

Start the Day

Badlands Bake Shop (345 Third Avenue; 701-623-4444): Coffee, caramel rolls, muffins, and bagels.

Joe Ferris General Store & Internet Café (251 Main Street; 701-623-4447): Sells coffee and pastries at the snack counter.

Gear Up

Dakota Cyclery (275 Third Avenue; 701-623-4808): Sells and rents bikes, provides shuttle service for the Maah Daah Hey. Open from Memorial Day to October.

Refuel

Pitchfork Fondue (Tjaden Terrace; 800-633-6721): Serves ribeye steaks fondued on pitchforks.

Maltese Burgers (336 Third Street; 701-623-4444): Try the buffalo burger, a local delicacy.

Bunk

Rough Riders Hotel and Dining Room (301 Third Avenue; 701-623-4422): A nine-room hotel and one of the town's four remaining buildings from the late eighteenth century.

Buffalo Gap Guest Ranch (701-623-4200; www.buffalogapguest ranch.com): A log cabin–style motel overlooking the badlands.

Can't Leave?

Nearest airport: Sloulin Field International, Williston, North Dakota (90 miles)

Primary industries: Service, retail, government

Spearfish, South Dakota

Population: 9,335

Action: Mountain and road biking, hiking, rock climbing, fishing, cross-country skiing

It took sixty million years for Spearfish Canyon to emerge from the inland seas and the forces of erosion that carved gorges, spires, and peaks in the mountains rising from the plains. So it's perfectly reasonable that the town that sits at the mouth of the canyon is taking its time in becoming an adventure boomtown.

Spearfish, South Dakota, was once just a gateway from Interstate 90 to the Spearfish Canyon National Scenic Byway, a eighteen-mile ribbon of pavement that wraps around the Black Hills, and a gathering spot for the half-million riders who rumble through western South Dakota for the nearby Sturgis Motorcycle Rally every August. But now, in addition to the leaf peepers and Spearfish's local population (defined by Rushmore Mountain Sports as the Black Hills State University students who toss beer cans and the retirees who pick them up) is a dedicated group of mountain bikers, hikers, and anglers who simply know of no better place to access the Black Hills of South Dakota. Spearfish sits at the doorstep to some of the country's best singletrack: a 10,000-square-mile playground that ranges from 2,500 to 7,200 feet in elevation, most of it protected as one of seven national parks, forests, grasslands, monuments, and memorials; state parks; and the towering Crazy Horse Memorial.

Two years after General Custer discovered gold in the Black Hills—long the sanctuary of the Great Sioux Nation and other tribes—in 1876, the city of Spearfish was surveyed and staked out; in 1888, it was officially incorporated, and a decade later President Grover Cleveland established the Black Hills Forest Reserve. Spearfish Creek, where Native Americans really did spear fish, is the city's namesake and still teems with rainbows, browns, and brookies. In September

Spearfish, South Dakota's namesake creek, teems with rainbow, brown, and brook trout.
(© Spearfish Convention & Visitors Bureau)

1935, Frank Lloyd Wright traveled through here, marveling at the natural architecture of Spearfish Canyon, including the great horizontal rock walls, which he called unique and unparalleled. You'll find some of the same sentiments among the rock climbers who hit these limestone walls today for routes of 5.6 to 15.3c that are climbable nearly year-round. It's an hour to the tower—Devil's Tower—across the Wyoming border; Mount Rushmore's granite and the Needles and Cathedral Spires are to the south, while Spearfish has bouldering problems right around town.

The mountain-biking trails are also as accessible as the post office. There is riding at Lookout Mountain—one of the three peaks that form a crown around Spearfish—via nearby trails. Some of the closest Black Hills rides are the Rimrock and Little Spearfish trails, which create twelve miles of singletrack loops in the hilly forests of Spearfish Canyon; the narrow and panoramic trail up Old Baldy Mountain, at just over six miles; and the thirteen and a half miles of the Big Hill Trails looping above the canyon. It's no surprise that Spearfish's Dakota Five-O, a fifty-mile mountain-biking race, is held around here every Labor Day weekend. Running the through the heart of the Black Hills is the 111-mile long Centennial Trail, a rugged route that passes Mount Rushmore, through Custer State Park, and into Wind Cave National Park, and the Mickelson Rail Trail, an easier, 114-mile ride among cliffs and ponderosa pine. The epic, ninety-six-mile Maah Daah Hey Trail in North Dakota's Theodore Roosevelt National Park isn't exactly near Spearfish—it's a 200-mile drive—but doable on a weekend. And for road biking, the Spearfish Canyon Scenic Byway has a wide, cyclist-friendly shoulder. Plan to dismount plenty of times, though, for the canyon

Local Legend

The Crazy Horse Memorial

Sculptor Gutzon Borglum and his son, Lincoln, spent fourteen years carving the faces of four presidents into Mount Rushmore. But that's just a blip in time to the carvers of the Crazy Horse Memorial in Crazy Horse, South Dakota, eighty miles south of Spearfish and seventeen miles southwest of Mount Rushmore. Sculptor Korczak Ziolkowski, an assistant to Borglum, began the project, a tribute to the Native American leader, in 1948, and work on what is the largest sculpture in the world is still ongoing. Ziolkowski died in 1982, but his family and other supporters continue the carving, making no firm predictions on when it might be completed. On the project's fiftieth anniversary, Crazy Horse's face was unveiled and dedicated; by 2006, his horse's eye had begun to appear. The progress would please Ziolkowski, whose parting words to his wife were, "You must work on the mountain, but go slowly so you do it right."

views, particularly if you're here in the fall, when the aspens, oak, and birch turn.

There's more to Spearfish than just climbing and biking, though; many of the fat-tire trails also host hikers and cross-country skiers. The 1.2-million-acre Black Hills National Forest, in fact, has more than 450 miles of trails. In Spearfish Canyon, the short Spearfish Falls Trail leads to an eighty-foot waterfall. Farther south, the 5.4-mile Willow Creek Trail is a challenging climb to the highpoint of the hills, 7,242-foot Harney Peak, which looks down at the back of Mount Rushmore. In the winter, cross-country skiers glide along the Big Hill and Eagle trails, the silence of the Black Hills allowing contemplation of just how long it might take to exhaust all the outdoor options. Sixty million years sounds about right.

Start the Day

Alpine Coffee (503 North Main Street; 605-722-7603): Coffee and espresso drinks, along with biscuits and gravy, breakfast sandwiches, oatmeal, and Belgian waffles.

Gear Up

Rushmore Mountain Sports (505 North Main Street; 605-642-2885): Bike rentals and repairs, accessories, climbing gear, maps, trail shuttles, and information.

Refuel

Sanford's Pub and Grub (545 West Jackson Street; 605-642-3204): More than 300 items on the menu, from burgers to deep-fried pickles, plus 100 beers in the fridge and twenty on tap. Decorated with countless junkyard treasures; part of a regional chain.

Seven Grill & Pub Room (447 North Main Street; 605-717-5701): Next to Rushmore Mountain Sports, it's both an eclectic eatery with artichoke and chicken curry soup and a casual hangout with burgers and beers; the back Club Room is a white-tablecloth steakhouse.

Bay Leaf Café (126 West Hudson Street; 605-642-5462): A bistro serving such specialties as elk fettuccine and herb-crusted walleye.

Bunk

Black Hills National Forest (2014 North Main Street; 877-444-6777; www.reserveusa.com): Thirty campgrounds with 682 sites throughout the Black Hills.

Spearfish Canyon Lodge (10619 Roughlock Falls Road; 605-584-3435; www.spfcanyon.com): A log lodge with fifty-four rooms and suites, near biking, fly-fishing, and hiking destinations.

Can't Leave?

Nearest airport: Rapid City Regional, Rapid City, South Dakota (64 miles)

Primary industries: Retail, hospitality, health care, financial services

Bayfield, Wisconsin

I f sea kayakers could design their afterworld, it would probably look something like the Apostle Islands: an archipelago of twenty-two islands scattered like skipping stones across Lake Superior, each with its own wow factor best seen from the hull of low fiberglass boat. There are the eroded sandstone sea caves, created by Superior's wild waves, on Devils Island; the shoreline waterfalls of Stockton Island; the old-growth forests of Raspberry and Outer islands; and the skeletal remains of brownstone quarries and loading docks on Hermit Island. As subtle reminders of civilization, lighthouses stand among the thick groves of pine trees. With the exception of one island, the entire heavenly constellation, along with twelve miles of shoreline, in an area of more than 700 square miles, is protected as the Apostle Islands National Lakeshore. And best of all, the Apostles are easily navigated by paddlers. They are speckled with remote private campsites that an RV couldn't even think about parking at; there are no roads and no cars here, unless you're on Madeline Island.

Population: 602
Action: Paddling, sailing, diving, downhill and cross-country skiing, mountain and road biking, fishing, hiking

At the gates to this paddlers' promised land is the postcard-pretty town of Bayfield, surrounded by berry farms and apple orchards and speckled with farmers' markets, Victorian architecture, and island-inspired art galleries. Sandstone cliffs spill down to marinas; eateries sauté or deep-fry whitefish livers, a local specialty, and a few pubs pour ice-cold pints of beer. The number and variety of amenities belong to a much bigger place than one with less than 1,000 year-round residents, which is partly due to the influx of visitors—October's Apple Festival draws more than 50,000 to its parades, pie contests, and fish boils.

But Bayfield's constant thrum is also the result of an enthusiasm for all things outdoors. Even when winter whips across Lake Superior, shuttering the paddling season and freezing the once-welcoming

From Bayfield, Wisconsin, kayakers can launch paddling tours of Lake Superior's Apostle Islands.

liquid trails with temperatures well below zero, there's a silver lining to the storm clouds. Now, cross-country skiers can participate in the Book Across the Bay 10K; the race takes place at night, and candles and bonfires lighting the skiers' way. Runners can brag to their friends in warmer climates about their ability to run on water, thanks to a road race of the same name that takes place on the ice road between Bayfield and Madeline Island. Snowshoers can hike to the spectacular ice caves at Squaw Bay. There are also the Apostle Islands Sled Dog Races, and, for those who can resist the allure of being on the frozen lake, downhill skiing, snowboarding, and forty kilometers of nordic trails at Mount Ashwabay. It's no Vail, but the Bayfield area receives 120 inches of snow each year, and where else are you going to find a season pass for less than the cost of a nice dinner out—and one that promises views of Lake Superior?

Sweater-weather lingers into summer evenings—a plus for paddlers cozying up to campfires and sleeping bags—but winter recedes by May, when locals participate in the tent-raising social for Big Top Chautauqua, a 900-seat arts venue at the base of Mount Ashwabay. Divers pull on dry suits to explore some of the wrecks of Lake Superior, including the *Fedora*, which went down in 1901 when a kerosene lamp exploded. More than twenty wrecks lie around the Apostles, and the exposed *Coffinberry* can be explored by snorkel.

SAIL magazine has called the Apostle Islands one of America's ten best places to sail, thanks to the area's deep passages and anchorages and the brisk, steady winds. In another outdoors-oriented party, June sees the annual Blessing of the Fleet, which is open to any waterborne vessel. (Along with numerous sailing charter operations, the marinas around Bayfield are stocked with fishing charters departing to catch red fin lake trout.) For landlubbers, there is road biking among the orchards; you can also mountain bike on Madeline Island's old dirt country roads and more than fifty miles of trails throughout the Apostle Islands National Lakeshore. The best plan of action? Throw a pair of hiking shoes into the kayak for the seven-mile hike along the Sandspit Trail on Outer Island, which is a twenty-four-mile paddle from Bayfield. As you camp at the single site on the island, watch the sunset over Lake Superior and wonder if you could ever design something better.

Start the Day

The Egg Toss Bakery Café (41 Manypenny Avenue; 715-779-5181): Specialties for the fisherman (two eggs, two sausage links,

Local Legend

Whitefish Livers

They may not sound as appetizing as, say, a Maine lobster roll, but Bayfield's whitefish livers are equally as legendary around northern Wisconsin. Once they were the sustenance of Scandinavian fishermen—today, they're the staple of many restaurants around town, and the debate over exactly how to serve them can be as contentious as whether lobster rolls should be drizzled with butter or tossed with mayonnaise. Greunke's claims to have expanded the lowly livers' popularity in the 1940s, when Victor Greunke began putting batter-fried whitefish livers on the menu; today the restaurant reports calls from as far as Chicago reserving a whitefish-liver dinner. Some say the livers, which are about the size of a chicken's, are an aphrodisiac and taste, well, just like chicken.

two slices of bacon with potatoes) and the logger (three buckwheat cakes with bacon, sausage, or ham), plus french "ecstasy" toast, waffles, and more.

Greunke's (17 Rittenhouse Avenue; 715-779-5480): The local spot for blueberry pancakes; also open for lunch, dinner, and snacks at the soda fountain. Hosts fish boils and serves world-famous fried whitefish livers.

Gear Up

Trek & Trail (7 Washington Avenue; 800-354-8735): Kayak and mountain-bike rentals, plus guided day and overnight trips throughout the Apostle Islands.

Superior Charters (34475 Port Superior Road; 800-772-5124): Captained and bareboat sailing charters.

Refuel

Morty's Pub (108 Rittenhouse Avenue; 715-779-3996): Microbrews and burgers, along with pizza, sandwiches, and a jukebox.

Maggie's (257 Manypenny Avenue; 715-779-5641): Creative and casual fare, from garlic polenta fries and black-bean nachos to Thai noodles and whitefish sandwiches.

Old Rittenhouse Inn (301 Rittenhouse Avenue; 715-779-5111): Five-course dinners featuring such fare as Lake Superior smoked trout, maple-seared duck breast, and cherry pie à la mode; dinner concerts in November and December.

Bunk

Apostle Islands National Lakeshore (415 Washington Avenue; 715-779-3398; www.nps.gov/apis): Established campsites and wilderness camping on the Apostles.

Winfield Inn (225 East Lynde Avenue; 715-779-3252): Thirty-one rooms overlooking Lake Superior, plus cabins, condominiums, and cottages in Bayfield.

Old Rittenhouse Inn (301 Rittenhouse Avenue; 800-779-2129): A bed-and-breakfast with rooms and suites housed in four Victorian houses.

Can't Leave?

Nearest airport: Duluth International, Duluth, Minnesota (95 miles)

Primary industries: Tourism, agriculture, commercial and recreational fishing, arts

fort Atkinson, Wisconsin

Population:

11,949

Action: Paddling,
hiking, mountain
and road biking,
cross-country
skiing

If you have time to look around when you are skydiving from a Cessna at 12,500 feet in southeastern Wisconsin, you might see a checkerboard of dairy farms that crumble into rolling hills. A wide river, speckled with a few canoes, widens into a large, teardrop-shaped lake. And maybe, if you look closely, you'll see a town along the river, just northeast of the lake, where historic buildings house folk-music cafés and a few local paddlers constructing their own canoes and kayaks from strips of cedar. This town is Fort Atkinson, an hour southwest of Milwaukee and just a few minutes from some of the state's best paddling, biking, and hiking.

The town's name stems from a fort built here in 1832 during the Black Hawk War, when Abraham Lincoln, Jefferson Davis, and Zachary Taylor fought Native Americans attempting to reclaim their homelands. (The area around Fort Atkinson contains dozens of Indian effigy mounds, some shaped like birds and turtles and others turned into a golf course; a few of the best-preserved mounds can be found at the open-prairie Aztalan State Park, north of town, and at the Jefferson County Indian Mounds and Trail Park, off State Highway 26.) But Fort Atkinson's outdoor-oriented history really stretches back 25,000 years, when melting ice from massive glaciers created kettle-shaped depressions in the land, along with hills and ridges. Today, a 100-mile stretch of those depressions is preserved as Kettle Moraine State Forest, a 50,000-acre park split into two units.

The Southern Unit of Kettle Moraine lies just east of Fort Atkinson and has 160 miles of trails that are not only quickly gaining recognition for their mountain-biking value, but also open to hiking and cross-country skiing. Wisconsin's hiking-only Ice Age Trail passes through here, and the three northerly Scuppernong loops, two to five miles

Fort Atkinson is an hour west of Milwaukee and just a few minutes from some of Wisconsin's best paddling, biking, and hiking. (© Fort Atkinson Chamber of Commerce)

long, are for hiking and classical skiing only. Along with the Scuppernong, the Nordic (toward the southern end of the forest), and McMiller (in the center) trails are groomed for cross-country skiers, and there's a biathlon range at the McMiller system. With fifty-four miles of horseback-riding trails, the Southern Kettles would already be a popular spot. Today, more fat-tire riders are discovering the John Muir and Emma Carlin systems, both of which are open to mountain bikers for a total of more than thirty-five miles of mostly singletrack. On loops from a mile and a half to eleven miles long, the John Muir trails roll through open fields and tight stands of pine trees; the steep and rocky Blue Loop was designed specifically for mountain biking. A five-mile connector trail leads up to the shorter, and some say, tougher Emma Carlin system. (For cycling, the Glacial River Bike Trail runs through Fort Atkinson, while the fifty-three-mile-long Glacial Drumlin Trail runs nearby.)

Paddlers might be more interested in the geological history that left behind the Rock River, whose placid waters create instant canoe and kayak trips from downtown Fort Atkinson. More recently, the Indianford Dam has created Lake Koshkonong, the second-largest body of water of Wisconsin. In the summer, it buzzes with fishing boats out for walleye; winters, it echoes with the sounds of miles of ice expanding, so loud that sometimes the booms can shake the lakeside cottages.

The Wild Side

The Ice Age National Scenic Trail

If you were to start hiking at the northwestern edge of Wisconsin, at the St. Croix Dalles, wander eastward to the center of the state, suddenly head south past Madison, and then abruptly northeast toward the Door County peninsula, you wouldn't be lost; you'd be following the Ice Age Trail. Given national scenic designation in 1980, the trail traces the recent glacial history of Wisconsin—just 15,000 years ago, ice sheets covered most of the state. The meandering footpath is planned to be 1,000 miles long; more than 600 miles are now open for use by hikers, and 30 miles pass through Kettle Moraine State Forest near Fort Atkinson. The forest is also the location of the Ice Age Trail 50, a hilly ultrarunning race that began in 1981 and can be competed at fifty miles or fifty kilometers.

Start the Day

Beauty & the Bean (207 East Milwaukee Avenue; 920-563-4937): Coffee shop with muffins, bagels, and scones.

Gear Up

Rock River Canoe (99 North Main Street; 920-222-6276): Canoe, kayak, and bike rentals, plus bike repair, tents, books, stoves, packs, and other outdoor gear.

Refuel

Bienfang's Bar (28 North Water Street East; 920-563-8046): Cheer for the Green Bay Packers at this 1907-established sports pub.

Salamone's (1245 Madison Avenue; 920-563-9217): Pizza and Italian specialties.

Café Carpe (18 South Water Street West; 920-563-9391): Microbrews on tap, grilled sandwiches, and nightly specials including jambalaya; folk music or jazz performances most weekend evenings.

Bunk

Kettle Moraine State Forest (S91 W39091 Highway 59, Eagle; 262-594-6200; www.dnr.wi.gov/land/parks/specific/kms): Three backpacking shelters along the Ice Age Trail and three campgrounds with walk-in sites.

La Grange Bed & Breakfast (1050 East Street; 920-563-1421; www.1928barn.com): Three French-country rooms in restored barns; breakfast might be quiche or caramel french toast.

Sunset Shores Resort (W7889 High Ridge Road; 920-563-2233; www.sunsetshore.com): Basic two-bedroom cabins with kitchens on Lake Koshkonong.

Can't Leave?

Nearest airport: Southern Wisconsin Regional, Janesville, Wisconsin (26 miles)

Primary industries: Food processing, printing and publishing, manufacturing

Hayward, Wisconsin

Population: 3,279

Action: Mountain biking, cross-country skiing, hiking

Northwestern Wisconsin is known as Indian Head Country for the way, some say, its borders, chiseled by Minnesota, the St. Croix River, and Lake Superior, resemble the profile of a Native American chief looking out toward California. If that's true, then right at his temple you'd find Hayward and nearby Cable, both throbbing with the pulse of the Great North Woods and parties for every pursuit. September sees the Chequamegon Fat Tire Festival, the largest mass-start mountain-biking race in the country. Cross-country skiers get their due in February, when the American Birkebeiner races storm through the Hayward-Cable area during a three-day skinny-ski extravaganza. June means the Musky Festival, and in July, the axe-plaid look makes a comeback at the Lumberjack World Championships. It's all fueled by Friday-night fish fries, Leinenkugel's beer, and potato pancakes. But whenever they need some peace and quiet, locals easily escape to one of the hundreds of lakes and trails weaving throughout Indian Head Country.

It's no accident that the Lumberjack World Championships are held in Hayward, in the aptly named Sawyer County. The three-day competition of chopping, logrolling, sawing, tree-climbing, and axe-throwing—which draws lumberjacks and lumberjills from as far as New Zealand—was founded in 1960 as a tribute to the U.S. logging industry, which long had a seat in Hayward. The pine-tree surrounded town sits not only on Lake Hayward but also on the Namekagon River, which in the 1870s town founder Anthony Judson Hayward saw as an ideal spot for storing timber and transporting it by means of the developing railroad. In 1922, Hayward's main lumber mill burned down, signifying a formal end to the diminishing logging economy. Now the pine trees are part of the Hayward allure for vacationers who flock to

The Chequamegon Fat Tire Festival, the largest mass-start mountain-biking race in the country, takes off from Hayward, Wisconsin. (Chequamegon Fat Tire Festival photo by Tom Kelly)

the log-cabin resorts that have been popping up on the cluster of lakes since the 1800s.

Perhaps as fierce as—and, collectively, a greater force than—the lumberjacks are the mountain bikers who wheel through the area for the Chequamegon Fat Tire Festival. Imagine 1,700 riders taking off at once for a forty-mile race from Hayward to Cable on forest roads and the American Birkebeiner ski trail, and you start to get the picture. The festival is rounded out by mountain-bike orienteering events and a dirt criterium on a half-mile course. It has been happening since 1983, indicating Hayward-Cable's deep connections to the sport. The Chequamegon Area Mountain Bike Association has a system of more than 300 miles of trails in and around the Chequamegon-Nicolet National Forest. Near Cable, you'll find the 15.1 mile Short and Fat, a mix of singletrack, doubletrack, and dirt roads that undulates through the woods, while Hayward's Mosquito Brook Trail Head leads to six different trails from 4.3 to 11.8 miles long.

The 1.5-million-acre Chequamegon-Nicolet National Forest, meanwhile, is equally as rich for hikers and cross-country skiers. Hikes can be as short as the interpretive Forest Lodge Nature Trail, at 1.5 miles, or as long as the Ice Age Trail, a Wisconsin-wide footpath with 600 miles now complete, and the North Country National Scenic Trail, a 4,600-mile network of interstate off-road options that is in development. In the Chequamegon, the North Country trail winds more than sixty miles through forests of pine, birch, and aspen, skirting glassy lakes and creating a five-day backpacking trip. Another nationally recognized recreation resource is the Rock Lake Trail, a series of groomed, classic-style cross-country-ski trails from two to sixteen kilometers long that lead past frozen lakes and stands of maple and oak trees.

On the other side of the nordic-skiing spectrum is the annual American Birkebeiner, or Birkie. The event's history stretches way back to before Hayward and Cable were settled, to 1206, when skiers carried the King of Norway's eighteen-month-old son to safety during a civil war. In 1973, a group of Wisconsin athletes decided to honor the legend by skiing forty-five kilometers from Hayward's Lumberjack Bowl to Cable's Telemark Lodge while wearing Norwegian knickers and woolen sweaters. Today, more than 9,000 skiers and 15,000 spectators show up for the now fifty-one-kilometer race, as well as a twenty-three-kilometer race, shorter sprints, kids events, and Birkie festivities. Here, you can see the elite cross-country skiers of nineteen countries, including Estonia and Finland, compete alongside costumed amateurs—and some lumberjacks and mountain bikers, disguised in Lycra.

Start the Day

The Norse Nook Restaurant & Bakery (10436 Highway 27 South; 715-634-7928): Homemade cinnamon and caramel rolls, plus a full breakfast menu and twenty-eight kinds of pies in a Norwegian-themed Wisconsin eatery and emporium; you can even register for wedding gifts here.

The Robin's Nest (11014 Highway B; 715-462-3132): Eggs Benedict, applewood-smoked bacon, biscuits and

The Wild Side

Namekagon River

One of the country's classic canoe-camping trips lies just outside of Hayward on the Namekagon River. The river's headwaters are trout stream near Cable, and from there it flows ninety-eight miles toward the St. Croix River, which forms part of the border between Minnesota and Wisconsin. To arrange a guided trip when the water's high enough—during which you'll paddle through Class I rapids, pass hills of sand, and glide beneath soaring bald eagles—contact Big Brook Paddlesports in Cable.

gravy, omelets, Bloody Marys, and
potato pancakes.

Gear Up

Outdoor Ventures (10579N Main
Street; 715-634-4447): Cross-country
skis, kayaks, snowshoes, camping gear,
and clothing.

New Moon Ski & Bike (15569 U.S.
Highway 63 North; 715-634-8685):
Mountain-bike and cross-country ski
rentals (call ahead to reserve), sales,
and service.

Big Brook Paddlesports (43055 U.S.
Highway 63, Cable; 715-798-3310):
Canoe and kayak rentals and sales, plus
guided river trips; open summers.

Refuel

Angry Minnow Restaurant & Brewery
(10440 Florida Avenue; 715-934-3055):
Brewmaster Jason Rasmussen crafts
Honey Wheat, Minnow Lite, and River
Pig American Pale Ale beers, among
others; the restaurant menu includes
burgers, cedar-plank mango salmon,
stuffed portabella mushrooms, and a
Friday-night fish fry.

Karibali's (10562 Main Street; 715-634-
2462): A 1922 pool emporium that now
serves burgers, sandwiches, and burri-
tos; also has a salad bar and Friday-night fish fry.

Chippewa Inn (9702N County Road B; 715-462-3648): Supper
club with Kansas City steaks, chops, lobster, bratwurst, and
schnitzels; closed on Tuesdays.

Bunk

Dun Rovin Lodge (9404 Dun Rovin Road; 715-462-3834;
www.dunrovinlodge.com): Includes six cabins on the Chippewa

Local Legend

The Musky

New York may have the Empire State Building and Statue of Liberty, but Hayward has a four-and-one-half story, 143-foot-long musky, whose mouth you can climb into and peer out over town from. The fish is easy to find at the National Fresh Water Fishing Hall of Fame, where you can find out the truth behind some of those fish tales and learn that Louis Spray caught the current world-record musky—sixty-nine pounds, eleven ounces—in 1949. Or did he? Some fish historians dispute the record because Spray shot the fish when he landed it—a practice that was legal back then. The Moccasin Bar in Hayward holds the runner-up (or the winner, depending on which side you stand)—the sixty-seven-and-a-half-pound musky caught by Cal Johnson, also in 1949. To settle it once and for good, and win $100,000 from the Moccasin Bar, you can make an attempt at a new record on Hayward's lakes.

Flowage, a restaurant, and unofficial world-record muskie whose seventy pounds were weighed with uncertified scales.

Spider Lake Lodge (10472 West Murphy Boulevard; 800-653-9472; www.spiderlakelodge.com): A bed-and-breakfast in a 1923 log lodge with seven rooms.

Telemark Resort (42225 Telemark Road; 877-798-4718; www.tele markresort.com): 193 guest rooms, suites, and condos at a full-service resort with downhill and cross-country skiing, snowboarding, snowmobiling, and mountain biking.

Can't Leave?

Nearest airport: Duluth International, Duluth, Minnesota (75 miles)

Primary industries: Forest management, timber and forest products, tourism

Sturgeon Bay, Wisconsin

There's more to Door County than dairy, cherry pies, and lighthouses. Take the fish, for example—and not just the kind that show up slathered in butter and served with potatoes and onions after a dramatic, fiery fish boil. On either side of the nearly ninety-mile-long peninsula that juts out into Lake Michigan are the swimming waters of thirty-pound king salmon; twenty-pound lake trout, northern pike, and musky; and ten-pound walleye, along with tough smallmouth bass. Or consider the cycling: 100 miles of back roads, along with off-road trails that wind past those famous cherry orchards. And below all those lighthouses (ten of them, at last count) lies more than 300 miles of shoreline from which to launch sea kayaks and sailboats.

Population: 9,180
Action: Fishing, road and mountain biking, hiking, paddling, sailing, cross-country skiing

Tucked into a crook at the middle of it all, and less than an hour from Green Bay, is the city of Sturgeon Bay, where sawmills and stone quarrying gave way to shipbuilding in the early nineteenth century, thanks to a canal that allowed vessels to avoid the perilous Porte des Morts, or Death's Door Strait. (At the tip of the peninsula, the water is littered with the bones of ships—part of the Lake Michigan scuba-diving lore that's also missed by the cherry- and lighthouse-obsessed.) Today, while some other towns along the peninsula bank on their quaint charm, Sturgeon Bay remains a working port and a down-to-earth launching pad for exploring the outdoor bounty of Door County.

Sturgeon Bay lies just southeast of Potawatomi State Park, one of five state parks that have helped to preserve the peninsula's wilder side. Here, nearly six miles of fast, flat mountain-biking trails loop through hemlock, birch, and maple forests and near limestone cliffs along the water's edge; the same trails convert to a cross-country skier's playground in the winter. (The park also connects to the statewide Ice Age Trail.) Stretching south from Sturgeon Bay—near the headquarters for

Sturgeon Bay is a working port and a down-to-earth launching pad for exploring the outdoor bounty of Wisconsin's Door County. (Door County Visitors Bureau/DoorCounty.com)

September's Door County Century Ride, by the way—is the thirty-mile Ahnapee State Trail, a former railroad bed now shared by bikers, hikers, and horseback riders; naturally, it's another skinny-ski outlet when the snow flies. North along the peninsula lies Whitefish Dunes State Park, where skiers can glide past icy Lake Michigan. In the summer, it's a beach destination, but one where the boardwalk is lined by marshes and rocky shoreline rather than cotton-candy vendors.

At 2,373-acre Newport State Park, also on the Lake Michigan side, nearly seventeen miles of trails are open to mountain bikers. As Wisconsin's only state park with a wilderness designation, its campsites are for backpackers who can carry their gear, not behemoth RVs, and its sea kayaking and hiking (up to thirty miles of it) will trick you into thinking you're much farther from the day-tripper-packed peninsula; try the seven-mile Europe Bay/Hotz Loop. Wind around

Northport, past the Porte des Morts and back south again, and you'll hit Peninsula State Park, where nearly 3,776 acres of old farm fields, forests, bluffs, and beaches are shared among backpackers, mountain bikers, and deer.

For sailing and fishing, it's nearly impossible not to hit a marina around Door County. But you can certainly find small sailboat rentals near Peninsula State Park at the town of Ephraim, and a bevy of fishing charters—and, January through March, ice-fishing operations—back at home base, Sturgeon Bay. After a day on the water, there's an even sweeter tang to the cherries, and you know already that those are everywhere.

Start the Day

Kick Coffee (148 North Avenue; 920-746-1122): Espresso drinks, coffee, baked goods, and local artwork.

Gear Up

D.C. Bikes (20 North Third Avenue; 877-322-4531): Rent bikes, canoes, kayaks, snowshoes, and cross-country skis; from Memorial Day to mid-October, there's another seasonal location at Potawatomi State Park.

Reel Action Charters (1802 Morning View Road, Brussels; 920-360-2136): Just outside of Sturgeon Bay, this is the Door County pick for ESPN and OLN; hook salmon, smallmouth bass, and walleye with Captain Scott Gutschow.

Refuel

Vans Bar & Grill (253 North Third Avenue; 920-743-9339): Get burgers, beers, and sour-cream-and-onion fries at this downtown bar, next to the movie theater.

Mill Supper Club (4128 Highway 42/57; 920-743-5044): Local families

The Wild Side

Rock Island

When you invent the world's first million-volt electrical transformer, you earn enough money to buy an entire island—and then turn the island into a mini Iceland, complete with Viking-inspired buildings decorated with runic carvings. Which is exactly what Chester Thorardson did with 912-acre Rock Island, which lies off the tip of the Door County peninsula, between 1910 and 1945. Today, the island is a state park, closed to cars and bikes and dotted with primitive campsites. Skip the two ferry rides it takes to get here and instead slip inside a sea kayak for the challenging, fifteen-mile paddle from Newport State Park to Rock Island. (You'll be crossing the Porte des Morts, or Death's Door Passage, known for its violent weather and passing Plum Island, the private Detroit Island, and Washington Island.) Camp on the southwest side, near the Viking boat-house. To stretch your legs, hit the 6.5-mile Thorardson Loop Trail, which circumnavigates the island.

head here for überfriendly service, chicken dinners, fish boils, and cherry-cheese torts.

Sage Restaurant & Wine Bar (136 North Third Avenue; 920-746-1100): Contemporary and upscale restaurant that's earned acclaim as one of Door County's best; entrées include ahi tuna, barbecued quail, and Provençal penne.

Bunk

Potawatomi State Park (3740 County PD; 920-746-2890; www.dnr.state.wi.us): At the mouth of Sturgeon Bay, this park has 123 wooded campsites, 25 with electrical service, near the Ice Age Trail and short hiking trails; it also has a small boat landing.

Reynolds House Bed and Breakfast (111 South Seventh Avenue; 877-269-7401; www.reynoldshousebandb.com): Famous for its breakfasts, including blueberry-walnut bread and almond egg puffs; four guest rooms.

Leathem Smith Lodge (1640 Memorial Drive; 800-366-7947; www.leathemsmithlodge.com): A former country club with thirty-two guest rooms and sixteen suites, in a resort setting on twelve acres of grounds.

Can't Leave?

Nearest airport: Austin Straubel International, Green Bay, Wisconsin (57 miles)

Primary industries: Shipbuilding, manufacturing, tourism, services

The Rockies

Alamosa, Colorado

Even though Alamosa is the center of recreation and
commerce in an alpine valley that's larger than the
state of Massachusetts, getting there isn't easy. To
approach from the east or north, you've got to navigate
through the serrated, 14,000-foot peaks of the Sangre de
Cristo (or "blood of Christ") Mountains. From the west
and south, you need to deal with the pesky, vast San
Juans. No wonder the interstate highway gods bypassed the entire area
when they plotted the main routes across Colorado. In turn, the people of Alamosa and the smattering of others who live across the broad
San Luis Valley at 7,500 feet in elevation are able to claim practically all
its outdoor treasures, like the Great Sand Dunes National Park and
Preserve, for themselves.

Population: 8,682
Action: Hiking,
mountain biking,
downhill skiing

Using Alamosa as your headquarters, you can fan into the surrounding landscape for hiking, mountain biking, and skiing, or head
straight to the national park and explore the tallest sand dunes in North
America (some stretching as high as 750 feet). Because the San Luis
Valley is so difficult to reach, it remained largely untouched by
European settlers until the mid-1800s, when they began to plant farms
there. Only about eight inches of rain falls each year on the grassy, treeless valley floor, but underground water is remarkably abundant
because the area is like a giant bathtub, retaining runoff from the surrounding mountains underground. Alamosa, named for a Spanish
word for "cottonwood grove," was established on the chocolate Rio
Grande River in 1878 and drew its prosperity from the new railroad.
Eventually it transformed into the mining and agriculture hub of the
entire valley.

Today farming is still an important part of the local economy, as
is Adams State College, founded in 1921. The school's 1,900 undergrads
inject a youthful vibe into the shops, coffeehouses, and restaurants that

Great Sand Dunes National Park and Preserve, near Alamosa, Colorado, contains the highest sand dunes in North America; some reach as high as 750 feet. (© NPS photo)

occupy the western-style buildings along Alamosa's wide main avenues. Tourism, too, is a vital local industry, especially since Alamosa is the closest sizeable town to the main entrance of the dunes (about twenty-five minutes away), which were designated a national park in 2004. These massive, constantly moving towers of khaki-colored sand cover thirty square miles of the eastern edge of the San Luis Valley and are contrasted by the green, often-snow-capped mountains rising so abruptly above them. They're formed when wind-carried sand is deposited at the foot of the Sangre de Cristos and held in place by a moat of creeks.

There are two ways to explore the park: in the dunes and around them. When you trek into the dunes, bring water and wear shoes, because the sand can get scorchingly hot in the middle of the day. Close to the visitor's center on the southern end is 650-foot, appropriately named High Dune. From its peak, you can peer across the valley and gain perspective on the scope of the park. You can hike wherever you want on the sand, and while you're there you're likely to see people flying kites, building castles by the creeks, or even riding a snowboard down the steep slopes. You can make quicker progress by hiking around the dunes. The barely used but spectacular Sand Creek Trail is a ten-mile route that contours the eastern edge of the park and terminates at its northern tip, passing through aspen groves and pine forests and crossing occasional dune fields along the way. Another five-star footpath is the 4.5-mile Mosca Pass Trail, which starts by the visitor's center and rises through subalpine forest along Mosca Creek until it reaches a mountain pass at higher than 9,000 feet.

For hiking outside the park, Blanca Peak is as close to Alamosa as the dunes, and climbing the rugged Lake Como Trail to the top is a fifteen-mile, two-day affair. The favorite trek from town is a gravelly path, barely a half-mile long, to thirty-foot-high Zapata Falls, which lies within a cleft in the bedrock. You can access the falls by rock-hopping across, or wading through, an icy creek. The area surrounding it has four short loops that are popular with mountain bikers and total about ten miles of trail. Fat-tire aficionados also head west of town to the three Limekiln singletrack loops, called C, D, and E (A is on private property and now off limits), that fan into the foothills that peer across at the dunes. Kristi Mountain Sports provides maps. Many of the rides close to the valley floor are open year-round because of the area's temperate climate and scant precipitation.

The encircling mountaintops, on the other hand, get buried under snow. The 11,000-foot summit of Wolf Creek Ski Area is about an hour and forty-five minutes away from Alamosa and averages 465 inches of the white stuff a year. Despite its great conditions, the resort— all 1,600 acres and fifty-five trails of it— is often overlooked because reaching it

The Wild Side

Great Sand Dunes National Preserve

The preserve portion of the Great Sand Dunes National Park and Preserve is a 41,676-acre swath of land that climbs east of the dunes into the Sangre de Cristo range. As you ascend through this portion of the park, you'll pass through cottonwood stands and spruce forests, beside crystal lakes and into alpine tundra; trails here wind among six mountain peaks higher than 13,000 feet. The three main hikes are to Medano Lake (at 11,500 feet); to Music Pass (11,380 feet), which offers vantages of Music Mountain and Cleveland Peak; and to Lower Sand Creek Lake (11,473 feet) and Upper Sand Creek Lake (11,745 feet), where you'll need a wetsuit if you plan to take more than a quick plunge in the water.

Local Legend

Alligators

Just past the Mosca turnoff toward the sand dunes on State Route 17 lives a prolific movie star who has supposedly made appearances in such classics as *Blues Brothers 2000, Happy Gilmore, Eraser,* and *Interview with the Vampire*. His name is Morris, and you'll find him and more than 400 other alligators at Colorado Gators, a reptile farm open every day except Thanksgiving and Christmas. The operation was created by a couple who also own a tilapia farm in the geothermally heated waters on their property. They began to import rescued gators to feed on the fish-farm waste products. The ponds are a little stinky, but block your nose and prepare to be entertained—and a little wigged out—by the gator-wrestling demonstrations.

within the Rio Grande National Forest isn't easy. Sound familiar?

Start the Day

Milagros (529 Main Street; 719-589-9299): A traditional college-town coffeehouse, with Internet access and a bakery.

Gear Up

Kristi Mountain Sports (3217 Main Street; 719-589-9759): Sells bike, ski, and snowboard gear and is the authority on local rides.

Skiball's Running World (622 Main Street; 719-589-6923): A running shop owned by a former All-American track runner from Adams State.

Refuel

True Grits Steakhouse (100 Santa Fe Avenue; 719-589-9954): Where the portions are plentiful and named after John Wayne movie characters.

Nino's (617 Sixth Street; 719-587-0101): The green chile (in mild, medium, and hot) comes on almost every dish and is the reason the lines for a dinner table at this Tex-Mex joint are so long.

Bunk

Cottonwood Inn (123 San Juan Avenue; 719-589-3882; www.cottonwoodinn.com): A six-room bed-and-breakfast in a Craftsman-style house decorated with works from local artists. Terrific breakfasts.

Inn of the Rio Grande (333 Santa Fe Avenue; 719-589-5833; www.innoftherio.com): A clean, dependable motel with an indoor swimming pool.

Great Sand Dunes Lodge (7900 Highway 150 North, Mosca; 719-378-2900): A motor lodge close to the national park; its rooms have spectacular patio views of the dunes.

Can't Leave?

Nearest airport: San Luis Valley Regional, Alamosa (5 miles)

Primary industries: Education, agriculture, tourism

Fruita, Colorado

Population: 6,878

Action: Mountain biking, hiking, rafting, downhill skiing

fruita is the kind of town where the mountain-biking shop's staff will point you not only in the direction of the best singletrack and slickrock, but also to the location of the post-ride party; there's a unique, friendly vibe here that has turned many visiting riders into full-time residents—that and the mighty Colorado River, which has scoured a spellbinding, sandstone canyon landscape on the western slope of the Rockies. For years, mountain bikers predicted that Fruita, hidden off Interstate 70 near the Utah border, would become the next Moab, Utah. But this laid-back little town has retained an altogether different flavor from Moab. That flavor comes from a famous fat-tire festival, yes, but also from dinosaurs, Mexican diners, and rodeos. And the town is missing the fancy frills that can spoil a special place.

Fruita (*FRUIT-ah*) earned its name in the late 1800s, when a developer named William Pabor founded the Fruita Town and Land Company. He later claimed he had seen, in the fertile Grand Valley, visions of "vineyards and orchards and rose-embowered cottages in which love, happiness and contentment abode." Aspiring agriculturists struck fertile soil in plots of land purchased from Pabor, while paleontologists—including Elmer Riggs of Chicago's Field Museum—discovered that the soil was also rich with dinosaur bones. The latter find explains why a giant green dinosaur named Greta greets visitors from Circle Park (the town green) and why the town has an official dinosaur (the Ceratosaurus).

The unofficial welcome center, on the other hand, is Over the Edge Sports, which began outfitting folks for the outdoors in 1995; it's found smack downtown in a functional, square facility that once housed the Fruita Furniture and Undertaking Company. The building's past use contrasts sharply with its present, as owner Troy Rarick and his employ-

Hundreds of miles of singletrack snake through dramatic deserts around Fruita, Colorado.
(© Jeff Cricco/Colorado Tourism Office)

ees are ebullient enthusiasts of all things biking, hiking, and kayaking. Rarick wrote the book on mountain biking in the area—literally. *The Fruita Fat Tire Guide* compiles all the tips that the store has been sharing since its inception and serves as a tribute to the massive trail-building efforts that have taken place around the funky farming town. More than 400 miles of mountain-biking trails snake through the Grand Valley, and a large chunk of them is singletrack, designed specifically for dizzying thrills on two wheels. While many other mountain-biking meccas throw in a mix of fire roads and doubletrack, it's possible to bike all day, or even all week, around Fruita on a narrow rope of trail that rolls along ridgetops and spirals into canyons, mixing Rocky Mountain greenery with desert drama.

Some of Fruita's most prized riding—such as the fifteen-mile Western Rim loop—is found in the Rabbit Valley area, which contains part of the Kokopelli Trail, a 142-mile mountain-biking corridor that winds through the desert to Moab. The area is crisscrossed with excellent hiking trails as well, including Devils Canyon and Pollock Bench. Multiday excursions and backcountry camping options are seemingly endless in the McInnis Canyons National Conservation Area; Fruita is also surrounded by rock art and historic and active dig sites, reachable by short exploratory hikes through cactus and berry bushes.

Fruita has a refreshing number of water sports, too. One-day rafting trips on the Colorado River lead paddlers through red sandstone canyons and on Class III to IV rapids, while overnight journeys rollick along the Gunnison or Dolores rivers. Highline Reservoir, just west of town, provides kiteboarding, windsurfing, and fishing (largemouth and smallmouth bass) opportunities, while Powderhorn Ski Resort, on the sprawling Grand Mesa, keeps adventurers entertained with downhill skiing and snowboarding when the frozen stuff falls.

The mild climate and year-round recreation make any month a fine time to visit Fruita. But the town itself is liveliest in the springtime, when the Fruita Fat Tire Festival celebrates mountain biking with endurance races, road-bike tours, and barbecues. Spring also means the Mike the Headless Chicken Days, where you can play football with a frozen chicken, eat fried chicken, and run like a chicken with its head cut off in a 5K foot race. On a weekday night in the summertime, you might just find yourself ringside at the Tuesday rodeo or park-bound for the Thursday-night variety shows, which feature free music at the Civic Center Pavilion. And if you still have energy to burn, Over the Edge's staff will point you in the right direction.

Local Legend

Mike the Headless Chicken

Fruita's most famous resident was a chicken named Mike who lived for eighteen months without a head. Really. It all happened in the mid-1940s, after Lloyd Olsen, a Fruita farmer, set out to fetch some supper with his ax. But when he cut off a chicken's head, the bird stayed alive. Surprised at—at impressed by—the bird's resilience, the Olsen family then began feeding "Mike" with an eyedropper until scientists from the University of Utah whisked the chicken to Salt Lake City for further study. They figured out that most of Mike's brain stem had survived the blow, allowing him to live a fairly normal existence. The Olsens then began touring the country with Mike the Headless Chicken until one day in 1947 when his esophagus closed. Today, Fruita's folks celebrate Mike's will to live with a raucous yearly festival.

Start the Day

Aspen Street Coffee House (136 East Aspen Avenue; 970-858-8888): Offers free wireless Internet access and has local artwork on display.

Gear Up

Over the Edge Sports (202 East Aspen Avenue; 970-858-7220): Full-suspension mountain bikes, and custom-made road bikes and hiking gear, plus maps and guides. Also has coffee and espresso drinks.

Refuel

The Hot Tomato Café (201 East Aspen Avenue; 970-858-1117): Gourmet pizza and sandwiches.

Pancho's Villa II (229 East Aspen Avenue; 970-858-9380): Real-deal Mexican joint.

Rib City Grill (455 Kokopelli Drive; 970-858-6566): Baby-back ribs, crunchy grouper salad, and other comfort foods.

Bunk

Casa Fruita (180 South Orchard Avenue; 720-840-8102): A three-bedroom house for rent in downtown Fruita; includes air conditioning, bike-tuning tools, and Wi-Fi.

The Wild Side

Colorado National Monument

Colorado National Monument is a 20,500-acre playground of sheer-walled canyons, steep cliffs, monoliths, and other geologic formations straight out of a Dr. Seuss book. Carved by the Colorado River, the monument is one of the least visited attractions of the Southwest, which makes explorations of its features like walking on the moon. For a quick trip, cruise along twenty-three-mile Rim Rock Drive—just don't park your rig anywhere near the precipitous overlooks. Or hike among the Coke Ovens, sharp fins of rock, and around Independence Monument, a 450-foot sandstone tower.

Stonehaven Inn (798 North Mesa; 800-303-0898): A Victorian bed-and-breakfast with bike-and-wine packages.

Serenity Bed & Breakfast (1763 K 6/10 Road; 970-858-6645): An Oriental health spa with three rooms and big breakfasts.

Can't Leave?

Nearest airport: Walker Field, Grand Junction, Colorado (12 miles)

Primary industries: Retail, services, manufacturing, transportation and utilities, wholesale trade

Gunnison, Colorado

Population: 5,298

Action: Downhill skiing, hiking, mountain biking, rafting, paddling, fishing

Offering to give hotel guests a free meal every gloomy day is generally not a good business plan, but when managers at the La Veta Hotel created such a gimmick in the early 1900s, they had Mother Nature on their side. "We had sunshine in Gunnison every day in 1912, every day in 1913 (except one day)," boasted a sign behind La Veta's check-in desk. "1914???"

More than 100 years later, the constant sunshine ensures that a similar bet could still lure guests to the western-slope town of Gunnison, Colorado—if these visitors weren't already captivated by the Gunnison National Forest, the Curecanti National Recreation Area and its Blue Mesa Reservoir, the Gunnison Whitewater Park, the nearby Fourteeners (mountains over 14,000 feet high) and countless hiking and biking trails that surround town, and the blue-ribbon fly-fishing waters of Gunnison River. (There are nearly 4,000 miles of fishable rivers and streams in Gunnison County.)

Less than thirty miles from Crested Butte, Gunnison has all the same access to the outdoors without the expense and with milder weather. Instead of upscale resorts there are simple motels—places to shower and trade a sleeping bag for a bed—that seem to dismiss the importance of rest when one could be out playing. The four-year choice for students of Western State College of Colorado—where student life revolves around the wilderness and wellness and which has its own gear shop—Gunnison has also become the choice for adventurers seeking a weekend or a lifetime in the real West.

Despite such creative marketing schemes as the La Veta's, and the presence of numerous saloons, Gunnison nearly became a Colorado ghost town in the late 1800s thanks to a rapid rise and fall of the mining and railroad industries. But ranching survived, as did education (Western State was founded as the Colorado State Normal School in

The challenging singletrack at Hartman Rocks has made sunny Gunnison, Colorado a popular mountain-biking destination. (© Tom Stillo, Photographer, & Gunnison-Crested Butte Tourism Association)

1911) and, of course, recreation. There were ski races in town as early as 1887, and snowshoe clubs at the turn of the next century; by the winter of 1961–1962, trails from the Crested Butte Ski Area (now Crested Butte Mountain Resort) had begun to spill down from the pointy, 12,162-foot peak of Mount Crested Butte.

Far from most everything, and ferociously steep at the Extreme Limits terrain, the ski area remains a Shangri-la for serious skiers and snowboarders who don't mind hiking for the hard stuff in feathery-soft snow. There's even more powder at Monarch Mountain, an 800-acre area east of Gunnison and along the Continental Divide.

Crested Butte's mountain-biking culture has also carried over to Gunnison, where Hartman Rocks Multi-Use Recreation Area, or the Rocks, offers more than fifty miles of singletrack trails, some as steep and as banked as a luge track, winding through otherworldly rock formations and over slickrock. The Rocks, sometimes compared to Moab, Utah, is the site of 24 Hours in the Sage, a mountain-bike endurance race held every August in which expert riders compete alone, with a partner, or with three to four teammates. The Rocks also has some rock-climbing routes, but climbers are more apt to head to Taylor Canyon Road, northeast of Gunnison.

The most spectacular canyon around, however, is the Black Canyon of the Gunnison—twice as high as the Empire State Building in some parts and infinitely more interesting. Northwest of Gunnison and a national park since 1999, the Black Canyon is actually a rainbow-colored landscape of knife-edge cliffs, cut by the Gunnison River, that tell stories of geologic history.

The Wild Side

Fourteeners

Northeast of Gunnison, the Sawatch Range contains fifteen of Colorado's fifty-four Fourteeners, or peaks over 14,000 feet. The tallest of all of them—Mount Elbert, at 14,433 feet—is in the Sawatch Range and is one of the easiest to climb. Give yourself a full day, starting just after sunrise, to hike the North Elbert Trail.

Some 180 miles long, the Gunnison River has been called one of the most complex and fascinating trout rivers in Colorado by *Fly Fisherman* magazine, thanks to its native cutthroats, rainbows, and browns; it's also been declared a gold-medal trout stream by the Colorado Wildlife Commission. And where the Gunnison empties into the twenty-mile-long Blue Mesa Reservoir in the Curecanti National Recreation Area, it has created fjordlike areas best explored by a canoe or kayak. (Kayakers can also hit the Gunnison Whitewater Park, the source of stickers around town that read "Surf Gunny.") Windsurfers and winter snowkiters skim across the Bay of Chickens, their sails looking like tiny butterflies to the hikers and backcountry skiers who've scaled the heights of the surrounding peaks. Twinkling across the Blue is the sun—you can bet on it.

Start the Day

Mochas (710 Main Street; 970-641-2006): A drive-through coffee shop with espresso drinks, bagels, sandwiches, and smoothies.

Gear Up

Scenic River Tours, Inc. (703 West Tomichi; 970-641-3131): Rafting and fishing trips on the Gunnison and Taylor rivers, plus climbing in Taylor Canyon.

TuneUp (222 North Main Street; 970-641-0285): Bike shop.

Refuel

The Gunnison Brewery (138 North Main Street; 970-641-2739): Brew-pub fare and Dunkel Weisen beers.

Blue Iguana (303 East Tomichi Avenue; 970-641-3403): Hand-mashed beans and ice-cold drinks; order the green-chile–smothered chimichanga and grab a seat on the outdoor deck.

Garlic Mike's (2674 North Highway 135; 970-641-2493): Italian fare, from calamari and antipasto to ravioli, pizza, and parmigiana; overlooking the Gunnison River.

Bunk

Curecanti National Recreation Area (970-641-2337; www.nps .gov/cure): Ten campgrounds surrounding the Blue Mesa Reservoir; the best for tents is the Ponderosa, with twenty-nine sites.

The Wildwood Motel (1312 West Tomichi; 970-641-1663; www.wildwoodmotel.net): Eighteen basic cabins and cabinettes on a quiet property with its own fish-cleaning station.

Can't Leave?

Nearest airport: Gunnison–Crested Butte Regional (2 miles)

Primary industries: Tourism, education, ranching

Salida, Colorado

Population: 5,476
Action: Paddling, rafting, mountain biking, hiking, downhill skiing

To the Gucci-wearing types who jet over to Colorado's resort communities every weekend for fun, Salida—in the Upper Arkansas Valley of the south-central part of the state—might as well be Siberia. They generally don't pay attention to a place where there's no gondola access to a major ski resort within walking distance of the local sushi bar. But to true all-around outdoor lovers, Salida may just be the ultimate Colorado mountain town. It's surrounded by fifteen peaks higher than 14,000 feet; it's the epicenter for whitewater paddling action in the West; it's accessible to mountain biking, rock climbing, backcountry skiing, and fly-fishing; and thanks to quirks in geography, it stays mild and dry all winter (unlike Siberia).

Salida lies under the morning shadow of the Sawatch Range of the Rockies to the west; the Sangre de Cristo Mountains are to the southeast and the Mosquito Range is to the east. Located about seventy-five miles southwest of Colorado Springs, it sits on the banks of the frothy Arkansas River at 7,100 feet in elevation, in a spot where the sun shines for more than 300 days a year and mild air drifts from the south to keep the average high temperature in the coldest months in the high forties. Established as a railroad outpost in 1880, it's home today to many artists and entrepreneurs transplanted from California and the nearby Front Range. These folks have restored many of the historic Victorian homes downtown and set up shop in the old Western storefronts. And if these people didn't come to Salida for the paddling, they're no doubt whitewater addicts by now.

The town is near the midsection of the Arkansas Headwaters Recreation Area, a legendary, roughly 150-mile stretch of river from Leadville to Pueblo Lake that is chock-a-block with Class III and IV rapids during spring runoff and early summer. The first fifty miles of this route plummet almost 3,000 feet in elevation, ending with the popular ten-

On-street kayak parking reflects the fact that Salida, Colorado is the epicenter for whitewater paddling action in the West. (© Heart of the Rockies Chamber of Commerce)

mile Browns Canyon run that leads into Salida. Downtown, there are even two municipal playholes in the artificial whitewater park on the Arkansas, the lower one alongside the recently revitalized Riverside Park. They're joined by a paved trail and form the nexus of the annual FIBArk ("First in Boating on the Arkansas River") festival, held every June since

1949. The event is renowned for its downriver race, the oldest and longest paddling competition in North America, running 25.7 miles from Salida to Cotopaxi. The freestyle and slalom championships also draw contestants from around the world. During the rest of the white-water season, the river is dominated by recreational kayakers and rafters and the eighty or so outfitters in the Arkansas River Valley.

The area's mountain biking might not share the same reputation as the paddling, but riding is nearly as big of an obsession among the locals. Hundreds of miles of singletrack zigzag the three major mountain ranges looming over Salida, and the 2,500-mile Great Divide Mountain Bike Route passes through the valley floor. People in town brag about how they can ski at Monarch Mountain, about twenty minutes away, in the morning and pedal wearing just a sweatshirt in the afternoon. Salida's most famous ride, the Monarch Crest Trail, is open only in the summer, because it starts on the Continental Divide above the treeline at 11,312 feet before plummeting 4,000 feet over its forty or so miles into the village center. High Valley Bike Shuttle provides rides to the top, usually from July to late September. Along its path, the Monarch Crest overlaps with stretches of the 3,100-mile Continental Divide Trail and the 470-mile Colorado Trail.

The town is also a supply stop and base camp for hikers headed into the Sangre de Cristo Range and the Collegiate Peaks Wilderness. The latter, a 168,000-acre preserve straddling the Continental Divide largely in the Sawatch Range, is home to eight 14,000-foot peaks. In the evenings, it seems as if everyone pours from the nearby mountains into downtown Salida—where you'll also find the largest historic district in Colorado—to grab a drink or a bite to eat. It also seems as if everyone strolling among the art galleries, bed-and-breakfasts, restaurants, and gear shops knows everyone else, giving Salida a down-home vibe that the visitors to Gucci havens like Vail and Aspen will never experience.

Local Legend

The FIBark Festival

The downriver race held nowadays at the FIBark Festival is nearly twenty-six miles, but in the beginning, it was more than twice that length, according to event historians. In 1949, twenty-three paddlers put in at Salida for the fifty-six-mile run. The course, before terminating in Canon City, passed through the treacherous, ten-mile-long Royal Gorge Canyon, which has granite walls as high as 1,200 feet and a base width of only fifty feet in spots. Only two men completed the race. The next year, Royal Gorge was cut out from the course, but still only one competitor passed the finish line. So in the third year, the race was cut to its current 25.7-mile length. Even shortened, the race is considered one of the most grueling events in North America.

Start the Day

Bongo Billy's Salida Café (300 West Sackett Avenue; 719-539-4261; www .salidacafe.com): Grab a coffee and a breakfast burrito and sit on the balcony facing the Arkansas.

Patio Pancake Place (640 East Rainbow Boulevard; 719-539-9905): Opens at 6 AM and serves breakfast all day.

Gear Up

Arkansas River Fly Shop (7500 West U.S. Highway 50; 719-539-4223): Experts on the region's waters; also runs a fly-fishing school.

Absolute Bikes (330 West Sackett Street; 888-539-9295): A bike shop offering rentals, guide service, and more knowledge on the local riding than you'll even need.

Bill Dvorak's Rafting and Kayak (17921 U.S. Highway 285, Nathrop; 719-539-6851): This highly respected outfit runs trips throughout the Southwest and Rockies, including on the Arkansas River.

The Wild Side

Mount Harvard

There's one way to say you've conquered the challenges of Harvard without ever setting foot in Massachusetts: climb 14,420-foot Mount Harvard, the third-highest peak in Colorado and one of eight summits over 14,000 feet in the Collegiate Peaks Wilderness west of Salida. Of course, if you prefer Princeton (14,197 feet), Yale (14,194), or Oxford (14,153), you can take a shot at those mountains, as well. The preserve traces forty miles of the spine of the Sawatch Range, along the Continental Divide. There are about 105 miles of hiking trails in the Collegiates, leading to jagged mountain tops, among hidden lakes and streams, and down to empty alpine valleys at 8,000 feet in elevation. Talk about higher learning.

Refuel

First Street Café (137 East First Street; 719-539-4759): Serves great steaks and Southwestern-style American food; located in an 1885 brick building.

Amicas Pizza (136 East Second Street; 719-539-5219): Wood-fired-oven pizzas and microbrew beers.

Country Bounty Restaurant and Gift Shoppe (413 West U.S. Highway 50; 719-539-3546): Grab some melt-in-your-mouth pot roast and some jewelry from the gift shop at the same time.

Bunk

Aspen Leaf Lodge (7350 West U.S. Highway 50; 719-539-6733; www.aspenleaflodge.com): A well-kept, single-story motel with a hot tub and views of the mountains.

River Run Inn (8495 County Road 160; 719-539-3818; www.river runinn.com): A magnificently restored 1892 former farmhouse, on its own stretch of the Arkansas River, with private-access fishing.

Beddin' Down Bed, Breakfast and Horse Hotel (10401 County Road 160; 800-470-1888; www.beddindown.com): A log cabin–style bed-and-breakfast with horse stables available.

Can't Leave?

Nearest airport: Gunnison–Crested Butte International (65 miles)

Primary industries: Recreation, art, retail

Silverton, Colorado

The precious metal that gave Silverton its name and onetime wealth has long since vanished from the surrounding San Juan Mountains, but the town lives on, drawing vitality from tourists, history buffs, and hardcore outdoor adventurers. Its resilient nature and homey aura make it as appealing as its better-known sister, Durango, fifty miles south near the New Mexico border. People need to be resilient when they live in a town plopped in a round valley at 9,300 feet, where the weeks of the growing season can be counted on two fingers. Their reward: it's also a gold mine—pardon the expression—for world-class hiking, biking, skiing, and paddling.

Population: 548
Action: Hiking, mountain and road biking, downhill skiing, paddling

The main source of recreation is the San Juan National Forest—the same Rhode Island–sized playground on the Continental Divide's western slope that put Durango on the outdoor-sports map. Within the 1.8-million-acre park are roughly 500 miles of trails spiderwebbed among lakes, canyons, thick aspen groves, frothing rivers, and peaks stretching higher than 14,000 feet. Some of the West's toughest, and most rewarding, hikes and rides—both singletrack and road—are found there and accessed from town, along with the wildest lift-accessed ski mountain ever conceived.

Miners first began to flock to Silverton in the mid-1870s, and it soon exploded with growth, prosperity, and the seedier aspects of the Old West that usually accompanied them. At one point, about forty saloons graced wide Blair Street, along with more than a few brothels, according to the Silverton Historical Society. Dodge City hero Bat Masterson was even supposedly hired as sheriff for a while to clean up the place. If you step into the Gold King Restaurant and Saloon on Greene Street, you can see the bullet hole in the back bar that the owners claim came from a shot fired by his gun. The last local mining

Silverton, Colorado rests in a round valley of the San Juan Mountains, at an elevation of 9,300 feet. (© Tom Stillo/Colorado Tourism Office)

operation closed in the 1990s, and by that time gold, silver, lead, and zinc had all been extracted from the peaks that ring the town like a jagged crown.

Now when people head into the mountains, the only gold they'll find comes from the sunset views over the San Juans and the only silver from the clouds wafting around them. With so many trails in the area, the biggest challenge for backpackers is deciding which route to take. The first choice is usually the ten-mile Needle Creek Trail, accessed by the narrow-gauge train that has run between Silverton and Durango for more than 130 years. It starts at the Needleton Stop—the site of an old mining camp—and climbs about 3,000 feet to Chicago Basin above the treeline, providing unhindered views of a handful of 14,000-foot peaks along the way. The 3,100-mile Continental Divide Trail veers close to town, as does the 500-mile Colorado Trail as it travels its course through eight mountain ranges and six national forests from Durango to Denver.

The biking is no less thrilling. The forty-seven-mile road climb from Durango, at 6,500 feet, to Silverton is a prime example; in addition to gaining 2,800 feet along the way, you also have to pass through Coal Bank Pass at 10,640 feet and Molas Divide at 10,910 feet. The course is used every May for the Iron Horse Bicycle Classic, a race against the narrow-gauge train and hundreds of other cyclists that is usually won in just over two hours and ten minutes (by a person). The area mountain biking, over equally as steep and spectacular terrain, is what has turned the Durango area into renowned fat-tire destination. Close to Silverton is the popular and fairly forgiving Lime Creek Trail, a former ten-mile stagecoach road leading to Purgatory; the trail also links to the smooth, legendary twenty-mile Hermosa Creek Trail, a technical stream-crossing forest ride with many open views.

If you're looking for a straight shot of adrenaline, bring your bike to the Silverton Mountain ski area and hop on its lone lift, which climbs 2,000 vertical feet to an elevation of 12,300 feet. In the winter—when most businesses in Silverton are closed down—this experts-only resort opens up to provide the closest experience to heli-skiing you can get without a helicopter. As many as 475 skiers take to the mountain each day during peak season, some unguided, some led by guides, and armed with avalanche beacons, probes, and shovels. The steeps there are not for the weak-kneed—figuratively or literally. The slope on its easiest run is thirty degrees, and its most treacherous stretch plummets at fifty-five degrees.

Maybe the town's biggest thrill ride, though, isn't a ski slope, but a stretch of water. The Animas River drops more than eight feet per mile through a barrage of Class III through V rapids from Silverton to Durango. Several outfitters run regular trips down the Animas in the summer. Coordinate your schedule so you can take the train back to town with your treasured memories—a prize maybe more valuable

Local Legend

The Railroad

In 1882, the narrow-gauge railroad connecting Durango to Silverton was completed, and since that time, it has hauled an estimated $300 million in precious metals. Although the area's mining industry has largely vanished, the line continues to carry passengers on its coal-powered, steam-driven trains. Its route through the San Juans along the Animas River is lined with stunning mountain vistas and the remains of old mining camps. It also makes two stops along the way to give bikers, hikers, and mountaineers access into the surrounding wilderness. Most of its locomotives and passenger cars date from late nineteenth and early twentieth centuries, capturing not only the imagination of riders, but also of Hollywood. The railroad has been used in several movies, including *Butch Cassidy and the Sundance Kid.*

The Wild Side

The Weminuche Wilderness Area

The rugged Weminuche Wilderness Area spreads across 490,000 acres of the San Juan and Rio Grande national forests, making it the largest wilderness area in Colorado. The average elevation within its boundaries is over 10,000 feet, meaning that much of its 500 miles of trails lies either in grassy open stretches above the timberline or in the forests just below it. It boasts three peaks over 14,000 feet—Mount Eolus, Mount Windom, and Sunlight Peak—and the headwaters for the San Juan and Rio Grande rivers. Need more incentive to check it out? It lies only about five miles outside of Silverton.

than the silver that once came from these hills.

Start the Day

Mobius Cycles & Café (1309 Greene Street; 970-387-0777): Get your bike repaired while you're served a mocha latte and bacon-and-grits breakfast burrito.

Avalanche Coffee House and Café (1067 Empire Street; 970-387-5282): Grab a cappuccino and roost on the welcoming front porch.

Gear Up

Outdoor World (1234 Greene Street; 970-387-5628): A full selection of camping, hunting, and fishing gear—and knowledgeable advice from owners Wiley and Wyatt Carmack.

Mobius Cycles: See above.

Refuel

The Explorers Club Southwest (1332 Blair Street; 970-387-5006): A hiking and mountain-biking guide service with a pub at its headquarters. Order a steak from the menu and grill it yourself.

The Pickle Barrel Restaurant (1304 Greene Street; 970-387-5713; www.thepickelbarrel.com): A family restaurant in the town's oldest standing structure—a former mercantile shop built in 1880 and later turned (surprise) into a saloon.

Bunk

The Grand Imperial (1219 Greene Street; 970-387-5527; www.grandimperialhotel.com): A forty-room hotel built in the rough-and-tumble nineteenth-century heyday of Silverton, complete with a bullet still embedded in the wall at the bar.

The Wyman Hotel and Inn (1371 Greene Street; 970-387-5372; www.thewyman.com): The seventeen Victorian-style rooms are furnished with bona fide Victorian-era antiques in this century-old hotel, and its restaurant serves the finest food in town.

Inn of the Rockies at the Historic Alma House (220 East Tenth Street; 800-267-5336; www.innoftherockies.com): An immaculate ten-room, 100-year-old Victorian bed-and-breakfast gives you a refined taste of the old Silverton.

Can't Leave?

Nearest airport: Telluride Regional (19 miles)

Primary industries: Construction, tourism

Driggs, Idaho

Population: 1,197

Action: Downhill, backcountry, and cross-country skiing, hiking, fishing, mountain biking, rafting, paddling

Driggs is just forty-five minutes from Jackson, Wyoming, but you won't find any Million Dollar Cowboy Bar here, or many million-dollar houses, either. Driggs—which stares up at the same Teton Mountains—tends to work in slightly smaller numbers than Jackson: 84,000 tons of potatoes are grown in the surrounding Teton County every year, while more than 4,000 miles of hiking trails are accessible from the one (or two) horse town. The backyard ski area of Grand Targhee in the Caribou-Targhee National Forest gets 500 annual inches of snow—nearly fifty more than Jackson Hole—while the backcountry ski options could easily fill the entire 365-day span of a calendar. Locals boast of more than 200 miles of mountain-biking routes while anglers tell tales of eighteen-inch trout along the Teton River. The rafting and kayaking rapids are Class IV and V, while the lifestyle is singular.

Incorporated in 1910, Driggs is wedged between Wyoming and potato land, and identifies with both; farmers work the fields, movie-goers head to the Spud Drive-In (where naturally you can snack on french fries, "spud buds," and spicy fries), and many homeowners head over to jobs in Jackson. In the neat grid of streets, the sheriff's office, city hall, forest service office, hospital, and mountaineering shops are all within a short walk. Your spuds are everywhere; your suds are at the Royal Wolf, the local watering hole on Depot Street.

One of the most important roads in Driggs, Targhee Ski Hill Road, leads away from Little Avenue and toward Grand Targhee Ski and Summer Resort, just twelve miles from town and the kind of place where lifties wear cowboy hats. On the western slope of the Grand Tetons, Grand Targhee lives up to all the grandeur-nomenclature; it has chest-high powder across its nearly 2,000 acres (more than 1,000 of

A backcountry ski trip is the ultimate way to experience winter in the Tetons, on the Wyoming-Idaho border, near Driggs, Idaho. (© Teton Valley Chamber of Commerce)

which are reserved for snowcat skiing and snowboarding, where runs are an average of 2,000 feet long). The majority of the lift-served trails are intermediate, but you can find some tough stuff off Peaked Mountain or hike to the notorious Mary's Nipple (now called just Mary's by the resort). Grand Targhee's nordic program oversees fifteen kilometers of groomed cross-country skiing at Rick's Basin and teaches telemark, classic, and skate skiing. In the winter, you can also go tandem paragliding, snowshoeing, snowmobiling, or dogsledding, all arranged through the resort.

The ultimate way to experience winter on the Wyoming-Idaho border, however, is to take on a hut-to-hut or single-hut-based backcountry ski trip. Deep within the Tetons, there are three yurts perched at 8,000-plus feet, each outfitted with bunks, kitchens, and latrines. You can rent them on your own, or book a classic tour with guides from Rendezvous Backcountry Tours; the Teton Crest Traverse is a five-day expedition along the Haute Route of the Tetons, while another five-day trip leads skiers throughout the Jedediah Smith Wilderness between the Baldy Knoll and Plummer Canyon yurts. In the summer—enhancing the hiking options offered by eleven- to twenty-mile loops in the Jedediah Smith Wilderness—the Family Yurt becomes base camp for those hiking the Teton Crest Trail and touring Grand Teton National Park.

The warm-weather vehicle of choice for many Driggs residents is a mountain bike, useful for navigating to Pendl's for a pastry before tackling the twenty-five-mile Pole Canyon and Black Canyon Ride, which involves 4,000 feet of climbing. There's also the Big Hole Challenge, a system of trails and a mountain-biking race named after the western Teton Valley Mountains in which the singletrack sits. For a much different feel (and a look at another outdoor-based town), try the seven-mile paved trail between Driggs and Victor.

Watery routes abound in every direction, from the quiet canoe creeks that wander from downtown Driggs to the whitewater-rafting playground of the Snake River. Near Driggs is the Teton River, which winds 143 miles near the Continental Divide, creating a yin-yang destination for mellow fly-fishing and rollicking kayaking. (Among the best spots for both is the tricky Narrows section.) The river's a bit like the town of Driggs, which proudly proclaims itself the quiet side of the Tetons—but is anything from boring.

Start the Day

Pendl's Bakery & Café (40 Depot Street; 208-354-5623): Warm Linzer tortes and other Austrian pastries, along with coffee.

Bunk House Bistro (285 North Main Street; 208-354-3770): Full breakfasts, all served with Idaho potatoes.

The Wild Side

Gliding from Grand Teton

You don't need climbing experience to see the views from the summit of Grand Teton Mountain, at 13,770 feet. In fact, you don't even need hiking shoes—you just need to head to Teton Aviation, where a one-hour scenic glider ride will tow you up the west side of Grand Teton and release you and your motorless glider to soar back toward Driggs with only the sound of the wind—and your gasps—to accompany you.

Gear Up

Peaked Sports (70 East Little Avenue; 800-705-2354): Bike, canoe, kayak, and snow-sports rentals, plus sales of hiking and camping gear, maps, and books.

Yöstmark Mountain Equipment (12 East Little Avenue; 208-354-2828): Backcountry and nordic touring shop with rentals, sales, and guide service.

Rendezvous Backcountry Tours (1110 Alta North Road; 877-754-4887): Day and overnight tours for alpine, telemark, and cross-country skiers, snowboarders, snowshoers, hikers, and backpackers; also hut-to-hut trips and yurt rentals.

Refuel

O'Rourkes (42 East Little Avenue; 208-354-8115): A sports bar that serves standard pub grub such as burgers, fish and chips, and large salads alongside on-tap microbrews.

Tony's Pizza and Pasta (364 North Main Street; 208-354-8829): Pizza with homemade sauces; also sandwiches and microbrews.

Warbirds Café (675 Airport Road; 208-354-2550): An upscale eatery at an up-and-up location: the airport. Entrées include seared elk medallions and crispy polenta cakes; there's sushi and lunch here, too, and breakfast on weekends.

Bunk

Teton Canyon Campground (Teton Basin Ranger District, Targhee National Forest; 877-444-6777; www.reserveusa.com): Twenty campsites near the Jedediah Smith Wilderness, nine miles east of Driggs.

Movin' Sol Hostel (110 East Little Avenue; 208-354-5454; www.tetonhostel.com): Inexpensive dorm beds in an outdoor-oriented hostel run by instructors from the National Outdoor Leadership School (NOLS).

Intermountain Lodge (34 East Ski Hill Road; 208-354-8153; www.intermountainlodge.com): Cabins on the road to Grand Targhee.

Can't Leave?

Nearest airport: Jackson Hole, Jackson, Wyoming (28 miles)

Primary industries: Government, construction, retail, leisure and hospitality, education, professional and business services

McCall, Idaho

Population: 2,415
Action: Downhill
and cross-country
skiing, hiking,
paddling, moun-
tain biking, raft-
ing, fishing

for a town of 2,415, McCall has a suspicious number of restaurants, bars, bakeries, shops, and services. The reasons are rooted in pure selfishness: everyone wants to figure out how to stay in McCall and make enough cash to keep their garages stuffed with skis, kayaks, bikes, and backpacks. Take Bill and Corey McDonald, two brothers and avid anglers who were deciding between bread and beer as a McCall moneymaker. They eventually opened Evening Rise Bakery (named after a fly-fishing phenomenon) as a way to raise some dough. Or Kevin Truesdell and Lisa LaFond, who fled six-figure careers and city life in Washington State to hike Idaho's peaks—and open the Hartland Inn near prime trails.

Stories like these abound around McCall, where summers on sparkling, 5,500-acre glacial Payette Lake contrast with winters during which more than 300 inches of snow will fall in the mountains surrounding town. Not that people in McCall mind all that white stuff—Brundage Mountain Resort, with its 7,640-foot elevation and 1,300 acres of lift-served terrain, is just eight miles from downtown. The recently developed Tamarack Resort, just south of McCall, opened in the winter of 2004–2005 and has nearly 2,000 acres of groomed and off-piste terrain, plus thirty kilometers of nordic trails. There's another thirty kilometers of groomed cross-country trails, night skiing, a biathlon range, and Olympic training opportunities at Little Ski Hill and even more skinny-ski choices at Spring Mountain Ranch and Ponderosa State Park. Backcountry skiers earn their turns on Jughandle Mountain, while snowshoers find unlimited options throughout Long Valley. For sledheads, McCall has been named one of the best places to snowmobile in the Northwest, thanks to nearly 1,000 miles of trails. There's even the cult-favorite sport of curling here at the

Each year, more than 300 inches of snow falls in the mountains surrounding McCall, Idaho, beckoning backcountry and nordic skiers. (© Idaho Travel Council)

Manchester Ice and Event Centre; local business owners face off in a surprisingly competitive league.

One of McCall's premier events, held every year since 1965, is Winter Carnival, when ten days of snow-sculpture contests, masquerade balls, beer gardens, sleigh rides, and 20,000 snow- and ice-crazed people make St. Moritz look like a quiet cow town. And sorry, Swiss Miss, but east of Payette Lake lies an uninhabited (and uninhibited) alpine land, larger than Switzerland, littered with hiking and biking trails, mountain streams, and whitewater. The Payette National Forest sprawls more than 2.3 million acres, while the nearby Frank Church-River of No Return Wilderness is the largest such protected piece of land in the lower forty-eight states.

Rock-climbing cliffs and bouldering areas, such as the Thinking Spot, speckle the land around McCall. Jughandle Mountain has a dozen different climbing routes, rated 5.10a to 5.13b, and is also a popular hike. Many of the best hikes, however, are around McCall's many lakes; they range from easy walks to fishing areas (such as Boulder Lake) to longer loops like the ten-mile Loon Lake. July and August are the best months for fishing the cool alpine lakes.

At the big momma lake itself, Payette, you can keep your eyes peeled for Sharlie, the so-called lake monster, or reel in a more manageable rainbow trout, with which the lake is stocked. Payette has plenty of flatwater paddling spots; for whitewater rafting and kayaking, choose from the Middle and Main Forks of the Salmon River and the Snake River's Hell's Canyon National Recreation Area—home to the deepest gorge in North America.

To dry off, hit the lift-served mountain-biking trails at Brundage, which hosts world-class racing events on its singletrack, or at Tamarack, which worked with the International Mountain Biking Association to create twenty-five miles of trails. A different sort of saddle can be found at one of the many McCall ranches.

Soothe either kind of saddle sores at one of Idaho's hot springs; Burgdorf, north of town, was once a favorite of loggers and miners and remains rustic, while the full-facility ZIMS has a more modern approach. Try not to linger too long before making your way back to McCall—you'll want to leave just enough time left in the day to figure out which business scheme will allow you to stay here for good.

Local Legend

Smokejumpers

Skydiving? You'll think about it. Skydiving into a forest fire? Unthinkable—except to the seventy-member crew at the McCall Smokejumper Base, one of seven national locations managed by the U.S. Forest Service and staffed by nearly 300 smokejumpers. Forester T. V. Pearson first proposed smokejumping in 1934; the McCall Smokejumper Base started in 1943. It sends out parachuting firefighters on DC-3s and Twin Otters. The McCall Smokejumper Base is near six national forests—the Boise, Nez Perce, Payette, Sawtooth, Salmon-Challis, and Wallowa-Whitman—and open to the public for tours in the summer.

Start the Day

Common Ground Café (303 East Colorado Street; 208-634-2846): One-stop shopping for organic coffee, indie-rock CDs, live music, burritos, beer, and gallery art.

Gear Up

Gravity Sports (503 Pine Street; 208-634-8530): They'll rent you just about any toy you need, from skis and mountain bikes to kayaks and canoes, to defy, or give way to, gravity.

Refuel

McCall Brewing Company (807 North Third Street; 208-634-1010): Watch the sunset over Payette Lake with a pint of hand-crafted Hefeweizen on the rooftop.

Bryan's Burger Den (600 North Third Street; 208-634-7964): Veggie burgers— or the double beef special piled with cheese and bacon.

Lardo's (600 West Lake Street; 208-634-8191): A locals' favorite since 1973, serving pastas, steaks, sandwiches, and seafood on a large outdoor deck.

Bunk

The Wild Side

The Frank Church–River of No Return Wilderness

At nearly 2.4 million acres—more than ten times the size of all five New York City boroughs combined—the Frank Church–River of No Return Wilderness is the largest single wilderness in the lower forty-eight. It's possible to spend a week in this land and see dozens of bears and hundreds of rattlesnakes but not a single other human. To explore the Frank Church in the company of a slightly less intimidating creature, find information on horse-supported outfitted trips from the Idaho Outfitters and Guides Association (www.ioga.org).

Hotel McCall (1101 North Third Street; 208-634-8105): Reasonable rates, après-activity wine in the afternoon, and bedtime cookies and milk; near Payette Lake.

Brundage Bungalows (10005 East Lake Street; 208-634-8573): Log cabins, some with fireplaces, for rent across on Payette Lake.

Whitetail Club (501 West Lake Street; 208-634-2244; www.white tailclub.com): Luxurious, seventy-seven-room sporting-lodge resort with golf, racquet sports, marina, kayaks, and sailboats on Payette Lake.

Can't Leave?

Nearest airport: Boise Air Terminal/Gowen Field, Boise, Idaho (94 miles)

Primary industries: Tourism

Sandpoint, Idaho

Population: 8,105

Action: Downhill and cross-country skiing, mountain and road biking, kayaking, sailing, fishing

The beach volleyball season in Sandpoint, Idaho, ends a little soon—around late September, when the ospreys begin to leave, the bald eagles arrive, snow begins to crown the 8,000-foot peaks of the surrounding Selkirk and Cabinet Mountains, and people's thoughts turn toward skiing Schweitzer Mountain Resort's 2,900 acres. But still, there's beach volleyball, its presence in the Idaho panhandle as astonishing as the sudden sight of glaciated Lake Pend Oreille, a cobalt blue comma that curves forty-three miles through the pine-tree wilderness near the Canadian border. Even more refreshing is the discovery of the lake's 111-plus miles of shoreline, mostly empty of development and instead dotted with a few kayakers, sailors, and anglers. And in the tiny town of Sandpoint itself, there's the surprising find of not only big-city-worthy restaurants and shops, but also big-city people who just couldn't leave this place.

Even when the volleyball courts are quiet, Lake Pend Oreille (pronounced *pon-duh-RAY*) is Sandpoint's centerpiece. The lake is so deep—1,160 feet at some spots—that the U.S. navy conducted submarine research and training here during World War II. Long before that, the lake was named by French settlers, who noticed the ear pendants—the *pen d'oreille*—of the Kalispell tribe who populated northern Idaho when explorers arrived. One of these explorers was Canadian David Thompson, who in the early 1800s noticed the sandy point on which Sandpoint now sits. The town didn't really grow, though, until a general store, the Great Northern Railroad, and the timber industry arrived in the late 1880s. There's still a naval station and a logging community in Sandpoint, but the organized activity on Lake Pend Oreille and among its heavily treed shores is today more likely to come from the annual triathlon, the two-mile Long Bridge Swim, or lakefront festivals.

Lake Pend Oreille, the centerpiece of Sandpoint, Idaho, is mostly empty of development, leaving more room for kayakers, sailors, and anglers. (© Dick O'Neil)

Only eleven miles north of town, Schweitzer Mountain Resort has also had an impact on Sandpoint's growth since it first opened in 1963. The resort received a financial boost and the first of many improvements when a new owner bought the resort in 1998. Now you'll find a few more fieldstone-fireplaced lodges and hot-tubbed condominiums around the mountain than in the past, but the 6,400-foot summit still has the same camera-worthy views of Lake Pend Oreille, Canada, and three states. Schweitzer's average annual snowfall is 300 inches, and it's not Northwest cement, but fluffy stuff. It settles into open bowls and onto eighty-two trails (the bulk intermediate or advanced) for regular powder stashes. A nordic center offers thirty-two kilometers of cross-country skiing and snowshoeing, while the Selkirk Powder

Company whisks skiers and riders to off-piste playgrounds by snow-cat or snowmobile. Back on-mountain, the scene alternates between quiet weekdays; serious races, such as telemark competitions and the Schweitzer Alpine Racing School's events; and serious fun at January's Winter Carnival, In April, Sandpoint residents get ready for the beach with reggae and tropical drinks at the Caribbean Carnival.

The beach would be City Beach, eighteen acres of tanning terrain, boat ramps, and picnic areas. There's still plenty of square footage left, however, thanks to the fact that many Sandpointers head back to Schweitzer, where twenty-five miles of singletrack, doubletrack, and screaming downhills open for lift-served mountain biking in early July. At Farragut State Park, south of Sandpoint, there's more fat-tire action on the 10.5-mile North Perimeter Trail and the six-mile Shoreline Trail; Wednesdays in July see a weekly race series here. For road cycling, there are paved trails, built by North Idaho Bikeways, spiderwebbing out from Sandpoint and near limitless options on the tree-lined and deserted roads that surround the town.

There's no better post-ride place than the lake itself, where you can probably also catch your supper. Kamloops rainbow trout swim the deep waters, from which several true fish tales have started—thirty-two-pound, world-record rainbows; Dolly Varden (bull trout, now restricted to catch-and-release); and forty-three-pound lake trout have all been caught in Lake Pend Oreille. At one of Sandpoint's many marinas, you can book a fishing charter and rent sailboats. Or just climb into a kayak for a paddle of the sinuous shoreline, where (in between gaping at the Selkirks and Cabinets) you'll find quiet creeks, rocky coves, and maybe even a beach volleyball court or two.

Start the Day

Monarch Mountain Coffee (208 North Fourth Avenue; 208-265-9382): Fresh-roasted international coffee, including organic and fair trade, plus baked goods.

Panhandler Pies (120 South First Avenue; 208-263-2912): Full breakfasts and nearly two dozen kinds of pie made from scratch.

Gear Up

Full Spectrum Kayak Tours (321 North Second Avenue; 208-263-5975): Kayak rentals and tours of Lake Pend Oreille and Priest Lake.

Selkirk Powder Company/All About Adventures (Schweitzer Mountain Resort; 866-464-3246): Cat-skiing and guided snowmobile tours in the winter; biking, hiking, and kayaking trips in the summer.

Outdoor Experience (314 North First Avenue; 208-263-6028): Hiking, paddling, snowshoeing, and telemark gear, plus books and maps.

Refuel

Eichardt's Pub, Grill, and Coffeehouse (212 Cedar Street; 208-263-4005): This year-round local hangout has microbrews on tap, live music, a game room, and cheap burgers and sandwiches.

Dukes Cowboy Grill (30340 Highway 200, Ponderay; 208-263-0600): Barbecue joint featuring buffalo chili, Frito pie, pulled pork, ribs, and beer by the quart.

The Hydra Restaurant (115 Lake Street; 208-263-7123): Steakhouse with twenty-eight-day-aged filets and strips, along with seafood, chicken, a sixty-item salad bar, and Sunday brunch.

Bunk

K2 Inn (501 North Fourth Avenue; 208-263-3441; www.k2inn.com): Downtown motel with eighteen rooms.

Selkirk Lodge (10000 Schweitzer Mountain Road; 800-831-8810; www.schweitzer.com): Eighty-two slopeside rooms, an outdoor pool, and hot tubs on Schweitzer Mountain.

Western Pleasure Guest Ranch (1413 Upper Gold Creek; 208-263-9066; www.westernpleasureranch.com): Cabins and lodge rooms on 960 acres; the ranch also offers horseback riding.

Can't Leave?

Nearest airport: Coeur D'Alene Air Terminal, Coeur D'Alene, Idaho (40 miles)

Primary industries: Tourism and recreation, light manufacturing, timber

The Wild Side

The Selkirk Mountains

Idaho has more undeveloped forests than anywhere else in the lower forty-eight states, and the Panhandle contains some of its wildest terrain and some of the last of the woodland caribou. To increase your chances of spotting one of the animals, book a backcountry hike in the Selkirk Mountains with All About Adventures (www.allaboutadventures.com).

Livingston, Montana

Population: 6,851

Action: Fishing, hiking, mountain biking, downhill and cross-country skiing

America's largest undammed waterway, the Yellowstone River, forms a 150-yard-wide border on the southeastern fringe of Livingston. Railroad tracks, punctuated by a majestic 1902 Italiante-style train depot, cleave the town's center. Angular Mount Livingston pierces the broad horizon above the nineteenth-century red-brick buildings on Main Street. Art from the fifteen or so local galleries sits on display on the sidewalks as bikers, hikers, fly-fishers, and occasional celebrities pass by. This is Montana.

To be more precise, this is Montana's aptly named Paradise Valley, crowned by the Crazy Mountain and Gallatin ranges, where the western prairies collide with the Rockies. While throngs of tourists and nature-loving migrants continue to bloat Bozeman in the Gallatin Valley twenty-five miles west, Livingston keeps to itself—though not completely out of the limelight. So picture-perfect are its historic buildings and alpine backdrop in the heart of the country's premier fly-fishing territory that Hollywood has actually brought its cameras here several times. Most notable was the movie that shall remain nameless—at least in these parts—made by Robert Redford and starring Brad Pitt, which inspired so many people to pick up a fly rod and crowd Montana's trout waters. (Hint: The film's title rhymes with "A Liver Runs Through It.") Yet the fishing is only a small part of what there is to do in the untamed territory around town.

Livingston was more or less created by the Northern Pacific Railroad in the early 1880s. Within a decade it became a thriving stop on the ride west from Minnesota, as well as the main junction for tourists going to Yellowstone National Park, about sixty miles south. At the turn of the twentieth century, the railroad company employed the architects of New York's Grand Central station to design a town

With its picture-perfect historic buildings and alpine backdrop, Livingston, Montana has been the setting for several Hollywood films. (© Travel Montana)

depot that would be one of the largest west of the Mississippi at that time—a size that signified Livingston's importance. You can still find some of the 100-year-old buildings that were a part of the booming red-light district on B Street, and many of the magnificently preserved storefronts on Main Street look almost no different than they do in photos from the early 1900s. The depot, which went out of commission in the 1970s, is now a museum and the focal point for an annual arts festival put on in late June.

The town, much quieter now than it was in its heyday, is still considered an entry point for Yellowstone, but more importantly, it's a fishing and adventure outpost for the backcountry just outside its door. It sits in the center of Montana's fly-fishing country, offering easy access to more than 100 miles of creeks and rivers, including the famed waters of the Yellowstone, Gardiner, and Madison rivers. Thousands of fish per mile often lurk in these waters, and you can find an experienced fishing guide and instructor in Livingston faster than you can say "early hatch." If you want to take a few fly-casting lessons, learn about the history of the sport, or check out what some of the local fish species look like, head for the Fly Fishing Discovery Center on the corner of B and Lewis streets.

The options for backpackers and mountain bikers are even greater than for anglers. Livingston is surrounded by the 2,000 miles of trails spiderwebbed throughout the 2.1-million-acre Gallatin National Forest, a preserve that spans six mountain ranges. Stretching partially within the forest's borders, just south of town, is the Absaroka-Beartooth Wilderness, home to Livingston Peak, one of the summits of the verdant Absaroka Range. Absaroka-Beartooth also includes the tallest mountain in Montana, 12,799-foot Granite Peak in the jagged Beartooth Range. Mountain biking is prohibited in wilderness areas of the national forest, but is permitted on all of the Gallatin's trails outside of them. For maps and descriptions of the best hikes and rides, go to Timber Trails on West Park Street. In the winter, the local footpaths make for spectacular snowshoeing, but for other prime snow sports, you'll need to go a little farther afield. Cross-country skiers usually head for Yellowstone, and alpine skiers and snowboarders go to Bridger Bowl, a little more than thirty miles away. Not that the cold weather means an end to fly-fishing. Just about any day makes for a good day to put on a pair of waders in Livingston. This is Montana, after all.

Local Legend

The Livingston Roundup Rodeo

Cowboys don't exactly cram the streets of Livingston anymore, but it's still home to the state's largest professional rodeo, established in the early 1920s. The Livingston Roundup Rodeo lures the top wranglers in the country to compete in bull riding, steer wrestling, calf roping, team roping, and other events over the course of July 2, 3, and 4. The festivities start with a parade down Main Street, and its end is highlighted by the crowning of the Roundup Rodeo Queen, who is chosen for her speaking ability, modeling talent, and horsemanship.

Start the Day

Caffe d'Arte (1404 East Park Street; 406-222-2231): Bagels and lattes; drive through or eat in.

Northern Pacific Beanery (108 West Park Street; 406-222-7288): Under different names, this breakfast and lunch counter has been serving people at the train depot for the past century.

Gear Up

Timber Trails (309 West Park Street; 406-222-9550): The definitive mountain-biking and hiking shop in town. Owner Dale Sexton is a wealth of information on the local trails.

Dan Bailey's Fly Shop (209 West Park Street; 406-222-1673): A fly shop and guide service that has been a Livingston institution since it opened in 1938.

George Anderson's Yellowstone Angler (5256 Highway 89 South; 406-222-7130): A guide service and oversized store on the outskirts of town; sells flies of more than 1,500 patterns and sizes.

Refuel

The Stockman Bar (118 North Main Street; 406-222-8455): Agreeably priced steaks accompanied by the best fries in town.

The Sport (114 South Main Street; 406-222-9500): Animal heads and artifacts hang on the walls, and beneath them, great South-western dishes (using organic beef) are served.

Mark's In & Out Drive-In (Eighth and Park; 406-222-7744): Roller-skating waitresses come to your car at this drive-in open since—and still trapped in—the 1950s.

Bunk

Chico Hot Springs Resort (1 Old Chico Road, Pray; 406-333-4933; www.chicohotsprings.com): A century-old lodge and cabins on 150 acres south of town toward Yellowstone National Park; includes two natural, spring-heated mineral pools that are open year-round.

Murray Hotel (201 West Park Street; 406-222-1350; www.murray hotel.com): A 1904 railroad hotel with a towering neon sign out-side. Calamity Jane, Buffalo Bill, and Will Rogers have all set foot in it.

Can't Leave?

Nearest airport: Gallatin Field, Bozeman, Montana (45 miles)

Primary industries: Hospitality, health care, forestry/parks service

Red Lodge, Montana

Population: 2,401

Action: Downhill skiing, hiking, rafting, kayaking, fishing, rock climbing

There is a stark contrast between the peaks and folds of Montana's Beartooth Mountains and the town that nudges against them. In the Beartooths, the 12,799-foot Granite Peak—the state's highest point—can sneakily lure hikers into the maw of ferocious and fast-moving winter weather and an unforgiving wilderness. But in Red Lodge, it's a fun, friendly, and altogether straightforward vibe that greets visitors, whether it be at the post office, Café Regis, the motorcycle rallies, the rodeos, the ski-joring championships, or the rock-climbing routes. While dozens of hikers have disappeared in the Beartooths, dozens more out-of-towners are appearing as permanent residents of Red Lodge, thanks to the town's thriving cultural and recreational offerings, which are sprinkled with just the right amount of irreverence to prevent you from taking yourself too seriously. (Local adventurers save that serious approach for their own backcountry expeditions.)

Red Lodge was once a coal-mining town with nearly as much action as it has today, except most of the activity was happening underground or at the twenty saloons instead of in the rivers and mountains or at the coffee shop. According to varying versions of history, the town got its name from the Crow Indians, whose shelters included red-painted teepees. The Crow were displaced from their lands in 1882, but many tribal members stayed and were soon joined by immigrant miners from Italy, Ireland, Finland, and beyond. (Today, Red Lodge honors this infusion with summer's Festival of Nations, each day of which is dedicated to a different country and its heritage.) The population peaked at 5,000 in 1911, then began to decrease when mines closed in the 1920s. Bootlegging then became the business of choice; you can still check out the home of bootlegger Punch Cowboy on South Broadway today.

Many of the historic downtown buildings in Red Lodge, Montana now house gear shops, restaurants, and other businesses. (© Donnie Sexton/Travel Montana)

Most of the historic downtown buildings have since turned into gear shops, bars, and the occasional tourist trap for drivers on the stunning Beartooth Highway. Opened in 1936, the sixty-eight-mile long National Scenic Byway emerges from a thick layer of snow every May to take cars up Rock Creek Canyon to Beartooth Pass and an elevation of nearly 11,000 feet. With scant evidence of humanity, it could be called empty were it not for the abundant alpine meadows, glacially carved rock formations, and wildflowers that have only until the snows of October to make their appearance. The Beartooth Highway leads to a number of hiking trailheads, including the eight-mile (round-trip) Beartrack Trail, which connects Rock Creek Canyon to the 10,000-foot Silver Run Plateau, and the four-mile (out-and-back) journey to Glacier Lake. More hikes, such as the renowned Hellroaring Lakes Trail, abound around town, and Red Lodge is also just sixty-five miles from the northeast entrance to Yellowstone National Park.

Many of the alpine lakes and streams that you see from your perch at Beartooth Pass are excellent fly-fishing waters, while rainbow and brown trout swim the Rock Creek, which flows right through Red Lodge. The Rock Creek, a tributary of the Clarks Fork of the Yellowstone, also has Class III and IV rapids for whitewater. Longer kayaking or rafting options lie along the deceptively named Stillwater River, another Yellowstone tributary that ranges from lively, at the Class I and II Buffalo Jump, to downright ill tempered, at the Class V stretch near Woodbine.

Some of the area's closest mountain biking and cross-country skiing is found on the Silver Run Trails, where you'll find four loops of singletrack. The most easily accessed climbing routes (think pitches of up to 5.10b) lie in the Rock Creek drainage area. With the early arrival of winter every year, Red Lodge climbers also take advantage of frozen spots for ice climbing around the Rock Creek, East and West Rosebud Lakes, and the Stillwater River.

But winter around here really means Red Lodge Mountain, or RLM, just six miles west of town. The ski area spills through 1,600 acres of Custer National Forest. With a vertical drop of 2,400 feet and a balanced mix of trails, it makes an ideal local family resort. There's not much truly expert stuff, but the proximity and affordability of season passes still make it a top draw. You'll see the same people here that you will at annual Fun Run for Charities, at the rodeo, and at the post office. Red Lodge is that kind of place.

Start the Day

Café Regis (206 West Sixteenth Street; 406-446-1941): A local favorite for breakfast, which can include portabella mushroom omelets, tofu scrambles, and huevos rancheros with queso blanco.

Coffee Factory Roasters (6 1/2 South Broadway; 406-446-3200): Coffee by

The Wild Side

The Wild Side: The Absaroka-Beartooth Wilderness

The Absaroka-Beartooth Wilderness is more than a mouthful—it's also a lifetime's worth of remote backpacking routes in nearly one million acres of roadless lands. The Absaroka portion, named after what Crow Indians called themselves, is slightly softer, with forests and meadows, while the Beartooth portion has harsher, steeper, and more treeless terrain and spots with such names as Froze to Death Plateau. The safest way into the wilderness? With someone from Beartooth Mountain Guides (www.beartooth mountainguides.com), who'll lead you on a multiday climb up Granite Peak, take you ski mountaineering in the Twin Lakes Drainage, or just show you the rock- and ice-climbing skills you'll need to sample a taste of the place.

the pound or the cup, plus espresso drinks, smoothies, sandwiches, and free Internet access.

Gear Up

Sylvan Peak Mountain Shoppe (9 South Broadway; 406-446-1770): Hiking, camping, and backcountry-ski gear and clothing.

Hellroaring Cycle & Ski (105 West Twelfth; 406-446-0225): Has mountain and road bikes for rent, nordic equipment, and reports on trail and road conditions; espresso, fresh bread, and pastries are available from the "Bikery."

Local Legend

Local Legend: Racing Pigs

Aside from the hogs that roll into town every summer for the Beartooth Rally, Red Lodge's claim to porcine fame are the pig races held every summer weekend at the Bearcreek Saloon, seven miles east of town. Bring some extra cash for a steak dinner and to bet on the jersey-clad porkers (it's legal). You'll see what happens when pigs fly.

Refuel

Bridge Creek Backcountry Kitchen & Wine Bar (116 South Broadway; 406-446-9900): Serves microbrews, locally raised beef, huckleberry salads, and fry bread topped with local honey; also has the only Starbucks coffee in town.

Bogart's (11 South Broadway; 406-446-1784): A hamburger and Mexican-food eatery in a rustic cabin; serves homemade salsa, great Bloody Marys and margaritas, and vegetarian selections.

Red Lodge Pizza Company (115 South Broadway; 406-446-3333): Hand-tossed pies (try the barbecue-chicken-based Cliff Claven), calzone-like Montana Rolls, a wide selection of beers, and six-inch, deep dish, ice-cream- and chocolate-sauce-topped cookies for dessert.

Bunk

Alpine Lodge (1105 North Broadway; 406-446-2213; www.alpine redlodge.com): Basic motel with rustic pine paneling; picnic tables and grills outside each room.

Rocky Fork Inn (718 South Broadway; 406-446-2967; www.rocky forkinn.com): Centrally located bed-and-breakfast with six suites.

Pollard Hotel (2 North Broadway; 406-446-0001; www.thepollard .net): Historic downtown hotel with thirty-nine rooms and suites, a health club and racquetball courts; reasonable rates include a full breakfast.

Can't Leave?

Nearest airport: Billings Logan International, Billings, Montana (65 miles)

Primary industries: Agriculture, tourism, health care

West Yellowstone, Montana

When you go mountain biking and trail running around West Yellowstone, Montana, you might just need to reserve part of your lungs for an unusual custom around here: whooping and hollering to warn off the bears that occasionally rumble over from Yellowstone National Park. The town lies just a few feet from the west entrance of the park and all of the park's flotsam and jetsam—bison, birds, bears, and, yes, tourists included.

Population: 1,223
Action: Cross-country skiing, mountain biking, hiking, fishing, kayaking, rafting

But in the past few years, West Yellowstone, or West, has become much more than motels and an IMAX theater. Sure, the town sprouted up as a tourist resource in 1908, when the first trains of the Oregon Shortline Railroad arrived, and flourished when car traffic, winter travel, and overnight lodging became a reality in Yellowstone National Park. Now, however, bordered on its other sides by the Gallatin National Forest and Targhee National Forest, West—at an elevation of precisely 6,666 feet—can't help but morph into an adventure capital, one where bike outfitters, bookstores, and breweries have now staked their claim next to postcard and T-shirt shops. West's Rendezvous Ski Trails—just a few pedals away from the coffee shops—hosts one of North America's premier cross-country-skiing events every November and then converts to a mountain-biking haven in the spring. The locals cool off in nearby Hebgen Lake Reservoir by kayaking, swimming, and fishing (as if Yellowstone's rivers didn't offer enough trout opportunities). And lest West lose touch of reality, there are places like Strozzi's bar, where regulars with lumberjack names have their own bar stools.

Your first stop, winter or summer, is Free Heel and Wheel to rent bikes or cross-country skis for a ramble through the Rendezvous Ski Trails. (Or just bring your trail-running shoes for a loop around the

Visitors to Yellowstone National Park and the Gallatin and Targhee national forests can fuel up (or refuel) in West Yellowstone, Montana. (© Donnie Sexton/Travel Montana)

18.9-kilometer Perimeter Trail.) Originally old logging roads, the thirty-five kilometers of rolling terrain among lodgepole pine trees and open meadows were fashioned into a skinny-ski, and then fat-tire, playground in the 1970s. They soon proved to have enough early, consistent snow for the U.S. Nordic Team to train here in November. (There's also a biathlon range.) Now, dozens of college and junior teams, along with hundreds of other amateur skiers, flock to the Yellowstone Ski Festival every Thanksgiving week to train, race, demo gear, and participate in clinics. Book-ending West's cross-country ski season is the Rendezvous Race in March, a series of 2K to 50K competitions that draws nearly 1,000 top skiers. And in between the two events are months of nordic backcountry touring in the more than two million acres of Yellowstone National Park. Around Old Faithful, you can take on the three-mile Divide Lookout Trail to a perch on the Continental Divide, or embark on the Fairy Falls Trail, an eleven-mile trip around frozen waterfalls. Either way, you'll see a far different side of Old Faithful than you would in the summertime.

There's more skiing closer to West on the Riverside Ski Trail and its nearly ten kilometers of loops, and from a series of trailheads on U.S. Highway 191, the road to Big Sky and Moonlight Basin for lift-served alpine skiing and snowboarding. West of town, the Nemesis Mountain Hut clings to the Centennial Range and provides an ideal destination for a 3.5-mile backcountry climb up and slide down.

When summer arrives in West, there's still plenty of solitude to be found in Yellowstone National Park: along the Madison River, where trout easily outnumber the distant passing cars; and also on the Yellowstone, Missouri, and Beaverhead rivers. Hebgen Lake Reservoir, only a few miles from West, is another spot for rainbows and browns. (Among scientists and old-timers around here, the body of water is best known for the Hebgen Lake Earthquake of 1959, a 7.5-magnitude quake that reminded residents of Yellowstone's volatile nature.) The sixteen-mile-long lake is a prime flatwater paddling spot, while whitewater kayakers and rafters head to the Yellowstone River.

Even without Yellowstone National Park, the hiking options around West would seem nearly endless: thirty-six miles of the Continental Divide National Scenic Trail run through Targhee National Forest and 2,600 miles of hiking and horseback-riding trails wind through the Gallatin National Forest. And at the end of the day, the week, or the weekend, you'll be grateful for a bit of whooping and hollering—at bears or at the bars—in West Yellowstone.

Start the Day

Mocha Mamma's (40 Yellowstone Avenue; 406-646-7744):
Espresso drinks and coffee in Free Heel and Wheel.

Three Bear Lodge (217 Yellowstone Avenue; 406-646-7353):
Pancakes, omelets, and other full-breakfast fare.

Gear Up

Free Heel and Wheel (40 Yellowstone Avenue; 406-646-7744):
Mountain bike and cross-country ski rentals and sales, plus clothing, maps, and other outdoor gear.

Hellroaring Ski Adventures (406-570-4025): Backcountry ski tours
in the Centennial Range of southwestern Montana.

Blue Ribbon Flies (305 North Canyon Street; 406-646-7642):
Fly-fishing gear and guided trips throughout Yellowstone country.

Local Legend

Doug Edgerton

West Yellowstone's own celebrity is
prized for his grooming—his trail
grooming, that is. His name is Doug
Edgerton, and he is one of the nation's
top nordic-trail tamers. After moving
to West Yellowstone in the 1970s,
Edgerton began volunteering on the
trails around town, work that eventually
led him to design special attachments
for grooming machines. At the 2002
Salt Lake Olympic Winter Games, he
was appointed chief of grooming for
Soldier Hollow, the cross-country and
biathlon venue. He has since returned
to West to keep its trails more buttery
smooth than any others in North
America.

Refuel

Wolf Pack Brewing Company (139
North Canyon Street; 406-646-7225):
Microbrews, from Wapiti Wheat to
Storm Castle Irish Stout, to wash
down Rocky Mountain oysters,
bratwursts, soups, beer-battered
fries, and sandwiches.

TJ's Bettola (721 Yellowstone Airport
Road; 406-646-4700): Authetic Italian
food at the most unusual—or perhaps
most appropriate—location: the airport.

Wild West Pizzeria (14 Madison
Avenue; 406-646-4400): Pizza made
from scratch.

Bunk

Bakers Hole Campground (three miles
northwest of West Yellowstone on U.S.
Highway 191; 406-823-6961; www.fs
.fed.us/r1/gallatin): Seventy-three sites

on the Madison River in the Gallatin National Forest; open from May 15 to September 15.

Madison Hotel & Motel (139 Yellowstone Avenue; 406-646-7745; www.wyellowstone.com/madison hotel): A downtown, 1912 log building with dormitory rooms, private hostel rooms, or motel units.

Hibernation Station (212 Gray Wolf Avenue; 406-646-4200; www .hibernationstation.com): Offers forty-four cabins within walking distance of shops and trails.

Can't Leave?

Nearest airport: Gallatin Field, Bozeman, Montana (76 miles)

Primary industry: Tourism

The Wild Side

Yellowstone's Bechler Canyon

The conga line of cars along Yellowstone's roads is only one side of the oldest U.S. national park; the other sides are more remote than any ice-cream-slurping geyser watcher could ever imagine. For a three- to five-day backpacking trip, hit the Bechler Canyon area in the park's southwestern corner. A forty-mile round-trip trail leads through forests, meadows, canyons, and to waterfalls and your very own hot springs.

Whitefish, Montana

Population: 7,067

Action: Downhill and cross-country skiing, hiking, rafting, paddling, mountain biking, fishing

Among the most unusual regular happenings in the town of Whitefish, Montana, is the Monday night grizzly bear slide show. But the weekly event, held at Kandahar Lodge at Big Mountain ski area, which stands guard over the town like an overprotective boyfriend, is also one of the most useful. It's not some wildlife photographer's tales from afar, but a hard lesson in how to safely protect yourself from a grizzly in bear country, which happens to be right about where your car is parked, or anywhere else around Whitefish.

Just twenty-five miles from Glacier National Park and only a few miles more from Alberta and British Columbia, Whitefish lies in a wild corner of northwestern Montana, where grizzlies roam the streets and it's the residents who learn to adjust to the intruders. It's the price they pay for living in a mountain town (elevation: 3,033 feet) that boasts not only its own world-class ski resort, but also rivers, lakes, and mountain-biking trails in the 525-plus-square-mile Flathead County. And unlike some other of the state's outdoorsy outposts, where the coffee and the beer are served at a single joint and taste about the same, Whitefish has espresso cafés, brew pubs, and tasty eateries to seal the deal for anyone considering a move to Montana.

Whitefish earned its name from the fish that Native Americans were catching when fur trappers arrived in the 1850s, but also earned the nickname of Stumptown when loggers began felling trees in the thickly forested settlement. The fledgling town's future was secured with the arrival of the Great Northern Railway in 1891, and it was officially incorporated in 1905. Even as Whitefish lumbered along as a timber and railroad town, recreation appeared to be a viable, alternate means of income; golf courses and landing strips appeared in the first half of the twentieth century, and members of the Whitefish Lake Ski

Whitefish Lake's calm waters draw paddlers to Whitefish, Montana. (© Donnie Sexton/Travel Montana)

Club began poking around for trails in the 1930s. Ten years later, their endeavors had become Big Mountain, one of two natural features that simultaneously invites and controls the town's current growth.

The other is Whitefish Lake. (Development here can only go so far before hitting the mountain or water.) Seven miles long, two and a half miles wide, and 222 feet deep, the lake draws beachgoers (yes, beach-goers in Montana), waterskiers, wakeboarders, canoeists, and kayakers to the mostly wind-free, cobalt blue waters, and anglers and campers to Whitefish Lake State Park.

East and south of Whitefish, the Flathead River, which flows into to Flathead Lake, creates ideal fly-fishing conditions. Near the river's headwaters at Schaffer Meadows in the Great Bear Wilderness, Westslope cutthroat trout as long as twenty inches and as heavy as three pounds reach their prime in July and August, swimming the Upper Middle Fork. The South Fork teems with as many as 1,000 cut-throat per mile, while rainbow trout and Whitefish's namesake are also abundant throughout the area. These same glacially fed waters froth with rapids in the spring, when snowmelt can swell the rivers to fifteen times their normal levels, sending rafters tumbling over such Class III to IV rapids as Jaws and Bone Crusher on the Upper Middle Fork.

For a crash course in glacial history, though, there's little that rivals Glacier National Park, a million-plus-acre preserve of Ice Age descendants from 10,000 years ago. There are some 750 miles of hiking trails that wind through the Glacier, which in 2000 was voted the best backcountry park in America by the readers of *Backpacker* magazine. So while there are shorter day hikes near the West Entrance to Glacier, such as the four-mile climb to Scalplock Lookout, you shouldn't pass up the chance to embark on a longer expedition, such as the fifty-one-mile Highline Trail, which dances along the backbone of the Continental Divide. Going-to-the-Sun Road, which links cars to many of the park's trailheads, is also a challenging cycle. Glacier's spectrum of bright green lakes and, in winter, pale blue mountains, are wide open to anglers, nordic skiers, and snowshoers.

Or you can just roll out of your bunk in Whitefish and head eight miles to Big Mountain, where 3,000 acres of winter skiing and snowboarding terrain morph into a massive mountain-biking, hiking, and huckleberry-picking park in the summer. Just watch out for those other huckleberry fans—the ones with all the fur and an equal fondness for Whitefish and the Flathead Valley.

Local Legend

The Glacier Challenge

In the booming sport of adventure racing, a 10K run, 8-mile canoe, 27-mile road bike, 8-mile mountain bike, 2.5-mile kayak, and a final 5K run, is no big deal, especially if you have several teammates to help shoulder the physical burden. But every July in the Glacier Challenge, there are a few Whitefish locals who tackle the entire race all by themselves, posting times of four and half hours—times that rival the teams' top finishes. Whitefish, as it turns out, has bred some of the country's top adventure racers, who brag about the training terrain in their backyard and like to show off their skills at the Glacier Challenge. Or maybe it's one of the prizes— free bagels for a year—that keep these carbo-loaders returning.

Start the Day

Montana Coffee Traders (100 Central Avenue; 406-862-7667): Big mugs of joe in the shadow of Big Mountain; open since 1981, when the first bean was roasted in a popcorn popper.

Buffalo Café (516 Third Street; 406-862-2833): Go for what the locals eat: Buffalo Pie (two poached eggs atop ham, hash browns, and cheese); there's fruit, granola, pancakes, and french toast here, too.

Gear Up

Glacier Cyclery (326 East Second Street; 406-862-6446): Mountain-bike rentals, information on local rides and trails, and more.

Ski Mountain Sports (242 Central Avenue; 406-862-7541): Skiing, snowshoeing, paddling, and hiking equipment.

Glacier Outdoor Center (6 Going-to-the-Sun Road and Highway 2, West Glacier; 800-235-6781): Rafting and fly-fishing trips on the Flathead River system, plus backpacking, fishing, and cabin, cross-country ski, and snowshoe rentals, from a duo that began in 1976 and outfitted Meryl Streep and Kevin Bacon for *The River Wild*.

The Wild Side

Bob Marshall Wilderness

At more than a million acres, the Bob Marshall Wilderness, southeast of Whitefish, rivals Glacier in size, but has just a smidgen of the visitors (unless you count the elk, grizzlies, moose, mountain lions, and wolverines). You cannot drive through this area, so to immerse yourself in what *National Geographic* has called one of the last wild places in America, book a stay at the Bob Marshall Wilderness Ranch (www.wildernessranch.com). From there you can take a horseback ride into a landscape forgotten by the twenty-first century.

Refuel

Great Northern Brewing Company (2 Central Avenue; 406-863-1000): Linger until 8 PM in the tasting room, where Bear Naked Amber, Wheatfish Hefeweisen, and five other brews are served; also has free wireless Internet access.

Mambo Italiano (234 East Second Street; 406-863-9600): A rowdy pizza and pasta bistro; order the Italian nachos and save room for classic tiramisu.

McGarry's Roadhouse (510 Wisconsin Avenue; 406-862-6223): A refined roadhouse, serving smoked duck quesadillas, shrimp pad thai, and Montana steaks.

Bunk

Whitefish Lake State Park (Whitefish Lake; 406-862-3991): An eleven-acre park with twenty-three campsites for tents and RVs.

North Forty Resort (3765 Highway 40 West; 800-775-1840; www.northfortyresort.com): Twenty-two log cabins for rent on forty wooded acres; property includes hot tubs and nature trails.

Good Medicine Lodge (537 Wisconsin Avenue; 406-862-5488; www.goodmedicinelodge.com): A green-minded bed-and-breakfast with three suites and six rooms, but without the grandmotherly feel.

Can't Leave?

Nearest airport: Glacier Park International, Kalispell, Montana (10 miles)

Primary industries: Tourism, construction, health care

Heber City, Utah

early as staggering as the peaks surrounding Park City, Utah, are the prices of the old Victorians clustered around its steeply sloping Main Street and Old Town. But skiers, snowboarders, mountain bikers, and others who want easy access to the town's three ski resorts and 100-plus bars and restaurants—and to still be able to afford a season pass and a garage full of gear—have a choice: move to one of the outlying developments sprawling across the sagebrush between Old Town and Interstate 80, or pop over the Wasatch Mountains to Heber City. Here, in a wide, pastoral valley that serves as the yin to Park City's precipitous, sometimes chaotic yang, home prices are lower and the pace is slower. But the views of the surrounding mountains, including 11,750-foot Mount Timpanogos, are perhaps even more staggering.

Population: 9,147
Action: Downhill and cross-country skiing, mountain biking, hiking, fishing

Heber has been on the map since the mid-1800s, when a new road between Provo and the Heber Valley was completed, and the first permanent homes, many made of the local red sandstone, began sprouting among the farm fields. Made up of a mostly Mormon population initially, Heber earned its town incorporation in 1889 and then became a city in 1901.Today, its attitude is more country than city, and there are lumberyards, the restored "Heber Creeper" train, and old-fashioned ice-cream stands mixed in among the business outlets on Main Street. You can also throw in a bit of *A River Runs Through It* flavor, thanks to the Provo River that wanders through the valley and toward Robert Redford's Sundance Resort, twenty-five miles southwest of here. And there's even a *Sound of Music* ring to the hills west of Heber, as the town of Midway displays its Swiss heritage in its buildings, homes, and Swiss Days every Labor Day.

While nearby Park City boomed from silver mines and then turned to skiing, the Heber Valley's own rich resources (beyond agriculture)

Heber City, Utah offers plenty of scenery and outdoor recreation options without the high Park City prices. (© Utah Office of Tourism)

have long been more recreationally oriented, both aboveground and below it. In the late 1800s, hot springs were discovered and developed in the area; today, the Homestead Resort's beehive-shaped limestone crater contains one of the most unusual après-ski activities in the country: scuba diving in ninety- to ninety-six-degree water while sunlight pours in through the open aperture. At the site of the present-day 21,592-acre Wasatch Mountain State Park, federal soldiers once camped in the shadow of Mount Timpanogos, or Mount Timp. In 2002, Olympic biathletes and cross-country skiers aimed for gold medals at the park's Soldier Hollow. The Olympic venue remains one of the Games' premier legacies; there are thirty-six kilometers of cross-country skiing and snowshoeing trails, a biathlon range open in winter and summer (for hikers and mountain bikers who want to test out their marksmanship), mountain biking, golf, and a charter school for students in first through eighth grades.

While Heber has a couple of bars, its more notable watering holes are two reservoirs that flank town. Jordanelle Reservoir, north of Heber, has 3,068-acres of wakeboarding, waterskiing, fishing, and sailing, while windsurfers often find a good breeze ripping from the Provo Canyon at Deer Creek Reservoir, southwest of town. Running between the two reservoirs is a long stretch of the blue-ribbon Provo River. There are numerous access points for fly-fishing along the river, which is full of rainbow, brown, and cutthroat trout. The Provo then runs into Sundance Resort, where you'll find a confluence of angling and the arts (including artists in residence and an outdoor film festival every summer). There's also mountain-biking, horseback-riding, and hiking trails that lead around the 8,250-foot Sundance Mountain—an intermediate-friendly ski resort in the winter—and back down to the famed Owl Bar and Foundry Grill.

The opposite end of the cushiness scale lies east of Heber, in the High Uintas Wilderness, which features some of northern Utah's most spectacular and rugged alpine mountains and basins. The 456,705-acre area wears a thick coat of pine forests, speckled with remote lakes and canyons, making it a backpackers' dream, and one that stays off the radar of most Utah visitors who come for the mountain biking and the skiing and snowboarding. You'll find other visitors—but still room for yourself—at Deer Valley Resort, Park City Mountain Resort, and the Canyons, the three sprawling ski areas that surround Park City. And when you need more space, simply head back to Heber, where there's plenty to go around.

Start the Day

Sidetrack Café (98 South Main Street; 435-654-0563): Coffee shop with breakfast sandwiches, pastries, and quiches.

Gear Up

Rocky Mountain Outfitters (Soldier Hollow; 435-654-1655): Orvis-endorsed fly-fishing guide service, plus horseback riding and snowmobile trips.

The Wild Side

The Wasatch Front 100

If you're staying at the Homestead Resort in September, expect to see some wild-looking creatures staggering down from the mountains. These are the athletes in the Wasatch Front 100 Mile Endurance Run, one of the country's top—and toughest—ultramarathons. The course stretches from Kaysville, Utah, to the finish line at the Homestead, gaining 26,882 feet in elevation (and losing another 26,131 feet) as it crosses the ridges and valleys of the Wasatch Mountains.

Refuel

Dairy Keen (199 South Main Street; 435-654-5336): Fast-foot fare in a depot-themed drive-in; try the Train Burger and the thick milkshakes.

The Other End Bar and Grille (1223 North Highway 40; 435-654-5532): Local roadhouse with microbrews on tap, cheeseburgers, and sandwiches; also has an outdoor deck.

Snake Creek Grill (650 West 100 South; 435-654-2133): In a restored railway village, this restaurant offers items such as corn cakes with shrimp and sweet pepper cream, vegetarian risottos, and Belle Isle baby-back ribs; leave room for the gingerbread cookie sandwich.

Bunk

Wasatch Mountain State Park (435-654-1791; www.stateparks .utah.gov): Fifty-seven tent sites in this park at the foot of the Wasatch Mountains; head to the Little Deer Creek campground.

Homestead Resort (700 North Homestead Drive, Midway; 888-327-7220; www.homesteadresort.com): A full-service resort just west of Heber, offering ninety-seven guest rooms, twenty-seven suites and executive rooms, and twenty-three condos and homes; also has a hot-springs crater for swimming and scuba diving, a pool, golf course, cross-country skiing trails, and tennis courts.

The Lodge at Stillwater (1364 West Stillwater Drive; 435-940-3800; www.lodgeatstillwater.com): Near the Jordanelle Reservoir; has 174 rooms, pool, hot tubs, and transportation to area ski resorts.

Can't Leave?

Nearest airport: Salt Lake City International, Salt Lake City, Utah (43 miles)

Primary industries: Tourism

Moab, Utah

oab has become so famous as a mountain-biking mecca, you almost expect the streets to be paved with rubber, the bar stools to be shaped like bike saddles, and the residents never to unclip their Giro helmets. Instead, despite, yes, fantastic fat-tire options and the fast growth of the gearhead population, the town is more complex than a single-sport Shangri-la. Hippies still hang out here, as do artists and ranchers, rafters and rock climbers, truck drivers and desert dwellers. There are hikers, too, who dump the dust out of their boots after a day at Arches or Canyonlands national parks, both within kissing distance of Moab.

Population: 4,807

Action: Mountain biking, hiking, rock climbing, rafting, paddling, cross-country skiing

You might be bragging to all your friends about your upcoming adventures in Uvadalia if a certain Mormon postmaster had gotten his way. In 1885, he tried to change the name of Moab to Uvadalia. But the name Moab stuck, and its cliffs and canyons drew uranium, potash, and manganese miners, whose industry eventually crumbled and gave way to tourism in the 1970s.

It's Moab's geologic history, however, that really wows outdoors people. Some 300 million years ago, this place, along with nearly all of surrounding Utah, was covered by ocean, which eventually retreated to leave sand dunes and deposits of sandstone. The receding waters, along with erosion, formed many of the Dr. Seuss–like spires, arches, and needles that surround Moab. River floodplains, returning seas, and continental uplift created more layers of sandstone and shale, which can be identified in the Slickrock area and along many other hiking and biking trails.

Though the Slickrock Trail has become a fat-tire phenomenon, it was actually first developed in 1969 by motorcyclists, who, like the seas, have since mostly retreated. The roar of an engine is mostly relegated

A minivan bears mountain bikers and their gear to Moab, Utah. (© Utah Office of Tourism)

to off-road jeeping, which involves lumbering over the rocks in, you guessed it, a Jeep. When many are about to unwrap chocolate eggs or don bonnets, the Red Rock 4-Wheelers are celebrating the Easter Jeep Safari, when hundreds of off-road vehicles veer in every direction from downtown to thirty different trails.

Even if you prefer a little more peace and quiet, spring and fall are the best times to make a pilgrimage to Moab, as summer temperatures can soar to a scorching 100-plus degrees Fahrenheit. Newer knobby-tire trails include the seventeen-mile Baby Steps in the Klondike Bluffs area and the Moonlight Meadows, a downhill ride in the La Sal mountains; both areas are for nonmotorized use only. In Canyonlands National Park, you can hop on the dramatic White Rim Trail in the Island in the Sky district, wind your way through the Maze, or dart among the Needles. Guided explorations of these areas, along with trips on Kokopelli Trail, which runs 142 miles to Grand Junction, Colorado, and other classic mountain-biking areas can be arranged through Moab's Rim Tours.

Hikers' only limitation, in terms of where they can head from Moab, is how much water they can carry on their backs. You'll find mountain lakes and meadows in the La Sals. The La Sals also have some of Utah's best backcountry skiing in the winter; there are no lifts, lines, or fancy lodging—just high mountain huts equipped with stoves and mattresses.

For rock climbing, head for the Wall Street area, ten minutes from town on Potash Road, to scramble up sandstone on routes mostly 5.8 and up, or to Indian Creek, which is full of crack climbs. Cool off in the Colorado River, which flows through Moab's tall red canyons. Trips range from calm floats to rollicking rafting and rip-roaring jetboating and can be found through the Moab Area Travel Council. For a do-it-yourself option, hop in a canoe or kayak and take on the Class I through III rapids on the 16.5-mile section from Dewey Bridge to Castle Creek.

Start the Day

Jailhouse Café (101 North Main Street; 435-259-3900): Southwestern eggs Benedict, good coffee, and a plant-filled patio that's the center of Moab's scene on weekend mornings; as the slogan says, it's "good enough for a last meal."

Gear Up

Rim Cyclery (94 West 100 North; 435-259-5333): Moab's original bike shop opened in 1983 and rents a full line of bikes; reservations are recommended.

Rim Tours (1233 South Highway 191; 800-626-7335): Leads mountain-bike tours throughout the Moab area.

Tag-A-Long Expeditions (452 North Main Street; 800-453-3292): River trips and jeep safaris throughout southeastern Utah.

Pagan Mountaineering (59 South Main Street, number 2; 435-259-1117): Rock-climbing gear and guide services.

Refuel

Eddie McStiff's (57 South Main Street; 435-259-2337): Brews of thirteen varieties and burgers; Stiff is not the atmosphere, but an owner's nickname.

Moab Brewery (686 South Main Street; 435-259-6333): Beehive Brew root beer,

Local Legend

The Slickrock Trail

Unless your doctor has prescribed a strict, saddle-free regimen, you shouldn't skip riding the twelve-mile long Slickrock Trail, which put Moab on the map back in the 1990s. More than 100,000 people visit the trail each year, but you can avoid the crowds by going early in the morning, when the sun is turning the Navajo sandstone an egg-yolk yellow. Mountain-biking tires can actually get a good grip on the so-called slickrock, which makes tackling the tough, steep sections easier than it looks. Test your skills on the 2.3-mile Practice Loop, then let it roll on the main Slickrock, where climbs, banks, and berms provide even more thrills than the surrounding scenery of the 12,000-foot La Sal Mountains.

The Wild Side

Arches National Park

Declared a national park in 1971 and now encompassing some 74,000 acres, Arches is a symbol of Utah and home to more than 2,000 natural sandstone arches, the world's largest collection. The way to explore this profound park is the way that author Edward Abbey did for his book *Desert Solitaire:* by foot. A 7.2-mile hike leads backpackers to eight arches in Devils Garden. Shorter trips lead to Delicate Arch, the Windows, and Fiery Furnace. And because, as they say, geologic time is now, there's even a chance of spotting a new arch eroding.

and plenty other potent picks, brewed on site; wide selection of vegetarian fare.

Slickrock Café (5 North Main Street; 435-259-8004): Salads, sandwiches, soups, and pasta, plus breakfast burritos and an upstairs Internet café.

Bunk

Arches National Park, Devils Garden (Arches Scenic Drive; 435-719-2299): Tent sites only (fifty-three of them), plus drinking water, picnic tables, and prime views.

The Gonzo Inn (100 West 200 South Street; 800-791-4044): Southwest marries the '70s; hip, colorful rooms, bike storage, and a swimming pool and hot tub.

Los Vados Canyon House (801-532-2651, www.losvados.com): A remote, unique two-bedroom home, designed by a San Francisco architect, at the end of a red-rock canyon, accessible by four-wheel drive. Includes a pool and upscale furnishings; three-night minimum.

Can't Leave?

Nearest airport: Walker Field, Grand Junction, Colorado (81 miles)

Primary industries: Tourism

Cody, Wyoming

Buffalo Bill was many things—an army scout, buffalo hunter, gold miner, cattle herder, and Pony Express rider. But he was not an ice climber. So in 1895, when Colonel William F. "Buffalo Bill" Cody named a town along the Shoshone River in Wyoming, in between Yellowstone National Park and the plains of the Bighorn Basin, he missed the fact that he was also choosing one of the best spots in the country for accessing frozen waterfalls—not to mention the wooded hiking and mountain-biking trails of Shoshone National Forest, the Class II to IV rapids on the Shoshone River, and the snow-blessed areas for cross-country and backcountry skiing.

Population: 9,100

Action: Ice climbing, hiking, downhill and cross-country skiing, fishing, windsurfing

And today, many of the visitors to Cody also miss out on this outdoor-adventure buffet, preferring instead to taste the Wild West atmosphere on their way to or from Yellowstone, just fifty-two miles to the west. It's hard to blame them, considering the distractions of the Cody Stampede, which has happened every Fourth of July since 1922; the staged shootouts outside the Irma Hotel (named after Buffalo Bill's daughter) at night; and the myriad shops selling authentic western belt buckles and cowboy hats.

But mosey into Sunlight Sports or Core Mountain Sports, and you'll hear an earful about the real Wild West of today, starting with, in winter, the South Fork of the Shoshone River. Deep in the 170-mile-long range of the Absaroka Mountains, which top out at more than 11,000 feet, the South Fork holds the largest collection of frozen waterfalls in the lower forty-eight states. Most climbs are rated WI 3 to 7. (The names of Classroom Bully, Joy After Pain, and the Mile of Ice are indications of their difficulty and remote location.) Since 1998, Cody's squadron of ice climbers has been growing with the Waterfall Ice Festival, which takes place every February in the South Fork Valley. The event includes

The Buffalo Bill Historical Center pays tribute to Cody, Wyoming's favorite outdoor adventurer. (Courtesy of Park County Travel Council, Cody, WY)

clinics and contests among the 100 or so named climbs. Or you can name your own route by venturing deeper into the wilderness of the 2.4-million-acre Shoshone National Forest from October until April, when the ice there is usually climbable.

Shaped like a fat exclamation point and resting against Yellowstone in its northern reaches, the Shoshone has more than just spectacular scenery in common with its national-park neighbor. Just as Yellowstone was the first U.S. national park, Shoshone was the first national forest (established in 1891); it is also one of the largest national forests. Buffalo Bill and his followers did explore much of the Shoshone, but you won't find much Wild West kitsch here—just deep canyons, alpine lakes and meadows, and lodgepole-pine forests. Among the hiking highlights is the ten-mile Dead Indian Trail, which leads from a trail-head west of Cody toward Sunlight Basin. Then, at the basin, the Clarks Fork Trail stretches for 17.5 miles through sun-dappled mountains. In the winter, the area is not only a top ice-climbing destination, but also provides incredible cross-country and backcountry skiing opportunities. There are lifts and downhill-skiing and snowboarding trails at Sleeping Giant Ski Area, near the entrance to Yellowstone, but recent permit problems have closed the area; check with the Cody Chamber of Commerce before packing your planks or board.

You can guarantee use, however, from a fishing rod, as Cody is close to trout fishing in Yellowstone, along the Shoshone River and its creeks, and on Newton and other area lakes. There are some 2,000 miles of fishing waters around here. For whitewater rafting and kayaking, you can float the mostly gentle Shoshone or head to the area around DeMaris Springs, where there are also hot, sulfurous waters whose purported healing properties Buffalo Bill promoted to help draw settlers to the area.

Today, some might find more refreshment in the waters of Buffalo Bill State Park, where the surface of an 8,000-acre reservoir froths with wind from the surrounding gorges, creating a premier windsurfing spot for a few avid locals. Though just a few miles west of Cody, it's also wide open for fishing and boating. You can thank Buffalo Bill and Cody's current gunslingers for providing plenty of other diversions.

Start the Day

The Beta Coffeehouse (1132 Twelfth Street; 307-587-7707): Espresso drinks, pastries, and free Wi-Fi.

Peter's Café & Bakery (1219 Sheridan Avenue; 307-527-5040): Go for the two-eggs, two-pancakes, two-slices-of-bacon special, the pecan rolls, or the oversized cinnamon buns.

Gear Up

Sunlight Sports (1251 Sheridan Avenue; 307-587-9517): Ski, climbing, and hiking gear, plus some winter-sport rentals.

Core Mountain Sports/Jackson Hole

Local Legend

Heart and Cedar Mountains

Two of Cody's nearby mountains are more than just natural landmarks—both Heart and Cedar mountains are also touchstones of controversy. Near Heart Mountain, more than 10,000 people with Japanese ancestry were confined in an internment camp during World War II. Today, the Nature Conservancy owns a 15,000-acre ranch near the relocation camp, and hikers can climb to the summit for 360-degree views of the area, but only through Jackson Hole Mountain Guides (www.jhmg .com). Meanwhile, the summit of Cedar Mountain is rumored to be the real resting place of Buffalo Bill, whose official gravesite is atop Lookout Mountain in Golden, Colorado.

Mountain Guides (1019 Fifteenth Street; 877-587-0629): Guided climbing, ice-climbing, rafting, and kayaking trips and equipment.

Absaroka Bicycles (2201 Seventeenth Street; 307-527-5566): Bike rentals, sales, and repair.

Refuel

Tommy Jack's (1134 Thirteenth Street; 307-587-4917): A Cajun-style eatery with crawfish-topped catfish, shrimp etouffee, and fried alligator bites—for real.

Cassie's Supper Club (214 Yellowstone Avenue; 307-527-5500): This restaurant opened in 1922 and as entertaining as it is sustaining; it has multiple bars, stuffed and mounted animals, live music, and a cowboy- and cowgirl-filled dance floor.

Bunk

Buffalo Bill State Park (47 Lakeside Road; 307-587-9227; www.wyoparks.state.wy.us/Bbslide.htm): Two campgrounds with a total of nine tent sites and eighty-five RV sites.

Bison Willy's (1625 Alger Avenue; 307-250-0763; www.bisonwillys .com): Downtown hostel with private and dorm rooms, plus a South Fork bunkhouse in winter for ice climbers.

Irma Hotel (1192 Sheridan Avenue; 307-587-4221; www.irmahotel .com): Historic downtown hotel built by Buffalo Bill; has suites and regular rooms.

Can't Leave?

Nearest airport: Yellowstone Regional, Cody (3 miles)

Primary industries: Agriculture/ranching, mineral extraction, tourism

Saratoga, Wyoming

Other towns may have all-night diners or dance clubs that close at dawn, but the most happening joint in Saratoga, Wyoming, is a mineral hot springs, open twenty-four hours a day, seven days a week, and free to anyone and everyone. Known as the Hobo Hot Pool, its natural presence on the North Platte River, along with that of other spring waters, is why the town shares its name with a New York resort area. (*Saratoga* is derived from an Iroquois word meaning "the place of miraculous water in the rock.") And like its eastern cousin, this town draws some VIPs and celebrities. But the similarities mostly stop there: instead of horse races, polo matches, and floppy hats, Saratoga, Wyoming, has blue-ribbon trout fishing, brew festivals, and cowboy hats. Nestled between the Snowy Range and the Sierra Madres, it's a mining town that still has plenty of untapped resources in the outdoors.

Population: 1,714
Action: Fishing, rock climbing, hiking, mountain and road biking, downhill and cross-country skiing

Saratoga lies west of Cheyenne and Laramie and north of Steamboat Springs, Colorado, in a land of both prairies and mountains known as the Good Times Valley. This moniker was appropriate in the late 1800s and early 1900s, when the logging industry boomed and more than two million dollars in copper was pulled from the Sierra Madres, but not so accurate when fake stock sales and other scandals closed down the major mining company. Townspeople can thank the North Platte River, and its 2,300 catchable fish per mile, for bringing the good times back; the Wyoming Game and Fish Department considers the stretch near Saratoga to have the best wild trout fishing in the state. With sixty-five miles of rich waters, you can amble right from your downtown lodging to start reeling them in (town officials boast that the trout leap right onto Main Street), head to the Miracle Mile—actually 7.5 miles—near the Kortes Dam for a float trip, or hike or

After long days of fishing, hiking, and mountain biking in Saratoga, Wyoming, you can enjoy outdoor adventure of a different sort. (© Saratoga/Platte Valley Chamber)

horsepack into the wilderness around the Encampment River near the Colorado border. Depending on where you choose, you'll be surrounded by golden-hued ranches, the green and yellow high-desert plains, or fog pulling through the mountains.

The fishing stays hot through the winter, when the 284-acre Saratoga Lake, a mile and a half north of town, freezes over and fills with ice-fishing shacks for the annual game-fish derby on the third weekend in January. (In the summer, the lake is used by windsurfers and waterskiers.) Snowmobiling is also big around Saratoga, but cross-country and backcountry skiing in the Snowy Range and Sierra Madres are given their due, too. The U.S. Forest Service maintains trails on Little Laramie and Corner mountains and at Brush Creek, Chimney Park, and Bottle Creek; it also keeps up the nearly three million powdery acres of Medicine Bow National Forest, which contains the two mountain ranges. For alpine skiing and snowboarding, the well-off-the-radar Snowy Range Ski and Recreation Area sits at a base elevation of 9,000 feet; it features five lifts, 250 acres, and bargain-basement prices for sky-high snow stashes.

And in the warmer months, while most everyone else around Saratoga is out fishing, hikers, backpackers, and mountain bikers are happy to have the Medicine Bow Mountains mostly to themselves. East of town in the Snowy Range, you can hike the 4.5-mile trail to the summit of 12,013-foot Medicine Bow Peak or backpack for days among the lakes of the Sugarloaf Recreation Area. In the Sierra Madre Range, west and south of Saratoga, hit the forty-six-mile stretch of the Continental Divide National Scenic Trail that runs through here, or hop on part of the Great Divide Mountain Bike Route that shares and crosses the trail. U.S. Highway 130, meanwhile, provides some of the area's best cycling as it runs south from Interstate 80 through Saratoga and east toward Centennial and Laramie.

On the third weekend of August, however, you'll want to stick around town for two events that go hand in hand: the "Taste of the West" chili and salsa cookoff and Wyoming's official state microbrewery competition, when brewmeisters go after the Saratoga Steinley Cup. When you find yourself lured to the Hobo Pool at some point in the weekend, just be sure to finish off your Snake River pale ale or Sierra Madre pilsner beforehand. There's no nudity and no booze allowed at Saratoga's hottest spot.

Start the Day

Lollypops (107 East Bridge Avenue; 307-326-5020): Eggs Benedict, croissant sandwiches, and espresso drinks.

Gear Up

Stoney Creek Outfitters (216 East Walnut; 307-326-8750): Fly-fishing shop that offers guided trips on the Upper North Platte and Encampment rivers.

The Wild Side

Vedauwoo

For a rock-climbing road trip, head about an hour and a half east from Saratoga past Laramie to Vedauwoo, whose wild rock formations and nearly 1,000 climbs of 5 to 5.14 have led many avid climbers to relocate to Laramie. The name is pronounced *VEE-da-voo* and means "land of the earth-born spirit" in Arapaho.

Hack's Tackle and Outfitters (407 North First Street; 307-326-9823): Fly and tackle shop that sells fishing supplies, guides trips, and rents canoes and rafts.

Refuel

Lazy River Cantina (110 East Bridge Avenue; 307-326-8472): Margaritas and other Mexican specialties.

Stumpy's Eatery (218 North First Street; 307-326-8132): Pizza, burgers, and sandwiches.

Hotel Wolf (101 East Bridge Street; 307-326-5525): Opened in 1893, the restaurant has bacon-wrapped filet mignon, king crab legs, vegetarian kabobs, burgers, and a salad bar; there's a pool table in the historic saloon.

Bunk

Saratoga Lake Campground (State Road 130/230; 307-326-8335; www.saratoga.govoffice2.com): On Saratoga Lake; forty-six campsites split between tents and RVs.

Stoney Creek River Cottages (216 East Walnut; 307-326-8750; www.fishstoneycreek.com): Two fishing-oriented cottages and a suite next to Hobo Pool and the North Platte River.

Hotel Wolf (101 East Bridge Street; 307-326-5525; www.wolfhotel .com): Saratoga's landmark downtown hotel has twenty-one reasonably priced rooms.

Can't Leave?

Nearest airport: Hayden/Yampa Valley Regional, Hayden, Colorado (74 miles)

Primary industry: Tourism, hospitality

Sheridan, Wyoming

When Queen Elizabeth II visited Sheridan, Wyoming, in 1984, she went shopping at two notable places. One was King's Saddlery, a 1940s-era purveyor of cowboy couture—ropes, bridles, blankets, slickers, and, of course, saddles—that has won honors from the National Endowment for the Arts for its excellence in American folk art. The other was Ritz Sporting Goods, where one could buy a custom-made rod from one of the world's top fly-fishermen who learned to cast in the nearby Big Horn Mountains, called "the heart of the heart of the West" by *Outside* magazine. The Ritz has since closed its doors, but flies, reels, and rods are still to be found at Fly Shop of the Big Horns. And King's Saddlery is still open; its craftwork is said to have landed on President Bill Clinton's belt and to have attracted even the crown prince of Saudi Arabia.

Population: 16,333

Action: Hiking, fishing, mountain biking, rock climbing, cross-country skiing

The two royal choices reveal the two sides of Sheridan: the authentic Western town of leather, spur, and ranchwear shops, and the adventure maniac boasting angling, hiking, and mountain-biking stores. Both types of establishments stand along historic Main Street, so perfectly preserved it can seem like a movie set. OK, so there is a Quizno's in the former department store. But the more notable neon lights are on the cowboy sign outside the Mint Bar, still in business since 1907 and the place for a whiskey, a dance by the Wurlitzer, and a whistle at the cattle brands worn into the woodwork. Not bad for a town that was plotted in 1882 on a sheet of wrapping paper and has since embraced both its inner wrangler (despite an economy that has depended more on mining) and its outdoor enthusiast.

Sheridan sits just south of Montana, just east of the Big Horn Mountains and a couple of hours west of Devil's Tower. Considered by the U.S. Forest Service to be a sister range of the Rocky Mountains, the

After tackling the trails in Big Horn Mountains or Cloud Peak Wilderness, you can get in touch with your inner cowboy at Sheridan, Wyoming's Mint Bar. (© Sheridan Travel and Tourism, www.sheridanwyoming.org)

Big Horns are a seventy-mile long buffet of weekend (or weeklong) play options, include the 9,585-foot Sheep Mountain in the north; the central, rugged Cloud Peak Wilderness, capped by the 13,167-foot eponymous peak; and the southerly Big Horn Ski Resort, whose powder has earned praise from Olympic gold medalist snowboarder Ross Powers. Jackson Hole is a full day's drive from Sheridan, but there's enough backcountry stuff in the Big Horns to keep telemarkers and cross-country skiers much closer to home. Among the four groomed nordic areas in the Bighorn National Forest are the Sibley Lake Ski Trails, fifteen miles of trails and old timber roads that loop among lodgepole-pine and spruce forests, leading to a warming hut. For cross-country skiers with canines, the Cutler Ski Trails allow dogs.

When the snow melts, backcountry hikers head to the 189,039-acre Cloud Peak Wilderness, where 100 miles of trails wind among fields of Indian paintbrush, the Wyoming state flower, and other blooming wildflowers bloom in June and July. The fifty-three-mile long and aptly named Solitude Loop circumnavigates the wilderness; take it for a five- to six-day ramble through Bighorn's biggest mountains, jagged ridges, and alpine tundra. The climb up to the summit of Cloud Peak is nearly eleven miles and includes scrambles that turn treacherous in fickle weather. Bighorn's friendlier hikes include the twelve-mile trip to Bucking Mule Falls and the eight-mile loop around Willow Lake.

Those bound for the Big Horn Mountains with only a pair of hiking shoes, however, are missing out on the multisport adventures allowed by the forest service. Most of the trails are open to mountain biking, including the Tongue River Trail, which drops 4,000 feet and eleven miles into Tongue River Canyon. Climbing gear is critical for the more than fifty routes around the Tongue River Canyon. A box of flies is essential for catching the rainbows, browns, and cutthroats in the North Tongue, South Tongue, and Little Bighorn rivers and in the alpine lakes and streams. And for adventuring by horseback into the deepest parts of the Cloud Peak Wilderness and the heart of the heart of the west, there's also the matter of a saddle. All such items can be found just where Queen Elizabeth shopped more than two decades ago—on Main Street, Sheridan.

Start the Day

Sheridan Palace (138 North Main Street; 307-672-2391): Full breakfasts starting at 6 AM.

Java Moon/Over the Moon (176 North Main Street; 307-673-5991): Coffeehouse and bistro.

Gear Up

Big Horn Mountain Sports (334 North Main Street; 307-672-6866): Mountain bike rentals at the store's own shop; also hiking, backpacking and skiing gear, clothing, maps, and more.

Fly Shop of the Big Horns (227 North Main Street; 307-672-5866): Fly-rods, reels, and ties, plus lessons and guided trips throughout the area.

Refuel

Sanford's Grub & Pub (5 East Alger; 307-674-1722): Tip back a pint of

Local Legend

Spear-O-Wigwam Ranch

Sheridan has long had ties with It-list names; even Prince premiered a movie here after a local motel maid won an MTV contest. But perhaps the most appropriate celebrity to hang around town was Ernest Hemingway, who finished *A Farewell to Arms* while staying at the Spear-O-Wigwam Ranch (www .spear-o-wigwam.com). The classic Wyoming dude ranch has been operating since the 1920s, offering extended pack and hiking trips, fishing lessons, and enough riding to perhaps inspire some of your own writing.

Sanford's own Cloud's Peak Raspberry Wheat and order the Cajun-fried chicken breast Franchise burger.

Pony Bar & Grill (3 South Gould Street; 307-674-7000): Wings and other sports-bar food.

Oliver's Bar and Grill (55 North Main Street; 307-672-2838): Artisan breads, also sold in the next-door gourmet shop, and a good wine list kick off creative meals of steaks from a local farm and seafood flown in from Seattle; finish with the espresso crème brûlée.

Bunk

Sibley Lake Campground (Bighorn National Forest; 877-444-6777; www.reserveusa.com): One of dozens of established campgrounds in the national forest and one of the closest to Sheridan; has twenty-five RV and tent sites at 7,900 feet.

Mill Inn (2161 Coffeen Avenue; 307-672-6401; www.sheridan millin.com): Forty-four rooms and suites in a restored flour mill.

Spahn's Big Horn Mountain Bed & Breakfast (307-674-8150; www.bighorn-wyoming.com): Two log cabins and three rooms in the Big Horn Mountains, fifteen miles west of Sheridan.

Can't Leave?

Nearest airport: Sheridan County (3 miles)

Primary industries: Mining, tourism, ranching

The West

Jerome, Arizona

W hen it snows in Arizona, the town of Jerome resembles the Grinch's lair in the Dr. Seuss tale, clinging to a steep hillside that has fifty-mile views of the Verde Valley instead of Whoville. The hill, named Cleopatra, nearly claimed this tiny mining settlement. In the first half of the twentieth century, underground dynamite explosions shook the area, dislocating buildings and even sending the jail down the slope. The mines had made Jerome Arizona's fourth largest city, but also carried a bit of the Grinch's devilish spirit, helping to support more than twenty bars and such prostitution houses as "cribs." In 1903, the *New York Sun* wrote, "This Jerome is a Bad One. The Arizona Copper Camp Now the Wickedest Town." But by the time the mines closed for good in the 1950s, people were calling the place a ghost town.

Population: 343
Action: Hiking, mountain biking, downhill skiing

But Jerome still clings to Cleopatra Hill and its thirty-degree incline today. Its cluster of museums and shops wink at the town's ups and downs. The sign outside the House of Joy emporium features a gartered-and boot-clad woman's leg; the "Sliding Jail" still teeters near a parking area. Underneath it all are more than eighty miles of underground mining tunnels. But at 5,200 feet, Jerome is more about what's above the ground: Mingus Mountain, Prescott National Forest, and Dead Horse Ranch State Park. The San Francisco Volcanic Field and Peaks and Sedona's Red Rock Country are just a bit further afield. The town itself is less than a square mile in area, but the surrounding wilderness extends far beyond what one can see from the top of Cleopatra Hill.

In the cooler winter months, Jerome hikers, mountain bikers, and paddlers head down to Dead Horse Ranch State Park, which sits on the nearly 180-mile-long Verde River at 3,300 feet. There are short trails of a quarter-mile to two-plus miles; for an hour's mountain-bike ride, it's possible to combine a few of the trails for a larger loop. And when it's

333

Jerome still clings to Arizona's Cleopatra Hill, but now its wealth lies aboveground—in the outdoor-recreation opportunities. (© B. Smith)

warm, the Woodchute Wilderness, which rises up from the Sonoran desert to juniper trees and oak forest, offers relief from the heat. Mingus Mountain, at 7,500 feet, features hiking trails through ponderosa pine for views of Jerome. Mingus lies in Prescott National Forest, which has 450 miles of trails in its 1.2 million acres. Also near Jerome is the two-mile-long Coleman Trail, which looks out toward Sedona, the San Francisco Peaks, and the Mogollon Rim.

Some 200 miles long and up to 8,000 feet high, the Mogollon Rim is topped with ponderosa-pine forests and overlooks lakes, creeks, and canyons, giving way to more hiking and mountain biking around Sedona. Farther northwest from Jerome is Humphrey's Peak, the high-point of Arizona at 12,633 feet. Humphrey's is found in the San Francisco Peaks, as is the Arizona Snowbowl, where there are thirty-two skiing and snowboarding trails. It's just over an hour from Jerome—and views from the chairlift are almost as good as the ones from town.

Start the Day

English Kitchen (119 Jerome Avenue; 928-634-2132): Built in 1899 by a Chinese immigrant, it's the oldest continually operating restaurant in Arizona; serves full breakfasts.

Gear Up

Ghost Town Gear (415 Hull Avenue; 928-634-3113): Hiking and outdoor gear, plus maps and information on local trails.

Refuel

Jerome Brewery (111 Main Street; 928-634-8477): In a renovated firehouse; serves microbrews, burgers, crispy-crusted pizza, salads, and such appetizers as artichoke bruschetta.

Belgian Jennie's Bordello Bistro & Pizzeria (412 Main Street; 928-639-3141): The eatery and the pizzas are named after some of Jerome's notorious entertainers—the Tijuana Tina has spicy sausage; also serves pasta, steaks, and Italian specialties.

The Asylum Restaurant (200 Hill Street; 928-639-3197): Views and a menu featuring such dishes as grilled-achiote-rubbed pork tenderloin and mesquite-bacon-wrapped filet mignon; in the Jerome Grand Hotel.

Bunk

Potato Patch Campground (Forest Road 106, Prescott National Forest; 928-443-8000; www.fs.fed.us/r3/Prescott): On Mingus Mountain, near the Woodchute Wilderness trailhead; offers twenty-eight campsites and twelve RV sites.

Local Legend

Jerome's Ghosts

While Jerome may not be a ghost town, it may be home to a few ghosts. Some folks believe that spirits haunt some of the historic buildings, including the Jerome Grand Hotel. The hotel was built in 1926 as the United Verde Hospital and then closed from 1950 to 1994. According to some accounts, there were not only mining-accident deaths in the hospital, but also the mysterious deaths of two orderlies, as well as a suicide. After it was closed, screams reportedly were heard coming from the vacant building, and since it was reopened as a hotel a decade ago, the sounds of heavy breathing and coughing have been noted. In 2002 and 2005, the Southwest Ghost Hunters Association conducted an investigation of the hotel, doing paranormal readings and taking nearly 700 photos. The group reported at least one photo with a mysterious shadow lurking in the background, as well as cold spots, unusual electromagnetic fields, and a possible moving "ecto cloud."

The Connor Hotel (164 Main Street; 800-523-3554; www.connor hotel.com): Ten rooms in downtown hotel, built in 1898.

Jerome Grand Hotel (200 Hill Street; 888-817-6788; www.jerome grandhotel.net): A historic (and some say haunted) Spanish Mission–style building originally built as a hospital; one of the highest structures in the Verde Valley, it has more than thirty rooms and a 1926 self-service Otis elevator.

Can't Leave?

Nearest airport: Ernest A. Love Field, Prescott, Arizona (23 miles)

Primary industries: Arts, tourism

Springerville, Arizona

L ife sure has gotten better over the past 150 years for the rugged types who make their way to Springerville, at the foot of the untamed White Mountains of east-central Arizona. One look at the eighteen-foot-tall Madonna of the Trail on Main Street is proof. It's a statue of a pioneer woman in a bonnet, carrying a rifle in one hand and a baby in the other, while a boy clutches her long skirt. Needless to say, she's not smiling. The five-ton sculpture is one of twelve identical poured-stone creations placed by the Daughters of the American Revolution in the late 1920s along the wagon route from Maryland to California, as a tribute to the courageous women who pushed the frontier westward. If there were a monument to today's women of the trail in Springerville, the gun would be swapped for a fly rod, the baby would be in a backpack, and the corners of her mouth would be turned emphatically upward.

Population: 1,956
Action: Fishing, mountain biking, hiking, cross-country and downhill skiing

The town offers plenty to smile about, given all of the fishing, hiking, and mountain biking in the nearby White Mountains and Apache-Sitgreaves national forests; managed as one entity, the preserve is three times larger than Rhode Island and has kept miraculously off the tourist map. Springerville sits with its sister community Edgar in the quiet Round Valley, wreathed by tall peaks at 7,000 feet in elevation. Make the four-hour drive there from Phoenix, and you'll slowly ascend into an alpine area carpeted with fir and spruce forests, where the average high temperature in August doesn't even crack eighty degrees Fahrenheit and the locals store snowshoes and ice-fishing gear in their garages for the winter.

Upon reaching downtown, your first stop should be to the Speckled Trout tackle shop on East Main Street; its staff are authorities on the prime places to cast a line among the thirty-four lakes and reservoirs and 680 miles of waterways—including the headwaters of four rivers—

Madonna of the Trail statue in Springerville, Arizona.
(© Sprngerville-Eagar Chamber of Commerce)

inside Apache-Sitgreaves. Arctic grayling and cutthroat, brown, rainbow, and rare Apache trout all thrive in these parts, and if you go deep into the backcountry, you can reach spots where a fish can turn belly-up from old age before crossing paths with someone carrying a rod. Within easier access is 575-acre Big Lake, south of Springerville, at 9,000 feet in elevation. Its cold, clear waters are stocked with more than 30,000 trout each year.

The options for hiking and mountain biking seem just as limitless. There are almost 1,000 miles of trails in the forest, and too many old dirt roads and wooded singletrack to count outside of it. Most are open to both foot and bike traffic, including the locally maintained 140-mile White Mountain Trail System, marked by blue diamonds. The system varies in elevation from 6,900 to 7,800 feet as its network of loops wind among open meadows and forests of pinon-juniper and ponderosa pine. If you only have a day to hike, take the fourteen-mile round-trip West Baldy Trail through aspen and spruce up the side of 11,590-foot Mount Baldy. You'll catch some amazing views of the White Mountains on the ridgeline near the top, but you're not allowed to summit, because the land falls within the Fort Apache Indian Reservation and is sacred ground. Also within the lands of the

White Mountain Apache Tribe are the three peaks that make up the Sunrise Park Resort ski area, a few miles due north. Its sixty-five runs, served by ten lifts, see an average of 250 inches of snow a year. Yes, the higher elevations around Springerville get buried with snow, making for prime backcountry and cross-country skiing—and another reason for rugged outdoorsy types to smile.

Start the Day

Java Blues (341 East Main Street; 928-333-5282): Espresso shop that serves hearty breakfasts to an eclectic mix of locals.

373 Bar and Grill (44 Main Street, Greer; 928-735-7216; www.greer lodgeaz.com): A warm restaurant at the Greer Lodge, overlooking trout ponds and the Little Colorado River in the friendly resort town of Greer.

Gear Up

The Speckled Trout (224 East Main Street; 928-333-0852): A fly shop and guide service.

Refuel

Booga Red's (521 East Main Street; 928-333-2640): Fast, affordable, and good Mexican food.

Wild Weede Brewery (173 West Main Street; 928-333-4826; www.wildweedebrewery.com): All-American food served with its five different microbrews. Try the Apricot Pilsner.

Bunk

X Diamond Ranch (County Road 4124, Greer; 928-333-2286; www.xdiamondranch.com): Six cabins a short walk from the Little Colorado River, just outside of Springerville.

Local Legend

Casa Malpais

Only a couple of miles north of Springerville, you'll find the ruins of Casa Malpais—considered to be remains from the Mogollon Culture, whose people lived there sometime during the eleventh and twelfth centuries. Among its most impressive structures are the circular observatory, which marks the solstices, and the Great Kiva, a massive pueblo that includes three stairways and is built of volcanic rock.

Reed's Lodge (514 East Main Street; 928-333-4323; www.k5reeds
.com): A roomy 1949 motor lodge with pine walls; John Wayne
used to play cards here with the owner when he lived in the area.

Can't Leave?

Nearest airport: Williams Gateway, Mesa, Arizona (175 miles)

Primary industries: Government, retail, health care, agriculture

Williams, Arizona

A man is shot every summer day in Williams, and the chamber of commerce actually brags about it. This recurring violence is part of the celebration of the town's history as a rough-and-tumble nineteenth-century Western outpost, where a cowboy or logger could get a bottle of rotgut and a meeting with a lady of questionable repute—plus a belly full of lead if he wasn't careful. Re-enactments, including the occasional gunfight, take place throughout the day in the heart of the brick-sidewalked downtown district on Railroad Avenue, which was nicknamed Saloon Row in its heyday. The only aspect of Williams that could be called rough-and-tumble now is its stunning backcountry on the lush Kaibab Plateau, interrupted by the Grand Canyon about fifty-five miles north. The town is used as the staging area for day-hiking adventures on the South Rim of the nation's greatest natural wonder—though people truly in the know also come for the hiking and mountain biking in Williams's own backyard.

Williams is the headquarters for the Kaibab National Forest, a 1.6-million-acre preserve that flanks the northern and southern sides of the Grand Canyon National Park and is home to one of the largest ponderosa-pine forests in the world. The half of the national forest south of the Colorado River is garnished with meadows, trout-stocked reservoirs, forests, and modest hills that hover mostly around 7,000 feet, except where the plateau is interrupted by occasional peaks like 9,264-foot Bill Williams Mountain, overlooking town. Williams was originally known as a trapping destination for mountain men like the legendary "Old Bill" Williams—hence the name of the town and summit—in the early 1800s, but by the end of the century, it had turned into an important railroad stop, carting away lumber and carting in tourists who wanted to make the eleven-hour stagecoach ride from town to see the Grand Canyon. In 1926, Williams became a stop on

Population: 3,094
Action: Hiking, mountain biking

Williams, Arizona is a staging area for adventure in the Kaibab National Forest and South Rim of Grand Canyon National Park. (© Williams-Grand Canyon Chamber of Commerce)

the new Route 66, and visitors could take a 2.5-hour ride on a spur rail line out to the South Rim.

The stores and restaurants downtown still cater to tourists, who are largely unaware of the local natural wonders that fall outside of the national park. Your options for gearing up are limited to Sportway Supplies—a hunting, camping, fishing, and drive-through liquor store in Williams—and stopping in Flagstaff, a half hour east. Once properly equipped, you should get a perspective on your surroundings by hiking the summit of Bill Williams Mountain. A handful of rocky footpaths, sprinkled with occasional open vistas, will take you there: the Bill Williams Mountain Trail (eight miles out and back) that climbs the north face, the Benham Trail on the south slope, and the Bixler Saddle Trail on the west. Williams is also the access point for relatively unknown Sycamore Canyon, a deep ravine carved into the red rock and nearly as spectacular as Oak Creek Canyon by Sedona. The eleven-mile

Sycamore Rim Trail encircles it, marked by rock cairns as it passes through pine forests, along pond shores and cliff ledges, and by the face of Sycamore Falls—where rock climbers gather when the intermittent creek runs dry. Parts of the trail are open to mountain bikers— one of many top-notch fat-tire routes around town. And if you ever get tired of the rocky technical switchbacks and long, rugged forest roads around town, you can always make the one-hour drive to the traffic-clogged singletrack of Sedona. The people of Williams won't mind if you escape for a little while—although there's always the chance they might shoot you when you return.

Start the Day

Java Cycle (326 West Route 66; 928-635-1117): The site used to be a bike shop, but now it's an upscale coffee bar and Internet café.

Grand Canyon Coffee Café (125 West Route 66; 928-635-1255): Traditional breakfasts, espresso, and cappuccino at this restaurant on old Route 66.

Gear Up

Sportway Supplies (400 West Route 66; 928-635-4571): Sells fishing, hunting, and camping gear—and beer.

Absolute Bikes (18 North San Francisco Street, Flagstaff; 928-779-5969): Rents bikes, sells bikes, fixes bikes, and organizes Tuesday, Friday, and Saturday rides.

Babbit's General Store (Main Park Loop Road, Grand Canyon; 928-638-2854): A deli and gift shop across from the visitor's center in Grand Canyon Village; sells and rents backpacking and camping equipment.

Refuel

Pancho McGillicuddy's (141 East Railroad Avenue; 928-635-4150): In the building of a former saloon built in the late nineteenth century is this Tex-Mex joint, serving specialties like jalapeño

Local Legend

The Grand Canyon Railway

In 1901 the Sante Fe Railway completed a spur line from Williams to the South Rim. Taking the iron horse to the Grand Canyon was a much more appealing option than a grueling, bumpy stagecoach route from Flagstaff, and the spur line became an immediate success. As automobiles gained steam, though, the number of riders on the train dwindled, until its passenger cars stopped operating altogether in 1968. A little more than two decades later, Max and Thelma Biegert became owners of the line and restored it to its former glory. Now the Grand Canyon Railway carries more than 200,000 people a year into the park.

poppers (which they call armadillo eggs) and more than twenty flavored margaritas.

Cruisers Café 66 (233 West Route 66; 928-635-2445): Kitschy, living piece of 1950s Americana. Great barbecue.

Bunk

Canyon Motel (1900 East Rodeo Road; 928-635-9371; www.the canyonmotel.com): A popular 1940s-style Route 66 motel. It even has a room in a 1929 railroad caboose.

Grand Canyon Railway Hotel (223 North Grand Canyon Boulevard; 800-843-8724; www.thetrain.com): A grand old Southwestern-style railroad hotel—with modern amenities—owned by the train company.

Can't Leave?

Nearest airport: Flagstaff Pulliam, Flagstaff, Arizona (40 miles)

Primary industries: Retail, tourism, forest service

Arcata, California

No one can accuse Arcata of being dull. From the outspoken politics of its Birkenstock-wearing, granola-munching residents, to the readily available marijuana (for medicinal purposes, of course), to the majesty of is surroundings, this place will keep you entertained. Entrenched beneath a belt of coastal mountains on the northern end of the Pacific's Humboldt Bay, the town is a 275-mile drive from San Francisco into the heart of northern California's redwood country. Combine its location among a vast patchwork of local, state, and national protected lands with its mild climate, and you've got a year-round hiking, biking, and paddling paradise—as long as your idea of paradise includes carrying a rain shell in your pack.

Population:
16,914
Action: Mountain biking, hiking, paddling

So many adventure options lie so close to downtown Arcata, your biggest challenge during a visit here is deciding what to do and where to do it. To the east is the million-acre Six Rivers National Forest, the reported mountainous stomping grounds of Bigfoot. There, 1,500 miles of waterways, including the Smith, Klamath, Trinity, Mad, Van Duzen, and Eel rivers interconnect with 400 miles of trails. North is Redwood National Park and its thirty-story-high living monuments. South is the Humboldt Bay National Wildlife Refuge, and to the west is the rugged Pacific coast. The first explorers of European descent to make the treacherous journey to this remote stretch of shoreline were sailors in the early 1800s, followed by prospectors almost fifty years later. Arcata became a supply stop for the mines, and its central plaza was often clogged with pack mules.

Today, the same grassy square is still surrounded by bars, restaurants, and stores, but the corrals and miners have been replaced by park benches and book-reading locals, and students from Humboldt State University, who make up almost half of the town's population. Arcatans

Restaurants, stores, and park benches surround the central plaza in Arcata, California.
(© Don Forthuber)

are extremely environmentally conscious, often with more city council members representing the Green Party than Republicans or
Democrats. They're also passionate about their two remarkable local
preserves. The first is the Arcata Marsh and Wildlife Sanctuary, a 154-
acre swath of swamp, marsh, and estuaries that serves not only as a
stopover for more than 200 types of birds, including the arctic loon,
but also as the town's natural wastewater treatment plant. The second
is the 622-acre Community Forest, open to hikers, horseback riders, and
mountain bikers. Its ten miles of smooth, hilly paths make for fun,
high-speed, fat-tire rides, and there are tons of singletrack options that
break off from the main trail. Keep your head up, though, because college kids like to hang out there.

For something a little quieter, head to Redwood National Park and
ride the Prairie Creek/Ossagon Trail, a nineteen-mile loop of single- and
doubletrack along ocean bluffs and through massive redwoods; here
you've got to keep an eye out for lazy elk rather than dazed students.
On the to-do list of many hardcore California hikers is the twenty-four-

mile trek on the Lost Coast Trail, along the slim, rocky shore to south of town. Buffered from civilization by the King Mountain Range, it's a prime viewing area for seals, sea lions, whales, and rare birds. Paddlers are equally as passionate about the Burnt Ranch Gorge in Six Rivers National Forest; the narrow, nine-mile whitewater obstacle course on the Trinity River has Class IV and V rapids. Novices, though, might prefer the Class III hazards of the five-mile Pigeon Point run, a popular trip for rafting outfitters.

Even taking a rest in Arcata can be exhilarating, if you do it by the ocean on Mad River Beach—a six-mile ride from downtown through pastures and dairy farms. Take along some granola and a pair of Birkenstocks, and you'll blend right in with the smattering of people you'll see there.

Start the Day

Jitter Bean Coffee Company (900 G Street; 707-822-0671): A lively coffeehouse on the edge of the plaza.

Mosgo's (180 Westwood Center; 707-826-1195): Coffee, pastries, and live music.

Daybreak Café (678 Eighteenth Street; 707-826-7543): Get your granola here (seriously). Also eggs, tofu cutlets, french toast, or even vegan potatoes.

Gear Up

Revolution Bicycle Repair (1360 G Street; 707-822-2562): Their business is renting and servicing bikes, but they're the ultimate resource on the local trails and group rides.

Life Cycle (1593 G Street; 707-822-7755): Sells bikes and bike gear and organizes Sunday morning road rides.

Adventures Edge (650 Tenth Street; 707-822-4673): The full-service outfitter of Arcata, selling hiking, biking, paddling, and climbing gear—and renting

Local Legend

Bigfoot

That mythical (or not) creature Bigfoot has been spotted throughout the West and western Canada, but if there's an unofficial home for him, it's in Arcata's surrounding Humboldt County—and specifically the hamlet of Willow Creek, just down State Route 299. There have been many supposed sightings by locals over the past century, but the first time the area caused a national stir in the Sasquatch legend was in the late 1950s, when the *Humboldt Times* ran a story on the beast and a photo of a plaster cast of its footprint. The second was in 1967, when Roger Patterson and Bob Gimlin made their famous grainy film capturing a cameo of Bigfoot in nearby Bluff Creek. There's a statue of Bigfoot in town and a display about him at the China Flat Museum.

The Wild Side

Humboldt Redwoods State Park

If the mountain biking, hiking, and horseback riding among the redwoods in Arcata isn't enough for you, head an hour south to Humboldt Redwoods State Park. Among the 100 miles of trails, you'll also find the 10,000-acre Rockefeller Forest, the largest cluster of old-growth redwoods in California. There, the trees date back as far as two millennia and rise higher than a thirty-story building. The park lies just off the thirty-two-mile Avenue of the Giants Highway, on State Route 101. Along the drive, you'll find a house in Philipsville built from a single redwood log and the Shrine Drive-Through Tree in Myers Flat.

boats, backcountry skis, and miscellaneous backpacking equipment.

Refuel

Crosswinds (860 Tenth Street; 707-826-2133): Vegetarian-friendly restaurant that serves excellent pasta and Mexican food. Go for the chicken crêpe.

Folie Douce (1551 G Street; 707-822-1042): Uses only locally produced, organic produce for its salads, entrées, and wood-fired pizzas.

Plaza Grill (780 Seventh Street; 707-826-0860): If you're tired of grazing on veggies, you'll find the best burgers in town here.

Bunk

Lady Anne Bed and Breakfast Inn (902 Fourteenth Street; 707-822-2797): A warm, ornate, five-room Queen Anne–style home built in the late 1880s, and now owned by a former mayor of Arcata.

Fairwinds Motel (1674 G Street; 707-822-4824; www.fairwinds motelarcata.com): A clean, inexpensive motor lodge.

Hotel Arcata (708 Ninth Street; 707-826-0217; www.hotelarcata .com): A stately, historic hotel facing the plaza downtown. Rooms have clawfoot bathtubs.

Can't Leave?

Nearest airport: Arcata/Eureka, Eureka, California (10 miles)

Primary industries: Education, health care, forestry

Bishop, California

As if the prime rock climbing and bouldering nearby isn't enough to draw adventure seekers from around the world to Bishop—and it is—this small valley town is also the jumping-off point for hiking, mountain biking, and fly-fishing in perhaps the country's largest and most varied outdoor playground. Consider: within the boundaries of surrounding Inyo County lie the highest point in the continental United States (14,497-foot Mount Whitney) and the lowest (Death Valley, 282 feet below sea level). Bishop is due east of San Jose, near the Nevada border, but it's actually easier to reach from Southern California—about a five-hour drive—because the towering, 300-mile-long Sierra Nevada range blocks direct access to it from the western half of the state.

Population: 3,606
Action: Rock climbing, hiking, fishing, mountain biking

The town is the largest in Inyo County and lies at 4,100 feet in elevation on the northern end of the long Owens Valley. Although it sits in the rain shadow of the Sierra Nevada, the area benefits from abundant mountain runoff. Bishop was established as an agricultural and ranching community in the late 1800s, and the town is still crisscrossed by canals and irrigation ditches dug by farmers from that time. The water was so plentiful that at the turn of the twentieth century the City of Los Angeles began to buy massive chunks of real estate to control the area's water rights. In 1913, a 223-mile-long aqueduct from the local Owens River to the city was completed, drying up the local waters—and in turn the livelihood of the farmers. Today, the rivers flow somewhat more freely, even though the aqueduct is still in operation, and Bishop's economy relies largely upon the tourism created by the area's vast recreational opportunities. About fifteen historic, Western-style storefronts still line Main Street, the spine of the cozy downtown, along with sports shops, thrift shops, galleries, and diners.

Sure, you can go rock-climbing, bouldering, hiking, or mountain biking in Bishop, California, but the real outdoor action happens at the town's annual Mule Days celebration. (© Bishop Mule Days)

In recent years, Bishop has served as bouldering's unofficial Western capital. Climbers make the pilgrimage there to drop their crashpads among the handful of legendary areas that lie within fifteen minutes of Main Street. About seven miles north of town are Happy Boulders and Sad Boulders, lying within two shallow drainages formed in the area's volcanic crust. To the west is Buttermilk Country, a sprawling cluster of massive granite stones that include famed Grandma

Peabody and Grandpa Peabody. Set farther into the backcountry is the Druid Stone, an intimidating, seventy-foot-tall tower of rock with more than 100 problems.

With so much world-class bouldering, the rock climbing tends to get overshadowed, though it shouldn't. The Owens River Gorge north of town is a worthy alternative to nearby Yosemite National Park, farther up U.S. Route 395. Wide cracks and short overhangs punctuate the 600 routes on the gorge's tall, vertical volcanic walls that rise into the mountains. Staying closer to Bishop would also give you more time to mountain bike its spectacular open, hilly terrain. Loops from town weave among Buttermilk Country and on the volcanic tablelands of Happy and Sad Boulders, alongside creeks and irrigation canals, and through alpine meadows.

Then there's the hiking. A backpacker could spend a lifetime in the mountains that flank Bishop and still not set foot on every trail. Directly east of town are trailheads leading into the semiarid White Mountains, where the 14,246-foot summit White Mountain Peak rises above thickets of scrubby bristlecone pines; the most ancient trees on the planet, at forty centuries old, these pines live at elevations between 10,000 and 11,000 feet. West of Bishop is the stunning 580,000-acre John Muir Wilderness, encompassing a 100-mile expanse of the Sierra Nevada ridgeline. The preserve stretches south until it almost reaches the summit of 14,494-foot Mount Whitney, which officially lies within the boundaries of Sequoia National Park. In all, almost 600 miles of hiking trails crisscross the John Muir Wilderness, including a stretch of the Pacific Crest Trail.

Even if you come to Bishop simply to fly-fish, you'll leave happy. The chilly, pristine, and well-stocked Owens River, which originates north of Mammoth and flows south into Bishop, holds some of the richest trout waters in the state. The four-mile Wild Trout Section above town can be fished year-round and is said to be home to 4,000 fish per mile, although that might be a stretch. The Owens River Gorge, since it's more challenging to

Local Legend

Bishop Mule Days

There's no bigger mule show in the country than the Bishop Mule Days, held every Memorial Day weekend at the Tri-County Fairgrounds. It's a Wild West celebration of the start of the summer packing season and draws more than 30,000 people along with 700 mules and their trainers and riders, who compete in shows like coon jumping, chariot racing, and driving. There's also a country-music concert, along with dances and barbecues. Yes, it's as cheesy as it sounds, which is why it's so much fun.

reach, is as empty as it is spectacular—and the recently revitalized population of brown trout there is surprisingly feisty. The fishing also provides Bishop with an excuse to hold one of its biggest festivals of the year—the Blake Jones Trout Derby. It's held every March at the Pleasant Valley Reservoir as a warm-up to the April start of the fishing season on most of the local creeks. The event awards nearly $10,000 in prizes for various categories, but is as much of an outdoor social celebration as it is a competition—not that the townsfolk need any more excuses to get outside.

Start the Day

Kava Coffeehouse (206 North Main Street; 760-872-1010): Local crunchy types get their granola here—along with bagels and espresso.

Jack's Waffle Shop (437 North Main Street; 760-872-7971): Classic greasy-spoon breakfasts.

Gear Up

Wilson's Eastside Sports (224 North Main Street; 760-873-7520): The town's all-around backcountry outfitter.

Sierra Mountain Center (174 West Line Street; 760-873-8526): Known as the premier mountaineering and rock-climbing guide service this side of the Sierra.

Brock's Flyfishing Specialists (100 North Main Street; 760-872-3581): A fly shop, guide service, and fishing school.

Refuel

Whiskey Creek (524 North Main Street; 760-873-7174): Saloon fare, steaks, microbrews, and a sizeable gift shop to boot.

Upper Crust Pizza (1180 North Main Street; 760-872-2410): Tasty soups and salads.

The Wild Side

Inyo National Forest

Bishop is sandwiched between two sections of the sprawling, 165-mile-long Inyo National Forest, which stretches from the edge of Yosemite National Park in the north down to near the border of Death Valley National Park in the south. It lies on the dry, eastern side of the Sierra, incorporating the John Muir and Ansel Adams wilderness areas—along with five others—in its two million acres of 14,000-foot peaks, desert scrublands, vast meadows, and clear lakes. More than five million people visit Inyo a year.

Erik Schat's Bakery (763 North Main Street; 760-873-7156):
Hearty sandwiches served on all-natural, hand-shaped sheepherder
bread.

Bunk

Joseph House Inn (376 West Yaney Street; 760-872-3389;
www.josephhouseinn.com): Homey five-room bed-and-breakfast
on three garden-filled acres.

Vagabond Inn (1030 North Main Street; 800-522-1555): Pink
motel with a swimming pool and a diner.

Mountain View Motel (730 West Line Street; 760-873-4242): Tidy
lodging and a common space for cleaning and freezing the day's
catch.

Can't Leave?

Nearest airport: Mammoth Yosemite, Mammoth Lakes, California
(35 miles)

Primary industries: Recreation, health, retail

Downieville, California

Population: 391

Action: Mountain biking, hiking, backcountry skiing, rafting

True hardcore mountain bikers are more likely to hand you their Social Security numbers than divulge the locations of their favorite rides. So if you ask any of them out West for the best directions to Downieville, California—about forty-five minutes northeast of Nevada City and two and a half hours from Sacramento—they'll probably try to send you to somewhere in New Mexico. The trails are that amazing, especially the stomach-in-throat descents from the surrounding mountains into the town's location at the confluence of the North Fork of the Yuba River and the Downie River, in a verdant, tree-filled canyon at 2,900 feet.

Downieville was founded more than 150 years ago as a mining outpost and quickly became the one of the top commerce centers in gold country. Prospectors were unearthing massive nuggets while hotels and shops were being built, and the population swelled to more than 5,000. The town became so prosperous that it was almost nominated as the capital of California before the selection of Sacramento.

Many of the nineteenth-century structures—built largely out of brick after two catastrophic fires—in the five-block downtown remain, as do the old-fashioned wooden sidewalks. Yet Downieville is no dusty ghost town. Its population is an eclectic mix of retired military veterans; lifelong natives; well-educated, telecommuting transplants; and, of course, mountain bikers. There are two local bike shops, Yuba Expeditions and Downieville Outfitters, which are as much social centers as they are retail and guiding operations, especially during the famed Downieville Classic Mountain Bike Festival held every July. The festival attracts thousands of pro and amateur riders from around the world to compete in or watch its three main competitions: a grueling point-to-point race, a big-air river jump, and the Downieville Downhill Race. This third event is the longest of its kind in the country—a mad

The mountain bike descents into Downieville, California are some of the West's biggest thrill rides. (© Muknud Photo and Sierra Buttes Trail Stewardship)

dash that drops 4,700 vertical feet in fifteen miles and ends in town. The record winning time is a staggering thirty-eight minutes and thirty-two seconds.

The festival and races are the creations of Greg Williams, the town's godfather of biking and owner of Yuba Expeditions. There's no truth to the rumor that he can walk atop the water of the Yuba River, as some local gearheads attest. It is true, though, that his shop will shuttle riders to the top of the Downieville Downhill course at 7,100-foot Packer Saddle. The ride follows singletrack trails and abandoned mining roads over wooden footbridges, around tight s-turns, alongside creek banks, and through thickly wooded forests. It starts on the wooded Butcher Ranch Trail, which has sheer rock drop-offs, then climbs shortly to connect with the Third Divide Trail. The Third Divide plummets to Lavezzola Creek before leveling off on the First Divide Trail, which leads into Downieville. For people who like climbs as much

Local Legend

The Gallows

The object of pride for most towns isn't usually an object of death—except in the case of Downieville. Sitting outside the courthouse is a nineteenth-century gallows so immaculately restored, it looks like it's ready for use today. Built to replace an older gallows, it was used only once: to execute an Irishman named James O'Neill, who shot and killed his employer, according to the official county account. Yet the gallows symbolizes the town's rough-and-tumble Gold Rush past, when it was known for executing criminals and for being the only community in California ever to lynch a woman. Today the gallows is an official state historic landmark.

as descents—or who don't have a dual-suspension bike—there are several other extensive trail circuits within town, all of them world class and almost completely empty.

Downieville lies in the center of the 800,000-acre Tahoe National Forest, which spreads across the crest of the Sierra Nevada Mountains to Lake Tahoe. Within the preserve's boundaries are more than 500 miles of hiking trails, and access to the Pacific Crest Trail is only a twenty-minute drive from Downieville in Sierra City. Rafting on the Class IV and V rapids of the Yuba River, which drains into and out of the village center, is also popular. In winter, the backcountry skiing possibilities are endless, and the resorts of Lake Tahoe are less than two hours away. While this tiny community will never again be considered for the political or economic capital of California, it can stake a reasonable claim as the adventure capital.

Start the Day

Red Moose Café (224 Main Street, Sierra City; 530-862-1502): Sticky cinnamon rolls and stick-to-your-ribs breakfasts in a cabin-style building.

Gear Up

Yuba Expeditions (105 Commercial Street; 530-289-3010): Sells gear, demos bikes, runs a biker shuttle, maintains trails, guides rides, and provides a social outlet.

Downieville Outfitters (208 Main Street; 530-289-0155): Sells and rents bikes, operates a shuttle, and provides a wealth of knowledge about the local trails and terrain.

Sierra Hardware (305 Main Street; 530-289-3582): Sells a limited but quality supply of camping gear and fishing tackle.

Refuel

Gallows Cafe (101 Nevada Street; 530-289-3540): Its riverside deck is the favorite post-ride gathering spot in town.

Grubstake Saloon (315 Main Street; 530-289-0289): Burgers and pasta in a family-style setting.

St. Charles Place Saloon (301 Main Street; 530-289-3237): A good ol' Western bar, complete with dead animal heads on the wall and draft beer served very cold.

Bunk

Lure Resort (100 Lure Bridge Lane; 800-671-4084; www.lureresort.com): Clean, low-cost cabins on the banks of the North Fork of the Yuba River.

Carriage House Inn (110 Commercial Street; 800-296-2289; www.downieville carriagehouse.com) A downtown bed-and-breakfast offering river-view rooms and bike storage.

The Weaver Building (208 Main Street; 510-501-2516; www.sierra retreats.com): A posh, recently remodeled loft with two gas fireplaces; can accommodate as many as eight people. It takes up the top floors of the 1867 building that houses Downieville Outfitters.

Can't Leave?

Nearest airport: Reno/Tahoe International, Reno, Nevada (90 miles)

Primary industries: Government, lumber, retail

The Wild Side

The Yuba River

Only three rafting operations are permitted to run trips down the North Fork of the Yuba River, and for good reason, considering how treacherous the whitewater is. This narrow, thirty-mile stretch of tight drops and boulder fields makes a precipitous descent—nearly 100 feet per mile in spots like Class V Rosassco Ravine, on the upper portion—as it slices through the forested mountains into Downieville and then on to nearby Sierra City. The most famous rapid is the frothing Maytag, a Class V that even veterans of the water scout each time before tackling, if they dare to run it.

June Lake, California

Population: 612

Action: Fishing, hiking, downhill skiing, mountain biking, paddling

You know there's a lot to do outdoors in a place when the gate to Yosemite National Park lies a half-hour away, yet is practically an afterthought. Such is life in June Lake, wedged between the wing-shaped Gull Lake and the slim, one mile by half-a-mile body of water that shares the town's name. Etched into the eastern slope of the Sierra Nevada, at 7,600 feet, it serves as its own gateway to adventure. Just past the doorsteps of its rustic lodges are epic fishing on prime trout waters, paddling on ancient glacial lakes, rugged hikes and mountain-bike rides with camera-dropping views, easy-access ice climbing, and skiing and snowboarding on an impressive, underappreciated mountain that's never crowded.

While the hip crowds flock twenty miles south to Mammoth Mountain Resort—quickly becoming Whistler South, where people come to see and be seen—the smattering of folks who frequent June Lake simply come to be. To get to the town, you need to turn off U.S. Route 395 and drive a few miles down State Route 158—a spur road also known as the June Lake Loop. In its fourteen miles, the loop connects with four crystal lakes beneath the shadow of stark, 10,909-foot Carson Peak. There's almost no way to drive the length of it without stopping to appreciate the views—or, if you have the gear and license, casting a line. The snow-fed waters along the road may be chilly for swimming, but they're rich with rainbow, brook, brown, and cutthroat trout.

Fishing is probably the biggest obsession in June Lake, but not the only one. Skiing and snowboarding aren't far behind, and boating and hiking after that. The people you'll find among the four-block cluster of general stores, art galleries, pubs, tackle shops, and gift shops that make up the tiny downtown get their downhill fix on local June Mountain. It isn't mammoth—or Mammoth—but it tops out at 10,135

The slopes at June Mountain, in June Lake, California offer views of nearby Carson Peak.
(© June Lake Chamber of Commerce)

feet and has a 2,600-foot vertical with thirty-five trails, two well-maintained terrain parks, and a half pipe. Most of the time the mountain's 500 acres stay blissfully uncrowded—a situation that leads the locals to fear that Intrawest, which owns it and the megaresort down the road, may some day close it down.

The hiking in the area feels equally free from the masses, largely because it's so extensive. Trailheads off the June Lake Loop can lead you deeper into the Inyo, as well as the Hoover, John Muir, and Ansel Adams national wilderness areas. The Rush Creek Trail by Silver Lake, outside of town, eventually links to the 211-mile John Muir Trail and to the Pacific Crest Trail, which slices across the eastern half of Yosemite. Even a short afternoon's trek can lead you to pristine backcountry lakes, hidden among the Jeffrey and lodgepole pines and the occasional aspen groves.

Mountain bikers also use the town as a jumping-off point into the woods, where there are a handful of thigh-scorching climbs into the high alpine passes on trails like Hartley Springs. For more manicured singletrack, Mammoth opens its forty miles of its trails—and the Panorama Gondola—to fat tires, as well. Paddlers have even easier access to action from town, if they don't mind sharing the waters of June Lake, Gull Lake, and Silver Lake with anglers, and those of Grant Lake with occasional waterskiers (it's the only lake on the Loop with a speed limit above ten miles per hour). Now do you understand why even Yosemite can get lost in the shuffle?

Start the Day

Eagle's Landing Restaurant
(5587 Highway 158; 760-648-7897; www.doubleeagleresort.com): Located within the Double Eagle Resort near Silver Lake, beneath views of Mount Carson, it serves traditional breakfasts beside the fireplace.

Silver Lake Café (6957 Highway 158; 760-648-7525): Its three-egg omelets will keep you going for the morning; part of the Silver Lake Resort, it's only open in the summer.

Local Legend

Sierra Mountain Guides

June Lake is home to one of the West's premier guide services: Sierra Mountain Guides. Led by Doug Nidever, an expert on Yosemite, the company attracts mountaineers, rock climbers, and backpackers from across the country in summer; and mountaineers, ice climbers, backcountry skiers, and snow campers in winter. Their location makes sense, given the proximity to Yosemite—where most of their trips take place—and the jagged, often ice-coated peaks of the eastern slope of the Sierra Nevada.

Gear Up

Ernie's Tackle and Ski Shop (Boulder Drive; 760-648-7756): An institution in June Lake for more than seven decades, its name almost says it all. (It also sells snowboard gear.)

June Lake General Store (Main Street; 760-648-7771): Sells basic camping supplies and plenty of munchies for the trail.

Refuel

The Tiger Bar & Café (Main Street; 760-648-7551): The evening hangout for everyone in town—whether they're there for the Tiger Burgers and home-made potato chips or just a beer.

Alpine Delicatessen and Pizza (Boulder Drive; 760-648-7633): June Lake's pizza and sandwich joint, housed in a cozy cabin.

Bunk

Double Eagle Resort (5587 Highway 158; 760-648-7004; www.doubleeagleresort.com): A quiet luxury cabin resort with a spa that is recognized as one of the finest in the country.

Boulder Lodge (2282 Highway 158; 760-648-7533, www.boulder lodge.net): Clean, welcoming cabins and a lakefront house above June Lake.

Can't Leave?

Nearest airport: Reno/Tahoe International, Reno, Nevada (150 miles)

Primary industries: Recreation, forestry, retail

The Wild Side

Tuolumne Meadows

The nearby Tioga Pass gate to Yosemite is the park's only entrance on the eastern side of the Sierra. It also provides easy access to stunning Tuolumne Meadows. At 8,600 feet in elevation, this verdant subalpine valley is laced with trails, including the John Muir and Continental Divide trails. Surrounded by round domes and far from the park's main western entrance, it's quieter than Yosemite Valley. For rock climbers, Tuolumne's crack-filled, knobby granite routes aren't as long as on the park's big walls, but the options are nearly endless. The Tioga Pass entrance is usually closed between November and June, so there's only a short window for visiting this area before it's covered in snow.

Truckee, California

Population:

15,737

Action: Downhill, cross-country, and backcountry skiing; hiking; mountain biking; paddling

They call Lake Tahoe the Blue World, but in Truckee, there's more to the spectrum than just the incomparable color of the 193-square-mile, 989- to 1,645-foot-deep lake twelve miles to the south. First, there is white, as in the 206 inches of snow that the Sierra Nevada town receives each winter. Without the white stuff, the eight major alpine resorts and premier nordic areas that surround Truckee would be a lot less lively in the winter, when below-zero nighttime temperatures (which earn the town a reputation as one of the coldest spots in the country) slowly rise to skier-, snowboarder-, and snowshoer-friendly thermometer readings during the day. Yellow matters—it's in the pale morning light over 7,239-foot Donner Summit and Donner Lake, the backyard spot for fishing and wakeboarding, and in the omelets that slide onto plates at the Squeeze Inn. In the ponderosa pine and Douglas fir of the 800,000-acre Tahoe National Forest—and in the increasingly eco-conscious home building—there is green. And finally, there are the multicolored hues of the store façades along Commercial Row, where Truckee's been able to preserve a piece of the Old West.

To the tourists who swing through here to peer in at the Jail Museum and sip an ice cream soda from Bud's Sporting Goods and Fountain on their way to Donner Memorial State Park, which honors the ill-fated traveling party, it may seem hard to believe that Truckee wasn't incorporated until 1993. That's nearly 150 years after the town's namesake, a Paiute Indian chief whose real name sounded like *Tro-kay* to western-migrating families, guided parties through the area. In the decades that followed, the small settlement that had been a rest area for wagon parties turned into a lumber and railroad town, serviced by Chinese immigrants, and home base for prosperous ice and beer-

Truckee, California is a premier snow-sports destination, thanks to the 200-plus inches of snow the Sierra Nevada town averages each year. (© Truckee Donner Chamber of Commerce)

brewing companies. Hundreds of historic buildings from Truckee's heyday still stand—albeit with different interiors—and have long drawn the interest of traveling families and film companies alike. But by the turn of the twentieth century, Truckee had already become a top snowsports destination—with ice palaces and toboggan runs—whose reputation was cemented with the arrival of the Squaw Valley 1960 Olympic Winter Games and, in 1964, Interstate 80.

And thanks to Mother Nature, it's tough to decide whether Truckee's best in winter or summer. Come November, snowstorms sweep across the Sierra Nevada, dumping some thirty-three feet of snow on more than 18,000 acres of lift-served ski and snowboard terrain. Ringing Lake Tahoe (and blessed with nearly guaranteed bluebird days) are Alpine Meadows, Heavenly, Kirkwood, Mount Rose–Ski Tahoe, Northstar-at-Tahoe, Sierra-at-Tahoe, Squaw Valley, and Sugar Bowl resorts. Readers of the *Sierra Sun,* Truckee's newspaper, recently picked Sugar Bowl—the provenance of Olympic skier Daron Rahlves—

as the best ski resort (it's also the closest), while Northstar-at-Tahoe won top honors for its snowboard park. And nordic skiers can't find a much better place than Tahoe Donner Cross Country Center, Truckee's local area; it boasts 115 kilometers of diverse trails that meander to warming huts and climb steep Sierra hills over more than 4,800 acres of terrain. All this plus hundreds of cross-country, snowshoeing, and backcountry skiing and riding options in the Tahoe National Forest, make Truckee one of the best places to hunker down or, rather, get out, in winter.

But then there are the warm-weather months, when such ski areas as Northstar-at-Tahoe turn into mountain-biking havens; the Tahoe Rim Trail opens to hikers, horseback riders, and bikers; and the lakes wake up to waterskiers, anglers, sailors, and wakeboarders. For the latter few sports, Truckee's local hangout is 1.5-square-mile, glacial Donner Lake, where rainbows and brown trout swim and where a 23-mile rim trail is in the works. The granddaddy of rim trails, however, is the 165-mile circle around Lake Tahoe, a thru-hiker's dream that has also become a hotspot for day hikes. On the North Shore, you'll find the 13.4-mile Brockway to Watson Lake route, which leads to a dramatic rock overlook on Lake Tahoe, and the six-mile Mount Rose Loop, which features a waterfall. Fifty percent of the Tahoe Rim Trail is now open to mountain bikers, who already had an entire summer's worth of choices at their disposal. Down on Lake Tahoe itself, you'll want to climb into a kayak—at the end of a dusty day around Truckee, it's the best way to see the Blue, and the not-so-blue, World.

Start the Day

Squeeze Inn (10060 Donner Pass Road; 530-587-9814): Enormous omelets of nearly every imaginable variety, as creatively named as the lunchtime sandwiches.

Gear Up

Paco's Bike & Ski (11200-6 Donner Pass Road; 530-587-5561): Mountain- and road-bike and cross-country ski rental and service, plus snowshoes and clothing.

Porters Sport (11391 Deerfield Drive; 530-587-6363): Alpine, backcountry, and snowboard gear, along with camping, hiking, wakeboarding, and waterskiing supplies.

Bud's Sporting Goods and Fountain (10043 Donner Pass Road; 503-587-3177): Fishing gear and malted milks.

Refuel

Casa Baeza (10010 Bridge Street; 530-587-2161): Truckee's best Mexican food, served with renowned margaritas.

OB's Pub & Restaurant (10046 Donner Pass Road; 530-587-4164): Steaks, ribs, seafood, and pasta, along with wild mushroom and spinach strudel and a bar menu; live music on Fridays and karaoke on Thursdays.

Cottonwood Restaurant and Bar (1042 Rue Hilltop; 530-587-5711): Overlooking Truckee from the Hilltop Lodge; start with crispy-fried, jerk-spiced baby-back ribs or a chèvre salad and move on to tofu stir fry, Thai prawns, or free-range rabbit cassoulet.

The Wild Side

Pacific Crest Trail

One of the closest hiking trails to Truckee is also one of the world's longest, toughest, and most diverse backpacking routes—the 2,650-mile Pacific Crest Trail that zigzags between Canada and Mexico. While thousands attempt the Appalachian Trail, only a few hundred thru-hikers hit the P.C.T. each year, thanks to its remoteness and wildly fluctuating terrain and elevation changes. You'll find the trailhead just west of Truckee, near Donner Summit.

Bunk

Tahoe National Forest (631 Coyote Street, Nevada City; 530-265-4531; www.fs.fed.us/r5/tahoe): Three different camping areas in the Truckee Ranger District: at Boca Stampede, Highway 89 North, and Highway 89 South.

The River Street Inn (10009 East River Street; 530-550-9290; www.riverstreetinntruckee.com): An 1885 former brothel turned bed-and-breakfast.

The Truckee Hotel (10007 Bridge Street; 800-659-6921; www.thetruckeehotel.com): This historic, Old West hotel has twenty-nine European rooms with shared baths and eight American rooms with private baths, plus Moody's Bistro and Lounge.

Can't Leave?

Nearest airport: Reno/Tahoe International, Reno, Nevada (32 miles)

Primary industries: Tourism, retail, government, mining, construction

Wrightwood, California

Population: 4,247

Action: Hiking, mountain biking, downhill skiing, fishing

What's most surprising about Wrightwood isn't that a place so close to Los Angeles (about fifty-five miles) can seem so rugged and remote, or that it can have four distinct seasons, and prime skiing, mountain biking, fishing, and backpacking. What's surprising is that a place so close to Los Angeles can remain so blissfully undiscovered. This no-stoplight town of nearly 4,000 people, etched into the Swarthout Valley of the northeastern San Gabriel Mountains, is almost completely bypassed by outdoorsy Southern California weekenders, who head to larger, more crowded resort destinations like Big Bear and Mammoth. Their loss.

Wrightwood was established as a ranching community in the late nineteenth century by the Wright family—go figure—who also planted apple orchards throughout the area. (These orchards still partly exist today.) In the early twentieth century, a developer bought much of the town and tried to subdivide it into a resort community, with very limited success. Now it remains an untapped gem, its tiny downtown a smattering of antique shops, tchotchke stores, and restaurants shaded by tall pines and aimed at snagging skiers headed to the three peaks of the cozy Mountain High Resort nearby. People who idly pass through rarely realize that they've entered a hub of outdoor adventure.

The town sits in the heart of the Angeles National Forest, a chaparral-covered patch of land the size of Rhode Island, adorned with lakes, sparkling rivers, mountain peaks stretching as high as 10,000 feet, and 490 miles of trails. With its elevation at 5,900 feet, Wrightwood is high enough to stay cool in the summer, yet low enough to remain mild and fairly dry in the winter. Meanwhile, an average of almost eighteen feet of snow gets dumped annually on the summits around it—a boon to Mountain High, about fifteen minutes west of town on

Flying high at Mountain High Resort. (© Mountain High)

State Route 2. What the resort lacks in vertical drop (about 1,600 feet) and size (290 acres) it makes up for with variety of terrain. Its East Resort mountain is known for its long, traditional groomers. On a clear day at the summit, you can stare across the Mojave Desert and even spot Catalina Island jutting out of the Pacific. The West Resort mountain, open at night seven days a week during peak season, attracts shredders to its jumps and rails throughout. The North Resort, which used to be the Ski Sunrise resort, is mostly for beginners and boasts a twenty-acre tubing park.

The landscape around Wrightwood is even more appealing after the snow melts, though. In spring, the whites, yellows, and purples of wild-flowers burst into the canyons, and in summer the mountains beckon hikers and bikers onto their trails, as the sun shines above them nearly 90 percent of the time. Skirting town is the Pacific Crest Trail, which continues through Mountain High and to the peak of 9,400-foot Mount Baden-Powell, about fourteen miles west, along the ridgeline of the San Gabriel Mountains. Wrightwood is a favorite stop among thru-hikers who drop in via the three-mile Acorn Trail access route.

Although the P.C.T. bars mountain bikes, most of the local footpaths also double as singletrack routes. A popular choice for hikers and riders is the four-mile, box-shaped Blue Ridge Trail, about five minutes west of downtown on State Route 2; the trail gains 1,000 feet in elevation among the pine and firs. About fifteen minutes further down the highway is the four-mile Dawson's Saddle Trail, which climbs along the ridgeline of Throops Peak until it reaches its turnaround point at the P.C.T.

As rugged and exhilarating as the steep trails of Wrightwood can be for hikers and riders, it's downright grueling for a trail runner. For more than twenty years, the town has been the starting point for the annual Angeles Crest 100-Mile Trail Run. The course climbs up the Acorn Trail onto the P.C.T. and heads west before ending in Pasadena. A maximum of 150 competitors can enter the race, and the record-setting time is an astonishing seventeen hours, twenty-five minutes.

A more cerebral alternative is to grab a fishing rod and head for Silverwood Lake Recreation Area, ten minutes east of town. The 1,000-acre lake created by Cedar Springs Dam teems with trout, largemouth bass, and record-setting stripers—not to mention waterskiers and pleasure boaters, who fill the campground there on weekends. The sublime fishing is yet another reason to visit Wrightwood—and to keep the secret of this place to yourself.

The Wild Side

Mount Baden-Powell

Mount Baden-Powell, the second-tallest peak in the San Gabriel range at 9,399 feet, was named after Boy Scouts founder Robert Baden-Powell, a former British army general. It's also a favorite summit among hikers in the Los Angeles area—especially for its four-mile Vincent Gap Trail, which begins about nine miles west of Wrightwood. The trail has forty-one switchbacks through oak, sugar pine, cedars—and near the top is a forest of knotty limber pines, which can only live above 9,000 feet. Some of these trees are as old as 2,000 years. The trail's total elevation gain is 2,800 feet.

Start the Day

Cinnamon's Bakery and Sandwich Shoppe (1350 Route 2; 760-249-5588): Owners Linda and Steve not only make a mean cinnamon roll, but they also welcome the classic cars that converge there and park in the back of the lot every Saturday at 7:30 AM.

The Village Grind (6020 Park Drive; 760-249-5501): Serves hot music and espresso on the outdoor deck.

Gear Up

McGrath's Ski and Snowboard Rentals (1327 Route 2; 760-249-3055): Rents equipment, but dishes out the most knowledgeable info about the local ski mountains for free.

Mountain Hardware (1390 Route 2; 760-249-3653): A solar-powered shop that stocks camping equipment alongside power drills and interior latex paint.

Refuel

Grizzly Café (1455 Route 2; 760-249-6713): Grab some pub grub at a table beside the stone fireplace in the dining room.

Blue Ridge Inn (6060 Park Drive; 760-249-3440): An old, down-home lodge building and bar where the menu is simple—scallops, porterhouse steak, burgers—but the food is the best in town.

Bunk

Table Mountain Campground (2 Table Mountain Road; 877-444-6777): The trailhead for eight hiking paths, it's adjacent to Mountain High North and has 111 spacious, private sites.

Canyon Creek Inn (6059 Pine Street; 760-249-4800; www.canyon creekinn.com): This chalet-style motel by the elementary school is simple but comfortable.

Can't Leave?

Nearest airport: San Bernardino International, San Bernardino, California (34 miles)

Primary industries: Tourism, service

Elko, Nevada

Population: 16,685

Action: Back-country skiing, hiking, rock climbing, mountain and road biking, fishing

four hundred miles north of Las Vegas, Elko might pine for a marketing slogan similar to that of the city of sin—what happens here, stays here. Not because of the shady, after-hours happenings (though Elko does have a few casinos and legal brothels), but rather because word about the daytime activities has started to spread beyond Nevada borders. Once, residents of this crossroads of cowboy culture, Basque history, and Interstate 80 were able to keep the sixty-mile-long Ruby Mountain Range and its deep stashes of spun-sugar powder skiing to themselves. Once, the Jarbidge Wilderness belonged mostly to those who had grown up learning to walk along Idaho Street, learning to ranch in the high desert, and learning what makes a saddle at J. M. Capriola's western-wear shop.

But then somebody founded a heli-skiing company, somebody moved the annual Cowboy Poetry Gathering here, and somebody else proclaimed Elko the best small town in America. Still, not everybody knows about all the adventure-related bells and whistles surrounding town, because most people are too concerned with the kind that come from the ubiquitous one-armed bandits.

Though Native Americans had lived here for thousands of years, it was the railroad industry that gave Elko its name—a Central Pacific developer named towns after animals—and its beginnings as a shipping center for Western mines. In the late 1800s, Basque shepherds from the Pyrenees Mountains on the French-Spanish border arrived to bolster a ranching economy that had begun with cattlemen; today, Elko dines heartily on Basque fare while celebrating the National Basque Festival every Fourth of July weekend.

The Basque may have been drawn, in part, by the Ruby Mountains, which rival the Pyrenees in height—having ten peaks more than

The Ruby Mountains overlook the ranches near Elko, Nevada. (© Nevada Commission on Tourism)

10,000 feet high—and length. Southeast of Elko, the range is home to the Ruby Dome (11,387 feet), more than twenty alpine lakes, and glacier-carved canyons. Since 1977, it's also been the sight of whirlybirds ferrying skiers to backcountry descents. (Ruby Mountain Helicopter Skiing was founded by a Utah-powder enthusiast looking for comparable conditions, but far fewer crowds.) Closer to town, never-evers can practice their turns at the Elko SnoBowl, a family resort that has 650 vertical feet, before tackling the Rubies.

Sometimes called the Alps of Nevada for their lush, snow-covered peaks, the Ruby Mountains and the 113,167-acre Jarbidge Wilderness glitter just as brightly in the warm-weather months. The U-shaped Lamoille Canyon—the Yosemite of Nevada, to throw out another comparison—is full of climbing and hiking routes. Walls are more than 800 feet tall, and there are more than 100 established rock routes surrounded by bouldering areas.

The Rubies are part of the 6.3-million-acre Humboldt-Toiyabe National Forest, the largest national forest in the continental United States. But even less impressively sized patches of protected land around Elko have an allure that should beat out casinos and brothels, at least among adventure travelers. There's boating and fishing on the South Fork Reservoir, and more fishing on the Humboldt River, which runs right through town. What happens in Elko may not stay in Elko, but you just may—and you'll have a much clearer head in the morning.

Local Legend

Cowboy Poetry

There are cowboy poetry gatherings everywhere these days, but none like the weeklong National Cowboy Poetry Gathering held at Elko's Western Folklife Center every winter. For more than twenty years, cowboys and cowgirls from not only the United States but also Argentina, Brazil, and France have been swapping tales of life on the range. A sign that this country is now taking its cowboy poets seriously: they were featured in the 2002 Olympic Winter Games in Salt Lake City.

Start the Day

Cowboy Joe (376 Fifth Street; 775-753-5612): Coffee, espresso drinks, and baked breakfast goods, two doors down from the Western Folklife Center.

Gear Up

Cedar Creek Clothing Company (453 Idaho Street; 702-738-3950): Alpine and cross-country ski, snowboard, and snowshoe rentals, plus backpacking and climbing gear and accessories.

Ruby Mountain Helicopter Skiing (Lamoille; 775-753-6867): Helicopter and snowcat skiing and snowboarding; packages include meals and three nights at Reds Ranch.

Refuel

La Fiesta (780 Commercial Street; 775-738-1622): Mexican specialties in a local hangout.

Stray Dog Pub and Café (374 Fifth Street; 773-753-4888): Downtown venue serving microbrews and sports-bar fare such as pizza and calzones.

Star Hotel & Restaurant (246 Silver Street; 775-738-9925): Family-style Basque restaurant that serves seemingly endless steaks, spaghetti, french fries, and more, on long tables with red-and-white-checked tablecloths.

Bunk

South Fork State Recreation Area (353 Lower South Fork Unit 8, Spring Creek; 775-744-4346; www.parks.nv.gov/sf.htm): Twenty-five campsites at the 1,650-acre South Fork Reservoir.

Red Lion Inn & Casino (2065 Idaho Street; 800-545-0044; www.redlioncasino.com): Lively, large hotel with 223 rooms and a sprawling casino with 500 slot machines.

Can't Leave?

Nearest airport: Elko Regional (2 miles)

Primary industries: Gold mining, gaming

Cloudcroft, New Mexico

Population: 749

Action: Mountain biking, hiking, downhill and cross-country skiing

You won't find a better place in southeastern New Mexico to chill than in Cloudcroft, which lies at 9,000 feet in elevation. Not only does it have an artsy, laid-back vibe, but on a typical day, the air is twenty degrees cooler than even fifteen miles west in Alamogordo, a town that lies about 4,700 feet—and a few life zones—below it at the foot of the steep Sacramento Mountains. And the difference in temperatures between there and El Paso, ninety miles to the south, is even starker. Yet when you're in Cloudcroft, there's so much hiking, biking, and skiing in the surrounding Lincoln National Forest that the last thing on your mind is the thought of sitting around and cooling your heels—or the rest of your body.

This tiny, western-style mountain village has been a resort escape from the start. It was created by the El Paso and Northern Railroad in the late 1890s, after company officials in Alamogordo scouted the spot where Cloudcroft now stands and decided they could not only use it as a lumber source for rail construction, but also build a resort, and ferry overheated Texans to it. By 1899 a guest pavilion, tent area, and guest lodge were constructed for visitors, and a year later the railroad had completed the line extension that climbed the mountains into town. Trains would provide the only source of transportation into Cloudcroft for the next couple of decades. In those early years, the lodge and pavilion would each burn down, but both were rebuilt and are now a part of the majestic Lodge at Cloudcroft—one of the social and economic engines driving the town since the last railroad car disappeared in 1947.

The other tourist magnet is the national forest itself. Divided into three separate sections—the largest two separated by the rectangular Mescalero Apache Indian Reservation—the Lincoln covers 1.1 million acres. Within its boundaries, you'll find 200 miles of trails among a var-

There's so much to do in Cloudcroft that chilling, even in winter is almost impossible.
(© Gary Wood)

ied terrain, from cactus-draped desert canyons at 3,500 feet to spruce-adorned peaks as high as 11,500 feet in elevation. The Sacramento District, south of the reservation, is the largest of the three at 450,000 acres and is headquartered in Cloudcroft. Although the fishing isn't spectacular in this area, the hiking and mountain biking among the aspen, ponderosa pine, and Douglas fir are. The highlight is the rocky singletrack of the 13.5-mile Rim Trail, which has occasional vistas opening onto White Sands to the west.

You'll get even better views on the twisting Cloud-Climbing Rail-Trail, an ever-expanding network tracing the abandoned twenty-six-mile, trestle-filled railroad bed between Alamogordo and Cloudcroft.

It's the result of the determined efforts of the New Mexico Rails-to-Trails Association, which hopes to incorporate it into a fifty-mile multiuse loop with Cloudcroft as one of the hubs. High Altitude outfitters on Burro Avenue in town carries maps of the best local trails. The shop also organizes the High Altitude Classic cross-country and downhill mountain-bike races, an event sanctioned by the North American Off-Road Bicycle Association and part of the New Mexico Off-Road Series circuit. The cross-country course is an up-and-down nine-mile loop that starts in town and alternates between railroad grade, dirt road, and forest singletrack. The 700-foot, vertical, jump-filled downhill course lies on one of the slopes of the local Ski Cloudcroft ski hill. In winter, the open-again–closed-again facility maintains twenty-one trails on its sixty-eight acres, although you're probably better off driving the forty minutes north to Ski Apache if you want to spend a full day on the slopes. The area around Cloudcroft does see enough snow for quality cross-country skiing on its trails—making it tough to chill there even when it's cold.

The Wild Side

Tularosa Basin

Less than an hour removed from the alpine setting of Cloudcroft are the sprawling white sands of the Tularosa Basin. Encircled by the San Andres Mountains to the west and the Sacramento Mountains to the east, this area contains the ancient bed of former Lake Otero, which dried up 4,000 years ago. In its place is the largest gypsum dune field in the world. Its bleached, wavelike ripples rise as high as sixty feet and stay cool to bare feet, even in the dead of summer. The White Sands Missile Range occupies much of the basin, but 275 square miles of it falls within the White Sands National Monument. There you can hike the marked trails, sled the dunes, or explore the open sand as if you're hiking the Sahara. Just remember to bring a compass, to be safe.

Start the Day

Jamocha Bean (505 Burro Avenue; 505-682-2332; www.jamochabean.com): Coffeehouse that serves bagels, Belgian waffles, and egg sandwiches for breakfast.

Rebecca's (1 Corona Place; 800-395-6343; www.thelodgeresort.com): This refined restaurant at the Lodge Resort was named after a redheaded former waitress, whose ghost still resides there.

Gear Up

High Altitude (310 Burro Avenue; 505-682-1229): Mountain bike sales and rentals, outdoor gear supplier, and experts on the local trails.

Busick Ski Haus (1000 South Highway 130; 505-682-2144): A ski shack that sells backcountry, downhill, and nordic skis, and rents equipment.

Refuel

Big Daddy's Diner (1705 James Canyon, Highway 82; 505-682-1224): Burgers, sandwiches, and enchiladas at this lunch and dinner joint owned by Linda and Roger Loper.

Western Bar & Café (304 Burro Avenue; 505-682-2445): The local hangout for beers and steaks.

Bunk

The Lodge Resort & Spa (1 Corona Place; 800-395-6343; www.thelodgeresort.com): The legendary fifty-nine-room hotel, spa, and golf course (one of the highest in the country at 9,000 feet) has hosted the likes of Clark Gable and Pancho Villa over the years.

The Crofting Inn (300 Swallow Place; 877-682-3604): A bed-and-breakfast in an eighty-year-old, log-style, two-story home.

Can't Leave?

Nearest airport: Alamogordo-White Sands Regional, Alamogordo, New Mexico (19 miles)

Primary industries: Service, health care, government

Silver City, New Mexico

Population: 9,999

Action: Mountain and road biking, hiking, kayaking, rafting

Silver City locals will tell you that hometown boy Billy the Kid committed his first crime by stealing some clothes from the town's Chinese laundry as a young teenager. After being nabbed, he wriggled up the jail's chimney, escaped, and spent the rest of his life on the lam. Too bad for him. Silver City, on the eastern fringe of the Continental Divide in southwestern New Mexico, is a tough place to leave. Its Old West–style downtown, sprinkled with adobe homes and prim brick Victorian houses left over from Billy's time, makes for a cultured high-desert oasis in the foothills of the Mogollon Mountains. With such a spread of wilderness around it, you can see why he was able to slip out of sight. These days, mountain bikers and hikers pull the same kind of disappearing act—onto the thousands of miles of trails in the bordering Gila National Forest to the north.

Like so many other settlements around these parts, Silver City, a former Apache Indian camping area, came into existence in 1870 after prospectors discovered silver nearby. Development boomed, and saloons, hotels, shops, and houses sprouted with amazing speed throughout the downtown. After the silver business went bust in the early 1890s, the town was saved from extinction because copper took its place. Copper is still extracted from the area today, though when you walk down the main thoroughfare, Bullard Street, you hardly get the feel that this is a mining town. With the growing number of retirees, crunchy urban transplants, and 1,800 students from Western New Mexico University milling about the art galleries, coffeehouses, antique shops, and restaurants, it seems more like an earthier, mini Santa Fe.

Like its tony sister far to the north, Silver City serves a smorgasbord of adventure, most of it within the Gila. This 3.3-million-acre pre-

Downtown Silver City. (© Bob Pelham, www.pinosaltoscabins.com)

serve covers a diverse landscape of desert floor, deep canyons, aspen and spruce forests, and alpine peaks reaching as high as 10,900 feet. At its heart is the 560,000-acre Gila Wilderness Area, the country's first designated wilderness area, and its 700 miles of trails among an untouched backcountry of rivers, springs, woodlands, and jagged mountains in the Mogollon Range. Local backpackers generally flock to its confines, while mountain bikers—who are prohibited there—and day-hikers often stick closer to town, on paths like the section of the 3,100-mile Continental Divide Trail that passes nearby. From the trailhead about seven miles out of Silver City, head south for the most stunning ridgetop views. Another scenic, easily accessible area is Signal Peak, about fifteen miles away in the national forest; the views from the top in every direction will make you glad you put up with the agony of its steep climbs.

In spring, kayakers need only drive about twenty-five miles to reach Class II and III whitewater on the Gila River. And on pavement every May, Silver City hosts the Tour of the Gila, a five-stage bike race that

Local Legend

The Big Ditch

In Boston, they have the Big Dig, and in Silver City, they've got the Big Ditch. This narrow, fifty-five-foot-deep gulch running through the heart of town used to be Main Street, until a flood—the result of overgrazing in the hills above it—washed it out in 1895. Over the next decade, the deluges continued until the soil was washed away down to the bedrock. Businesses adjusted and moved to Bullard Street, and now the Big Ditch is a tree-shaded town park, where every Labor Day weekend an organization of local artists holds a popular art fair.

attracts some of the country's top road racers—and even some well-known mountain bikers—who compete for five consecutive days, covering 340 miles for men and 258 for women. The fourth stage is held completely on the streets of town, and after every stage the competitors come back to town in the evening to recover. Billy the Kid would be so jealous.

Start the Day

Nancy's Silver Café (514 North Bullard Street; 505-388-3480): Southwestern breakfasts at their very best.

Gear Up

Gila Bike and Hike (103 East College Avenue; 505-388-3222): A bike shop and the premier hiking and backpacking outfitter in town.

Twin Sisters Cycling (303 North Bullard Street; 505-538-3388): A bike and fitness shop downtown; owner Annie Crawford can give you the scoop on all of the local rides.

Refuel

Diane's Restaurant and Bakery (510 North Bullard Street; 505-538-8722; www.dianesrestaurant.com): A trendy restaurant by a former Sante Fe pastry chef.

The Jalisco Café (100 South Bullard Street; 505-388-2060): Great Southwestern food, low prices, and renowned sopapillas.

Buckhorn Saloon and Opera House (32 Main Street, Pinos Altos; 505-538-9911): Grab a steak in the Old West, 1860s saloon and then watch a melodrama in the adjacent opera house.

Bunk

Bear Mountain Lodge (2251 Cottage San Road; 505-538-2538; www.bearmountainlodge.com): Owned by the Nature Conservancy and located about three miles outside of town, this rustic hacienda on 178 acres has been the cushiest place to stay near Silver City for the past eighty years.

Palace Hotel (106 West Broadway; 505-388-1811): A twenty-two-room boutique hotel in a downtown building from the late nineteenth century.

Silver Creek Inn (HC 61, Mogollon; 866-276-4882; www.silver creekinn.com): Located two hours north of town, in the nearly abandoned former mining town of Mogollon (population fifteen) in the national forest is this exquisite nineteenth-century four-room hacienda-turned-inn.

Can't Leave?

Nearest airport: Las Cruces International, Las Cruces, New Mexico (100 miles)

Primary industries: Mining, retail, education

Taos, New Mexico

Population: 5,126

Action: Downhill and cross-country skiing, kayaking, fishing

How long does it take to become a Taoseño? Recently, the *Taos News* posed that question to its readers. It was partly tongue-in-cheek, but also a barometer of the changing cultural climate of this town. Steeped in Native American history and arts, Taos sits against the Sangre de Cristo Mountains and casts a New Age spiritual spell on so many who come for a short stay, but end up staking out their own piece of land somewhere near the central Taos Plaza. Julia Roberts and Donald Rumsfeld have joined micaceous-clay potter Felipe Ortega, Earthship-builder Michael Reynolds, and kayaker Yellowbird Zamora as local celebrities, while wine competitions now fill the calendar along with ski competitions on the steep Taos Ski Valley. The answers to the *Taos News* question ranged from "Fifteen minutes, if the vibes are right" to "All the slots are filled, no more left."

But the two most encouraging responses, at least for the adventure-minded, were "As soon as you like green chile" and "Two ski seasons." Others might have included a prowess for kayaking the Rio Grande, reaching the summit of 13,161-foot Wheeler Peak, or climbing Dead Cholla Wall—all some of the more fun (and quicker) ways to become a Taoseño or Taoseña.

Start with a crash course in skiing the steeps at Taos Ski Valley, long owned by the Blake family and one of the last four major resorts in the country to remain closed to snowboarders—a policy that is the source of the "Free Taos" bumper stickers around town. (Single-planked riders can head to the seventy trails at Angel Fire Resort, just east of Taos, or to Ski Santa Fe's 1,725 vertical feet; there's also another 200 acres at Ski Sipapu and backcountry snowboarding throughout the Sangre de Cristos.) Twenty minutes from the town, and at the same latitude as northern Africa, Taos Ski Valley boasts 300 days of sunshine and 300

The central plaza of Taos, New Mexico offers shade and shopping. (© New Mexico Tourism Department)

inches of snow per year. But the resort is best known for the half of its 1,294 acres of terrain that is classified as expert, including the stomach-lurching runs off the Ridge and the powder off Kachina Peak.

Catch your breath at Enchanted Forest, a cross-country skiing area that has thirty-three kilometers of groomed trails for classic and skate skiing and fifteen kilometers for snowshoeing. The area—one of the state's best for skinny skiers—is northeast of Taos in the Carson National Forest, a 1.5-million-acre preserve of Southwest terrain, ranging from high-desert elevations of 6,000 feet to alpine mountains and the 13,161-foot Wheeler Peak. Some of the premier hikes include the 3.7-mile Italianos Canyon Trail, which heads toward Lobo Peak, the moderate Cebolla Mesa and Big Arsenic trails and the strenuous eleven-mile out-and-back trip to 12,711 feet at Gold Hill.

For mountain biking, pedal ten miles through the wildflowers in the Rio de la Olla Canyon, where singletrack follows a mountain-fed stream, or hit the twenty-seven miles of the South Boundary Trail. The West Rim Trail, meanwhile, follows the Rio Grande gorge for nine miles.

The Wild Side

Wheeler Peak

Wheeler Peak, New Mexico's highpoint, can be hiked in a day, without technical climbing skills, from trailheads at Taos Ski Valley. Start early—you don't want to hit summer storms—and follow the eight-mile trail through Bull of the Woods Pasture and the La Cal Basin (where you can camp if planning an overnight) before the final approach to the summit. Alpine lakes dot glacial cirques, while vegetation turns to tundra. The views from the top are as captivating as the town of Taos below.

And it's the Rio Grande where you'll want to get wet, starting in March. The river runs for 1,865 miles from the Rockies to the Gulf of Mexico, but some of its best sections, especially for kayaking and fly-fishing, lie just outside of Taos Plaza. At the Taos Box, there are seventeen miles of Class IV whitewater, while Class III rapids run through the five-mile Racecourse and at such spots as Sleeping Beauty. Anglers also head to the Taos Box for rainbows and browns and what has been called black-belt fly-fishing.

If all else fails, getting the hang of Taos means loading up on green chiles and simply hanging around for a while. "You can be flaky, reserved, outgoing, completely pragmatic, blissful, cranky, clueless, clinical, highly intellectual, creative, fussy or incredibly silly, and yet be as normal as can be because you're from Taos County," writes the *Taos News*. "In fact, all that pretty much defines what it means to be a Taoseño or Taoseña, whether you've just set your suitcase down or can look down a bloodline that stretches back for centuries."

Start the Day

The Bean (1033 Paseo del Pueblo Sur; 505-758-5123): Coffeehouse and bakery with veggie omelets, green-chile-and-egg breakfast sandwiches, and the New Grounds Gallery showcasing local artwork.

Gear Up

Mudd-n-Flood (134 Bent Street; 505-751-9100): Outdoor gear including Arc'teryx, Western Mountaineering, Prana, and Chaco.

Taos Mountain Outfitters (114 South Plaza; 505-758-9292): Skiing, kayaking, rock-climbing, and hiking equipment and clothing.

Refuel

Pizaños Pizza (23 State Highway 150; 505-776-1050): Buffalo wings, beer, wine, salads, sandwiches, and pasta, along with pizza.

Orlando's (114 Don Juan Valdez Lane; 505-751-1450): Authentic New Mexican dishes; go for anything with chiles, or the Frito pie.

Joseph's Table (108-A South Taos Plaza; 505-751-4512): Chef Joseph Wrede prepares contemporary cuisine, including such dishes as wild mushroom and local duck-egg flan, molasses-cured Hawaiian yellowfin tuna with organic beets, and daily vegetarian specials.

Bunk

Carson National Forest (208 Cruz Alta Road; 505-758-6200; www.fs.fed.us/r3/carson): More than twenty campsites at three places—La Sombra, Capulin, and Las Petacas—along U.S. Highway 64 between Taos and Taos Ski Valley (next to Rio Fernando).

The Abominable Snowmansion (476 State Highway 150; 505-776-8298, www.abominablesnowmansion.com): An adobe hostel and ski lodge with dorm rooms and private rooms, plus a campground with tipis and tent space.

Hotel St. Bernard (112 Sutton Place; 505-776-2251; www.stbernard taos.com): Alps-style upscale hotel at the base of Taos Ski Valley.

Can't Leave?

Nearest airport: Albuquerque International, Albuquerque, New Mexico (118 miles)

Primary industries: Tourism, construction, real estate, retail

Astoria, Oregon

Population: 9,784

Action: Fishing, hiking, paddling, sailing, road and mountain biking

Okay, so those original American adventurers Meriwether Lewis and William Clark weren't exactly enamored by Astoria when they arrived here in 1805. Soaked by the Oregon rains and battered by the waves of the Columbia River crashing into the Pacific Ocean, they complained of the dreadful weather, soggy bread, and their disagreeable situation. But Lewis and Clark also lingered long enough to build a camp near Youngs Bay, from which they began to discover the friendliness of the locals, the bounty of salmon, and, eventually, dry conditions.

So, yes, it does rain in Astoria—about seventy inches per year—and winter storms can be ferocious. There's no better place, however, to reel in salmon, hike old-growth Sitka spruce forests, paddle whitewater, cycle the Pacific coast, and kayak the Columbia—all within the same weekend. And the comforts for which Lewis and Clark longed, such as good lodgings and sustenance, along with others they couldn't have envisioned, such as brewfests, are today found in abundance all over Astoria.

Of course, few things around this corner of the Pacific Northwest are more abundant than fish—or at least that's true in the minds of anglers, who push off from Astoria's docks in pursuit of salmon, sturgeon, halibut, albacore tuna, and crabs. Chinook and coho salmon runs stretch toward the 100,000 mark in the Lower Columbia and Pacific waters surrounding town, and rods reel in salmon of up to fifty pounds. And since that's more than enough fish than you need for dinner, Astoria has canning, smoking, and shipping facilities nearby, obliterating any need to pick up a souvenir at the airport on your way home. Sturgeon and Dungeness crab, meanwhile, are found along the Columbia.

The Columbia River is the heart of Astoria, Oregon, and the town's fishing and paddling opportunities. (© Astoria-Warrenton Chamber of Commerce)

The mighty Columbia, which has coursed 1,243 miles from its headwaters in British Columbia, is also a prime spot for paddling and has various levels of difficulty. Downtown, navigating the boat traffic on the four-and-a-half-mile-wide stretch of river can be a challenge in itself, but worth it for the experience of gliding among historic salmon docks and under the longest bridge in Oregon, the elegant Astoria-Megler. At the Nature Conservancy site of Blind Slough Sitka Spruce Swamp, you can see, at a placid pace, the same trees Lewis and Clark saw, while midriver islands—and river towns across the Columbia in Washington state—create longer destination trips. There are waves to surf on the Pacific side and, within a short drive of Astoria, Class III to V rapids on the Nehalem, Kilchis, and Wilson rivers in Oregon and on Naselle and Grays in Washington (all are less than an hour from town).

The power of the wind, and not just the paddle, is also widely celebrated throughout Astoria; every May, the Oregon Offshore International Yacht Race sets sail from here on the 193-mile course to

Local Legend

The Goonies

Steven Spielberg's 1985 film *The Goonies,* about kids searching for buried treasure, has given Astoria a serious case of life imitating art. Thousands of Goonies fans now come to search for the sites in Astoria where the movie was shot. The main house is open to the public, and one of the key venues for the yearly celebrations of the film. (The twentieth anniversary, in 2005, drew more than a thousand people.) *Kindergarten Cop, Free Willy,* and *Teenage Mutant Ninja Turtles III* were also filmed in Astoria, but none have inspired the allegiance to this Oregon town as *The Goonies.*

Victoria, British Columbia. August witnesses Astoria Regatta Week, when hundreds of white-sailed boats march along the water and parade participants march through the streets. The event has been going on since 1894 and avoids any snooty exclusivity by including pancake breakfasts, softball tournaments, and beer gardens. Astoria's other key events also pay tribute to the water: there is a crab and seafood festival in April and a salmon celebration in October.

Not quite as long as the offshore race, but equally important to the heritage of the region is a ninety-seven-mile section of the Lewis and Clark Trail—commemorating you know who—that's well suited to cyclists. Going in the opposite direction of the explorers, you start at the Columbia River Maritime Museum in Astoria and end in the biking-mad city of Portland, paralleling the Columbia River. (Or shuttle a car to Portland and end, as most cyclists do, in Astoria.) For mountain biking, a fifteen-mile network of singletrack (simply called Norm's Trails) lies just east of town, while Fort Stevens State Park has nine miles of easy and scenic biking and hiking trails, including a two-mile loop around Coffenbury Lake. And some of the Northwest's prized backpacking routes are less than two hours from Astoria, at Olympic National Park in Washington.

Of course, it's hard to leave the allure of Astoria, whose Victorian homes, the color of thin candy wafers, and maritime weather have earned it comparisons to San Francisco. And though it's the oldest American town west of the Rockies, it's shed a quaint image in favor of being a hip and up-and-coming place in which to rest, like Lewis and Clark, your canoe—or any other adventure vessel.

Start the Day

Espresso Peddler (345 West Marine Drive; 503-325-9012): Muffins, pastries, bagels, and, naturally, espresso drinks; it's one of twenty-some espresso joints here.

Pig 'n' Pancake (146 West Bond; 503-325-3144): Not an Astoria original, but the only place in town to find thirteen types of pancakes including the irresistible pigs in blankets.

Gear Up

Tiki Charters (350 Industry Street; 503-325-7818): Salmon and other fishing charters, plus crabbing trips.

Bikes & Beyond (1089 Marine Drive; 503-325-2691): Bike rentals, repairs, and tours from two local cyclists in business since 1988.

Pacific Wave (201 Highway 101, Warrenton; 888-223-9794): Kayak rentals and other water gear; located on the Columbia River and seven miles from the Pacific.

Refuel

Wet Dog Café (144 Eleventh Street; 503-325-6975): Find such Pacific Rim Brewery varieties as Admiral ESB and Rat City IPA, plus burgers, ribs, and other brewpub fare.

Baked Alaska (1 Twelfth Street; 503-325-7414): A former mobile soup trailer turned into a Pacific Northwest eatery—think grilled wild salmon—on a pier overlooking the Columbia River.

Bowpicker Fish & Chips (Seventeenth and Duane streets; 503-791-2942): Buy albacore tuna fish and chips (thick steak fries) right off an old gillnet boat.

Bunk

Fort Stevens State Park (800-452-5687; www.oregonstateparks .org/park_179.php): A sprawling campground with 530 campsites —busy, but well situated on the beaches.

Crest Motel (5366 Leif Erickson Drive; 503-325-3141): Comfortable and affordable rooms on a Columbia River cliff; spend extra on one with a view.

The Wild Side

The Oregon Coast Trail

Astoria marks not only one end of the Columbia River, but also one end of the Oregon Coast Trail. This 360-mile footpath traces the state's dramatic coastline and is punctuated by lighthouses, rocky beaches, and whales swimming the Pacific. If you don't have the whole summer off to hike the entire trail, simply head south from Fort Stevens State Park and wander the easy, northernmost stretch sixteen miles to the town of Gearheart.

Cannery Pier Hotel (10 Basin Street; 888-325-4996; www.cannery pierhotel.com): A luxury boutique hotel (with a Finnish sauna) on a former fish-cannery site.

Can't Leave?

Nearest airport: Astoria Regional (4 miles)

Primary industries: Fishing, timber, tourism

Hood River, Oregon

unch 386, the digits for Hood River, Oregon's exchange, into your Motorola, and you're also spelling out "fun."

Population: 6,480
Action: Windsurfing, kiteboarding, road and mountain biking, hiking, skiing

How perfect for a place that's been synonymous with fun ever since someone first figured out that the consistent, twenty- to thirty-knot westerly winds pumping up the eighty-mile-long Columbia River Gorge National Scenic Area, combined with the westbound current, the steep walls of the gorge and the Cascade Mountains, create optimal conditions in which to skim, jump, and flip over the water's surface with a board attached to a sail. Few would argue that Hood River, which lies at the narrowest part of the gorge, is the windsurfing capital of the world; locals who play hooky—with their bosses' permission—have plenty of fun beneath looming Mount Hood when the wind really blows. But there's also some serious business for the slew of manufacturers (such as DaKine) and gear shops. Despite the hardcore scene, you can forget about any exclusivity that might be associated with the sport: there are youth windsurfing nights, community windsurfing lessons, and "pray for wind" fundraisers, thanks to the Columbia Gorge Windsurfing Association. And soccer moms and dads regularly go windsurfing before and after their kids' games.

Is there anything else to do here? Well, sure—kiteboarding.

Actually, the gorge has plenty of kayaking, rafting, hiking, and biking, too, and the skiing and snowboarding at Mount Hood is just a thirty-minute drive to the south. Job openings at the local hospital tout the various hobbies of its current employees: kayaking, snowboarding, mountain biking. Even the editors at *Progressive Farmer,* enchanted by the 14,000 acres of fruit orchards in Hood River County, have named this is one of the best places to live in America. It's fruit that helped Hood River grow roots; the first commercial orchard was planted in the

Hood River, Oregon is an outdoor-sports playground, thanks to its eponymous river and Mount Hood. (© petermarbachphotography.com)

1876. The large-scale apple orchard proved the soil's fertility, which soon attracted pear, cherry, and berry growers to the region, along with wine makers.

The abundance of orchards and vineyards has created some excellent cycling routes. One is the Fruit Loop, a thirty-five-mile circle south from Hood River that connects country roads to more than thirty orchards, wineries, and farm stands. From June through October there are festivals and events just about every weekend, each celebrating a particular harvest. July means the Hood River Cherry Days, apples arrive in August, and September is pear season. The only trouble is determining a way to carry back all the bounty on your bike—or even getting back on your bike after too many huckleberry milkshakes.

Mountain bikers, meanwhile, face their own perils in focusing on the technical singletrack that twists around Hood River and the Columbia River Gorge when there are so many distracting views of Mount Hood, Mount Adams, Mount Jefferson, and the white-capped river. Practice around Post Canyon Road, east of town, then head toward the nineteen-mile Gunsight Trail, which rolls above Jean and Badger lakes; the eleven-mile East Fork Hood River Trail; and the Fifteen Mile Creek Trail, which is actually eleven miles of steep uphills and downhills with in-your-face views of Mount Hood. All three are in the Mount Hood National Forest.

Mount Hood itself has become a badge of honor for any aspiring skier or snowboarder, thanks to the summer race camps that have been held on Palmer Snowfield since 1956. Instead of hanging up their skis and boards in the spring, the country's best snow-sports athletes flock here to test out new equipment, scout out the upcoming competition, and chill out in skateboard parks and along the gorge. In the winter, the 11,235-foot mountain is home to five separate ski areas, as well as backcountry skiers hiking to non-lift-served terrain.

From the number of warm-weather hikers who clog many of the waterfalls west of Mount Hood, the trails may seem too crowded, but there are empty, scenic routes everywhere—you just have to hoof it a bit farther. Consider Mount Defiance, an 11.3-mile round-trip, or the 12-mile Starvation Ridge Trail. Both offer a perch from which to choose just which part of the Columbia River Gorge you'll plunge when you're back down in Hood River. Or maybe you've already booked a lesson or rental with one of the windsurfing shops in town—their phone numbers start with 386, or F-U-N.

Start the Day

Bette's Place (416 Oak Street; 541-386-1880): A windsurfers' hangout serving must-order cinnamon rolls.

Local Legend

Timberline Lodge

Mount Hood's summer skiing isn't restricted to sponsored athletes testing out new gear. At Timberline, the lifts are open through August, and the lodge is a National Historic Landmark built in 1937. If you're there with a romantic interest, book a fireplace room; if you've brought your buddies, go for the chalet rooms. Either way, you'll find that one of the best places in the world to be on a summer day is sipping a Bloody Mary in the Ram's Head bar, recounting what it's like to ski and snowboard in August while the rest of the country overheats. (See www.timberlinelodge.com for information.)

The Wild Side

Wind Power

If the names Rooster Rock, the Hatchery, Celilo Park, and Maryhill don't already give you goosebumps, they will. These are among the top windsurfing and kiteboarding spots on the Columbia River Gorge, where some thirty different sites are wide open to the public and whose locations are happily provided by the Hood River Chamber of Commerce. Beginners are best off at the easy Marina and Inn Beach areas, which have shallow, sandy starting areas, while expert boardheads hit the Wall, Doug's Beach, and Swell City.

10-Speed Coffee (1412 Thirteenth Street; 541-386-3165): Coffee and live music; run by a triathlete.

Egg Harbor (1313 Oak Street; 541-386-1127): A nine-page breakfast menu; go for the banana-and-blueberry Pancakes Supreme (made from scratch) or the smoked-salmon eggs Benedict.

Gear Up

Big Winds (207 Front Street; 541-386-6086): Windsurfing and kiteboarding lessons, sales, and rentals.

Discover Bicycles (116 Oak Street; 541-386-4820): Mountain biking rentals, sales, and maps.

Refuel

Brian's Pourhouse (606 Oak Street; 541-387-4344): A local favorite for its hip bar and deck and creative Asian and European menu twists; order the chili-crusted calamari.

Sixth Street Bistro (509 Cascade Avenue; 541-386-5737): Burgers and curries made with local, organic ingredients; thirteen microbrews on tap.

Andrews Pizza and Bakery (107 Oak Street; 541-386-1448): New York–style pizza, plus pastries, coffee, and more.

Bunk

Routson Park (U.S. Highway 35; 541-387-6888): A rustic campground (not for trailers) with twenty sites, near the Mount Hood National Forest.

Hood River Hotel (102 Oak Street; 800-386-1859; www.hoodriver hotel.com): Historic downtown hotel built in 1913; many rooms have a view of the river.

Columbia Gorge Hotel (4000 Westcliff Drive; 800-345-1921; www.columbiagorgehotel.com): A forty-room inn; rates include an enormous farm breakfast.

Can't Leave?

Nearest airport: Portland International, Portland, Oregon (74 miles)

Primary industries: Agriculture, tourism

Sisters, Oregon

Population: 1,212

Action: Hiking, downhill and backcountry skiing, fishing, rafting, mountain and road biking

When you learn that the town of Sisters, Oregon, was named for three siblings named Faith, Hope, and Charity, you're not getting the whole story. That's because Faith, Hope, and Charity are not old-fashioned Sunday-best wearing people, but three volcanic peaks that stand more than 10,000 feet tall and create a stunning southern backdrop for this town of 1,212 in the Cascade Mountains. (After locals disagreed on which mountain was which, they were renamed North, Middle, and South Sisters.) The peaks—along with Mount Jefferson, Three-Fingered Jack, Broken Top, Black Butte, and Mount Washington—are one part of a recreational panorama that also includes Sparks Lake, Suttle Lake, Hoodoo Mountain Resort, and the National Wild and Scenic Metolious River.

That's not to say that Sisters—twenty miles west of its better-known outdoorsy brother, Bend—lacks old-fashioned charm. Today, log cabins and nineteenth-century storefronts still grace the diminutive architectural skyline, leaving the grandeur to the High Cascades. There are still wooden boardwalks, a subtle reminder of the town's logging industry, which has since given way to outdoor-oriented tourism, thanks to the 300-plus days of sunshine each year. And a frontier ranching spirit also remains, seen in the Sisters Rodeo every June, in sprawling llama ranches, and in Bronco Billy's, an Old West Landmark Saloon where Stetsons and beer, rather than heels and martinis, rule.

But first you have to earn Bronco Billy's ribs. If it's a sunny day from August to mid-October (to avoid dangerous storms), start with a strenuous, but nontechnical, hike up to the summit of 10,358 South Sister, the youngest of the three volcanoes. The trail gains 4,900 feet of elevation in 5.5 miles, skirting glaciers and green lakes and offering regular wide-open views of the surrounding Cascades. From the summit,

Log cabins and nineteenth-century storefronts give Sisters, Oregon old-time charm.
(© Sisters Chamber of Commerce)

you can peer down on Sisters from Teardrop Pool, the state's highest lake. Middle and North Sisters are more challenging, but draw a number of mountaineers and telemarkers each year.

Ten miles west of Sisters are the headwaters of the Metolius River, a tributary of the Deschutes that gurgles from a wooded spot near the evergreen-covered volcanic cone of Black Butte, at 6,436 feet. There are some short hikes around here, as well as excellent fly-fishing holes for rainbows, bull, and brown trout and mountain whitefish. Along the Deschutes, steelhead run from late June to November, while there are also abundant rainbows known as redsides.

Both the Deschutes and the McKenzie River have become white-water rafting destinations, thanks to such rapids as the Class IV Big Eddy on the Upper Deschutes; the McKenzie rolls through forests of Douglas fir, hemlock, and red cedar trees while bumping rafters along the Class II and III Zipper Ripper, Shorts Rinser, and Boomerang.

The water is nearly as turbulent every summer on Suttle Lake, when swimmers in the Sisters High Cascades Off-Road Triathlon churn through 1,000 meters before mountain biking 17 miles and trail running another 6.2. The event has become one of the country's premier adventure races, and there is no shortage of local athletes who have hundreds of miles of biking trails and roads out their back door. For cycling, the thirty-mile Fryrear Loop glides through farmlands, sagebrush flats, and canyons and gives prime views of the vocanic peaks. The McKenzie Summit Ride, at fifty miles, leads to the McKenzie Pass and is a favorite of local rider and bike shop owner Brad Boyd. Fat-tire trails are found around Black Butte, where there are eleven and thirteen-mile loops in the thick evergreen forests, and on the steep Cache Mountain Downhill.

The most downhill action arrives every winter, when Hoodoo Mountain Resort's 806 acres and 1,035 feet of vertical drop open to skiers and snowboarders, who tackle such breathtaking steeps as Dante's Crater and Leap of Faith in between equally breathtaking views of Three Fingered Jack, Mount Jefferson, and the Three Sisters. (For less of a perch, but more lung busting, there are more than fifteen kilometers of trails at Hoodoo's nordic center.) The backcountry opportunities in the Cascades are bounded only by faith in the deep snows, hope for clear skis, and charity from local skiers to show the way.

Start the Day

The Depot Deli (250 West Cascade Avenue; 541-549-2572): Omelets any which way you choose, served in a train-station atmosphere that's just about as busy as Grand Central.

Sisters Coffee Company (273 West Hood Street; 541-549-0527): House-roasted brews and huckleberry tea; live folk performances on many evenings.

Sisters Bakery (251 East Cascade Avenue; 541-549-0361): Homemade doughnuts, bear claws, and jalapeño cheddar bread, along with bagels, pie, and espresso.

Gear Up

The Fly Fisher's Place (151 West Main Avenue; 541-549-3474): Guided trips on the Deschutes, along with lessons and angling accessories.

Eurosports (182 East Hood Avenue; 541-549-2471): A cycling, mountain biking, and ski and snowboard shop, offering rentals, maps, and guided rides.

Refuel

Bronco Billy's Ranch Grill and Saloon (190 East Cascade Avenue; 541-549-7427): Go for the ribs; if you're a vegetarian, go anyway for the salad bar and local banter.

Papandrea's Pizzeria (442 East Hood Street; 541-549-6081): Tossing dough since 1977, this family-run joint serves sixteen types of pizza that keeps foodies returning.

Gallery Restaurant (171 West Cascade Avenue; 541-549-2631): All the comfort-food favorites, from mac and cheese and fish and chips to meatloaf and prime rib.

Local Legend

The Sisters Rodeo

In Sisters, June means Father's Day, the official start of summer, and the Sisters Rodeo. The three-day event has featured the Pacific Northwest's top cowboys and cowgirls since 1940 and has even earned a visit from the David Letterman show. It features classic rodeo performances of bareback riding, team roping, bull riding, and more; it also includes parades, rodeo clowns, and a buckaroo breakfast.

Bunk

Blue Spruce Bed & Breakfast (444 South Spruce Street; 541-549-9644; www.blue-spruce.biz): Four rustically decorated rooms and hearty breakfasts.

Lake Creek Lodge (13375 Southwest Forest Service Road, Camp Sherman; 541-595-6331; www.lakecreeklodge.com): In the Metolius Recreation Area, offers twenty cabins and cottages near hiking, mountain biking, and fishing spots; includes a tennis court and pool.

Black Butte Ranch (541-595-6211; www.blackbutteranch.com): Full-service resort eight miles from Sisters; includes a golf course, sports field, tennis courts, and lake. Lodging ranges from hotel-style rooms to condos and private homes.

Can't Leave?

Nearest airport: Roberts Field–Redmond Municipal, Redmond, Oregon (29 miles)

Primary industries: Tourism, small business, light manufacturing

Eastsound, Washington

Population: 3,217
Action: Paddling, mountain and road biking, hiking

If you're convinced that palm trees, coral reefs, and tropical sunsets are essential ingredients for an island paradise, you've never been to fifty-eight-square-mile Orcas Island. Its secluded bays, thick forests, and mountaintop views are so captivating, it'll get you to rethink your equation. Eastsound, a three-block village of wood-frame shops, coffeehouses, restaurants, and bed-and-breakfasts, is the unofficial capital of this piece of land, which is shaped like two saddlebags, in the San Juan archipelago. And among the smattering of unincorporated towns on the island, Eastsound is also the most conveniently located for adventure. It rests on the innermost rim of the long, protected sound that creates the gap between the two saddle bags, making a central launching pad for paddling and biking—the two outdoor passions (if you don't count growing fruit trees or cultivating organic gardens) of the island's colorful residents.

Orcas is one of the largest of the 175 or so islands that buffer the northwestern border of Washington. (Among the others is Canada's Vancouver Island.) The surrounding mountains shield Orcas from storms, so that it enjoys nearly 250 days of sunshine a year. Because of its year-round mild temperatures, there's no bad time to visit—or stay—although crowds taking the one-hour ferry ride from Anacortes are quite a bit smaller during the damper winter months. The island's first settlers of European descent were trappers who arrived in the mid-nineteenth century, followed a couple of decades later by farmers, who were attracted by the rich soil and long growing seasons. Around the turn of the twentieth century, Eastsound was formed, and shortly after, the Seattle shipbuilding titan Robert Moran came to build an estate called Rosario—now the Rosario Resort and Spa.

Those who hike or bike to the top of Orcas Island's Mount Constitution, near Eastsound, Washington are rewarded with stunning views of the other San Juan Islands. (© J. Poth)

In 1921, Moran donated to the state 2,700 acres of land southeast of town, encompassing 2,409-foot-tall Mount Constitution. This is where your land-bound adventures should start. The parcel, expanded over the years to 5,200 acres, is now Moran State Park, the most rugged swath on the island. Incorporating virgin tree stands, five lakes, and a handful of hidden waterfalls, it is navigable by a thirty-mile network of hiking trails, mostly cut in the 1930s by the Civilian Conservation Corps. For bikers, there are eleven miles of forest roads and singletrack open year-round, and twenty-five miles open between mid-September and mid-May. The latter includes its share of thigh-screaming climbs and white-knuckle downhills. If the top of Mount Constitution isn't temporarily covered in snow, make your way to the stone summit observation tower at the end of the Cold Spring Trail. On a clear day, you can see surrounding islands, framed by the Cascade and Olympic ranges, and the mountains of Vancouver Island.

Road bikers can climb Mount Constitution on the five miles of hairpin-packed pavement that reaches the peak, and then use the vantage to get their bearings for exploring the rest of Orcas on its stoplight-free roads. The eastern half, occupied largely by the park, is steep and tree filled, while the rolling western side is sprinkled with farms, forestlands, and a handful of settlements like West Sound and Orcas—where the ferry dock is. Wildlife Cycles, the bike shop in Eastsound, can recommend the most picturesque routes, like the rolling six-mile (one-way) Deer Harbor Road ride to the edge of Deer Harbor, which gives views of Fawn and Crane islands.

Then there are the waters around Orcas Island itself. In the late summer, when the seas are generally the calmest, the entire San Juans are at your disposal, or you can stick within the hidden inlets and long sounds of Orcas's seventy-seven-mile shoreline. If you can, stop for the night at the boat-in/hike-in, primitive Obstruction Pass State Park on the southern tip of the eastern saddlebag. Body Boat Blade International paddling school in Eastsound organizes custom and group tours of the area. There are a few killer whale–watching tour boats that leave from Orcas Island, and you can also rent a sailboat to cruise around. Or you can always take a rest on one of the pebbly beaches along the coast. It isn't exactly the Caribbean—but that's the beauty of it.

Start the Day

Olga's Restaurant (Eastsound Square; 360-376-5862): The closest thing that the island has to a culinary legend; the presentation is nearly as exquisite as the food, which is made from fresh, local organic produce. The menu is ever changing, but hope they're serving cheese blintzes when you get there.

Orcas Village Store (ferry landing, Orcas Village; 360-376-8860): An espresso bar, market, and deli at the ferry dock. Good place to fuel up and supply yourself for the day.

Gear Up

Wildlife Cycles (350 North Beach Road; 360-376-4708): This cycling shop is the ultimate resource on rides on the island. Also rents mountain and road bikes.

Body Boat Blade International (310 Prune Alley Road; 360-376-5388): Some visitors are lured to Orcas Island solely by this paddling school and adventure-guide service. It also operates a kayak store in town.

Shearwater Adventures (138 North Beach Road; 370-376-4699): Sells new and used kayaks, and guides day trips in the San Juan Islands.

Refuel

Bilbo's Festivo (310 A Street; 360-376-4728): Southwestern and Mexican food made from scratch and served in a fireplace-heated dining room.

Christina's Food and Wine (310 Main Street; 360-376-4904; www.christinas .net): Foodies from across the West Coast come to taste owner and cookbook author Christina Reid Orchid's gourmet seafood creations.

Portofino Pizzeria (274 A Street; 360-376-2085): Checkered tablecloths, Mediterranean village scenes painted on the walls, and the best pies on the island.

Bunk

The Anchorage Inn (249 Bronson Way; 360-376-8282; www .anchorageonorcas.com): A three-suite bed-and-breakfast sitting atop a bluff on sixteen waterfront acres.

Inn at Ship Bay (326 Olga Road; 877-276-7296; www.innatshipbay .com): A luxurious inn overlooking the water and centered around a 1869 farmhouse. Its eleven rooms have gas fireplaces and private balconies.

Can't Leave?

Nearest airport: Eastsound–Orcas Island Airport (1 mile)

Primary industries: Tourism, retail, construction

Local Legend

Rosario Resort

The local story goes that forty-nine-year-old Robert Moran, a shipbuilder from Seattle, built his dream mansion on Orcas Island in 1906, after his doctors told him he only had a year to live. (He must have had faith that the builders could work fast.) He survived for another thirty-seven years–good thing, too, because he didn't move onto the property until 1909. Today, the home, named Rosario, is the poshest hotel on the San Juan Islands. Most of the Rosario Resort's 116 rooms are in outlying buildings, while the mansion houses the lounge, dining room, and music room, where you'll find the pipe organ with 1,972 pipes, installed in 1913.

Port Townsend, Washington

Population: 9,001

Action: Kayaking, road and mountain biking, hiking

These are some things you will need around Port Townsend, Washington. First, a kayak, for paddling Port Townsend Bay and the San Juan Islands. Then a bicycle or two—one for Highway 101 and the web of country roads, one for the singletrack at Fort Worden State Park and Anderson Lake. A backpack and a thick book will serve you well for the hundreds of miles of hiking trails that weave through Olympic National Park's rainforest and along its coastal wilderness. And finally, maybe a raincoat.

These are the things you won't need: a car, an iPod, or an itinerary. Lying at the tip of the Olympic Peninsula, Port Townsend is well served by ferries and public transit (including from as far as the Seattle airport; otherwise a two and a half-hour drive), and the year-round festivals make bringing your own music unnecessary. Finally, you'd simply crumple up your itinerary when you started to add on adventures.

This town of Victorian homes and well-kept mills has no fewer than nineteen city parks, ranging from the tiny Tyler Street Stairs to the eighty-acre Kah Tai Lagoon that greets visitors with a flurry of wildlife among the greenery. One of the premier pieces of protected land is Chetzemoka, which overlooks the Cascade Mountains from the side of a hill that spills down to beaches and marshes; it was named for the Native American leader of the Klallams, who lived in cedar lodges when white settlers arrived in the 1800s. From historical records, it might be presumed that the town's founders had delusions of grandeur—they called Chetzemoka the Duke of York and Port Townsend the City of Dreams when officially settling the area in 1851, and they envisioned it becoming the West Coast's biggest port. But initial prosperity and a busy shipping industry were failed by lack of railroad service; today, the town has been revived by a paper mill, tourism, and relocation

From Port Townsend, Washington, both big sailboats and small kayaks can explore the Olympic Peninsula and San Juan Islands. (© D. Kevin Mason, victorianwoodshop.com)

among retirees, small-business owners, and outdoor-minded escapees from the types of cities that Port Townsend once aimed to be.

More than a dozen state and county parks surround Port Townsend, including the 433-acre Fort Worden State Park at the tippy top of town. Originally built to protect Puget Sound (the Admiralty Inlet is the only way in or out for most ships), the fort is where much of the film *An Officer and a Gentleman* was filmed in the early 1980s. Parts of *The Ring* and *Enough* were also shot here. None of this is of much relevance to the mountain bikers and hikers who hit the twelve miles of trails and camp on the beaches, or to the kayakers who launch from here for journeys along the Admiralty Inlet or the Strait of San Juan de Fuca.

From Port Townsend, paddlers explore the shores of the Olympic Peninsula, head up Chimacum Creek, or venture out to the abundance of nearby islands in and around Puget Sound—Marrowstone and Bird,

Protection, and Indian, where seals swim along geologic creations of sandstone. Farther north, and accessible by ferry, are Whidbey Island and the San Juan Islands, an archipelago of nearly 200 forest-topped islands and the summer swimming waters of orca whales. For those who didn't bring a kayak, Port Townsend is home to major kayak symposiums and Pygmy Boats, where paddlers can learn how to build their own wooden kayaks.

For those who remembered a bike, there's the annual Rhody Tour, a metric and half-metric century (think rides of thirty-two, forty-five, or sixty-three miles) that takes place each May and follows the rural roads connecting the bays of the Olympic Peninsula. The course can be easily followed in other months, too. U.S. Highway 101, meanwhile, leads west from Discovery Bay to the Olympic National Forest, where a 15.5-mile mountain-biking loop on the Lower Dungeness and Gold Creek trails creates one of the Pacific Northwest's classic fat-tire routes. Mountain bikers and hikers also have the hundreds of old logging roads on the Olympic Peninsula, the former railroad beds, and remote Anderson Lake State Park. At the park, anglers can also fish for rainbows on a seventy-acre lake surrounded by cedar, fir, and alder forests. But thanks to the proliferation of seafood bistros back in Port Townsend, where grilled locally caught fish is washed down with pints of Boatyard Bitter or Bitter End India Pale Ale from the Port Townsend Brewing Company, a fishing rod is also one thing you can leave behind.

Start the Day

Madison Street Café (609 Washington Street; 360-379-6993): Glazed doughnuts, breakfast sandwiches, and coffee.

Gear Up

P.T. Outdoors (1017 Water Street; 888-754-8598): Kayak rentals, tours, and lessons, available downtown and at Fort Worden State Park.

P.T. Cyclery (252 Tyler Street; 360-385-6470): Road and mountain bike rentals and sales, plus accessories and maps of local routes and the Olympic Peninsula.

Refuel

Water Street Brewing & Ale House (639 Water Street; 360-379-6438): Live music, house-produced microbrews, and local cuisine in the Waterstreet Hotel.

The Landfall Restaurant (412 Water Street; 360-385-5814): Serves fish tacos, Gorgonzola and caramelized-onion burgers, and Reubens with homemade sauerkraut, along with breakfast specialties, at the water's edge.

The Wild Coho (1044 Lawrence Street; 360-379-1030): Chef Jay Payne brings local, organic ingredients to such dishes as roasted oysters, pepper-crusted pork loin, and cauliflower-cream king salmon.

Bunk

Fort Worden State Park (200 Battery Way; 360-344-4400; www.fortworden .org): A beach campground has fifty sites, while a forest campground has thirty; both are open to tents and RVs. Reservations (by mail, e-mail, fax, or in person) are recommended.

Water Street Hotel (635 Water Street; 800-735-9810; www.waterstreethotel porttownsend.com): Rooms and suites overlooking Port Townsend Bay.

Manresa Castle (651 Cleveland Street; 800-732-1281; www.manresacastle .com): An 1892 mansion built in the style of a medieval castle, it was once the mayoral home and, later, a Jesuit training college; rooms have views of town and the bay.

Can't Leave?

Nearest airport: Bellingham International, Bellingham, Washington (49 miles)

Primary industries: Services, government, retail trade

The Wild Side

Olympic National Park

Most backyards? An acre or two. But Port Townsend's is nearly a million acres, thanks to President Franklin D. Roosevelt, who signed a 1938 act turning this chunk of rainforest and glacier-capped mountains into Olympic National Park (the third feature of its stunning diversity, the coastal beaches, was added later). A full 95 percent is wilderness, and it has more than 600 miles of backcountry hiking routes. Though there are tamer trails around Port Townsend, backpackers will want to make a beeline for the fifty-seven-mile Olympic Coastal Strip that connects rocky, sea-sprayed shoreline to deserted beaches. There you can camp to the sounds of whales and the sight of bald eagles. Less popular hikes include the ten-mile trip around Mount Angeles and the eighteen-mile loop through the Seven Lakes Basin. For guided trips, contact the Olympic Mountain School (www.olympic mountainschool.com).

Winthrop, Washington

Population: 359
Action: Mountain and road biking, cross-country and backcountry skiing, hiking, rock climbing, kayaking, fishing

Cast aside your notions of the Pacific Northwest when you consider Winthrop. By the time the rain clouds of Seattle have climbed the high spine of the Cascade Range to get there, they've already exhausted most of their energy—and contents. In turn, this town at 1,760 feet in the narrow Methow Valley sees mostly sunny days in the summer and gets layered beneath dry, fluffy Western powder in the winter. Yet even more appealing than the weather is the mix of hikes, bike rides, ski routes, rock climbs, you name it, reachable out the back doors of its faux Old West downtown.

The pride of Winthrop is the vast trail network that fans into the surrounding Okanogan National Forest backcountry. During the snow-filled months, every one of its 125 miles is machine groomed for nordic skiing by the Methow Valley Sport Trails Association (MVSTA), and in the warmer part of the year, its singletrack and old dirt roads are waffle-marked by the treads of fat tires and trail running shoes. There are probably only two or three multiuse trail systems in the country comparable in quality and scope to the MVSTA ones, yet they remain remarkably unknown—much like this town itself at the confluence of the Methow and Chewuch rivers.

Winthrop was largely the creation of Guy Waring, a thirty-two-year-old Bostonian who started a general store for miners, trappers, and cowboys there in 1891. He would eventually give Winthrop its name and come to own almost every downtown building, including the Duck Brand Saloon, where anyone who got drunk was kicked out. (A rule popular with those cowboys, trappers, and miners, no doubt.) The palatial log-cabin home he built is now part of the Shafer Museum, and the saloon is the town hall. Most of the other rustic-looking buildings fronting the three-block downtown were actually built in the 1970s,

Downtown Winthrop. (© WST/Port of Seattle)

as a way to lure tourists driving the new east-west highway, State Route 20, which passes through the long, slim downtown.

Although the Old West premise is a tad hokey, it still seems to fit here given Winthrop's history—and local merchants don't get too over the top, because they don't need to. People mostly pack the town's outfitter shops, brew pub, java house, and restaurants looking for outdoor adventure, not a blacksmithing demonstration or pound of old-fashioned fudge. And they don't leave disappointed, if they leave at all. The options—mostly in the 1.7-million-acre Okanogan National Forest—seem endless; the MVSTA trails alone take a week to explore, even if you're nordic skiing or biking twenty miles a day. About fifteen miles west on State Route 20 is the burgeoning rock-climbing destination of Mazama Rocks; new routes are being established on its granite crags all the time. Near town, fly-fishers can wade into the empty waters of the Methow for cutthroat and rainbow trout, and paddlers can launch onto the twenty miles of Class III and IV rapids that course through the valley and end near the Columbia River.

Often overlooked is the prime road biking in Winthrop. There is an array of flat and steep routes among the ponderosa pine, including,

The Wild Side

Rendezvous Mountain

The most challenging section of the MVSTA trails for nordic skiers are the thirty miles draped around Rendezvous Mountain, at elevations between 3,500 and 4,100 feet, north of town. These trails are also the most inviting not just because they're the least traveled, but also because of the five Rendezvous Huts stationed roughly five miles apart on the groomed trails in the backcountry. Each of these one-room, fire-heated, propane-lit cabins sleeps about eight people. You can reserve an entire one ($150 to $175) or space for just one or two people ($25 to $35 per person). For an extra $85, a snowmobile will haul out a load of supplies so they're waiting when you get there. The operation is run by Rendezvous Huts, Inc., (509-996-8100).

most notably, the climb up to 5,477-foot Washington Pass, a section of State Route 20 to the west of town that closes throughout the winter because of snow. There's also a local heli-ski outfit in town. You can't get all of that in Puget Sound.

Start the Day

Duck Brand Restaurant (248 Riverside Avenue; 509-996-2192): It's not the same saloon as the original Duck Brand owned by Guy Waring, but it's still got old-time character and, most importantly, serves espresso.

Sun Mountain Lodge Dining Room (Patterson Lake Road; 800-572-0493; www.sunmountainlodge.com): Have a refined breakfast at this top-notch resort, overlooking the valley from 1,000 feet above town.

Gear Up

Winthrop Mountain Sports (257 Riverside Avenue; 509-996-2886): Its rental shop offers the best options for cross-country skis and mountain bikes in town; also sells and services gear.

The Outdoorsman (170 Main Street; 509-996-2649): A fishing, camping, and hunting outfitter.

Refuel

Winthrop Brewing Company (155 Riverside Avenue; 509-996-3183): Order a home-brewed Hopalong Red Ale and panko fish and chips. If you're there on Friday evening, you'll be treated to the sounds of the open-mic jam.

Three Fingered Jacks Saloon (176 Riverside Avenue; 509-996-2411; www.3fingeredjacks.com): Bask in the Old Western feel to this family restaurant—while watching a game on the big-screen TV.

Bunk

Sun Mountain Lodge (Patterson Lake Road; 800-572-0493; www.sunmountainlodge.com): A mountaintop lodge on 3,000 acres and maybe the most luxurious place to stay in all of the Cascades.

Freestone Inn (31 Early Winters Drive, Mazama; 800-639-3809; www.freestoneinn.com): A 120-acre ranch property northwest of town; includes a plush inn on a lake, cabins, and private lodges.

Can't Leave?

Nearest airport: Yakima Air Terminal, Yakima, Washington (130 miles)

Primary industries: Agriculture, forestry, government

Alaska and Hawaii

Girdwood, Alaska

f orget having to rise at the crack of dawn for first tracks at Alyeska: the lifts at this Alaska ski and snowboard resort don't open until 10:30 AM. For the opportunity to sleep off last night's revelries at the Sitzmark, load up on buttered sweet rolls at the Bake Shop, and still be one of the earliest birds to gaze around at the Chugach Mountains and Turnagain Arm from the summit, you can mostly thank planet earth. Its particular angle in winter means that daylight starts later and lingers longer; the lifts at Alyeska stay open until 5:30 PM or later. But you can also thank the laid-back attitudes of Girdwood residents. (They're so laid back, in fact, that they still haven't gotten around to incorporating their ski town.)

Population: 2,500
Action: Downhill skiing, hiking, ice climbing

Less than forty miles south of Anchorage, Girdwood has the best of both worlds—access to big-city perks such as movie houses with a pub attached and the grandeur of glaciers, rainforests, the Chugach Range, and the Northern Lights, with a funky, ski-mad community in between the two. Once a gold-mining town named Glacier City, it thrived off the Crow Creek Mine until around World War II and then again during the construction of the Seward Highway. The 1964 "Good Friday" earthquake flooded Girdwood, and the town relocated to a site more than two miles up the valley. In 1980, a Japanese corporation invested in Alyeska, giving this town on the northern shore of the Turnagain Arm just the shot it needed. Girdwood is the provenance of Olympic medalists Tommy Moe and Rosey Fletcher (who's said that Girdwood has more dogs than people), as well as a home base for Anchorage commuters and the retreat of longtime ski bums.

It's easy to slip into ski- or snowboard-bum life around Alyeska, not only because of its late lift-opening hours, but also because of the 631 annual inches of snow, 1,000 acres of terrain, a vibrant racing scene, a zippy 60-passenger aerial tram, and a yawning expanse of backcountry

415

With yawning expanses of backcountry and Alaska-size vertical drops, it's easy to see why Girdwood is mad for skiing and snowboarding. (© Tom Evans)

skiing and riding. The base elevation is just 250 feet (good for those who suffer altitude sickness), but the summit sits at nearly 4,000 feet—even the math-phobic can figure out the Alaska-sized vertical drop here. Despite the heavy investment into the resort and upscale amenities at the Alyeska Prince Hotel, the slopes—which include the above-treeline steeps on Glacier Bowl and Head Wall, the New Years and Christmas chutes, and glades at A La Carte—remain relatively empty.

Alyeska has a small nordic trail system, but the much bigger lift-free attractions are the heli-skiing and snowcat trips; Chugach Powder Guides leads both throughout the Chugach Range. Ice climbers head to glaciers and ice flows around the Portage Glacier, the Chugach Mountains, and the Seward Highway, while an Iditraod veteran leads dogsledding trips. Challenge Alaska, meanwhile, operates a premier nonprofit for people with disabilities, conducting an adaptive ski and snowboard school in winter and running sea-kayaking, horseback-riding, and hiking trips in the summer.

Alyeska and Girdwood don't miss a beat when the snow melts. They have 5K races and mountain runs, a paragliding fly-in, and a blueberry and mountain-arts festival in July and August, when temperatures range from fifty to seventy degrees. Paddling waters are just a short drive away, while several hiking trails run right from town and the mountain. (For an easy hike, the five-mile round-trip on the Winner Creek Trail, from the Prince Hotel, winds through the forest to a gorge. The more challenging Crow Pass Trail extends up to twenty-six miles and has a forest-service cabin near the pass.) Adventurers can also strap on crampons for excursions on the Alyeska Glacier, learn to rock climb at Tram Rock, or explore the surrounding rainforest.

When the sun begins to disappear again for the winter, it's possible to see the polar bears around the Arctic Circle by taking flights and four-wheel-drive tours from Anchorage. (These tours can be arranged by Alyeska.) October and November are the prime months to see the polar bears, and from then it's just a short wait until the mountain's skiing and snowboarding lifts start running again—at just around the perfect time for Girdwood.

Start the Day

The Bake Shop (Alyeska Boardwalk; 907-783-2831): The carbs you'll need for carving—sweet rolls, sourdough pancakes, and oatmeal—plus vegetable omelet, scrambled eggs, potatoes, and fried ham steaks.

Gear Up

Girdwood Ski & Cyclery (Alaska Highway; 907-783-2453): Ski, telemark, cross-country, and backcountry rentals and sales in the winter; bike rentals and sales in the summer.

Refuel

Chair 5 (Linblad Avenue; 907-783-0933): Lively bar and restaurant with ten beers on tap and many more Pacific Northwestern microbrews in bottles; burger options include reindeer and buffalo; house rules include no gun fights, fist fights, food fights, or cursing.

Double Musky Inn (Crow Creek Road; 907-783-2822): New Orleans–inspired cuisine a mile from Alyeska's lifts in a lodge/roadhouse decorated with Mardi Gras beads; go for the crab-stuffed halibut or spicy jambalaya.

The Wild Side

The Northern Lights

Winter in Alaska is one of the best chances in the world see the aurora borealis, or Northern Lights. To view them at their brightest and most colorful, you can go on a moonlight dogsledding trip with Chugach Express (www.chugachexpress.com). Or just stay at the Alyeska Prince Hotel, where, at your request, the hotel staff will wake you up when the Northern Lights are visible.

Seven Glaciers (Glacier Terminal; 907-754-2237): Take Alyeska's Aerial Tramway to this four-diamond restaurant at 2,300 feet for pesto-roasted scallop bisque, Alaskan king crab, grilled elk rib eye, and blond-brownie banana splits.

Sitzmark Bar & Grill (Alyeska Boardwalk): The post-snow hotspot for burgers, brews, and more.

Bunk

Alyeska Adventures (314 Cortina Road; 907-754-2400; www.alyeska adventures.com): A bed-and-breakfast between Girdwood and Alyeska, offering three rooms with views of the Chugach, Wrangell, and Brooks mountains, plus on-site access to salmon fishing, jet-boating, paragliding, and eco-tours.

Carriage House Bed and Breakfast (Mile 0.2 Crow Creek Road; 888-961-9464; www.thecarriagehousebandb.com): Two rooms and a suite in a timber-frame home across from the Double Musky; horses and carriage rides available.

Alyeska Prince Hotel (Alyeska Highway; 800-880-3880; www .alyeskaresort.com): An enormous, chateau-style resort at the base of the mountain that includes 304 luxury, smoke-free rooms and suites; a lounge; a Japanese restaurant; an expansive fitness center; and shops.

Can't Leave?

Nearest airport: Ted Stevens Anchorage International, Anchorage, Alaska (40 miles)

Primary industries: Tourism, recreation

Haines, Alaska

When you first arrive in Haines, Alaska, you'll want to tune into KHNS, 102.3 FM. The community radio station will help you leave a message for a friend who doesn't have a phone (yes, such a subculture does still exist in some parts of the country), discover local events, and find cheap gear for exploring the adjacent Glacier Bay National Park and Preserve. And once you've decided to stay in Haines, KHNS will even help you find employment through its job-opportunities report.

Population: 2,400
Action: Kayaking, hiking, fishing, rafting

If this reminds you of a certain radio station in the TV show *Northern Exposure,* you're not alone. Haines has earned countless comparisons to the fictional town of Cicely in the past fifteen years, thanks to its quirky, moosey appeal. (There's even a visiting doctor—a veterinarian.) But Haines is surrounded by twenty million acres of protected wilderness, so chances are you'll forget about fiction and focus on the reality of kayaking, hiking, sighting bald eagles, and fishing as soon as you've unloaded the car. It's not just any wilderness, either, but pure Alaskan, jaw-dropping stuff: 7,000-foot peaks; glittering, ice blue glaciers; and skies as clear as a squeaky clean windshield, thanks to Haines' peninsula position, which escapes much of the state's cloudy and soggy weather.

Haines is one of only three southeastern Alaska towns accessible by road. The Tlingit people once called it *Dtehshuh,* or "end of the trail," but it's really the trailhead to seemingly limitless land or sea adventures. The best days on this northern terminus of America's longest fjord arrive in the late spring and summer months, when fifty- to sixty-degree temperatures make the call of the wild even more appealing. But the fall is an excellent time for a scouting trip, too, as thousands of bald eagles gather in the 48,000-acre Alaska Chilkat Bald Eagle Preserve to gorge on late-running chum salmon during a phenomenon

From Haines, Alaska, hikers can explore the trails of adjacent Glacier Bay National Park.
(© Bart Henderson)

known as "the congregation." Along the four-mile stretch known as the "council grounds," you'll see, up close and personal, the birds whose wings stretch as wide as a basketball player is tall and that build nests as wide as twelve feet. The annual Alaska Bald Eagle Festival, held every November, coincides with peak of the congregation.

The council grounds for adventurers, meanwhile, lies just twenty-five miles from Haines, at Glacier Bay National Park and Preserve. The land once lay under an ice sheet more than 4,000-feet-thick in places. Today, some of the frozen stuff has retreated, leaving a sixty-five-mile-long fjord and Y-shaped bay that has become one of the world's best playgrounds for exploring by land or by sea. From the visitor's center at Bartlett Cove, near the southeastern tip of the park, kayakers can slip into the bay to island-hop among the Beardslee Islands, or venture farther toward the shores of the Beartrack Mountains and the Muir Glacier. (The daily tour boat drops paddlers at different spots around the bay.) Moose, bald eagles, seals, and grizzly and black bears are, quite simply, everywhere, along with chunks of ice that groan and tumble into the sea. For rafting, head to the park's Tatshenshini and Alsek rivers which have Class II through IV rapids, depending on water levels. A 140-mile Tatshenshini trip typically takes about a week.

The longest maintained hiking trail you'll find in Glacier Bay is the eight-mile round-trip on the Bartlett Lake Trail, one of just four foot-paths serviced by the park service and accessible from Bartlett Cove. For longer land-based expeditions consider climbing 15,300-foot Mount Fairweather and other peaks of the Fairweather range, which can take several weeks to complete and are completely empty of any day hikers from the cruise boats navigating the Inside Passage.

Much smaller than their *Celebrity* or *Princess* counterparts, fishing charters continuously chug in and out of Haines for salmon and halibut trips; salmon fiends can also get a taste of the fish's place in Alaska's history through tours of the Tsirku Canning Company, available mid-May to mid-September.

Winter means days as short as just six hours, but also the Northern Lights and a multitude of ways to travel across the snow and ice, starting with dogsledding among Itidarod and Yukon Quest competitors. Thanks to Chilkoot Sled Dog Adventures, you can mush through the backcountry with the top dogs trained by Dan and Chris Turner. About forty miles from Haines, there's backcountry skiing at Chilkat Pass. Or you can splurge on a chopper trip with Out of Bounds Adventures, whose guides also run surfing trips in the summer. Need a surfboard? Listen to KHNS, 102.3 FM, and you just might find one.

Start the Day

Chilkat Restaurant & Bakery (Fifth Street and Dalton Street; 907-766-3653): Breakfast and lunch.

Gear Up

Alaska Backcountry Outfitter (210 Main Street; 907-766-2876): Camping and skiing essentials.

Local Legend

The Hammer Museum

When Dave Pahl set out to create a unique attraction in Haines, he nailed it. In 2001, Pahl opened the Hammer Museum, which is the world's only hall solely dedicated to the tool. Found on Main Street and open May through September, the Hammer Museum displays more than 1,400 hammers, many of them from Pahl's personal collection. You can peruse everything from a Tlingit warrior's pick that Pahl found when digging the basement of the museum to a Roman battle hammer to one used at a Manhattan nightclub. Many of them are displayed "in action," gripped by hammer-holding mannequins that were originally part of the Smithsonian Institution.

Alaska Discovery (800-586-1911): Sea kayaking tours of Glacier Bay National Park.

Refuel

The Bamboo Room (corner of Second and Main streets; 907-766-2800): Halibut fish and chips, the house specialty.

Fort Seward Lodge & Restaurant (39 Mud Bay Road; 907-766-2009): Steaks and seafood, including all-you-can-eat crab specials.

Just for the Halibut (142 Beach Road; 907-766-3800): Seafood on the waterfront.

Bunk

Bear Creek Cabins and Hostel (1.5 miles Small Tracts Road; 907-766-2259): Cabins, hostel bunks, and tent sites near the trailheads for Mount Riley and Mount Ripinski.

Hotel Hälsingland (13 Fort Seward Drive; 907-766-2000; www.hotelhalsingland.com): Victorian hotel at historic Fort Seward; Belgian-tile fireplaces and claw-foot bathtubs.

Chilkat Eagle Bed and Breakfast (67 Soap Suds Alley; 907-766-3779; www.eagle-bb.com): Four-bedroom bed-and-breakfast with multilingual owners; rents kayaks.

Can't Leave?

Nearest airport: Juneau International, Juneau, Alaska (86 miles)

Primary industries: Tourism, fishing

Homer, Alaska

The highway into Homer is called Sterling, and everything about this place takes on a silvery sheen: the glittering blue-green waters of Kachemak Bay, the velvety fjords of the Kenai Peninsula, the snow-capped mountains that seem to drop into the sea, and the grains of sand on the 4.5-mile-long spit that stretches out from the cluster of canneries, wilderness lodges, galleries, and weather-beaten wharves. Homer is considered by many to be the jewel of Alaska and is, incidentally, the provenance of singer Jewel, along with such lesser known, but equally beloved, artists as Hobo Jim. Even the wings of the resident bald eagles—fed by the Eagle Lady, Jean Keene—and the 10,000 shorebirds that fly through here every May on their annual migration take on a certain, unmistakably Homer glint.

Population: 5,364
Action: Kayaking, hiking, mountain and road biking, fishing

The shorebirds are hardly the only ones traveling through Homer, as evidenced by the number of cruise ships that dock here every summer and the traffic that's now as predictable as the proliferation of goldenrod and purple lupine in fields around town. But more and more adventurers, captivated by the kayaking, hiking, cycling, and angling, are starting to settle alongside the fishermen, artists, and eccentrics who've long called Homer home.

Most everyone here is from somewhere else originally, and this has been true for hundreds of years. According to the *Homer Tribune,* the town's newspaper, the first residents were the Pacific Eskimos, who were followed by the Dena'ina Indians and then the Russians who came for the coal around Kachemak Bay. The coal left on Alaska's railroad and ships that waited by a dock at the end of the spit, while the miners stayed to eventually form a town named after gold prospector and con man Homer Pennock. The fishermen arrived for the salmon, the homesteaders for the rich soil, and the lumberjacks for the spruce. In 1964,

Kachemak Bay and the Kenai Peninsula welcome both anglers and paddlers to Homer, Alaska. (© Bill Scott/alaskaodyssey.com)

an earthquake shook the town, but not the resolve of the new residents, who incorporated Homer just a few days later.

Today, fishing remains lucrative for the town's economy—and for the locals who enter the Homer Jackpot Halibut Derby. From June to September, anglers can win up to $1,000 for their prize catches while the contest's kitty keeps growing from the number of paid entries. Recently, an Oregon angler out on a charter brought home nearly $50,000 along with his souvenirs from Homer. Cast for king, pink, and silver salmon swimming right off the Homer Spit, or fish for kings throughout the Kenai Peninsula and Kachemak Bay. And a fifty-mile stretch of coastline around Homer is dimpled with clamming holes, providing a vast raw bar and buckets of steamers for anyone willing to dig.

While town officials warn newcomers about the serious workout that catching a halibut engenders, there are Homer residents who prefer to use a bike or their feet to expend calories. Depending on the wildly fluctuating tides, you can hike for hours along Bishop's Beach. Or you can head up the 6.7-mile long Homestead Trail that winds through the woods and meadows around town. Kachemak Bay State Park sprawls over some 300,000 acres around the Halibut Cove lagoon, where a roadless artists' community is littered with wandering trails. Homer is also surrounded by gravel and dirt roads that, coupled with views of the spit, the Alaskan lakes, the wildflowers, and Kachemak Bay, keep mountain bikers happy; try the fifteen-mile loop around Caribou Lake or the seventeen-mile round-trip on Ohlson Mountain Road. On a road bike, head back out along the Sterling Highway to remind yourself of those first stunning views of Homer and perhaps see a humpback, killer, or beluga whale splashing through Kachemak Bay.

For an up-close-and-personal look at the bay and its wildlife, however, you'll need to climb into a kayak. Launch from the end of the spit and paddle just over three miles to Gull Island, the access point to Halibut Cove and other sheltered bays, including Peterson and China Poot, where there are campsites. Caves and tunnels cut through Yukon Island, beyond which volcanoes on the mainland are visible on clear days. On summer weekends, you may have to navigate around a few cruise ships, but they'll disappear by the fall, when you'll stay for winter and the even more brilliant silvery glow it brings to Homer.

Start the Day

Fresh Sourdough Express (1316 Ocean Drive; 907-235-7571): Sourdough pancakes, along with egg scrambles and biscuits and gravy, served until 4 PM.

Two Sisters Bakery (233 East Bunnell Avenue; 907-235-2280): Breakfasts, baked goods (including pecan sticky buns), coffee, and fresh bread; go on Monday for the whole-wheat raisin loaves or Thursday for the herbed ciabatta.

Mermaid Café (3487 Main Street; 907-235-7984): Smoked-salmon and vegetable quiche, plus scones, muffins, apple pancakes, and danish.

Local Legend

Brother Asaiah Bates

If you feel there's something cosmic about Homer, you're not alone. Among the groups of people who've been attracted to this Alaskan town are the barefooters, who arrived in the 1950s. They strived for world peace and an end to hunger by refusing to cut their hair or wear shoes. Among them was Brother Asaiah Bates, who proclaimed that Homer was the Cosmic Hamlet by the Sea. Not feeling it? You can no longer consult with Bates, who died in 2000, but you can still dine on some out-of-this-world Tex-Mex at Homer's Cosmic Kitchen.

Gear Up

True North Kayak Adventures (4300 Homer Spit Road; 907-235-0708): Kayak rentals and guided trips.

Central Charters (4241 Homer Spit Road; 907-235-7847): The company that helped reel in a derby-winning, 308-pound halibut, which fetched nearly $50,000.

Silverfin Guide Service (907-235-7352): Guided fishing trips on the lower Kenai Peninsula with veteran Gary Sinnhuber.

Refuel

Boardwalk Fish & Chips (4287 Homer Spit Road; 907-235-7749): Clam-chowder bread bowls and fried halibut or salmon on a stick; dine on the deck.

The Homestead (Mile 8.2 End Road East; 907-235-8723): A menu that changes weekly but often features fresh local oysters, Alaskan king crab, halibut, and steaks, plus featured wines; the fine dining is paralleled by the views.

The Saltry (Halibut Cove; 907-296-2223): Freshly caught seafood (think halibut ceviche and smoked-salmon pâté) and carafes of red or white wine.

Bunk

Homer Spit Campground (4611 Homer Spit Road; 907-235-8206): Just ten tent sites and 122 RV sites, but an unbeatable location, where the Eagle Lady, Jean Keene, feeds the birds. (She's now the only one in Homer allowed to do so, until 2010.)

The Surf Shack (939 Ocean Drive Loop; 907-235-7873; www.surfshack homeralaska.com): A private, two-story cabin on for rent on Kachemak Bay; from the fire ring on the bluff, watch owner Don "The Iceman" McNamara surf Homer's waves.

The Wild Side

Exit Glacier in Winter

Three and a half miles long and some 3,000 feet high, Exit Glacier is one of the top attractions of the 671,000-acre Kenai Fjords National Park, which shares Homer's eponymous peninsula. The glacier is not only stunning, but it's also melting—at a rate of up to 100 feet per year. To see it without the crowds (except for a couple of moose), go in winter, when Exit Glacier Road closes due to snow and Willow Cabin opens, creating an unparalleled overnight cross-country ski trip. (For Willow Cabin reservations, call the U.S. Park Service at 907-224-7500.)

Peterson Bay Lodge & Oyster Camp (866-899-7156; www.peterson baylodge.com): Lying five miles across Kachemak Bay from Homer, this eco-adventure lodge has two-room waterfront cabins; sea kayaking, hiking, fishing, and clamming are available on the premises.

Can't Leave?

Nearest airport: Kenai Municipal, Kenai, Alaska (67 miles)

Primary industries: Commercial and recreational fishing, tourism

Kenai, Alaska

Population: 7,464

Action: Fishing, paddling, hiking

When you're fishing on the Kenai River and catch a Chinook salmon—better known as a king salmon in these parts—you'll be able to recognize it by its distinctive black gums and by the black spots on its back and dorsal fins. You might also be clued in by the fact that it just fought you for the better part of a day and weighs around thirty pounds. Alaska's oversized official state fish is the obsession of all anglers who make the pilgrimage to Kenai on the central west coast of the Kenai Peninsula. They come between mid-May and early August for the first and second runs on the Kenai River, and have dreams of topping the world-record 97.25-pounder pulled from its waters in 1984. They also know that people sometimes don't even need to leave the confines of town, on the edge of the Cook Inlet, to reel in ones larger than seventy pounds. As if the king salmon isn't reason enough to come, Kenai will hook you with its magnificent black beach; friendly, untouristy feel; and hundreds of miles of hiking and flatwater kayaking in the adjacent Kenai National Wildlife Refuge.

The site where the town rests, at the confluence of the eighty-two-mile-long Kenai River and the Cook Inlet south of Anchorage, has been inhabited for thousands of years. The first settlers of European descent to venture into these parts were Russian trappers and fishermen in the late eighteenth century, followed by prospectors nearly 100 years later. In the early twentieth century, commercial-fishing companies took root in Kenai, and in July, 1957, the state's first major commercial oil discovery was made nearby, turning the town into an industry center. Tourism is a newer, but booming, phenomenon. Several guide services have set up shop in town, and they're essential. Without someone knowledgeable about the waters, the proper bait, and the king salmon itself, you're almost guaranteed to end the day empty-handed. Gary Kernan of Fish On is one of the better guides in town; he also runs trips

Fishing boats at the mouth of the Kenai River. (© Bill Heath)

for sockeye and coho salmon, and for Dolly Varden char on the Upper Killey River.

With its reputation for fishing, Kenai is underused as a gateway to the two-million-acre Kenai National Wildlife Refuge and its hundreds of miles of hiking and paddling trails. Unlike the mountainous southeastern fringe of this West Virginia–sized park, the portion accessed by town is dominated by spruce forests and glacial lakes. The Kenai Canoe Trails within it are one of only two wilderness paddling systems in the country and consists of the Swan Lake and Swanson River trails. The Swan Lake Trail stretches sixty miles across thirty lakes, and the Swanson covers forty lakes over forty-six miles. For hikers, the options near town seem almost limitless—kind of like the number and size of the king salmon running up the Kenai River in the summer.

Local Legend

Record King Salmon

The world record ninety-seven pound, four ounce king salmon was caught by longtime Soldotna resident Les Anderson on May 17, 1985, on the Kenai River. Don't believe it? The fish is now mounted and on display at the local visitor's center. Every year on the anniversary of the famous catch, the town commemorates Les Anderson Day with a king salmon fishing derby.

Start the Day

Veronica's Coffee House (1506 Tyoyn Way; 907-283-2725): Coffeehouse and music venue by the Russian church in Old Town.

Charlotte's (115 South Willow Street; 907-283-2777): Coffee shop and bakery.

Gear Up

Lee Young's Kenai Outfitters (Soldotna; 907-260-1901): One of the area's top guide and outfitter services.

Refuel

Katina's Greek and Italian Restaurant (1188 Kenai Spur Highway; 907-283-4403): Pizza, sandwiches, and homemade soups amid a Mediterranean décor.

Mykel's Restaurant (35041 Kenai Spur Highway, Soldotna; 907-262-4305; www.mykels.com): Attached to the Soldotna Inn; serves freshly caught local salmon and halibut.

Bunk

Log Cabin Bed & Breakfast Inn (49860 Eider Road; 907-283-3653): Nine rooms in a log house and three cabins next to a beaver pond.

Daniels Lake Lodge (Kenai Spur Highway; 907-776-5578; www.danielslakelodge.com): Guesthouse and three log cabins on a lake, twenty miles north of town.

Can't Leave?

Nearest airport: Kenai Municipal (1 mile)

Primary industries: Commercial fishing, oil, retail

Kapaa, Kauai, Hawaii

O f all the Hawaiian islands, Kauai tends to elicit the most oohs and aahs from envious adventure travelers. Tell friends you're headed here, and their eyes will glaze over with remembered magazine photos of velvety green folded canyons; raw, rainbow-kissed coasts; and beaches lapped by frothy turquoise waves. Tell them you're *moving* here, and their eyes may pop in astonishment: can it really be possible? In the Hawaiian village, luau hotspot, and resort town of Kapaa, halfway up Kauai's Coconut Coast (on the east side), the answer is yes. Here, a lively community of shop-owners, vegetarian chefs, and bed-and-breakfast owners have figured out how to afford a mortgage, or at least rent, in between paddling nearby rivers, mountain biking to waterfalls, and surfing.

Population: 9,472
Action: Surfing, kayaking, mountain biking, hiking, diving

If you lose something (other than yourself, which is likely) on Kauai, you might, like islanders, blame the Menehune, the leprechaunlike mythical tribe that is said to have inhabited Waimea Canyon and built stone walls, ditches, and fishponds in a single night under the light of the moon. The Kauai Historical Society prefers to begin the Garden Island's story more than five million years ago, when the Pacific tectonic plate began spewing the magma that would form Kauai and its mountains, valleys, and canyons, which made this area nearly as mythical as the Menehune. Polynesians from the Marquesas, and then from Tahiti, lived among only the thousands of plants and animals until Captain James Cook arrived in 1778. Cook would later be followed by missionaries, sugar-plantation owners, and tourists. The last king of Kauai was Kaumualii, who died in the early 1800s.

Today, the kings and queens of Kauai are those who can penetrate the otherwise impenetrable landscape by boat, foot, or bike, because 90 percent of the island is inaccessible by road. From Coconut Marketplace in Kapaa, where you'll find most of the restaurants and

Most of Kauai's beauty is inaccessible by car. But hikers, bikers, and paddlers can explore it easily, while using Kapaa as their home base. (© Kauai Visitors Bureau/kauaidiscovery.com)

shops, including Kayak Kauai, it's just a mile to the mouth of the Class I Wailua River, which tumbles fifteen miles from sacred, 5,148-foot Mount Waialeale, the wettest spot on earth. Inward-blowing tradewinds make paddling upstream easier than it sounds. Along the river, paddlers might find petroglyphs and the remains of temples, or *heiau*. You can also take-out to hike forty-five minutes through ginger and plum trees to 120-foot Secret Falls, or Uluwehi. Other top river-paddling spots include the Hanalei River, Bay Reef Lagoon, and the Huleia River, where the Huleia National Wildlife Refuge protects 241 acres of endangered Hawaiian bird habitat. Sea kayakers head to the Poipu area, the site of humpback-whale watching in the winter, and the Na Pali Coast.

Many of Kauai's best mountain-biking trails—made more challenging by slippery clay—begin around the Kapaa and Wailua areas. Sugar-cane plantation roads provide miles of riding between Kealia Beach and Anahola, while the Kuamoo-Nounou Trail winds around Nounou Mountain, or Sleeping Giant, and provides views of waterfalls and the Makaleha Mountains. For more views, hit the Kuilau Ridge and Moalepe trails, or the thirteen-mile-long (one-way) Powerline Trail, which climbs up to 2,000 feet and drops into the Hanalei Valley. On the other side of Kauai is the epic area of Waimea Canyon—called the Grand Canyon of the Pacific by Mark Twain—which is laced with a twenty-five-mile road-biking loop trail.

Waimea, ten miles long and 4,000 feet deep, is also one of Hawaii's top hiking destinations. Circle through the lush slopes and along a knife-edged ridge on the eleven-mile Nualolo-Awawapahui Trail, and you'll be convinced you've found the legendary Shangri-la. Or take nearly any of the trailheads toward waterfalls and fragrant tropical forests. Closer to Kapaa there is the three-hour hike up Sleeping Giant, while trails along the north shore of Kauai lead to botanical gardens, white-sand beaches, and, naturally, more waterfalls.

You probably won't be able to pry the absolute best surfing spots from the locals, but well-known swells of three to fifteen feet can be found at Kealia Beach and Donkey Beach near Kapaa, and at Acid Drops, PK's, and Cow's Head, all on the South Shore near Poipu Beach Park; the north shore features Hideaways, Tunnels, and Dump Truck at Hanalei Bay. And while Kauai's most legendary dive site lies out at the forbidden island of Niihau and Lehua Rock, there's snorkeling and diving to be found along the Coconut Coast at Lydgate Park, Anahola Bay, and Ahukini Landing.

Sound all too abnormally good to be true? Ground yourself in the fact Kapaa also has such mundane things as a Rotary Club, a grocery

The Wild Side

The Na Pali Coast

It has been called the Mount Everest of sea kayaking, and the roughest and longest sea-kayak trip on the planet—and the superlatives are accurate. Paddling Kauai's Na Pali Coast, a 6,000-acre stretch of pure wilderness, is the best, least popular, and sometimes most brutal, way to see the glowing green cliffs and footprint-free beaches. Let others hike the Kalalau Trail, book helicopter trips, and sign up for a day-long trip offered by Kayak Kauai from May through September. You'll paddle seventeen miles of shoreline splendor, bouncing through waves; passing seals, sea caves, dolphins, and sea turtles; dozing off after lunch on a beach; and stretching out under waterfalls. The seasick-prone need not apply.

store (the Wednesday-morning "sunshine market," abundant with fresh fruits and vegetables), and building codes (nothing can be higher than a coconut tree).

Start the Day

Eggbert's (4-484 Kuhio Highway; 808-822-3787): Banana pancakes and a dozen types of omelets.

Blossoming Lotus (4-1384 Kuhio Highway; 808-823-6658): Coffee, chai tea, granola, muffins, and breakfast burritos.

Gear Up

Kayak Kauai (Coconut Marketplace, Kuhio Highway; 800-437-3507): Kayak rentals and lessons, surfing lessons, beach-cruiser bike rentals, and hiking trips throughout Kauai.

Refuel

Bubba's Burgers (4-1421 Kuhio Highway; 808-823-0069): A greasy but good (and popular) hamburger joint; sides include chili rice and frings—an onion-ring, french-fry combo.

Caffe Coco (4-369 Kuhio Highway, Wailua; 808-822-7990): A lime-green cottage hidden by a cane field and with a backyard garden of mango and avocado trees; serves Greek salads, tofu-chutney pot stickers, muffins, fish wraps, and more.

Bunk

Kauai International Hostel (4532 Lehua Street; 808-823-6413; www.kauaihostel.net): Inexpensive dorm and private rooms in Kappa town; offers onsite kayak rentals.

Hale Lani Bed & Breakfast (283 Aina Lani Place; 877-423-6434; www.halelani.com): Four rooms and suites with kitchens; perched in the hills above Kapaa.

Kapaa Sands Hotel (380 Papaloa Road; 800-222-4901; www.kapaa
sands.com): Twenty beachfront condos, within walking distance of
hiking trailheads and the Coconut Marketplace

Can't Leave?

Nearest airport: Lihue Airport, Lihue, Kauai, Hawaii (9 miles)

Primary industries: Tourism, retail

Kaunakakai, Molokai, Hawaii

Population: 2,726

Action: Mountain biking, kayaking, hiking

occasin-shaped Molokai is small enough that you don't need a lead foot to get from one end to the other quickly. But in case you forget where you are, a sign outside the island's tiny airport reminds you. "Aloha," it reads, "slow down this is Molokai." Even the pace of life in its commercial center, the three-block, no-stoplight town of Kaunakakai, is so laid back that it makes sipping drinks on the beach back at one of Hawaii's four bigger islands seem like a harried experience by comparison. Only a smidgen of the tourist population ever makes the puddle jump to this thirty-eight by ten-mile volcanic protrusion. Molokai has views of Oahu to the west, Lanai to the south, and Maui to the east, and a majority of its 7,000 residents are actually native Hawaiians. The only drawback is that once you get caught up in its super slo-mo lifestyle, you'll need extra time to investigate all of its wild wonders—like the tallest sea cliffs in the world, the longest sandy beach and coral reef in Hawaii, and singletrack that would make most mountain bikers on the U.S. mainland jealous.

What's striking about Molokai is the diversity of its geography. The hills and grasslands of the western and central sections stay mostly dry, while the forests among the soaring, mountainous eastern half can see as much as thirteen feet of precipitation a year. On the northeastern edge—known as the Backside—the terrain comes to an abrupt end, as cliffs high as 2,600 feet plummet to a narrow strip of shore. On a flat stretch of red dirt on the south-central part of the island is its largest settlement, Kaunakakai. Here, among the two blocks of weather-beaten storefronts and wooden homes, you can get outfitted, hire a guide, grab a hot meal, or simply experience true, friendly Hawaiian culture like nowhere else. This is, after all, the island where hula was created.

The verdant Kabupapa Peninsula is separated from the rest of Molokai by a 1,600-foot cliff. (© Maui Visitors Bureau)

If you're fortunate enough to be on Molokai on the third Saturday in May, head for Papohaku Beach Park, on the western shore, for the Ka Hula Piko Festival, to take part in celebrating the famous hip-swaying dance. This three-mile stretch of bleached sand is worth visiting on the other 364 days as well; even though it's the largest sandy beach in Hawaii, it stays blissfully barren. Not that you're likely to spend much time sunbathing, given how much else there is to do. Buffering almost the entire length of the south coast is the state's longest coral reef, making for protected kayaking water. Here, a snorkel and mask are as essential as a personal flotation device or paddle. The seas on the north shore can be more treacherous, but during the relative calm of summer, you can immerse yourself among the hidden waterfalls and beaches along the cliff-shadowed inlets.

You can feel just as removed from civilization among the single-track that roller-coasters through Molokai's paradisiacal forests and grassy plains. There are almost 100 miles of hard-packed, marked trails on the 53,000-acre Molokai Ranch, in the island's midsection; flat sections are about as rare as other bikers, although sometimes maintenance can be lacking. For even steeper ups and downs, head up the jeep track that leads through thick wilderness to the plateau peak of the Molokai Forest Reserve; the track climbs a few thousand feet in less than ten miles.

Hikers face an even more precipitous route when they descend a trail with twenty-six tight switchbacks to reach the verdant Kalaupapa Peninsula, separated from the rest of the island by a 1,600-foot cliff. The peninsula is the home to the infamous leper community started in 1866, when victims of the disease were cast off from ships and sent here to live. Although drugs now hold the disease in check, and colony residents have been able to leave for more than thirty-five years, a handful of residents have chosen to remain at the settlement there, which is now protected within the borders of the Kalaupapa National Historic Park. The only way to visit the area is to be invited by a resident or on a guided hike led by Richard Marks, a resident and owner of Damien Tours. After climbing back up the trail, head in your car back to Kaunakakai to rest your weary legs. Remember to drive slow, though, because this is Molokai.

Local Legend

Father Damien

Afraid of the spread of leprosy on the Hawaiian Islands, King Kamehameha IV began sending victims of the disease to the Kalaupapa Peninsula in the 1860s. Conditions were deplorable, and patients were dropped by boats that sometimes wouldn't even pull up to shore, but instead forced people to swim to land. In 1883, Father Damien, a Catholic missionary in Hawaii, came to Kalaupapa to build a church and help the population. Over his years there, he helped establish a village and brought worldwide attention to the plight of its patients. He soon contracted leprosy himself and died in 1889. Now he is on the path toward sainthood in the Catholic Church.

Start the Day

Stanley's Coffee Shop (125 Puali Street; 808-553-9966): Buy a cup of coffee on the first floor of the shop and art on the second.

Sundown Deli (145 Puali Street; 808-553-3713): A tiny health food–oriented café.

Gear Up

Molokai Fish and Dive (808-553-5926): Outdoor gear shop and paddling, mountain-bike, and dive guide service owned by local author and entrepreneur Jim Brocker.

Molokai Outdoors (40 Ala Malama Street; 877-553-4477): Rents kayaks, snorkel gear, and boogie boards.

Refuel

Kanemitsu Bakery (79 Ala Malama Street; 808-553-5855): Heavenly bread. Line up at the back door at 10 PM on any night except Monday, and you can get a piping hot loaf, with cream cheese or jam, on the spot.

Molokai Drive-Inn (857 Ala Malama Street; 808-553-5655): A take-out joint with gloriously greasy honey-fried chicken and mahi mahi.

Bunk

Hotel Molokai (Kamehameha V Highway; 800-477-2329; www .hotelmolokai.com): Oceanfront Polynesian-style bungalows with balconies.

The Lodge at Molokai Ranch (100 Maunaloa Highway; 888-627-8082; www.molokairanch.com): One of the most exclusive hotels in Hawaii, this lodge is a country-style home on the sprawling ranch.

Can't Leave?

Nearest airport: Molokai Airport, Kaunakakai (5 miles)

Primary industries: Service, agriculture, tourism

Lanai City, Lanai, Hawaii

Population: 3,164

Action: Mountain biking, paddling, snorkeling, diving

It's no surprise that Bill Gates got married and honeymooned on Lanai. Of all tropical paradises, few can combine utter seclusion with magnificent scenery, yet still be so easy to reach. This fin-shaped island—Hawaii's sixth largest—in the rain shadow of Maui is also undeveloped enough that the software gazillionaire was able to rent out every room for his nuptials. At its center is Lanai City, a former pineapple-plantation town that's the hub for biking, paddling, and all-around adventure—and where you don't need Gates' bank account to be able to afford to stay.

Lanai, a fifteen-mile ferry ride from Maui, is only eighteen miles long and thirteen miles wide, yet rises to more than 3,300 feet in elevation at its highest point, atop Mount Lanaihale. It remained mostly uninhabited until James Dole bought about 98 percent of the island in the early 1920s for use as a pineapple plantation. Lanai City was created to house workers, and many of the pine-shaded tin-roofed homes in its tiny downtown are remnants from that time. In 1990, David Murdock bought almost all of Lanai, as the pineapple industry migrated from Hawaii, and he built two of the world's most exclusive hotels: the Manele Bay Hotel—where the Gates wedding took place—on Hulopo'e Beach, and the Lodge at Ko'ele, a high-elevation resort modeled after an old English lodge. Development has been slow and controlled since that time, leaving the rugged island largely untamed and open for exploration.

There are only thirty miles of pavement on Lanai, meaning its other 100 or so miles of narrow, red-dirt roads essentially double as mountain-bike trails. That's in addition to the established paths that snake through the island's many hidden valleys and above the cliffs that line much of its shores. Unless you're staying at one of the posh resorts, you won't be able to rent a bike on the island, so you'll need to bring

440

one on the ferry. You'll be rewarded with rides such as the Munro Trail, a five-mile, curvy, 1,500-foot ascent through Mount Lanaihale's thick pine forest. On a clear day, you can spot six islands from the summit. Another popular destination is the Garden of the Gods, roughly seven miles north of town, a bare badlands area packed with buttes and rock pinnacles that make a prism of colors.

The other way to discover the island's stark, hidden wonders is by kayak. You can spend hours hugging the shore, investigating sea caves beneath massive cliffs, and not see any other boaters besides your guide. The currents can be treacherous, especially on the northeast coast. Trilogy Oceansports Lanai is the only outfitter in town; the company also organizes dive trips to the island's famed underwater sites, like the stunning submerged caverns called the Cathedrals. The best snorkeling can be found in the bay that washes onto Hulopo'e Beach, a sparklingly clear, protected marine preserve teeming with tropical fish, especially near the rocky bluffs at the bay's fringes. This stretch of sand is often rated as one of the most romantic in the world. That's probably why the Manele Bay Hotel was built above it—and why Bill Gates got married there.

The Munro Trail makes a five-mile, curvy, 1,500-foot ascent through Mount Lanaihale's thick pine forest, on the island of Lanai, Hawaii. (© Maui Visitors Bureau)

Start the Day

Blue Ginger Café (Seventh Street; 808-565-6363): Go to this tiny café for the banana pancakes.

Local Legend

Puu Pehe

Protruding above the water at the end of Hulopo'e Bay, on the island's south shore, is an eighty-foot-tall formation called Puu Pehe, also known as Sweetheart Rock. It's shaped like a giant's battered top hat. According to legend, a warrior from the island brought his beautiful wife to a nearby sea cave to keep her away from other men, but the violent seas drowned her one day when he was away. He then buried her in the crater at the top.

Coffee Works (604 Illima Street; 808-565-6962; www.coffeeworkshawaii.com): Choose from its selection of Hawaiian and international blends, and drink your selection on the deck.

Gear Up

Richard's Shopping Center (434 Eighth Street; 808-565-6047): The oldest general store on the island; sells fishing gear, food, and basic supplies.

Refuel

Henry Clay's Rotisserie (828 Lanai Avenue; 877-665-2624; www.hotel lanai.com) Exquisite Cajun food where you would least expect it—in the Hotel Lanai.

Pele's Other Garden (Eighth Street; 808-565-9628): New York–style deli sandwiches for eat-in or takeout.

Bunk

Hotel Lanai (828 Lanai Avenue; 877-665-2624; www.hotellanai.com): Built by James Dole in the early 1920s as a place to stay for his company's executives, it's now a welcoming, eleven-room, South Pacific–style inn.

Lodge at Koele (Keomoku Highway; 808-565-4000; www.lodgeat koele.com): If you can pony up the $400 a night, you can live like a movie star, and maybe see a few of them in the lobby of this highbrow inland lodge.

Can't Leave?

Nearest airport: Lanai Airport (5 miles)

Primary industries: Service, tourism, retail

Top Towns

Top 10 Best Outdoor Towns
1. Lake Placid, New York
2. Hood River, Oregon
3. McCall, Idaho
4. Salida, Colorado
5. Livingston, MT
6. Boone, NC
7. Ely, Minnesota
8. Davis, West Virginia
9. Bethel, Maine
10. Haines, Alaska

Hiking
1. Lake Placid, New York
2. Damascus, Virginia
3. Kapaa, Hawaii
4. Red Lodge, Montana
5. Bethel, Maine

Mountain Biking
1. Fruita, Colorado
2. Downieville, CA
3. Moab, Utah
4. East Burke, VT
5. Davis, West Virginia

Whitewater Paddling
1. Salida, Colorado
2. Taos, New Mexico
3. Bryson City, NC
4. Moab, Utah
5. Ohiopyle, PA

Flatwater Paddling
1. Ely, Minnesota
2. Cedar Key, Florida
3. Bayfield, Wisconsin
4. Beaufort, SC
5. Homer, Alaska

Fishing
1. Kenai, Alaska
2. Edenton, North Carolina
3. Saratoga, Wyoming
4. Apalachicola, Florida
5. Alexander City, Alabama

Sailing/Kiteboarding/ Windsurfing

1. Hood River, Oregon
2. Tiverton, Rhode Island
3. Edenton, North Carolina
4. St. Michaels, Maryland
5. Alexander City, Alabama

Cross-Country Skiing

1. Winthrop, Washington
2. West Yellowstone, Montana
3. Hayward, Wisconsin
4. Jackson, NH
5. Driggs, Idaho

Outdoor College Towns

1. Middlebury, Vermont
2. Gunnison, Colorado
3. Boone, North Carolina
4. Williamstown, MA
5. Oxford, Mississippi

Rock/Ice Climbing

1. New Paltz, NY
2. Bishop, California
3. Cody, Wyoming
4. Brevard, North Carolina
5. Fayetteville, West Virginia

Downhill Skiing/Snowboarding

1. Truckee, California
2. Silverton, Colorado
3. Girdwood, Alaska
4. Whitefish, Montana
5. Lake Placid, New York

Road Biking

1. Fredericksburg, Texas
2. Port Townsend, Washington
3. Montpelier, Vermont
4. Silver City, New Mexico
5. Ellijay, Georgia

Index